CW00459353

1 MONTH OF
FREE
READING

at

www.ForgottenBooks.com

By purchasing this book you are
eligible for one month membership to
ForgottenBooks.com, giving you
unlimited access to our entire
collection of over 1,000,000 titles via
our web site and mobile apps.

To claim your free month visit:
www.forgottenbooks.com/free805647

* Offer is valid for 45 days from date of purchase. Terms and conditions apply.

ISBN 978-0-331-63042-8
PIBN 10805647

This book is a reproduction of an important historical work. Forgotten Books uses state-of-the-art technology to digitally reconstruct the work, preserving the original format whilst repairing imperfections present in the aged copy. In rare cases, an imperfection in the original, such as a blemish or missing page, may be replicated in our edition. We do, however, repair the vast majority of imperfections successfully; any imperfections that remain are intentionally left to preserve the state of such historical works.

Forgotten Books is a registered trademark of FB &c Ltd.
Copyright © 2018 FB &c Ltd.
FB &c Ltd, Dalton House, 60 Windsor Avenue, London, SW19 2RR.
Company number 08720141. Registered in England and Wales.

For support please visit www.forgottenbooks.com

HYMNS

ANCIENT AND MODERN

FOR USE IN THE SERVICES OF THE CHURCH

"Young men and maidens, old men and children, praise the Name of the LORD."

PRINTED FOR THE PROPRIETORS

NEW EDITION 1904

LONDON
WILLIAM CLOWES AND SONS, LIMITED
23 COCKSPUR STREET
1904

BIBLIOGRAPHICAL NOTE

FIRST EDITION. 1861

Supplement added 1868

SECOND EDITION 1875

Further Supplement added 1889

------

*Of the foregoing Editions many impressions have
been published.*

NEW EDITION . . (*thoroughly revised*) . . . 1904

EXTRACT FROM THE PREFACE.

THE Compilers of *Hymns Ancient and Modern* cannot issue this new edition of the book without expressing their deep thankfulness to Almighty God for the blessing which He has hitherto so richly bestowed upon their undertaking. The book has been so widely adopted as to make it manifest that in spite of defects, of which the Compilers are not unaware, the collection, both of hymns and of tunes, has met the wants of the English Church in a way that has surpassed the most sanguine anticipations. To God be the praise.

When the latest Supplement was added in 1889 to the Edition of 1875, it was evident that this was only a temporary expedient, and that at some future date a revision would be necessary which should at least fuse the supplement into one with the main body of the book. But it seemed desirable to those who were responsible for the issue of the hymnal that the work of revision should go further than this, and should comprise a thorough and comprehensive review of the whole collection, together with the introduction of new material. Negotiations which took place between the Compilers and a joint Committee of the two

EXTRACT FROM THE PREFACE.

Houses of the Convocation of Canterbury in 1892 gave further impetus to the work; and in the interval of twelve years that has elapsed it has gone continuously forward. The result is now offered for the service of God.

The principles by which the book was governed from the first have undergone no alteration. More than once in former prefaces the Compilers have expressed their desire "to do their work in the spirit of the English Prayer-book." This has been the aim of the present revision, no less than of those which preceded it.

A good many of the older English hymns have been added to the book. Extensive search has been made for new hymns which might suitably be added, and especially in connexion with certain sections of the book which seemed to need augmentation in order to secure a due proportion in the parts.

It is somewhat to be regretted that hymn writers have not been much drawn to some subjects which might well have occupied their attention. It is often urged as an objection to Christian hymn books, that so great a proportion of the hymns contained in them are addressed to our Blessed Redeemer, rather than to the Father to Whom He brings us. The defect lies largely with the composers of our hymns, and not with the compilers of the collections. Again, few hymn writers have applied themselves successfully to

EXTRACT FROM THE PREFACE.

writing hymns for particular Saints' Days; few apparently have been inspired by the social and national aspects of Christianity which appeal so largely to our time. There is no great choice of good hymns, even upon subjects like the Seven Words from the Cross, or for Holy Baptism, or about Holy Scripture. In these and other departments the Compilers would have been glad to enrich their book. In some few cases new hymns have been written for the purpose.

The omissions in this edition amount to a considerable number, but it is hoped that few, if any, of the omitted hymns will be widely missed, and their excision has made room for others of greater value.

In accordance with the original design and title of the book the foremost part of the work of the Revisers has been to present the best of the ancient hymns of the Western Church in as good a form as possible. Immense labour has been spent on improving the translations. Here and there new versions have been given in the metre of the original—in a few cases without displacing older versions in other metres, which were firmly established in popular favour.

In dealing with the English hymns, care has been taken to examine the most authentic text available. In many cases a return to the author's original has in consequence been made. But the Revisers have *felt* that they were preparing

EXTRACT FROM THE PREFACE.

a hymn book for use in public worship, and not an anthology of sacred verse for purposes of study.. Wherever, therefore, an alteration of the original, which had been long in current use, seemed to them a real improvement upon the original, they have not hesitated to perpetuate it. In some hymns they have deliberately made changes with this practical end in view.

With a view to guidance in the selection of hymns there is appended to the preface a table of the ancient English Office Hymns, and also a table of sets of hymns appropriate for the Three Hours' Service on Good Friday. The ordinary table of contents which was given in previous editions is now printed with a more ample and comprehensive classification, including a list of the various headings under which the General Hymns are grouped.

Trinity, 1904.

TABLE OF HYMNS.

TABLE OF HYMNS.

TABLE OF HYMNS.

TABLE OF ANCIENT ENGLISH OFFICE HYMNS.*

Advent.

43 Creator of the starry height. E.
44 O WORD, that goest forth on high. E.
45 Loud rings the warning voice around. L.
34 To Thee before the close of day. C.

Christmas.

55 O come, Redeemer of the earth. E.
57 O CHRIST, Redeemer of our race. M.
56 From east to west, from shore to shore. L. & E.
58 Of the FATHER'S love begotten. C. (York.)
67 O Saviour of the world, we pray. C.

Epiphany.

79 Why doth that impious Herod fear. E. & M.
80 The FATHER'S sole-begotten SON. L.
67 O Saviour of the world, we pray. C.

From the Epiphany to Lent.

2 O splendour of GOD'S glory bright. L.
15 O blest Creator of the light. E.
34 To Thee before the close of day. C.

[Before Septuagesima.

89 Alleluia, song of sweetness. (Anglo-Saxon Hymnals.)]

The first fortnight of Lent.

92 By precepts taught of ages past. E.
93 O Thou Who dost to man accord. (8.8.7 D.) M.
94 O merciful Creator, hear. L.
105 O CHRIST, Who art the Light and Day. C.

* Unless it is otherwise specified the Hymns represent the Sarum use and are translated in their original metres.
The initials represent the Ancient Services of Evensong, Mattins, Lauds, and Compline.

TABLE OF ANCIENT ENGLISH OFFICE HYMNS.

The second fortnight of Lent.

95 Lo! now is our accepted day. E.
96 It is the glory of this fast. M.
97 O JESU, Thou didst consecrate. (C.M.) L.
105 O CHRIST, Who art the Light and Day. C.

From Passion Sunday to the Wednesday before Easter.

106 The Royal banners forward go. E.
107 Sing, my tongue, the glorious battle. M. & L.
108 Servant of GOD, remember. C.

Eastertide.

141 Up, new Jerusalem, and sing. E.
142 Light's glittering morn bedecks the sky. M. & L.
143 The LAMB's high banquet call'd to share. E.
145 O CHRIST, the heav'ns' Eternal King. (Anglo-Saxon Hymnals.)
163 JESU, the world's redeeming LORD. C.

Ascensiontide.

167 O Thou Eternal King most High. E. & M.
168 O CHRIST, our Joy, gone up on high. L.
176 JESU, our Hope, our heart's Desire. (C.M.) C.

Whitsuntide.

178 Now CHRIST above the starry floor. E. & M.
179 Oh joy! because the circling year. E.
67 O Saviour of the world, we pray. C.

Trinity Sunday.

188 Be near us, Holy TRINITY. E. & M.
189 FATHER most Holy, merciful and loving. L.
190 All hail, adorèd TRINITY. (Anglo-Saxon Hymnals.)

From Trinity to Advent.

15 O blest Creator of the light. E.
36 O TRINITY, most blessèd Light. E. (Saturday.)
34 To Thee before the close of day. C.

Apostles and Evangelists.*

191 Let all on earth their voices raise. L. & E.
192 Th' eternal gifts of CHRIST the King. (York.) M.
67 O Saviour of the world, we pray. C.†

* In Eastertide, Hymn 142, Part 2 or 3 was sung on the Festivals of Apostles and Evangelists.
† This Hymn was sung at Compline on greater Festivals, except between Lent and Trinity Sunday.

TABLE OF ANCIENT ENGLISH OFFICE HYMNS.

Martyrs.

200 O God, Thy soldiers' faithful Lord. L. & E.
201 The triumphs of the Saints. E. & M.
202 Th' eternal gifts of Christ the King. (York.) M.

Confessor, Bishop.

209 O Thou Whose all-redeeming might. L. & E.

Virgin.

212 O Jesu, Thou the Virgins' Crown. L. & E.

The Blessed Virgin Mary.

232 The God, Whom earth, and sea, and sky. M.

S. John Baptist.

235 The high forerunner of the morn. (Bede.)

Michaelmas.

239 Thee, O Christ, the Father's splendour. E. & M.

Transfiguration.

249 O wondrous type, O vision fair. E.

Name of Jesus.

252 Jesu! the very thought is sweet. M.

Dedication.

253 Blessèd city, heav'nly Salem. E. M. L.

Note 1. The Hymns for the Lesser Hours of Prime, Terce, Sext, and None are given at Nos. 1, 9, 10, 11.

Note 2. No account is taken in the foregoing Table of the more modern Latin Office Hymns taken from French Breviaries of the XVIIth and XVIIIth centuries. Many of these will, however, be found useful in this connexion either in supplying some gaps, where the Sarum Hymns are not available—*e.g.*, **208** is suitable for Confessors, or **246** for All Saints' Day ; or else in giving variants for days and seasons where the older Breviaries made no special provision—*e.g.*, **76**, at the Feast of the Circumcision, or **90, 91** for Septuagesima.

A TABLE OF SETS OF HYMNS APPROPRIATE FOR USE AT THE THREE HOURS' SERVICE ON GOOD FRIDAY.

INTRODUCTORY : any of the following : —

128 O come and mourn with me awhile.
180 Come, HOLY GHOST, our souls inspire.
181 Come, HOLY GHOST, Creator Blest.
127 See the destined day arise.
470 JESU, meek and lowly.
116 In the LORD's atoning grief.
121 Sweet the moments, rich in blessing.
468 Behold the LAMB of GOD!

SET I.

ON THE WORDS FROM THE CROSS, **129-136.**

SET II.

114 O sinner, for a little space.
597 Approach, my soul, the mercy-seat.
132 At the Cross her station keeping.
467 Rock of ages, cleft for me.
116 In the LORD's atoning grief.
253 CHRIST is made the sure Foundation.
337 Praise to the Holiest in the height.

SET III.

470 JESU, meek and lowly.
344 Thou art the Way; by Thee alone.
543 O Thou Who makest souls to shine.
484 JESU, grant me this, I pray.
119 Glory be to JESUS.
120 When I survey the wondrous Cross.
14 O Strength and Stay upholding all creation.

or,

610 *O my Saviour, lifted.*

(xiii)

HYMNS FOR THE THREE HOURS' SERVICE.

SET IV.

282 O Thou, before the world began.
472 Come unto Me, ye weary.
426 Thy way, not mine, O LORD.
124 Alone Thou trodd'st the winepress.
122 O sacred head, surrounded.
345 Where high the heav'nly temple stands.
112 O'erwhelm'd in depths of woe.

At the close of the service.

17　The sun is sinking fast.

or,

16 As now the sun's declining rays.

SET V.

489 JESUS, LORD of life and glory.
384 There is a blessèd home.
448 LORD, as to Thy dear Cross we flee.
604 My GOD! my GOD! and can it be.
35 O JESU, crucified for man.
128 Go to dark Gethsemane.
490 When our heads are bow'd with woe.

At the close of the service.

23 Abide with me; fast falls the eventide.

or,

500 Thy life was given for me.

SET VI.

{118 Now, my soul, thy voice upraising.
{599 O come to the merciful Saviour,
{601 There is a fountain fill'd with Blood.
{606 JESU! Name all names above.
502 We sing the praise of Him Who died.
117 My GOD, I love Thee.
452 O Saviour, may we never rest.
107 (Pts. 1 & 3) Sing, my tongue, the glorious battle.
335 From highest heav'n th' Eternal Son.

HYMNS.

MORNING.

1 *Early in the morning will I direct my prayer unto thee.*

Jam lucis orto sidere.

NOW that the daylight fills the sky,
 We lift our hearts to GOD on high,
That He in all we dó or say
Would keep us frée from harm to-day;

Our tongues would bridle, lést they sin
By waking ánger's hateful din;
With tender care' would guárd our eyes
From giving héed to vanities.

O may our inmost héarts be pure,
From thoughts of fólly kept secure;
And pride of sinful flésh subdued
Through sparing úse of daily food.

So we, when this new dáy is o'er,
And shades of night return once more,
The path of holy témperance trod,
Shall give the glóry to our GOD.

All praise to GOD the FÁTHER be,
All praise, Etérnal SON, to Thee,
Whom with the SPIRIT wé adore,
For ever ánd for evermore.   Amen.

2 *He that followeth me shall not walk in darkness, but shall have the light of life.*

Splendor paternæ gloriæ.

O SPLENDOUR of GOD's glory bright,
 Who bringest forth the light from Light;
O Light of light, light's Fountain-spring;
O Day, our days enlightening;

MORNING.

Come, very Sun of truth and love,
Come in Thy radiance from above,
And shed the HOLY SPIRIT's ray
On all we think or do to-day.

Likewise to Thee our prayers ascend,
FATHER of glory without end,
FATHER of sov'reign grace, for power
To conquer in temptation's hour.

Teach us to work with all our might;
Beat back the devil's threat'ning spite;
Turn all to good that seems most ill;
Help us our calling to fulfil;

Direct and govern heart and mind,
With body chaste and disciplined;
Let faith her eager fires renew,
And hate the false and love the true.

On CHRIST the true Bread let us feed;
Let faith to us be drink indeed,
And let us taste with joyfulness
The SPIRIT's temperate excess.

O joyful be the livelong day,
Our thoughts as pure as morning ray,
Our faith like noonday's glowing height,
Our souls undimm'd by shades of night.

*The dawn begins to speed her way,
Let the true Dawn Himself display,
The SON with GOD the FATHER One,
And GOD the FATHER in the SON.   Amen.

or,

All praise to GOD the FATHER be,
All praise, Eternal SON, to Thee,
Whom with the SPIRIT we adore,
For ever and for evermore.   Amen.

This verse is only suitable for an early Service.

(2)

MORNING.

I myself will awake right early.

AWAKE, my soul, and with the sun
    Thy daily stage of duty run ;
Shake off dull sloth, and early rise
To pay thy morning sacrifice.

Redeem thy mis-spent moments past,
And live this day as if thy last ;
Improve thy talent with due care ;
For the great Day thyself prepare.

Let all thy converse be sincere,
Thy conscience as the noon-day clear ;
Think how th' all-seeing GOD thy ways
And all thy secret thoughts surveys.

Wake, and lift up thyself, my heart,
And with the Angels bear thy part,
Who all night long unwearied sing
High praise to their eternal King.

PART 2.

Glory to Thee, Who safe hast kept
And hast refresh'd me whilst I slept ;
Grant, LORD, when I from death shall wake,
I may of endless light partake.

LORD, I my vows to Thee renew ;
Disperse my sins as morning dew ;
Guard my first springs of thought and will,
And with Thyself my spirit fill.

Direct, control, suggest, this day,
All I design, or do, or say ;
That all my powers, with all their might,
In Thy sole glory may unite.

*The following Doxology should be used at the end of
either Part:*

Praise GOD, from Whom all blessings flow,
Praise Him, all creatures here below,
Praise Him above, ye heav'nly host,
Praise FATHER, SON, and HOLY GHOST. Amen.

(3)

4 *Unto you that fear my name shall the Sun of righteousness arise.*

CHRIST, Whose glory fills the skies,
    CHRIST, the true, the only Light,
Sun of righteousness, arise,
    Triumph o'er the shades of night ;
Dayspring from on high, be near ;
Daystar, in my heart appear.

Dark and cheerless is the morn
    Unaccompanied by Thee ;
Joyless is the day's return,
    Till Thy mercy's beams I see,
Till Thou inward light impart,
Glad my eyes, and warm my heart.

Visit then this soul of mine,
    Pierce the gloom of sin and grief ;
Fill me, Radiancy Divine,
    Scatter all my unbelief ;
More and more Thyself display,
Shining to the perfect day.   Amen.

5 *His compassions fail not : they are new every morning.*

NEW every morning is the love
    Our wakening and uprising prove ;
Through sleep and darkness safely brought,
Restored to life, and power, and thought.

New mercies, each returning day,
Hover around us while we pray ;
New perils past, new sins forgiven,
New thoughts of GOD, new hopes of heaven.

If on our daily course our mind
Be set to hallow all we find,
New treasures still, of countless price,
GOD will provide for sacrifice.

MORNING.

The trivial round, the common task,
Will furnish all we need to ask,—
Room to deny ourselves, a road
To bring us daily nearer GOD.

Only, O LORD, in Thy dear love
Fit us for perfect rest above;
And help us this and every day
To live more nearly as we pray.   Amen.

6 *I have set God always before me; for he is on my right
hand, therefore I shall not fall.*

FORTH in Thy Name, O LORD, I go
   My daily labour to pursue;
Thee, only Thee, resolved to know,
   In all I think, or speak, or do.

The task Thy wisdom hath assign'd
   O let me cheerfully fulfil;
In all my works Thy presence find,
   And prove Thy good and perfect will.

Thee may I set at my right hand,
   Whose eyes my inmost substance see,
And labour on at Thy command,
   And offer all my works to Thee.

Give me to bear Thy easy yoke,
   And every moment watch and pray,
And still to things eternal look,
   And hasten to Thy glorious day;

For Thee delightfully employ
   Whate'er Thy bounteous grace hath given,
And run my course with even joy,
   And *closely* walk with Thee to heaven.
                       Amen.

7   *Do all in the name of the Lord Jesus.*

MY FATHER, for another night
        Of quiet sleep and rest,
For all the joy of morning light,
        Thy Holy Name be blest.

Now with the new-born day I give
        Myself anew to Thee,
That as Thou willest I may live,
        And what Thou willest be.

Whate'er I do, things great or small,
        Whate'er I speak or frame,
Thy glory may I seek in all,
        Do all in JESUS' Name.

My FATHER, for His sake, I pray,
        Thy child accept and bless ;
And lead me by Thy grace to-day
        In paths of righteousness.   Amen.

8 *Hold thou me up, and I shall be safe: yea, my delig*
        shall be ever in thy statutes.

AT Thy feet, O CHRIST, we lay
        Thine own gift of this new day ;
Doubt of what it holds in store
Makes us crave Thine aid the more ;
Lest it prove a time of loss,
Mark it, Saviour, with Thy Cross.

If it flow on calm and bright,
Be Thyself our chief delight ;
If it bring unknown distress,
All is good that Thou canst bless ;
Only, while its hours begin,

We in part our weakness know,
And in part discern our foe ;
Well for us, before Thine eyes
All our danger open lies ;
Turn not from us, while we plead
Thy compassions and our need.

Fain would we Thy word embrace,
Live each moment in Thy grace,
All our selves to Thee consign,
Fold up all our wills in Thine,
Think, and speak, and do, and be,
Simply that which pleases Thee.

Hear us, LORD, and that right soon ;
Hear, and grant the choicest boon
That Thy love can e'er impart,
Loyal singleness of heart ;
So shall this and all our days,
CHRIST our GOD, show forth Thy praise.

Amen.

THE THIRD HOUR.

9   *They were all filled with the Holy Ghost.*

Nunc Sancte nobis Spiritus.

COME, HOLY GHOST, Who éver One
Art with the FÁTHER and the SON,
Come, HOLY GHOST, our sóuls possess
With Thy full flóod of holiness.

In will and deed, by héart and tongue,
With all our pówers, Thy praise be sung ;
And love light up our mórtal frame,
Till others cátch the living flame.

Almighty FATHER, héar our cry
Through JESUS CHRÍST, our LORD most High,
Who with the HOLY GHÓST and Thee
Doth live and réign eternally.   Amen.

THE SIXTH HOUR.

10

At noonday will I pray.

Rector potens, verax Deus.

O GOD of truth, O LORD of might,
  Who ord'rest time and change aright,
Arraying morn with joyful gleams,
And kindling noonday's fiery beams ;

Quench Thou on earth the flames of strife ;
From passion's heat preserve our life ;
Our bodies keep from perils free,
And grant our souls true peace in Thee.

Almighty FATHER, hear our cry
Through JESUS CHRIST, our LORD most High,
Who with the HOLY GHOST and Thee
Doth live and reign eternally.   Amen.

THE NINTH HOUR.

11

The hour of prayer, being the ninth hour.

Rerum Deus tenax vigor.

O GOD, the world's sustaining force,
  Thyself unmoved, all motion's source,
Who, from the morn till evening's ray,
Dost through its changes guide the day ;

O grant us light at eventide,
That life may unimpair'd abide,
And that a holy death may be
The door of immortality.

Almighty FATHER, hear our cry
Through JESUS CHRIST, our LORD most High,
Who with the HOLY GHOST and Thee
Doth live and reign eternally.   Amen.

MID-DAY.

12 *In the evening, and morning, and at noonday will I pray.*

UP to the throne of GOD is borne
    The voice of praise at early morn,
And He accepts the punctual hymn,
Sung as the light of day grows dim.
Nor will He turn His ear aside
From holy offerings at noon-tide ;
Then here to Him our souls we raise,
In songs of gratitude and praise.

Blest are the moments, doubly blest,
That, drawn from this one hour of rest,
Are with a ready heart bestow'd
Upon the service of our GOD.
Look up to heav'n ; th' industrious sun
Already half his race hath run ;
He cannot halt, or go astray,
But our immortal spirits may.

LORD, since his rising in the east
If we have falter'd or transgress'd,
Guide, from Thy love's abundant source,
What yet remains of this day's course.
Help with Thy grace, through life's short day,
Our upward and our downward way ;
And glorify for us the west,
When we shall sink to final rest.   Amen.

MID-DAY—FOR A TOWN CHURCH.

13 *The kingdoms of this world are become the kingdoms of
    our Lord and of his Christ.*

BEHOLD us, LORD, a little space
    From daily tasks set free,
And met within Thy holy place
    To rest awhile with Thee.

MID-DAY.

Around us rolls the ceaseless tide
  Of business, toil, and care;
And scarcely can we turn aside
  For one brief hour of prayer.

Yet these are not the only walls
  Wherein Thou may'st be sought;
On homeliest work Thy blessing falls
  In truth and patience wrought.

Thine is the loom, the forge, the mart,
  The wealth of land and sea;
The worlds of science and of art
  Reveal'd and ruled by Thee.

Then let us prove our heav'nly birth
  In all we do and know,
And claim the kingdom of the earth
  For Thee, and not Thy foe.

Work shall be prayer, if all be wrought
  As Thou wouldst have it done;
And prayer, by Thee inspired and taught,
  Itself with work be one.   Amen.

AFTERNOON.

14   *The Lord was my stay.*

Rerum Deus tenax vigor.

O STRENGTH and Stay upholding all creation,
  Who ever dost Thyself unmoved abide,
Yet day by day the light in due gradation
  From hour to hour through all its changes guide;

Grant to life's day a calm unclouded ending,
  An eve untouch'd by shadows of decay,
The brightness of a holy death-bed blending
  With dawning glories of th' eternal day.

AFTERNOON.

Hear us, O FATHER, gracious and forgiving,
  And Thou, O CHRIST, the co-eternal WORD,
Who, with the HOLY GHOST, by all things living
  Now and to endless ages art adored. Amen.

EVENING.

15   *The day is thine, and the night is thine.*

Lucis Creator optime.

O BLEST Creator of the light,
    Who makest day with radiance bright,
'Twas Thou Who o'er the forming earth
Didst give the golden light its birth ;
Who, joining eve with morning ray,
Didst bid them bear the name of day ;
Again the darkness gathers o'er ;
Thy pitying succour we implore.
O let us not by guilt oppress'd
Stray from the way of life and rest :
Lest thinking but the thoughts of time
We bind our souls in chains of crime.
Nay, let us aim beyond the skies,
And labour till we grasp the prize,
Eschew our own besetting sin,
And throughly cleanse our hearts within.
Almighty FATHER, hear our cry
Through JESUS CHRIST, our LORD most High,
Who with the HOLY GHOST and Thee
Doth live and reign eternally. Amen.

16   *I, if I be lifted up from the earth, will draw all men*
                      unto me.

Labente jam solis rota.

AS now the sun's declining rays
    At eventide descend,
So life's brief day is sinking down
  To its appointed end.

EVENING.

LORD, on the Cross Thine arms were stretch'd
   To draw Thy people nigh ;
O grant us then that Cross to love,
   And in those arms to die.

All glory to the FATHER be,
   All glory to the SON,
All glory, HOLY GHOST, to Thee,
   While endless ages run.   Amen.

17 *Let the lifting up of my hands be an evening sacrifice.*

Sol præceps rapitur.

THE sun is sinking fast,
   The daylight dies ;
Let love awake, and pay
   Her evening sacrifice.

As CHRIST upon the Cross
   His head inclined,
And to His FATHER's hands
   His parting soul resign'd,

So now herself my soul
   Would wholly give
Into His sacred charge
   In Whom all spirits live ;

So now beneath His eye
   Would calmly rest,
Without a wish or thought
   Abiding in the breast,

Save that His will be done,
   Whate'er betide,
Dead to herself, and dead
   In Him to all beside.

Thus would I live ; yet now
Not I, but He,
In all His power and love
Henceforth alive in me,

One sacred TRINITY,
One LORD Divine ;
May I be ever His,
And He for ever mine.   Amen.

18　　　　*The true Light.*

Φῶς ἱλαρὸν · ἁγίας δόξης.

HAIL, gladdening Light, of His pure glóry
　　pour'd
Who is th' immortal FATHER, heav'nly, blest,
Holiest of Holies, JESUS CHRIST, our LORD !
　Now we are come to the sun's hóur of rest,
　The lights of évening round us shine,
We hymn the FATHER, SON, and HOLY SPIRIT
　Divine.

Worthiest art Thou at all times tó be sung
　　　　With undefilèd tongue,
　SON of our GOD, Giver of life, Alone :
Therefore in all the world Thy glories, LORD, they
　own.   Amen.

19　　　*Lighten mine eyes that I sleep not in death.*

Τὴν ἡμέραν διελθών.

THE day is past and over ;
　　All thanks, O LORD, to Thee :
I pray Thee now that sinless
　The hours of dark may be :
O JESU, keep me in Thy sight,
And *guard me* through the coming night.

(13)

EVENING.

The joys of day are over ;
  I lift my heart to Thee,
And ask Thee that offenceless
  The hours of dark may be :
O Jesu, keep me in Thy sight,
And guard me through the coming night.

The toils of day are over ;
  I raise the hymn to Thee,
And ask that free from peril
  The hours of dark may be :
O Jesu, keep me in Thy sight,
And guard me through the coming night.

Lord, that in death I sleep not,
  And lest my foe should say,
"I have prevail'd against him,"
  Lighten mine eyes, I pray :
O Jesu, keep me in Thy sight,
And guard me through the coming night.

Be Thou my soul's preserver,
  For Thou alone dost know
How many are the perils
  Through which I have to go :
Lover of men, O hear my call,
And guard and save me from them all. Amen.

20   *He shall defend thee under his wings.*

GLORY to Thee, my God, this night
  For all the blessings of the light ;
Keep me, O keep me, King of kings,
Beneath Thy own almighty wings.

Forgive me, Lord, for Thy dear Son,
The ill that I this day have done,
That with the world, myself, and Thee,
I, ere I sleep, at peace may be.

EVENING.

Teach me to live, that I may dread
The grave as little as my bed ;
Teach me to die, that so I may
Rise glorious at the awful day.

O may my soul on Thee repose,
And may sweet sleep mine eyelids close,
Sleep that shall me more vigorous make
To serve my GOD when I awake.

When in the night I sleepless lie,
My soul with heav'nly thoughts supply ;
Let no ill dreams disturb my rest,
No powers of darkness me molest.

Praise GOD, from Whom all blessings flow,
Praise Him, all creatures here below,
Praise Him above, ye heav'nly host,
Praise FATHER, SON, and HOLY GHOST.

Amen.

21   *The Lord shall be thine everlasting light.*

THE radiant morn hath pass'd away,
   And spent too soon her golden store ;
The shadows of departing day
      Creep on once more.

Our life is but an autumn day,
Its glorious noon how quickly past !
Lead us, O CHRIST, Thou living Way,
      Safe home at last.

O by Thy soul-inspiring grace
Uplift our hearts to realms on high ;
Help us to look to that bright place
      Beyond the sky,

Where light, and life, and joy, and peace,
In undivided empire reign,
And thronging Angels never cease
      Their deathless strain ;

Where Saints are clothed in spotless white,
And evening shadows never fall,
Where Thou, eternal Light of Light,
    Art LORD of all. Amen.

22   *He shall give his angels charge over thee.*

GOD, Who madest earth and heaven,
    Darkness and light ;
Who the day for toil hast given,
    For rest the night ;
May Thine angel-guards defend us,
Slumber sweet Thy mercy send us,
Holy dreams and hopes attend us,
    This livelong night.

Guard us waking, guard us sleeping ;
    And, when we die,
May we in Thy mighty keeping
    All peaceful lie :
When the last dread call shall wake us,
Do not Thou our GOD forsake us,
But to reign in glory take us
    With Thee on high. Amen.

23 *Abide with us ; for it is toward evening, and the day is*
              far spent.

ABIDE with me ; fast falls the eventide ;
    The darkness deepens ; LORD, with me abide!
When other helpers fail, and comforts flee,
Help of the helpless, O abide with me.

Swift to its close ebbs out life's little day ;
Earth's joys grow dim, its glories pass away ;
Change and decay in all around I see ;
O Thou Who changest not, abide with me.

I need Thy presence every passing hour :
What but Thy grace can foil the tempter's power ?
Who like Thyself my guide and stay can be ?
Through cloud and sunshine, LORD, abide with me.

1 fear no foe with Thee at hand to bless ;
Ills have no weight, and tears no bitterness ;
Where is death's sting ? where, grave, thy victory ?
I triumph still, if Thou abide with me.

Hold Thou Thy Cross before my closing eyes ;
Shine through the gloom, and point me to the skies;
Heav'n's morning breaks, and earth's vain shadows
    flee ;
In life, in death, O Lord, abide with me.   Amen.

24   *Abide with us.*

SUN of my soul, Thou Saviour dear,
    It is not night if Thou be near :
O may no earth-born cloud arise
To hide Thee from Thy servant's eyes.

When the soft dews of kindly sleep
My wearied eyelids gently steep,
Be my last thought, how sweet to rest
For ever on my Saviour's breast.

Abide with me from morn till eve,
For without Thee I cannot live ;
Abide with me when night is nigh,
For without Thee I dare not die.

If some poor wand'ring child of Thine
Have spurn'd to-day the voice divine,
Now, Lord, the gracious work begin ;
Let him no more lie down in sin.

Watch by the sick ; enrich the poor
With blessings from Thy boundless store ;
Be every mourner's sleep to-night
Like infant's slumbers, pure and light.

Come near and bless us when we wake,
Ere through the world our way we take ;
Till in the ocean of Thy love
We lose ourselves in heav'n above.   Amen.

25 *The Lord is my light.*

SWEET Saviour, bless us ere we go,
  Thy word into our minds instil,
And make our lukewarm hearts to glow
  With lowly love and fervent will.
Through life's long day and death's dark night,
O gentle JESUS, be our Light.

The day is gone, its hours have run,
  And Thou hast taken count of all,
The scanty triumphs grace hath won,
  The broken vow, the frequent fall.
Through life's long day and death's dark night,
O gentle JESUS, be our Light.

Grant us, dear LORD, from evil ways
  True absolution and release ;
And bless us, more than in past days,
  With purity and inward peace.
Through life's long day and death's dark night,
O gentle JESUS, be our Light.

Do more than pardon ; give us joy,
  Sweet fear, and sober liberty,
And simple hearts without alloy
  That only long to be like Thee.
Through life's long day and death's dark night,
O gentle JESUS, be our Light.

Labour is sweet, for Thou hast toil'd ;
  And care is light, for Thou hast cared ;
Ah ! never let our works be soil'd
  With strife, or by deceit ensnared.
Through life's long day and death's dark night,
O gentle JESUS, be our Light.

For all we love, the poor, the sad,
  The sinful, unto Thee we call ;
O let Thy mercy make us glad :
  Thou art our JESUS, and our all.
Through life's long day and death's dark night,
O gentle JESUS, be our Light.   Amen.

26 *He that keepeth thee will not sleep.*

THROUGH the day Thy love has spared us ;
  Now we lay us down to rest ;
Through the silent watches guard us,
  Let no foe our peace molest :
    JESUS, Thou our guardian be ;
    Sweet it is to trust in Thee.

Pilgrims here on earth, and strangers,
  Dwelling in the midst of foes,
Us and ours preserve from dangers ;
  In Thine arms may we repose,
    And, when life's brief day is past,
    Rest with Thee in heav'n at last.   Amen.

27 *The Lord which giveth the stars for a light by night.*

NOW on land and sea descending,
  Brings the night its peace profound ;
Let our evening hymn be blending
  With the holy calm around.
Soon as dies the sunset glory,
  Stars of heav'n shine out above,
Telling still the ancient story,—
  Their Creator's changeless love.

Now our wants and burdens leaving
  To His ca e, Who cares for all,
Cease *we fearing,* cease *we* grieving ;
  At His touch our burdens fall.

EVENING.

As the darkness deepens o'er us,
 Lo ! eternal stars arise ;
Hope and Faith and Love rise glorious,
 Shining in the spirit's skies. Amen.

28 *The Lord's Name is praised from the rising up of the*
  sun unto the going down of the same.

THE day Thou gavest, LORD, is ended,
 The darkness falls at Thy behest ;
To Thee our morning hymns ascended,
 Thy praise shall sanctify our rest.

We thank Thee that Thy Church unsleeping,
 While earth rolls onward into light,
Through all the world her watch is keeping,
 And rests not now by day or night.

As o'er each continent and island
 The dawn leads on another day,
The voice of prayer is never silent,
 Nor dies the strain of praise away.

The sun that bids us rest is waking
 Our brethren 'neath the western sky,
And hour by hour fresh lips are making
 Thy wondrous doings heard on high.

So be it, LORD ; Thy throne shall never,
 Like earth's proud empires, pass away ;
Thy Kingdom stands, and grows for ever,
 Till all Thy creatures own Thy sway. Amen.

29 *At evening time it shall be light.*

HOLY FATHER, cheer our way
 With Thy love's perpetual ray :

EVENING.

HOLY SAVIOUR, calm our fears
When earth's brightness disappears;
Grant us in our latter years
    Light at evening time.

HOLY SPIRIT, be Thou nigh
When in mortal pains we lie;
Grant us, as we come to die,
    Light at evening time.

HOLY, Blessèd TRINITY,
Darkness is not dark with Thee;
Those Thou keepest always see
    Light at evening time.   Amen.

30 *And at even, when the sun did set, they brought unto*
him all that were diseased, and them that were
possessed with devils. And all the city was gathered
together at the door.

AT even, when the sun did set,
    The sick, O LORD, around Thee lay;
Oh in what divers pains they met!
    Oh with what joy they went away!

Once more 'tis eventide, and we
    Oppress'd with various ills draw near;
What if Thy form we cannot see,
    We know and feel that Thou art here.

O Saviour CHRIST, our woes dispel;
    For some are sick, and some are sad,
And some have never loved Thee well,
    And some have lost the love they had;

And some have found the world is vain,
    Yet from the world they break not free;
And some have friends who give them pain,
    Yet have not sought a friend in Thee;

And none, O LORD, have perfect rest,
  For none are wholly free from sin ;
And they who fain would serve Thee best
  Are conscious most of wrong within.

O Saviour CHRIST, Thou too art Man ;
  Thou hast been troubled, tempted, tried ;
Thy kind but searching glance can scan
  The very wounds that shame would hide ;

Thy touch has still its ancient power,
  No word from Thee can fruitless fall ;
Hear, in this solemn evening hour,
  And in Thy mercy heal us all. Amen.

31 *And all the angels stood round about the throne . . .*
and worshipped God.

OUR day of praise is done ;
  The evening shadows fall ;
But pass not from us with the sun,
  True Light that lightenest all.

  Around the throne on high,
    Where night can never be,
  The white-robed harpers of the sky
    Bring ceaseless hymns to Thee.

  Too faint our anthems here ;
    Too soon of praise we tire :
  But Oh, the strains how full and clear
    Of that eternal choir !

  Yet, LORD, to Thy dear will
    If Thou attune the heart,
  We in Thine Angels' music still
    May bear our lower part.

'Tis Thine each soul to calm,
Each wayward thought reclaim,
And make our life a daily psalm
Of glory to Thy Name.

A little while, and then
Shall come the glorious end ;
And songs of Angels and of men
In perfect praise shall blend.   Amen.

32 *The Lord shall give his people the blessing of peace.*

AT THE END OF DIVINE SERVICE.

SAVIOUR, again to Thy dear Name we raise
With one accord our parting hymn of praise ;
We stand to bless Thee ere our worship cease,
Then, lowly kneeling, wait Thy word of peace.

Grant us Thy peace upon our homeward way ;
With Thee began, with Thee shall end the day ;
Guard Thou the lips from sin, the hearts from
    shame,
That in this house have call'd upon Thy Name.

Grant us Thy peace, LORD, through the coming
    night ;
Turn Thou for us its darkness into light ;
From harm and danger keep Thy children free,
For dark and light are both alike to Thee.

Grant us Thy peace throughout our earthly life,
Our balm in sorrow, and our stay in strife ;
Then, when Thy voice shall bid our conflict cease,
Call us, O LORD, to Thine eternal peace.   Amen.

EVENING.

Praise him according to his excellent greatness.

AT THE END OF DIVINE SERVICE.

AND now the wants are told that brought
    Thy children to Thy knee ;
Here ling'ring still we ask for nought,
    But simply worship Thee.

The hope of heav'n's eternal days
    Absorbs not all the heart
That gives Thee glory, love, and praise,
    For being what Thou art.

For Thou art GOD, the One, the Same,
    O'er all things high and bright ;
And round us, when we speak Thy Name,
    There spreads a heav'n of light.

Oh wondrous peace, in thought to dwell
    On excellence divine ;
To know that nought in man can tell
    How fair Thy beauties shine !

O Thou, above all blessing blest,
    O'er thanks exalted far,
Thy very greatness is a rest
    To weaklings as we are ;

For when we feel the praise of Thee
    A task beyond our powers,
We say, "A perfect GOD is He,
    And He is fully ours."

All glory to the FATHER be,
    All glory to the SON,
All glory, HOLY GHOST, to Thee,
    While endless ages run.   Amen.

EVENING.

34 *Thou shalt not be afraid for any terror by night.*

Te lucis ante terminum.

FOR A LATE EVENING SERVICE.

TO Thee before the close of day,
    Creator of the world, we pray;
As Thou art wont, in mercy keep
Thy watch around us while we sleep.

Put every evil dream to flight,
And haunting visions of the night;
Keep far our ghostly foe, that we
Thy temples undefiled may be.

Almighty FATHER, hear our cry
Through JESUS CHRIST our LORD most High,
Who with the HOLY GHOST and Thee
Doth live and reign eternally.   Amen.

FRIDAY.

35 *The marks of the Lord Jesus.*

O JESU, crucified for man,
    O LAMB, all glorious on Thy throne,
Teach Thou our wond'ring souls to scan
    The mystery of Thy love unknown.

We pray Thee, grant us strength to take
    Our daily cross, whate'er it be,
And gladly, for Thine own dear sake,
    In paths of pain to follow Thee.

As on our daily way we go,
    Through light or shade, in calm or strife,
O may we bear Thy marks below
    In conquer'd sin and chasten'd life.

And week by week this day we ask
    That holy memories of Thy Cross
May sanctify *each* common task,
    And turn to gain each earthly loss.

FRIDAY.

Grant us, dear LORD, our cross to bear,
  Till at Thy feet we lay it down,
Win through Thy Blood our pardon there,
  And through the cross attain the crown.
                                Amen.

*Hymns on the Passion are suitable for use on this day of
the week. Also*

    448 LORD, as to Thy dear Cross we flee.
    452 O Saviour, may we never rest.
    610 O my Saviour, lifted.

SATURDAY.

36 *My heart was glad and my glory rejoiced, my flesh also
shall rest in hope.*

O lux beata Trinitas.

EVENING.

O TRINITY, most blessèd Light,
  O UNITY of sovereign might,
As now the fiery sun departs,
Shed Thou Thy beams within our hearts.

To Thee our morning song of praise,
To Thee our evening prayer we raise;
Thee may our glory evermore
In lowly reverence adore.

All praise to GOD the FATHER be,
All praise, Eternal SON, to Thee,
Whom with the SPIRIT we adore,
For ever and for evermore.   Amen.

The following Hymns are suitable for Saturday:

    138 Resting from His work to-day.
    381 Oh, what the joy and the glory must be.
    447 Great Mover of all hearts.

SUNDAY.

37 *When Jesus was risen early the first day of the week.*

En dies est dominica.

AGAIN the LORD's own day is here,
The day to Christian people dear,
As week by week it bids them sing
The Resurrection of their King.

For His return to live and reign
Is our most sure and certain gain ;
And we, who trust in Him to save,
With Him are risen from the grave.

We, one and all, of Him possess'd,
Are with exceeding riches bless'd ;
For all He did, and all He bare,
And all He won, with Him we share.

Eternal glory, rest on high,
A blessèd immortality,
True peace and gladness, and a throne,
Are all His gifts, and all our own.

To Thee, Who art the soul's true rest,
Who times and seasons orderest,
Be glory, honour, thanks, and praise,
To-day and through the length of days.
Amen.

38 *And God said, Let there be light: and there was light.
. . . And the evening and the morning were the
first day.*

Die parente temporum.

ON this day, the first of days,
GOD the FATHER's Name we praise,
Who, creation's Lord and spring,
Did the world from darkness bring.

SUNDAY.

On this day th' Eternal SON
Over death His triumph won ;
On this day the SPIRIT came
With His gifts of living flame.

O that fervent love to-day
May in every heart have sway,
Teaching us to praise aright
GOD the source of life and light.

FATHER, Who didst fashion me
Image of Thyself to be,
Fill me with Thy love divine,
Let my every thought be Thine.

Holy JESUS, may I be
Dead and risen here with Thee,
And upon love's fire arise
Unto Thee a sacrifice.

Thou Who dost all gifts impart,
Shine, good SPIRIT, in my heart ;
Best of gifts Thyself bestow ;
Make me burn Thy love to know.

GOD, the one GOD of my heart,
I am Thine, and mine Thou art ;
Take me, blessèd ONE in THREE,
Here I give myself to Thee.   Amen.

39   *I was in the Spirit on the Lord's day.*

THIS is the day of light :
  Let there be light to-day ;
O Day-spring, rise upon our night,
  And chase its gloom away.

This is the day of rest :
  Our failing strength renew ;
On weary brain and troubled breast
Shed Thou Thy freshening dew.

(28)

SUNDAY.

This is the day of peace :
Thy peace our spirits fill :
Bid Thou the blasts of discord cease,
The waves of strife be still.

This is the day of prayer :
Let earth to heav'n draw near ;
Lift up our hearts to seek Thee there,
Come down to meet us here.

This is the day of Bread,
The Bread that Thou dost give ;
To-day for us Thy feast is spread,
That hung'ring souls may live.

This is the first of days :
Send forth Thy quickening Breath,
And wake dead souls to love and praise,
O Vanquisher of death.   Amen.

*This is the day which the Lord hath made: we will
rejoice and be glad in it.*

O DAY of rest and gladness,
O day of joy and light,
O balm of care and sadness,
Most beautiful, most bright ;
On thee the high and lowly
Before th' eternal throne
Sing Holy, Holy, Holy,
To the great THREE in ONE.

On thee at the Creation
The light first had its birth ;
On thee for our salvation
CHRIST rose from depths of earth ;
On thee our LORD victorious
The SPIRIT sent from heaven ;
And thus *on thee* most glorious
A triple light was given.

(29)

Thou art a cooling fountain
  In life's dry dreary sand :
From thee, like Pisgah's mountain,
  We view our promised land ;
A day of sweet refection,
  A day of holy love,
A day of resurrection
  From earth to things above,

To-day on weary nations
  The heav'nly Manna falls ;
To holy convocations
  The silver trumpet calls,
Where Gospel-light is glowing
  With pure and radiant beams,
And living water flowing
  With soul-refreshing streams.

New graces ever gaining
  From this our day of rest,
We reach the rest remaining
  To spirits of the blest ;
To HOLY GHOST be praises,
  To FATHER, and to SON ;
The Church her voice upraises
  To Thee, blest THREE in ONE.
          Amen.

41 *Blessed is he that cometh in the name of the Lord.*

THIS is the day the LORD hath made ;
  He calls the hours His own :
Let heav'n rejoice, let earth be glad,
  And praise surround the throne.

To-day He rose and left the dead,
  And Satan's empire fell ;
To-day the saints His triumphs spread,
  And all His wonders tell.

Hosanna to th' anointed King,
  To David's holy Son !
Make haste to help us, LORD, and bring
  Salvation from Thy throne.

Bless'd be the LORD Who comes to men
  With messages of grace ;
Who comes in GOD His Father's Name
  To save our sinful race.

Hosanna in the highest strains
  The Church on earth can raise !
The highest heav'ns, in which He reigns,
  Shall give Him nobler praise.   Amen.

42   *There shall be no night there.*

O luce qui mortalibus.

EVENING.

GREAT GOD, Who, hid from mortal sight,
  Dost dwell in unapproachèd light,
Before Whose throne with veilèd brow
In awe Thy sinless Angels bow ;

Awhile in darkness here below
We lie oppress'd with sin and woe ;
But splendours of th' eternal day
Ere long shall chase the night away,—

The day prepared for us by Thee—
The day reserved for us to see ;
A day but faintly imaged here
By brightest sun at noontide clear.

Too long, alas ! it still delays ;
It lingers yet, that day of days ;
And we, before *its* joy we win,
Must leave the burd'ning flesh of sin.

SUNDAY.

Then from these earthy bonds set free
The soul shall fly, O GOD, to Thee ;
Her blissful task for evermore
To see Thee, love Thee, and adore.

All-bounteous TRINITY, prepare
Our souls Thy hidden joy to share,
That this brief daytime, used aright,
May issue in eternal light.   Amen.

The following Hymns are also specially suitable for Sunday :

392 JESUS, where'er Thy people meet.
393 Great Shepherd of Thy people, hear.

ADVENT.

43 *Which cometh forth as a bridegroom out of his chamber.*

Conditor alme siderum.

CREATOR of the starry height,
Thy people's everlasting light,
JESU, Redeemer of us all,
Hear Thou Thy servants when they call.

Thou, sorrowing at the helpless cry
Of all creation doom'd to die,
Didst save our sick and helpless race
By healing gifts of heav'nly grace.

When earth was near its evening hour,
Thou didst, in love's redeeming power,
Like bridegroom from his chamber, come
Forth from a Virgin Mother's womb.

At Thy great Name, exalted now,
All knees in lowly homage bow ;
All things in heav'n and earth adore,
And own Thee LORD *for evermore.*

To Thee, O HOLY ONE, we pray,
Our Judge in that tremendous day,
Ward off, while yet we dwell below,
The weapons of our crafty foe.

To GOD the FATHER, GOD the SON,
And GOD the SPIRIT, THREE in ONE,
Praise, honour, might, and glory be
From age to age eternally.   Amen.

44   *He shall judge the world in righteousness.*

Verbum supernum prodiens.

O WORD, that goest forth on high
    From GOD's own depths eternally,
Who in these latter days art born
For succour to a world forlorn ;

Our hearts enlighten from above,
And kindle with the fire of love,
That we, who hear the call to-day,
At length may cast our sins away.

And when as Judge Thou drawest nigh,
The secrets of all hearts to try ;
When vengeance falls on hidden sin,
And Saints their promised reign begin ;

O let us not through evil past
Be driven from Thy face at last,
But with the Saints in glory be
To endless ages pure and free.

To GOD the FATHER, GOD the SON,
And GOD the SPIRIT, THREE in ONE,
Praise, honour, might, and glory be
From age to age eternally.   Amen.

45 *Now it is high time to awake out of sleep.*

Vox clara ecce intonat.

LOUD rings the warning voice around,
  And earth's dark places hear the sound
Away, false dreams ; vain shadows, fly ;
Lo ! CHRIST, the Dayspring, shines on high.

Now let th' enfeebled soul arise,
That in the dust all wounded lies ;
To banish sin and heal distress
Comes forth the Sun of righteousness.

The LAMB is sent to earth below
To free us from the debt we owe ;
To seek His mercy let us all
With prayers and tears before Him fall ;

That, when again He shall appear,
And all the world is wrapp'd in fear,
He may not then our sins requite,
But shield us with His love and might.

To GOD the FATHER, GOD the SON,
And GOD the SPIRIT, THREE in ONE,
Praise, honour, might, and glory be
From age to age eternally.   Amen.

46 *Now it is high time to awake out of sleep.*

Vox clara ecce intonat.

HARK ! a thrilling voice is sounding ;
  "CHRIST is nigh," it seems to say ;
"Cast away the dreams of darkness,
  O ye children of the day !"

Waken'd by the solemn warning,
  Let the earth-bound soul arise ;
CHRIST, her Sun, all ill dispelling,
  Shines upon the morning skies.

Lo! the LAMB, so long expected,
  Comes with pardon down from heaven;
Let us haste, with tears of sorrow,
  One and all to be forgiven;

That, when next He comes with glory,
  And the world is wrapp'd in fear,
With His mercy He may shield us,
  And with words of love draw near.

Honour, glory, might, and blessing
  To the FATHER and the SON,
With the Everlasting SPIRIT, .
  While eternal ages run.   Amen.

47   *The Redeemer shall come to Zion.*
         Veni, veni, Emmanuel.

O COME, O come, Emmanuel,
    And ransom captive Israel,
That mourns in lonely exile here,
Until the SON of GOD appear.
      Rejoice! Rejoice! Emmanuel
      Shall come to thee, O Israel.

O come, Thou Rod of Jesse, free
Thine own from Satan's tyranny;
From depths of hell Thy people save,
And give them victory o'er the grave.
      Rejoice! Rejoice! Emmanuel
      Shall come to thee, O Israel.

O come, Thou Dayspring, from on high,
And cheer us by Thy drawing nigh;
Disperse the gloomy clouds of night,
And death's dark shadows put to flight.
      Rejoice! Rejoice! Emmanuel
      Shall come to thee, O Israel.

ADVENT.

O come, Thou Key of David, come
And open wide our heav'nly home ;
Make safe the way that leads on high
And close the path to misery.
    Rejoice ! Rejoice ! Emmanuel
    Shall come to thee, O Israel.

O come, Adonai, Lord of might,
Who to Thy tribes, on Sinai's height,
In ancient times didst give the law
In cloud and majesty and awe.
    Rejoice ! Rejoice ! Emmanuel
    Shall come to thee, O Israel. Amen.

48 *Tell ye the daughter of Sion, Behold, thy King com*
unto thee.

Instantis adventum Dei.

THE Advent of our King
    Our prayers must now employ,
And we must hymns of welcome sing
    In strains of holy joy.

The Everlasting Son
    Incarnate deigns to be ;
Himself a servant's form puts on,
    To set His servants free.

Daughter of Sion, rise
    To meet thy lowly King ;
Nor let thy faithless heart despise
    The peace He comes to bring.

As Judge, on clouds of light,
    He soon will come again,
And His true members all unite
    With Him in heav'n to reign.

ADVENT.

Before the dawning day
Let sin's dark deeds be gone,
The old man all be put away,
The new man all put on.

All glory to the SON,
Who comes to set us free,
With FATHER, SPIRIT, ever One,
Through all eternity.   Amen.

19 *The voice of one crying in the wilderness, Prepare ye
the way of the Lord, make his paths straight.*

Jordanis oras prævia.

ON Jordan's bank the Baptist's cry
　　Announces that the LORD is nigh ;
Awake and hearken, for he brings
High tidings of the King of kings.

Then cleansed be every breast from sin ;
Make straight the way for GOD within ;
Prepare we in our hearts a home,
Where such a mighty Guest may come.

For Thou art our salvation, LORD,
Our refuge, and our great reward ;
Without Thy grace we waste away,
Like flowers that wither and decay.

To heal the sick stretch out Thine hand,
And bid the fallen sinner stand ;
Shine forth, and let Thy light restore
Earth's own true loveliness once more.

All praise, Eternal SON, to Thee
Whose Advent sets Thy people free,
Whom with the FATHER we adore,
And HOLY GHOST for evermore.   Amen.

(37)

ADVENT.

50 *At midnight there was a cry made, Behold the bridegroom cometh; go ye out to meet him.*

'Ιδοὺ ὁ Νυμφίος.

"BEHOLD the Bridegroom draweth nigh :"
  Hear ye the oft-repeated cry ?
Go forth into the midnight dim ;
For bless'd are they whom He shall find
With ready heart and watchful mind ;
  Go forth, my soul, to Him.

"Behold the Bridegroom cometh by,"
The call is echo'd from the sky :
  Go forth, ye servants, watch and wait ;
The slothful cannot join His train ;
No careless one may entrance gain ;
  Awake, my soul, 'tis late.

The wise will plead with one accord,
"O Holy, Holy, Holy LORD,
  On us Thy quickening grace bestow,
That none may reach the door too late,
When Thou shalt enter at the gate
  And to Thy kingdom go."

"Behold the Bridegroom draweth near,"
The warning falls on every ear :
  That night of dread shall come to all :
Behold, my soul, thy lamp so dim,
Rise, rise the smoking flax to trim ;
  Soon shalt thou hear His call.   Amen.

51 *He hath sent me to bind up the broken-hearted, to proclaim liberty to the captives.*

HARK the glad sound ! the Saviour comes,
  The Saviour promised long :
Let every heart prepare a throne,
  And every voice a song.

(38).

He comes, the prisoners to release
  In Satan's bondage held ;
The gates of brass before Him burst,
  The iron fetters yield.

He comes, the broken heart to bind,
  The bleeding soul to cure,
And with the treasures of His grace
  To bless the humble poor.

Our glad hosannas, Prince of peace,
  Thy welcome shall proclaim,
And heav'n's eternal arches ring
  With Thy belovèd Name. Amen.

2 *Behold, he cometh with clouds : and every eye shall see
  him, and they also which pierced him.*

LO ! He comes with clouds descending,
  Once for favour'd sinners slain ;
Thousand thousand Saints attending
  Swell the triumph of His train :
    Alleluia !
GOD appears on earth to reign.

Every eye shall now behold Him,
  Robed in dreadful majesty ;
Those who set at nought and sold Him,
  Pierced and nail'd Him to the Tree,
    Deeply wailing,
Shall the true Messiah see.

* Every island, sea, and mountain,
  Heav'n and earth, shall flee away ;
All who hate Him must, confounded,
  Hear the trump proclaim the Day :
    Come to judgment !
Justice can no more delay.

(39)

ADVENT.

*Now redemption, long expected,
　See in solemn pomp appear !
All His saints, by man rejected,
　Now shall meet Him in the air :
　　　Alleluia !
　See the Day of GOD appear !

Those dear tokens of His Passion
　Still His dazzling Body bears,
Cause of endless exultation
　To His ransom'd worshippers :
　　　With what rapture
　Gaze we on those glorious scars !

Yea, Amen, let all adore Thee,
　High on Thine eternal throne ;
Saviour, take the power and glory :
　Claim the Kingdom for Thine own :
　　　Alleluia !
　Thou shalt reign, and Thou alone.　Amen.
　　　These verses can be omitted.

53 *The Lord himself shall descend from heaven with a
shout, with the voice of the archangel, and with the
trump of God.*

GREAT GOD, what do I see and hear ?
　　The doom of things created :
The Judge of all men doth appear,
　On clouds of glory seated :
The trumpet sounds, the graves restore
The dead which they contain'd before ;
　Prepare, my soul, to meet Him.

The dead in CHRIST shall first arise
　At that last trumpet's sounding,
Caught up to meet Him in the skies,
　With joy their LORD *surrounding :*

No gloomy fears their souls dismay ;
His presence sheds eternal day
  On those prepared to meet Him.

Th' ungodly, fill'd with guilty fears,
  Behold His wrath prevailing ;
In woe they rise, but all their tears
  And sighs are unavailing :
The day of grace is past and gone ;
Trembling they stand before His throne,
  All unprepared to meet Him.

Great Judge, to Thee our prayers we pour,
  In deep abasement bending ;
O shield us through that last dread hour,
  Thy wondrous love extending :
May we, in this our trial day,
With faithful hearts Thy word obey,
  And thus prepare to meet Thee.   Amen.

54   *I sleep, but my heart waketh.*

In noctis umbra desides.

FOR A LATE EVENING SERVICE.

WHEN shades of night around us close,
    And weary limbs in sleep repose,
The faithful soul awake may be,
And yearning sigh, O LORD, to Thee.

O Thou, for Whom the nations long,
O Word of GOD, Thou Saviour strong,
Turn unto us Thy pitying eyes,
And bid at length the fallen rise.

O come, Redeemer, come and free
Thine own from their iniquity ;
The gates of heav'n again unfold,
Which Adam's trespass closed of old.

(41)

ADVENT.

All praise, Eternal Son, to Thee
Whose Advent sets Thy people free,
Whom with the FATHER we adore,
And HOLY GHOST for evermore.   Amen.

The following Hymns are suitable for this season:

104 LORD, in this Thy mercy's day.
234 Lo! from the desert homes.
235 The high forerunner of the morn.
302 Day of wrath! O day of mourning!
335 From highest heav'n th' Eternal SON.
352 Thou art coming, O my Saviour.
354 Thou Judge of quick and dead.
355 That day of wrath, that dreadful day.
370 Thy kingdom come, O GOD.
371 O quickly come, dread Judge of all.
374 Hail to the LORD'S Anointed.
377 The world is very evil.
428 A few more years shall roll.
429 Days and moments quickly flying.
433 Ye servants of the LORD.
434 Christian! seek not yet repose.
527 LORD, her watch Thy Church is keeping.
632 Litany of the Four Last Things.

CHRISTMAS.

55 *Behold, a virgin shall be with child, and shall bring
forth a son.*

Veni Redemptor gentium.

O COME, Redeemer of the earth,
   Show to the world Thy virgin birth;
Let age to age the wonder tell;
Such birth, O GOD, beseems Thee well.

No earthly father Thou dost own;
By GOD's o'ershadowing alone
The WORD made flesh to man is come,
The fair fruit of a mother's womb.

A maiden pure and undefiled
Is by the SPIRIT great with child;
Like standard fair, her virtues tell,
'Tis GOD within her deigns to dwell.

(42)

CHRISTMAS.

Forth from His chamber cometh He,
The court and bower of chastity ;
Henceforth in two-fold substance one,
A giant glad His course to run.

From GOD the FATHER He proceeds,
To GOD the FATHER back He speeds ;
Runs out His course to death and hell,
Returns on GOD's high throne to dwell.

O ancient as the FATHER Thou,
Gird on our flesh for victory now ;
The weakness of our mortal state
With deathless might invigorate.

E'en now Thy manger glows ; new light
Is borne upon the breath of night ;
Let darkness ne'er eclipse the ray,
And faith make everlasting day.

All praise to GOD the FATHER be,
All praise, Eternal SON, to Thee,
Whom with the SPIRIT we adore,
For ever and for evermore.   Amen.

or,

O LORD, the Virgin-born, to Thee
Eternal praise and glory be,
Whom with the FATHER we adore
And HOLY GHOST for evermore.   Amen.

NOTE.—*The first Doxology is sung only on Christmas Eve
at Evensong.*

56 *Who being in the form of God . . . took upon him the
form of a servant, and was made in the likeness of men.*

A solis ortus cardine.

FROM east to west, from shore to shore,
    Let every heart awake and sing
The Holy Child Whom Mary bore,
    The CHRIST, the everlasting King.

CHRISTMAS.

The world's divine Creator wears
    The form and fashion of a slave ;
Our very flesh our Maker shares,
    His fallen creature, man, to save.

Soon, as the day of grace was come,
    A Holy Thing found place on earth,
And in a spotless Virgin's womb
    Was fashion'd day by day for birth.

She travail'd and brought forth the SON,
    Announced before by Gabriel's voice,
Whose presence made the unborn John
    Within his mother's womb rejoice.

He shrank not from the oxen's stall,
    He lay within the manger bed,
And He Whose bounty feedeth all,
    At Mary's breast Himself was fed.

While high above the silent field
    The choirs of heav'n made festival,
To simple shepherds was reveal'd
    The Shepherd Who created all.

All glory for this blessèd morn
    To GOD the FATHER ever be ;
All praise to Thee, O Virgin-born,
    All praise, O HOLY GHOST, to Thee.
                    Amen.

57   *Christ Jesus came into the world to save sinners.*
        Christe, Redemptor omnium.

O CHRIST, Redeemer of our race,
    Thou Brightness of the FATHER's face
Of Him, and with Him ever ONE,
Ere times and seasons had begun ;

CHRISTMAS.

Thou that art very Light of Light,
Unfailing hope in sin's dark night,
Hear Thou the prayers Thy people pray
The wide world o'er, this blessèd day.

Remember, LORD of life and grace,
How once, to save a ruin'd race,
Thou didst our very flesh assume
In Mary's undefilèd womb.

This day, as year by year its light
Sheds o'er the world a radiance bright,
Tells how descending from the throne
Thou saved'st man, and Thou alone.

Thou by the FATHER'S will didst come
To call His banish'd children home ;
And heav'n and earth, and sea and shore
His love Who sent Thee here adore.

And gladsome too are we to-day,
Whose guilt Thy Blood has wash'd away :
Redeem'd the new-made song we sing ;
It is the birthday of our King.

O LORD, the Virgin-born, to Thee
Eternal praise and glory be,
Whom with the FATHER we adore
And HOLY GHOST for evermore.   Amen.

58   *God was manifest in the flesh.*
Corde natus ex parentis.

OF the FATHER'S love begotten
Ere the worlds began to be,
He is Alpha and Omega,
  He the source, the ending He,
Of the things that are, that have been,
  And that future years shall see,
        Evermore and evermore.

CHRISTMAS.

*At His word they were created ;
   He commanded ; it was done :
Heav'n and earth and depths of ocean
   In their threefold order one ;
All that grows beneath the shining
   Of the moon and orbèd sun,
          Evermore and evermore.

*He is found in human fashion,
   Death and sorrow here to know,
That the race of Adam's children,
   Doom'd by law to endless woe,
May not henceforth die and perish
   In the dreadful gulf below,
          Evermore and evermore.

Oh that Birth for ever blessèd !
   When the Virgin, full of grace,
By the HOLY GHOST conceiving,
   Bare the Saviour of our race,
And the Babe, the world's Redeemer,
   First reveal'd His sacred face,
          Evermore and evermore.

O ye heights of heav'n, adore Him ;
   Angel-hosts, His praises sing ;
Powers, Dominions, bow before Him,
   And extol our GOD and King :
Let no tongue on earth be silent,
   Every voice in concert ring,
          Evermore and evermore.

This is He Whom heav'n-taught singers
   Sang of old with one accord ;
Whom the Scriptures of the Prophets
   Promised in their faithful word ;
Now He shines, the long-expected ;
   Let creation praise its LORD,
          Evermore and evermore.

CHRISTMAS.

*Righteous Judge of souls departed,
  Righteous King of them that live,
On the FATHER'S throne exalted
  None in might with Thee may strive ;
Who at last in vengeance coming
  Sinners from Thy face shalt drive,
      Evermore and evermore.

Thee let old men, Thee let young men,
  Thee let boys in chorus sing ;
Matrons, virgins, little maidens,
  With glad voices answering ;
Let their guileless songs re-echo,
  And the heart its music bring,
      Evermore and evermore.

CHRIST, to Thee, with GOD the FATHER,
  And, O HOLY GHOST, to Thee,
Hymn and chant, and high thanksgiving,
  And unwearied praises be,
Honour, glory, and dominion,
  And eternal victory,
      Evermore and evermore. Amen.
   These verses can be omitted.

59   *Let us now go even unto Bethlehem.*
Adeste fideles.

O COME, all ye faithful,
  Joyful and triumphant,
O come ye, O come ye to Bethlehem ;
  Come and behold Him
  Born the King of Angels ;
O come, let us adore Him, CHRIST the LORD.

  GOD of GOD,
  LIGHT of LIGHT,
Lo ! He abhors not the Virgin's womb ;
  Very GOD,
  Begotten, not created ;
O come, *let us adore* Him, CHRIST the LORD.

CHRISTMAS.

Sing, choirs of Angels,
  Sing in exultation,
Sing, all ye citizens of heaven above :
  "Glory to GOD
  In the highest ; "
O come, let us adore Him, CHRIST the]

Yea, LORD, we greet Thee,
  Born this happy morning ;
JESU, to Thee be glory given,
  WORD of the FATHER,
  Now in flesh appearing.
O come, let us adore Him, CHRIST the]

60 *And this shall be a sign unto you; ye shall find t*
     wrapped in swaddling clothes, lying in a mang(

Jam desinant suspiria.

GOD from on high hath heard ;
    Let sighs and sorrows cease ;
Lo ! from the opening heav'n descends
  To man the promised peace.

Hark ! through the silent night
  Angelic voices swell ;
Their joyful songs proclaim that GOD
  Is born on earth to dwell.

See how the shepherd-band
  Speed on with eager feet ;
Come to the hallow'd cave with them
  The Holy Babe to greet.

But, Oh what sight appears
  Within that lowly door !
A manger-bed and swaddling clothes,
  A Child and Mother poor !

Art Thou the CHRIST? the SON?
The FATHER's image bright?
And see we Him Whose arm upholds
Earth and the starry height?

Yea, faith can pierce the cloud
Which veils Thy glory now;
We hail Thee GOD, before Whose throne
The Angels prostrate bow.

A silent teacher, LORD,
Thou bidd'st us not refuse
To bear what flesh would have us shun,
To shun what flesh would choose.

Our sinful pride to cure
With that pure love of Thine,
O be Thou born within our hearts,
Most Holy Child Divine.   Amen.

81　　　　*Good tidings of great joy.*

HIGH let us swell our tuneful notes,
　　And join th' Angelic throng,
For Angels no such love have known
　To wake a cheerful song.

Good-will to sinful men is shown,
　And peace on earth is given:
For, lo! th' incarnate Saviour comes
　With grace and truth from heaven.

Justice and peace, with sweet accord
　His rising beams adorn:
Let heav'n and earth in concert join,
　To us a Child is born!

Glory to GOD in highest strains
　In highest *worlds* be paid,
His glory by our lips proclaim'd,
　And by our lives display'd.

When shall we reach those blissful realms
Where CHRIST exalted reigns,
And learn of the celestial choir
Their own immortal strains ! Amen.

62 *Glory to God in the highest, and on earth peace, good will toward men.*

*HARK ! how all the welkin rings,
    Glory to the King of kings,
Peace on earth, and mercy mild,
GOD and sinners reconciled.
Joyful, all ye nations, rise,
Join the triumph of the skies ;
With th' Angelic host proclaim,
"CHRIST is born in Bethlehem."
    *Hark ! how all the welkin rings,
    Glory to the King of kings.

CHRIST, by highest heav'n adored,
CHRIST, the Everlasting LORD,
Late in time behold Him come,
Offspring of a Virgin's womb.
Veil'd in flesh the GODHEAD see !
Hail, th' Incarnate Deity !
Pleased as Man with man to dwell,
JESUS, our Emmanuel !
    *Hark ! &c.

Hail, the heav'n-born Prince of peace !
Hail, the Sun of righteousness !
Light and life to all He brings,
Risen with healing in His wings.
Mild He lays His glory by,
Born that man no more may die,
Born to raise the sons of earth,
Born to give them second birth.
    *Hark ! &c. Amen.

* *Or,* *Hark!* the herald-angels sing
    Glory to the new-born King,

63 *Behold I bring you good tidings of great joy.*

CHRISTIANS, awake, salute the happy morn,
 Whereon the Saviour of the world was born ;
Rise to adore the mystery of love,
Which hosts of Angels chanted from above ;
With them the joyful tidings first begun
Of GOD Incarnate and the Virgin's Son.

*Then to the watchful shepherds it was told,
Who heard th' Angelic herald's voice, " Behold,
I bring good tidings of a Saviour's birth
To you and all the nations upon earth :
This day hath GOD fulfill'd His promised word,
This day is born a Saviour, CHRIST the LORD."

*He spake ; and straightway the celestial choir
In hymns of joy, unknown before, conspire :
The praises of redeeming love they sang,
And heav'n's whole orb with Alleluias rang :
GOD's highest glory was their anthem still,
Peace upon earth, and unto men good will.

*To Bethlehem straight th' enlighten'd shepherds
 ran,
To see the wonder GOD had wrought for man,
And found, with Joseph and the Blessèd Maid,
Her Son, the Saviour, in a manger laid :
Then to their flocks, still praising GOD, return,
And their glad hearts with holy rapture burn.

O may we keep and ponder in our mind
GOD's wondrous love in saving lost mankind ;
Trace we the Babe, Who hath retrieved our loss,
From His poor manger to His bitter Cross ;
Tread in His steps, assisted by His grace,
Till man's *first heav'nly* state again takes place.

Then may we hope, th' Angelic hosts among,
To sing, redeem'd, a glad triumphal song:
He that was born upon this joyful day
Around us all His glory shall display;
Saved by His love, incessant we shall sing
Eternal praise to heav'n's Almighty King.

Amen

* *These verses can be omitted.*

64 *Unto you is born this day in the city of David a Savi*
which is Christ the Lord.

WHILE shepherds watch'd their flo
      by night,
  All seated on the ground,
The Angel of the LORD came down,
  And glory shone around.

"Féar not," said he ; for mighty dread
  Had seized their troubled mind ;
"Glad tidings of great joy I bring
  To you and all mankind.

"To you in David's town this day
  Is born of David's line
The Saviour, Who is CHRIST the LORD ;
  And this shall be the sign :

"The heav'nly Babe you there shall find
  To human view display'd,
All meanly wrapp'd in swathing bands,
  And in a manger laid."

Thus spake the seraph ; and forthwith
  Appear'd a shining throng
Of Angels praising GOD, who thus
  Address'd their joyful song :

"All glory be to GOD on high,
  And on the earth be peace ;
Good-will henceforth from heav'n to men
  Begin and never cease." Amen.

35 *We are come to worship him.*

ANGELS, from the realms of glory,
  Wing your flight o'er all the earth ;
Ye who sang creation's story,
  Now proclaim Messiah's birth ;
    Come and worship,
Worship CHRIST, the new-born King.

Shepherds, in the field abiding,
  Watching o'er your flocks by night ;
GOD with man is now residing,
  Yonder shines the Infant Light ;
    Come and worship,
Worship CHRIST, the new-born King.

Sages, leave your contemplations,
  Brighter visions beam afar ;
Seek the great Desire of nations,
  Ye have seen His natal star ;
    Come and worship,
Worship CHRIST, the new-born King.

All creation, join in praising
  GOD the FATHER, SPIRIT, SON,
Evermore your voices raising
  To th' Eternal THREE in ONE ;
    Come and worship,
Worship CHRIST, the new-born King.   Amen.

36 *Jesus Christ is come in the flesh.*

CHRISTIANS, sing out with exultation,
  And praise your Benefactor's Name !
To-day the Author of salvation,
  The FATHER's Well-belovèd came.
Of undefilèd Virgin Mother
  An Infant, all Divine, was born,
And GOD Himself became your Brother
  Upon *this happy Christmas* morn.

CHRISTMAS.

In Him eternal might and power
    To human weakness hath inclined ;
And this poor Child brings richest dower
    Of gifts and graces to mankind.
While here His majesty disguising,
    A servant's form the Master wears,
Behold the beams of glory rising
    E'en from His poverty and tears.

A stable serves Him for a dwelling,
    And for a bed a manger mean ;
Yet o'er His head, His advent telling,
    A new and wondrous star is seen.
Angels rehearse to men the story,
    The joyful story of His birth ;
To Him they raise the anthem—" Glory
    To GOD on high, and peace on earth !"

For through this holy Incarnation
    The primal curse is done away ;
And blessèd peace o'er all creation
    Hath shed its pure and gentle ray.
Then, in that heav'nly concert joining,
    O Christian men, with one accord,
Your voices tunefully combining,
    Salute the Birthday of your LORD.   Ame

67   *With my soul have I desired thee in the night.*
Salvator mundi Domine.
FOR A LATE EVENING SERVICE.

O SAVIOUR of the world, we pray,
   As Thou hast saved us through the day
Now in the coming night defend
And save us alway to the end.

Be with us, LORD, in mercy nigh,
And spare Thy servants when they cry ;
Blot out our misdeeds from Thy sight,
And turn our darkness into light.

(54)

CHRISTMAS.

Let not dull sleep the soul oppress,
Nor stealthy foe the heart possess ;
Grant that our flesh may ever be
An holy temple meet for Thee.

To Thee, Who dost by rest renew
Our wasted strength, we humbly sue,
That when we shall unclose our eyes
All pure and chaste we may arise.

O LORD, the Virgin-born, to Thee
Eternal praise and glory be,
Whom with the FATHER we adore
And HOLY GHOST for evermore.   **Amen.**

or,

All praise to GOD the FATHER be,
All praise, Eternal SON, to Thee,
Whom with the SPIRIT we adore,
For ever and for evermore.   **Amen.**

ᴺᵀᴱ.—*When this Hymn is sung in other seasons the second
Doxology is used.*

The following Hymns are suitable for this season :
83 The people that in darkness sat.
335 From highest heav'n th' Eternal SON.

SAINT STEPHEN'S DAY.

8 *Be thou faithful unto death, and I will give thee a
crown of life.*

O qui tuo, dux martyrum.

FIRST of Martyrs, thou whose name
Doth itself a crown proclaim,
Not of flowers that fade away
Fashion we thy crown to-day.

Bright the stones which bruise thee gleam,
Sprinkled with thy life-blood's stream ;
Stars around *thy* sainted head
Such a radiance could not shed.

(55)

SAINT STEPHEN'S DAY.

Every wound upon thy brow
Sparkles with unearthly glow ;
Like an Angel's is the glance
Of thy shining countenance.

First to offer up for CHRIST
Life for His life sacrificed ;
By a death like His to be
Witness for His Deity.

First to follow where He trod
Through the deep Red Sea of blood ;
First, but after thee shall press
Ranks of Martyrs numberless.

Glory to the FATHER be,
Glory, VIRGIN-BORN, to Thee,
Glory to the HOLY GHOST,
Praised by men and heav'nly host. Am

The following Hymns are suitable for this Festival :

173 Part 2. HOLY GHOST, Illuminator.
200 O GOD, Thy soldiers' faithful LORD.
217 The SON of GOD goes forth to war.

SAINT JOHN THE EVANGELIST'S DAY.

69 *That which we have seen and heard declare we unto*
Quæ dixit, egit, pertulit.

THE life, which GOD's Incarnate WORD
 Lived here below with men,
Three blest Evangelists record
 With heav'n-inspirèd pen :

John soars on high, beyond the three,
 To GOD the FATHER's throne,
And shows in what deep mystery
 The WORD with GOD is One.

(56)

Upon the Saviour's loving breast
Permitted to recline,
'Twas thence he drew, in moments blest,
Rich stores of truth divine :
And thence did that consuming love
His inmost spirit fill,
Which, once enkindled from above,
Burns in his pages still.

O, dear to CHRIST !—to thee upon
His Cross, of all bereft,
Thou virgin soul, the virgin SON
His virgin Mother left.

JESU, the Virgin's Holy SON,
We praise Thee and adore,
Who art with GOD the FATHER One
And SPIRIT evermore.   Amen.

70   *The disciple whom Jesus loved.*

WORD Supreme, before creation
Born of GOD eternally,
Who didst will for our salvation
. To be born on earth, and die ;
Well Thy Saints have kept their station,
Watching till Thine hour drew nigh.

Now 'tis come, and faith espies Thee ;
Like an eaglet in the morn,
One in steadfast worship eyes Thee,
Thy beloved, Thy latest born :
In Thy glory he descries Thee
Reigning from the tree of scorn.

*He upon Thy bosom lying
Thy true tokens learn'd by heart ;
And Thy dearest pledge in dying,
LORD, Thou didst to him impart ;
Show'dst him how, all grace supplying,
Blood *and* water from Thee start.

*He first hoping and believing
   Did beside the grave adore ;
Latest he, the warfare leaving,
   Landed on th' eternal shore ;
And his witness we receiving,
   Own Thee LORD for evermore.

Much he ask'd in loving wonder,
   On Thy bosom leaning, LORD ;
In the secret place of thunder
   Answer kind didst Thou accord,
Wisdom for Thy Church to ponder
   Till the day of dread award.

Lo ! heav'n's doors lift up, revealing
   How Thy judgments earthward move ;
Scrolls unfolded, trumpets pealing,
   Wine cups from the wrath above ;
Yet o'er all a soft voice stealing—
   "Little children, trust and love !"

Thee, th' Almighty King Eternal,
   FATHER of th' Eternal WORD,
Thee, the FATHER'S WORD Supernal,
   Thee, of Both, the BREATH adored,
Heav'n, and earth, and realms infernal
   Own One glorious GOD and LORD.
                  Amen.

    * *These verses can be omitted.*

71 *I John . . . was in the isle that is called Patmos, fo*
the word of God, and for the testimony of Jesus Christ

Jussu tyranni pro fide.

A N exile for the faith
    Of his Incarnate LORD,
Beyond the stars, beyond all space,
   His soul in vision soar'd :

There saw in glory Him
Who liveth, and was dead,
There Judah's Lion, and the Lamb
That for our ransom bled :

There of the kingdom learn'd
The mysteries sublime.;
How, sown in Martyr's blood, the faith
Should spread from clime to clime.

There heard through highest heav'n
The Alleluia sound,
The loud Amen that ever rolls
Th' eternal throne around.

LORD, give us grace, like him,
In Thee to live and die ;
To spurn the fleeting things of earth,
And seek for joys on high.

JESU, our risen LORD,
We praise Thee and adore,
Who art with GOD the FATHER One
And SPIRIT evermore.   Amen.

THE INNOCENTS' DAY.

12   *The first-fruits unto God and to the Lamb.*

Salvete flores martyrum.

SWEET flow'rets of the martyr band,
    Pluck'd by the tyrant's ruthless hand
Upon the threshold of the morn,
Like rosebuds by a tempest torn ;

First victims for th' Incarnate LORD,
A tender flock to feel the sword ;
Beside *the very altar, gay*
With palm and crown, ye seem'd to play.

(59)

THE INNOCENTS' DAY.

Ah ! what avail'd king Herod's wrath ?
He could not stop the Saviour's path :
Alone, while others murder'd lay,
In safety CHRIST is borne away.

O LORD, the Virgin-born, to Thee
Eternal praise and glory be,
Whom with the FATHER we adore
And HOLY GHOST for evermore.   Amen.

73 *These are they which follow the Lamb whithersoere*
he goeth.

Hymnum canentes martyrum.

A HYMN for Martyrs sweetly sing ;
For Innocents your praises bring ;
Of whom in tears was earth bereaved,
Whom heav'n with songs of joy received ;
Whose Angels see the FATHER'S face
World without end, and hymn His grace ;
And, while they praise their glorious King,
A hymn for Martyrs sweetly sing.

A voice from Ramah was there sent,
A voice of weeping and lament,
While Rachel mourn'd her children sore,
Whom for the tyrant's sword she bore.
After brief taste of earthly woe
Eternal triumph now they know ;
For whom, by cruel torments rent,
A voice from Ramah was there sent.

Fear not, O little flock and bless'd,
The lion that your life oppress'd ;
To heav'nly pastures ever new
The heav'nly Shepherd leadeth you ;
Who, dwelling now on Sion's hill,
The Lamb's own footsteps follow still,
By tyrant there no more distrest ;
Fear not, O little flock and bless'd.

And every tear is wiped away
By your dear FATHER's hands for aye :
Death hath no pow'r to hurt you more ;
Your own is life's eternal shore.
And all who, good seed bearing, weep,
In everlasting joy shall reap,
What time they shine in heav'nly day,
And every tear is wiped away.   Amen.

14   *They are without fault before the throne of God.*

GLORY to Thee, O LORD,
　　Who from this world of sin
By cruel Herod's ruthless sword
　　Those precious ones didst win.

Baptized in their own blood,
　　Earth's untried perils o'er,
They pass'd unconsciously the flood,
　　And safely gain'd the shore.

Glory to Thee for all
　　The ransom'd infant band,
Who since that hour have heard Thy call,
　　And reach'd the quiet land.

O that our hearts within,
　　Like theirs, were pure and bright !
O that as free from wilful sin
　　We shrank not from Thy sight !

LORD, help us every hour
　　Thy cleansing grace to claim ;
In life to glorify Thy power,
　　In death to praise Thy Name.   Amen.

(61)

THE CIRCUMCISION.

75 *When eight days were accomplished for the circumcising of the child, his name was called JESUS.*

Debilis cessent elementa legis.

THE ancient law departs,
  And all its fears remove,
For JESUS makes with faithful hearts
  A covenant of love.

The Light of Light Divine,
  True brightness undefiled,
He bears for us the pain of sin,
  A holy spotless Child.

His infant body now
  Begins the Cross to feel;
Those precious drops of Blood that flow
  For death the victim seal.

To-day the Name is Thine
  At which we bend the knee;
They call Thee JESUS, Child Divine;
  Our JESUS deign to be.

All praise, Eternal SON,
  For Thy redeeming love,
With FATHER, SPIRIT, ever One,
  In glorious might above.   Amen.

76 *God sent forth his Son, made of a woman, made under the law, to redeem them that were under the law.*

Felix dies quem proprio.

O BLESSÈD day, when first was pour'd
  The Blood of our redeeming LORD!
O blessèd day, when CHRIST began
His saving work for sinful man!

While from His Mother's bosom fed,
His precious Blood He wills to shed;
A foretaste of His death He feels,
An earnest of His love reveals.

(62)

THE CIRCUMCISION.

Scarce come to earth, His FATHER's will
With prompt obedience to fulfil,
A victim even now He lies
Before the day of sacrifice.

In love our guilt He undertakes,
Sinless for sin atonement makes ;
The great Lawgiver for our aid
Obedient to the law is made.

The wound He through the law endures
Our freedom from that law secures ;
Henceforth a holier law prevails,
That law of love which never fails.

LORD, circumcise our hearts, we pray,
And take what is not Thine away ;
Write Thine own Name upon our hearts,
Thy law within our inward parts.

O LORD, the Virgin-born, to Thee
Eternal praise and glory be,
Whom with the FATHER we adore
And HOLY GHOST for evermore.   Amen.

The following Hymns are suitable for this Festival :
    338 To the Name of our salvation.
    341 Conquering kings their titles take.

NEW YEAR'S DAY.

'7 *Hear thou in heaven, and forgive the sin of thy
servants, and of thy people Israel, that thou teach
them the good way wherein they should walk.*

Lapsus est annus.

THE year is gone beyond recall,
    With all its hopes and fears,
With all its bright and gladd'ning smiles,
    With all its mourners' tears ;

NEW YEAR'S DAY.

Thy thankful people praise Thee, LORD,
  For countless gifts received ;
O may our country keep the faith
  Which Saints of old believed !

To Thee we come, O gracious LORD,
  The new-born year to bless ;
Defend our land from pestilence ;
  Give peace and plenteousness ;

Forgive this nation's many sins ;
  The growth of vice restrain ;
And help us all with sin to strive,
  And crowns of life to gain.

From evil deeds that stain the past
  We now desire to flee,
And pray that future years may all
  Be spent, good LORD, for Thee.

O FATHER, let Thy watchful eye
  Still look on us in love,
That we may praise Thee, year by year,
  As Angels do above.   Amen.

78 *So teach us to number our days, that we may apply ou*
hearts unto wisdom.

FOR Thy mercy and Thy grace,
  Faithful through another year,
Hear our song of thankfulness ;
Jesu, our Redeemer, hear.

In our weakness and distress,
Rock of strength, be Thou our stay ;
In the pathless wilderness
Be our true and living way.

Who of us death's awful road
In the coming year shall tread,
With Thy rod and staff, O GOD,
Comfort Thou his dying bed.

(64)

Keep us faithful, keep us pure,
Keep us evermore Thine own,
Help, O help us to endure,
Fit us for the promised crown.   Amen.

The following Hymns are suitable for this occasion:

354 Thou Judge of quick and dead.
403 O GOD, our help in ages past.
426 Thy way, not mine, O LORD.
428 A few more years shall roll.
429 Days and moments quickly flying.
636 Litany for the Rogation Days.

EPIPHANY.

79   *The Life was manifested.*
Hostis Herodes impie.

WHY doth that impious Herod fear
    When told that CHRIST the King is near ?
He takes not earthly realms away,
Who gives the realms that ne'er decay.

The Eastern sages saw from far
And follow'd on His guiding star ;
By light their way to Light they trod,
And by their gifts confess'd their GOD.

The Lamb of GOD to Jordan's wave
New virtue as it touch'd Him gave ;
No sins were His to cleanse that day,
His washing takes our sins away.

To manifest His power divine,
The water reddens into wine :
He spake the word, and forth it flow'd
In streams that nature ne'er bestow'd.

All glory, JESU, be to Thee
For this Thy glad Epiphany,
Whom with the FATHER we adore
And HOLY GHOST for evermore.   Amen.

EPIPHANY.

80 *The kindness and love of God our Saviour toward man appeared.*

A Patre unigenitus.

THE FATHER'S sole-begotten SON
 Came down, a Virgin's child, to earth ;
His Cross for all believers won
 The hallow'd font, the second birth.

Forth from the heav'ns the Highest came,
 In form of man with men abode ;
Redeem'd His world by death of shame,
 The joys of endless life bestow'd.

Redeemer, come with power benign,
 Dwell in the souls that look for Thee ;
O let Thy light within us shine
 That we may Thy salvation see.

Abide with us, O LORD, we pray,
 Dispel the gloom of doubt and woe ;
Wash every stain of guilt away,
 Thy loving remedies bestow.

Thou camest, LORD ; and well we know
 That Thou wilt likewise come again ;
Thy kingdom shield from every foe,
 Thy honour and Thy rule maintain.

All glory, JESU, be to Thee
 For this Thy glad Epiphany,
Whom with the FATHER we adore
 And HOLY GHOST for evermore.   Amen.

81   *We have seen his star in the east.*

Quæ stella sole pulchrior.

WHAT star is this, with beams so bright,
 More beauteous than the noonday light ?
It shines to herald forth the King,
And Gentiles to His crib to bring.

EPIPHANY.

True spake the seer who from afar
Beheld the rise of Jacob's star;
And Eastern sages with amaze
Upon the wondrous token gaze.

The guiding star above is bright:
Within them shines a clearer light,
And leads them on with power benign
To seek the Giver of the sign.

True love can brook no dull delay;
Nor toil nor dangers stop their way:
Home, kindred, father-land, and all
They leave at their Creator's call.

O Jesu, while the star of grace
Allures us now to seek Thy face,
Let not our slothful hearts refuse
The guidance of that light to use.

All glory, Jesu, be to Thee
For this Thy glad Epiphany,
Whom with the Father we adore
And Holy Ghost for evermore.   Amen.

2 *And thou, Bethlehem, in the land of Juda, art not the least among the princes of Juda: for out of thee shall come a Governor, that shall rule my people Israel.*

O sola magnarum urbium.

EARTH has many a noble city;
   Bethlehem, thou dost all excel:
Out of thee the Lord from heaven
   Came to rule His Israel.

Fairer than the sun at morning
   Was the star that told His birth,
To the world its God announcing
   Seen in fleshly form on earth.

EPIPHANY.

Eastern sages at His cradle
　　Make oblations rich and rare ;
See them give, in deep devotion,
　　Gold, and frankincense, and myrrh.

Sacred gifts of mystic meaning :
　　Incense doth their GOD disclose,
Gold the King of kings proclaimeth,
　　Myrrh His sepulchre foreshows.

JESU, Whom the Gentiles worshipp'd
　　At Thy glad Epiphany,
Unto Thee, with GOD the FATHER
　　And the SPIRIT, glory be.　Amen.

83　　*The people which sat in darkness saw great light.*

THE people that in darkness sat
　　A glorious light have seen ;
The Light has shined on them who long
　　In shades of death have been.

To hail Thee, Sun of righteousness,
　　The gathering nations come ;
They joy as when the reapers bear
　　Their harvest treasures home.

For Thou their burden dost remove,
　　And break the tyrant's rod,
As in the day when Midian fell
　　Before the sword of GOD.

For unto us a Child is born,
　　To us a Son is given,
And on His shoulder ever rests
　　All power in earth and heaven.

His Name shall be the Prince of peace,
　　The Everlasting LORD,
The Wonderful; the Counsellor,
　　The GOD by all adored.

(68)

His righteous government and power
 Shall over all extend;
On judgment and on justice based,
 His reign shall have no end.

LORD JESUS, reign in us, we pray,
 And make us Thine alone,
Who with the FATHER ever art
 And HOLY SPIRIT One. Amen.

84 *When they saw the star they rejoiced with exceeding
great joy.*

AS with gladness men of old
 Did the guiding star behold,
As with joy they hail'd its light,
Leading onward, beaming bright,
So, most gracious LORD, may we
Evermore be led to Thee.

As with joyful steps they sped,
Saviour, to Thy lowly bed,
There to bend the knee before
Thee Whom heav'n and earth adore,
So may we with willing feet
Ever seek Thy mercy-seat.

As they offer'd gifts most rare
At Thy cradle rude and bare,
So may we with holy joy,
Pure and free from sin's alloy,
All our costliest treasures bring,
CHRIST, to Thee our heav'nly King.

Holy JESUS, every day
Keep us in the narrow way;
And, when earthly things are past,
Bring our ransom'd souls at last
Where they need no star to guide,
Where no clouds Thy glory hide.

EPIPHANY.

In the heav'nly country bright
Need they no created light ;
Thou its Light, its Joy, its Crown,
Thou its Sun which goes not down ;
There for ever may we sing
Alleluias to our King.   Amen.

The following Hymns are suitable for this Festival :

372 GOD of mercy, GOD of grace.
373 JESUS shall reign where'er the sun.
374 Hail to the LORD'S Anointed.

FROM THE OCTAVE OF THE EPIPHANY TO

SEPTUAGESIMA.

85 *The light shineth in darkness ; and the darkness
comprehended it not.*

Christus tenebris obsitam.

NOW heaven's growing light is manifest
Through Judah's land, which in the dark
ness lies ;
But they have steel'd their breast,
And closed their earth-bound eyes.

Now signs of present Godhead teem around,
The dead are raised, feet to the lame are given,
The dumb a tongue hath found,
The blind man sees the heaven.

But Israel hath become blind, deaf, and dead :
He is their Sun ; but they, like birds of night,
To unclean haunts have fled,
And will not brook the light.

LORD, we would turn to Thee, and court the ray
Thou art th' Eternal FATHER's Charity ;
And never-setting day
For ever dwells in Thee.

FROM THE OCTAVE OF THE EPIPHANY TO SEPTUAGESIMA.

et not the night creep o'er us, Light Divine ;
et not the night creep o'er our hearts below ;
    With Thy truth may they shine,
    With Thy love burn and glow.

'o Thee, with FATHER and with SPIRIT bless'd,
ESU, to Thee, born of a Maiden pure,
    Be highest praise address'd,
    And evermore endure. Amen.

6 *And he went down with them, and came to Nazareth, and was subject unto them.*

Divine, crescebas, Puer.

THE Heav'nly Child in stature grows,
    And, growing, learns to die ;
And still His early training shows
    His coming agony.

The SON of GOD His glory hides
    To dwell with kinsfolk poor ;
And He, Who made the heav'ns, abides
    In village home obscure.

Those mighty hands that rule the sky
    No earthly toil refuse ;
The Maker of the stars on high
    An humble trade pursues.

He at Whose word swift Angels fly
    His dread commands to bear,
Obeys in deep humility
    A simple carpenter.

For this Thy lowliness reveal'd,
    JESU, we Thee adore,
And praise to GOD the FATHER yield
    And SPIRIT evermore. Amen.

87 *The Lord ... shall suddenly come to his temple.*

WITHIN the FATHER's house
  The SON hath found His home ;
And to His temple suddenly
  The LORD of Life hath come.

The doctors of the law
  Gaze on the wondrous Child,
And marvel at His gracious words
  Of wisdom undefiled.

Yet not to them is given
  The mighty truth to know,
To lift the fleshly veil which hides
  Incarnate GOD below.

The secret of the LORD
  Escapes each human eye,
And faithful pond'ring hearts await
  The full Epiphany.

LORD, visit Thou our souls,
  And teach us by Thy grace
Each dim revealing of Thyself
  With loving awe to trace ;

Till from our darken'd sight
  The cloud shall pass away,
And on the cleansèd soul shall burst
  The everlasting day ;

Till we behold Thy face,
  And know, as we are known,
Thee, FATHER, SON, and HOLY GHOST,
  Co-equal THREE in ONE. Amen.

8   *The Son of God was manifested.*

SONGS of thankfulness and praise,
   JESU, LORD, to Thee we raise,
Manifested by the star
To the sages from afar ;
Branch of royal David's stem
In Thy birth at Bethlehem ;
Anthems be to Thee addrest,
GOD in Man made manifest.

Manifest at Jordan's stream,
Prophet, Priest, and King supreme ;
And at Cana wedding-guest
In Thy Godhead manifest ;
Manifest in power divine,
Changing water into wine ;
Anthems be to Thee addrest,
GOD in Man made manifest.

Manifest in making whole
Palsied limbs and fainting soul ;
Manifest in valiant fight,
Quelling all the devil's might ;
Manifest in gracious will,
Ever bringing good from ill ;
Anthems be to Thee addrest,
GOD in Man made manifest.

Sun and moon shall darken'd be,
Stars shall fall, the heav'ns shall flee ;
CHRIST will then like lightning shine,
All will see His glorious Sign ;
All will then the trumpet hear,
All will see the Judge appear ;
Thou by all wilt be confest,
GOD *in Man* made manifest.

FROM THE OCTAVE OF THE EPIPHANY
TO SEPTUAGESIMA.

Grant us grace to see Thee, LORD,
Mirror'd in Thy holy word ;
May we imitate Thee now,
And be pure, as pure art Thou ;
That we like to Thee may be
At Thy great Epiphany,
And may praise Thee, ever Blest,
GOD in Man made manifest.   Amen.

During this period Hymns of a general character may be sung.

89   *And again they said, Alleluia.*

Alleluia, dulce carmen.

FOR THE WEEK BEFORE SEPTUAGESIMA.

ALLELUIA, song of sweetness,
    Voice of joy that cannot die ;
ALLELUIA is the anthem
    Ever dear to choirs on high ;
In the house of GOD abiding
    Thus they sing eternally.

ALLELUIA thou resoundest,
    True Jerusalem and free ;
ALLELUIA, joyful Mother,
    All thy children sing with thee ;
But by Babylon's sad waters
    Mourning exiles now are we.

ALLELUIA may not always
    Be our song while here below ;
ALLELUIA our transgressions
    Make us for a while forgo ;
For the solemn time is coming
    When our tears for sin must flow.

FROM THE OCTAVE OF THE EPIPHANY
TO SEPTUAGESIMA.

Therefore in our hymns we pray Thee,
　Grant us, Blessèd TRINITY,
At the last to keep Thine Easter
　In our home beyond the sky,
There to Thee for ever singing
　ALLELUIA joyfully.　Amen.

The following Hymns are suitable for this week:
328 The strain upraise of joy and praise.
383 Sing Alleluia forth in duteous praise.

SEPTUAGESIMA.

90 *How shall we sing the Lord's song in a strange land?*
Te læta, mundi Conditor.

CREATOR of the world, to Thee
　An endless rest of joy belongs ;
And heav'nly choirs are ever free
To sing on high their festal songs.

But we are fallen creatures here,
Where toil and travail daily come ;
And how can we in exile drear
Sing out, as they, sweet songs of home ?

O FATHER, Who dost promise still
That contrite souls shall mercy see,
Grant us to weep for deeds of ill
That banish us so long from Thee :

But let the wholesome sorrow blend
With hope, and faith which hope sustains ;
A little while, and it shall end
In Thine own rest and those glad strains.
　　　　　　　　　　　Amen.

91 *The God of heaven shall set up a kingdom, which shall never be destroyed.*

Rebus creatis nil egens.

NO want of Thine, O GOD, to meet,
   Who in Thyself art bliss complete,
Thou issuedst from Thy secret place
To set the world upon its base.

Things that were not, Thou, LORD, didst call,
And they obey'd Thee one and all,
And all to their Creator raise
A wondrous harmony of praise.

But while this visible fair earth
From Thy creative will took birth,
Thou in Thy counsel didst enfold
Another world of loftier mould.

That world doth our Redeemer frame,
And build upon His own great Name,
And sow, wherever speech is heard,
The seed of His almighty word.

When time itself has pass'd away,
That higher world shall share for aye
The throne and board of CHRIST in heaven,
By Him to GOD the FATHER given.

O FATHER, SON, and SPIRIT blest,
Thou GOD, Who all things orderest,
Preserve, direct, and sanctify
Thy realm below, Thy realm on high.   Amen.

From Septuagesima Sunday to Lent the following Hymns are
also suitable:
(For Septuagesima.)
15 O blest Creator of the light.
326 O worship the King.
331 There is a book, who runs may read.
(For Sexagesima.)
334 Almighty FATHER, Unoriginate.
337 Praise to the Holiest in the height.
(For Quinquagesima.)
363 Gracious SPIRIT. HOLY GHOST.
447 Great Mover of all hearts.

LENT.

92 *Now, saith the Lord, turn ye even to me with all your heart, and with fasting, and with weeping, and with mourning.*

Ex more docti mystico.

BY precepts taught of ages past,
 Now let us keep again the fast
Which, year by year, in order meet
Of forty days is made complete.

The law and seers that were of old
In divers ways this Lent foretold,
Which CHRIST Himself, the Lord and Guide
Of every season, sanctified.

More sparing therefore let us make
The words we speak, the food we take,
Deny ourselves in mirth and sleep,
Our bounden watch more strictly keep;

Avoid the evil thoughts that roll
Like waters o'er the heedless soul;
Nor let the foe occasion find
Our souls in slavery to bind.

In prayer together let us fall,
And cry for mercy one and all,
And weep before the Judge, and say,
O turn from us Thy wrath away.

Thy grace have we offended sore
By sins, O GOD, which we deplore;
Pour down upon us from above
The riches of Thy pardoning love.

Remember, fallen though we be,
That yet Thine handiwork are we;
Nor let the honour of Thy Name
Be by another put to shame.

(77)

Put all our evil deeds away,
Enlarge the good for which we pray ;
That we, though late, our wanderings o'er,
May please Thee now and evermore.

Blest THREE in ONE, and ONE in THREE,
Almighty GOD, we pray to Thee,
That Thou wouldst now vouchsafe to bless
Our fast with fruits of righteousness.   Amen

93   *In due season we shall reap, if we faint not.*
Summi largitor præmii.

O THOU Who dost to man accord
His highest prize, his best reward,
Thou hope of all our race ;
JESU, to Thee we now draw near
Our earnest supplications hear,
As we devoutly seek Thy face.

With self-accusing voice within
Our conscience tells of many a sin
In thought, and word, and deed ;
O cleanse that conscience from all stain,
The penitent restore again,
From all the load of trespass freed.

If Thou reject us, who shall give
Our fainting spirits strength to live ?
'Tis Thine alone to spare.
With cleansèd hearts to seek aright,
And find acceptance in Thy sight,
Be this, O LORD, our lowly prayer.

*'Tis Thou hast bless'd this solemn fast ;
So may its days by us be pass'd
In self-control severe,
That, when our Easter morn we hail,
Its mystic feast we may not fail
To celebrate with conscience clear.

(78)

LENT.

O Blessèd TRINITY, bestow
Thy pardoning grace on us below,
  And shield us evermore;
Until, within Thy courts above,
We see Thy face, and sing Thy love,
  And ever with Thy Saints adore. Amen.

* *If this verse be omitted, the Hymn can be used at other
Seasons.*

94 *O deliver us, and be merciful unto our sins, for thy
Name's sake.*

Audi, benigne Conditor.

O MERCIFUL Creator, hear;
  In tender pity bow Thine ear:
Accept the tearful prayer we raise
In this our fast of forty days.

Each heart is manifest to Thee;
Thou knowest our infirmity:
Repentant now we seek Thy face;
Bestow on us Thy pardoning grace.

Our sins are great and numberless,
But spare us who our sins confess,
And for Thine own Name's sake make whole
The sick and heavy-laden soul.

Grant us to mortify each sense
By use of outward abstinence,
That free from every stain of sin
The soul may keep her fast within.

Blest THREE in ONE, and ONE in THREE,
Almighty GOD, we pray to Thee,
That Thou wouldst now vouchsafe to bless
• Our fast *with fruits* of righteousness. Amen.

(79)

LENT.

95 *Behold, now is the accepted time; behold, now is the day of salvation.*

Ecce tempus idoneum.

LO! now is our accepted day,
The time for purging sins away,
The sins of thought, and deed, and word,
That we have done against the LORD.

For He, the merciful and true,
Hath spared His people hitherto,
Not willing that the soul should die
In all its great iniquity.

Then let us all with earnest care,
And contrite fast, and tear, and prayer,
And works of mercy and of love,
Implore forgiveness from above;

That He may all our sins efface,
Adorn us with the gifts of grace,
And join us in the heav'nly land
For ever to the Angel band.

All blessings with the FATHER be.
Only-begotten SON, to Thee,
And to the COMFORTER adored,
For ever THREE, and yet ONE LORD. Amen.

96 *Jesus answered him, saying, It is written, That man shall not live by bread alone, but by every word of God.*

Clarum decus jejunii.

IT is the glory of this fast,
Foreshadow'd in the ages past,
That CHRIST, our own Almighty LORD,
Did hallow it by deed and word.

'Twas while he fasted Moses saw
The LORD Who gave by him the Law;
Thus to Elijah Angels came,
And steeds of fire and car of flame.

(90)

Thus Daniel was empower'd to gaze
On visions of the latter days ;
And thus the Baptist to proclaim
Salvation through the Bridegroom's Name.

Grant us, good LORD, like them to be
Full oft in prayer and fast with Thee ;
Endue us with Thy heav'nly might ;
Be Thou our joy and true delight.

O FATHER, hear us through Thy SON
And HOLY SPIRIT, with Thee One,
Thou Whom our thankful hearts adore
And glorify for evermore.   Amen.

7 *I sat down and wept, and mourned, certain days, and
fasted, and prayed before the God of heaven.*

Jesu, quadragenariæ.

O JESU, Thou didst consecrate
    This fast of forty days,
That men might quit their dying state
    And learn Thy healthful ways :—

A time in which towards Paradise,
    Once lost by carnal sense,
The souls redeem'd by Thee might rise
    Through chastening abstinence.

Now with Thy Church be present, LORD,
    In all Thy saving grace,
And hear us as with one accord,
    Mourning, we seek Thy face.

Most Merciful, forgive the past,
    The sins which we deplore ;
Thy shelt'ring arms around us cast,
    That we may sin no more.

LENT.

To Thee our sacrifice we bring
  Of Lenten fast and prayer,
Till, cleansed by Thee, our GOD and King,
  Thy Paschal joy we share.

Grant this, O FATHER, through Thy SON,
  And through the SPIRIT Bless'd,
Who art with Them for ever One
  Eternally confess'd.   Amen.

98 *Rend your heart and not your garments, and turn unto
the Lord your God.*

Sollemne nos jejunii.

ONCE more the solemn season calls
  A holy fast to keep ;
And now within the temple walls
  Let priest and people weep.

But vain all outward sign of grief
  And vain the form of prayer,
Unless the heart implore relief,
  And penitence be there.

In sorrow true then let us pray
  To our offended GOD,
From us to turn His wrath away
  And stay th' uplifted rod.

O righteous Judge, O FATHER, deign
  To spare us in our need ;
Thou givest time to turn again,
  Give grace to turn indeed.

Blest THREE in ONE, to Thee we bow ;
  Vouchsafe us in Thy love
To gather from these fasts below
  Immortal fruit above.   Amen.

9

Redeeming the time.

En! tempus acceptabile.

LO ! now the time accepted peals
　Its tidings of release ;
A time that with salvation heals
And to repentant tears reveals
　The mercy-seat of peace.

Then let us wisely now restrain
　Our food, our drink, our sleep ;
From idle word and jest refrain,
And steadfastly begin again
　A stricter watch to keep.

Now heav'n-taught love will haste to rise,
　And seek the cheerless bed
Where cold and wan the sufferer lies,
And CHRIST Himself to heedful eyes
　Is hung'ring to be fed.

'Tis now that zealous charity
　Her goods more largely spends,
Lays up her treasure in the sky,
And freely yields, ere death draw nigh,
　To GOD the wealth He lends.

Then consecrate us, LORD, anew,
　And fire our hearts with love ;
That all we think, and all we do,
Within, without, be pure and true,
　Rekindled from above.

Now fuller praise and glory be
　To Thee, the First and Last ;
And make us, Blessèd TRINITY,
More faithful soldiers, worthier Thee,
　Through this our chastening fast. Amen.

100 *And Jesus . . . was led by the Spirit into the w:*
ness, being forty days tempted of the devil. A1
those days he did eat nothing.

FORTY days and forty nights
  Thou wast fasting in the wild ;
Forty days and forty nights
Tempted, and yet undefiled :—
Sunbeams scorching all the day ;
Chilly dew-drops nightly shed ;
Prowling beasts about Thy way ;
Stones Thy pillow ; earth Thy bed.

Shall not we Thy sorrow share,
And from earthly joys abstain,
Fasting with unceasing prayer,
Glad with Thee to suffer pain ?

And if Satan, vexing sore,
Flesh or spirit should assail,
Thou, his vanquisher before,
Grant we may not faint nor fail.

So shall we have peace divine ;
Holier gladness ours shall be ;
Round us too shall Angels shine,
Such as minister'd to Thee.

Keep, O keep us, Saviour dear,
Ever constant by Thy side ;
That with Thee we may appear
At th' eternal Eastertide.   Amen.

101   *Whom resist, steadfast in the faith.*

CHRISTIAN, dost thou see them
  On the holy ground,
How the troops of Midian
  Prowl and prowl around ?
Christian, up and smite them,
  Counting gain but loss ;
Smite them by the merit
  Of the holy Cross.

Christian, dost thou feel them,
  How they work within,
Striving, tempting, luring,
  Goading into sin ?
Christian, never tremble ;
  Never be down-cast ;
Smite them by the virtue
  Of the Lenten fast.

Christian, dost thou hear them,
  How they speak thee fair ?
" Always fast and vigil ?
  Always watch and prayer ? "
Christian, answer boldly,
  " While I breathe, I pray : "
Peace shall follow battle,
  Night shall end in day.

" Well I know thy trouble,
  O My servant true ;
Thou art very weary,—
  I was weary too ;
But that toil shall make thee
  Some day all Mine own,
And the end of sorrow
  Shall be near My throne." Amen.

102 *Hear my crying, O God, give ear unto my prayer.*
'Ιησοῦ γλυκύτατε.

SWEET Saviour, in Thy pitying grace
  Thy sweetness to our souls impart ;
Thou only Lover of our race
  Give healing to the wounded heart ;
O hear Thy contrite servants' cry,
And save us, Jesu, lest we die.

Long-suffering JESU, hear our prayer,
  Who weep before Thee in our shame ;
We have no hope but Thee ; O spare,
  LORD, spare us from th' undying flame ;
O hear Thy contrite servants' cry,
And save us, JESU, lest we die.

All we have broken Thy command ;
  LORD, help us for Thy mercies' sake ;
Deliver us from Satan's hand,
  And safely to Thy Kingdom take ;
O hear Thy contrite servants' cry,
And save us, JESU, lest we die.

We flee for refuge to Thy love,
  Salvation of the helpless soul ;
Pour down Thy radiance from above,
  And make these sin-worn spirits whole ;
Good LORD, in mercy hear our cry,
And save us, JESU, lest we die.   Amen.

103 *Enter not into judgment with thy servant ; for in thy*
     sight shall no man living be justified.

O LORD, turn not Thy face from me,
  Who lie in woful state,
Lamenting all my sinful life
  Before Thy mercy-gate ;
A gate which opens wide to those
  That do lament their sin ;
Shut not that gate against me, LORD,
  But let me enter in.

And call me not to strict account
  How I have sojourn'd here ;
For then my guilty conscience knows
  How vile I shall appear.
Mercy, good LORD, mercy I ask ;
  This is the total sum ;
For mercy, LORD, is all my suit,
  O let Thy mercy come.   Amen.

104 *The time of thy visitation.*

LORD, in this Thy mercy's day,
Ere the time shall pass away,
On our knees we fall and pray.

Holy JESU, grant us tears,
Fill us with heart-searching fears,
Ere the hour of doom appears.

LORD, on us Thy SPIRIT pour,
Kneeling lowly at Thy door,
Ere it close for evermore.

By Thy night of agony,
By Thy supplicating cry,
By Thy willingness to die;

By Thy tears of bitter woe
For Jerusalem below,
Let us not Thy love forgo.

Judge and Saviour of our race,
When we see Thee face to face,
Grant us 'neath Thy wings a place.   Amen.

105 *I am the light of the world: he that followeth me
shall not walk in darkness.*

Christe, qui lux es et dies.

FOR A LATE EVENING SERVICE.

O CHRIST, Who art the Light and Day,
Thou drivest night and gloom away;
O Light of light, Whose word doth show
The light of heav'n to us below.

All-Holy LORD, in humble prayer,
We ask to-night Thy watchful care;
O grant us calm repose in Thee,
A quiet *night from* perils free.

LENT.

Our sleep be pure from sinful stain ;
Let not the Tempter vantage gain,
Or our unguarded flesh surprise,
And make us guilty in Thine eyes.

Asleep though wearied eyes may be,
Still keep the heart awake to Thee ;
Let Thy right hand outstretch'd above
Guard those who serve the LORD they love.

Behold, O GOD our Shield, and quell
The crafts and subtleties of hell ;
Direct Thy servants in all good,
Whom Thou hast purchased with Thy Blood.

O LORD, remember us who bear
The burden of the flesh we wear ;
Thou, Who dost e'er our souls defend,
Be with us even to the end.

All praise to GOD the FATHER be,
All praise, Eternal SON, to Thee,
Whom with the SPIRIT we adore,
For ever and for evermore.   Amen.

The following Hymns are suitable for this season :

PASSIONTIDE.

06 *Tell it out among the heathen that the Lord is king.*

Vexilla regis prodeunt.

ROM THE FIFTH SUNDAY IN LENT TO THE WEDNESDAY BEFORE EASTER.

THE Royal banners forward go,
 The Cross shines forth in mystic glow;
Where He in flesh, our flesh Who made,
Our sentence bore, our ransom paid.

His feet and hands outstretching there,
He will'd the piercing nails to bear,
For us and our redemption's sake
A victim of Himself to make.

There whilst He hung, His sacred side
By soldier's spear was open'd wide,
To cleanse us in the precious flood
Of water mingled with His Blood.

Fulfill'd is now what David told
In true prophetic song of old,
How GOD the heathen's King should be:
For GOD is reigning from the Tree.

O Tree of glory, Tree most fair,
Ordain'd those holy limbs to bear,
How bright in royal hue it stood,
The purple of a Saviour's Blood!

Upon its arms, like balance true,
He weigh'd the price for sinners due,
The price which none but He could pay,
And spoil'd the spoiler of his prey.

To Thee, Eternal THREE in ONE,
Let homage meet by all be done:
As by the Cross Thou dost restore,
So rule *and guide* us evermore.   Amen.

(89)

PASSIONTIDE.

107 *Blessed is the wood by which cometh righteousness.*

Pange lingua gloriosi Prælium certaminis.

PART 1.

SING, my tongue, the glorious battle,
 Sing the last, the dread affray ;
O'er the Cross, the victor's trophy,
 Sound the high triumphal lay,
How a victim's death enduring,
 Earth's Redeemer won the day.

Outraged He, and deeply grieving
 That the first man Adam fell,
When he took the fruit forbidden,
 Which to taste was death and hell,
Mark'd e'en then a Tree the mischief
 Of the first tree to dispel.

This alone was found befitting
 Our salvation's well-laid plan,
By a better craft to baffle
 Him whose craft had ruin'd man,
And to find the healing medicine
 Where our foe the hurt began.

PART 2.

Therefore when at length the fulness
 Of the sacred time was come,
He was sent, the world's Creator,
 From His FATHER'S heav'nly home,
And appear'd on earth incarnate,
 Offspring of a Virgin's womb.

Laid within a narrow manger,
 Uttering but an infant sound,
While the Virgin Mother fastens
 Swaddling clothes His limbs around,
In the tightly girded linen
 GOD'S own hands and feet are bound.

PASSIONTIDE.

He in Body now made perfect
  By the thirty years and three
Meets full willingly the Passion
  Which He came on earth to see ;
On the Cross the LAMB is lifted,
  To be slain upon the Tree.

There the nails and spear He suffers,
  Vinegar, and gall, and reed ;
From His gentle Body piercèd
  Blood and water both proceed :
Things on earth and things in heaven
  By that flood from sin are freed.

PART 3.

Faithful Cross, in fame exalted
  High o'er every earthly tree ;
Leaf, bud, blossom—never forest
  Bore another like to thee :
Sweet the wood, and sweet the iron,
  And thy Load, most sweet is He.

Lofty Tree, thy branches soften,
  And thy stiff-set fibres bend ;
Suffer now the inborn hardness
  Of thy wood to have an end ;
Let the King of heav'n His members
  On thy yielding trunk extend.

Thou alone wast counted worthy
  This world's ransom to sustain,
That by thee a wreck'd creation
  Might its ark and haven gain,
With the sacred Blood anointed
  Of the LAMB that hath been slain.

The following Doxology may be used at the end of any P(

Praise and honour to the FATHER,
　Praise and honour to the SON,
Praise and honour to the SPIRIT,
　Ever THREE and ever ONE,
One in might, and One in glory,
　While eternal ages run.　Amen.

108 *Come not near any man upon whom is the mark.*

Cultor Dei, memento.

FOR A LATE EVENING SERVICE.

SERVANT of GOD, remember
　The holy Font's bedewing,
And in thy Confirmation
　The seal of thy renewing.

When on chaste bed thy body
　To slumber thou dost fashion,
Bethink thee of the symbol
　Of CHRIST's redeeming Passion.

The Cross dispels all evil ;
　Beneath its hallowing token
The soul, in spite of darkness,
　Stands firm with hope unbroken.

Begone, thou arch-deceiver,
　And trouble not our slumber
With haunting dreams of evil,
　And wiles that none can number.

CHRIST, CHRIST Himself is with us ;
　Thou crookèd serpent, vanish !
His sign, full well ye know it,
　Thy crew and thee shall banish.

Awhile the tirèd body
　With outstretch'd limbs reposes,
*Yet e'en in sleep the spirit
　Bright* thoughts of CHRIST encloses.

PASSIONTIDE.

Glory to GOD the FATHER,
  To CHRIST the King of nations,
And to the HOLY SPIRIT,
  Throughout all generations.   Amen.

109   *Let us also go that we may die with him.*

HOLY WEEK.

LORD, through this Holy Week of our salva-
    tion,
  Which Thou hast won for us who went astray,
In all the conflict of Thy sore temptation
  We would continue with Thee day by day.

We would not leave Thee, though our weak
    endurance
  Make us unworthy here to take our part ;
Yet give us strength to trust the sweet assurance
  That Thou, O LORD, art greater than our heart.

Thou didst forgive Thine own who slept for
    sorrow,
  Thou didst have pity, O have pity now,
And let us watch through each sad eve and
    morrow
  With Thee, in holy prayer and solemn vow.

Along that Sacred Way where Thou art leading,
  Which Thou didst take to save our souls from
    loss,
Let us go also, till we see Thee pleading
  In all-prevailing prayer upon Thy Cross ;

Until Thou see Thy bitter travail's ending,
  The world redeem'd, the will of GOD complete,
And, to Thy FATHER'S hands Thy soul com-
    mending,
  Thou lay the work He gave Thee at His feet.
                                           Amen

PASSIONTIDE.

110 *Out of the mouth of babes and sucklings thou hast perfected praise.*

Gloria, laus et honor.

PALM SUNDAY.

ALL glory, laud, and honour,
　　To Thee, Redeemer, King,
To Whom the lips of children
　　Made sweet hosannas ring.

Thou art the King of Israel,
　　Thou David's royal Son,
Who in the LORD's Name comest,
　　The King and Blessèd One.
　　　　　　　　All glory, &c.

The company of Angels
　　Are praising Thee on high,
And mortal men and all things
　　Created make reply.
　　　　　　　　All glory, &c.

The people of the Hebrews
　　With palms to meet Thee went ;
Our praise and prayer and anthems
　　Before Thee we present.
　　　　　　　　All glory, &c.

To Thee before Thy Passion
　　They sang their hymns of praise ;
To Thee now high exalted
　　Our melody we raise.
　　　　　　　　All glory, &c.

Thou didst accept their praises,
　　Accept the praise we bring,
Who in all good delightest,
　　Thou good and gracious King.
　　　　　　　All glory, &c.　Amen.

111 *And the multitudes that went before, and that followed, cried, saying, Hosanna to the son of David.*

PALM SUNDAY.

RIDE on ! ride on in majesty !
   Hark ! all the tribes hosanna cry :
O Saviour meek, pursue Thy road
With palms and scatter'd garments strow'd.

Ride on ! ride on in majesty !
In lowly pomp ride on to die ;
O CHRIST, Thy triumphs now begin
O'er captive death and conquer'd sin.

Ride on ! ride on in majesty !
The wingèd squadrons of the sky
Look down with sad and wondering eyes
To see th' approaching sacrifice.

Ride on ! ride on in majesty !
The last and fiercest strife is nigh ;
The FATHER on His sapphire throne
Awaits His own anointed SON.

Ride on ! ride on in majesty !
In lowly pomp ride on to die ;
Bow Thy meek head to mortal pain,
Then take, O GOD, Thy power, and reign.
                       Amen.

112 *All the people that came together to that sight, beholding the things which were done, smote their breasts and returned.*

Sævo dolorum turbine.

THE PASSION.

O'ERWHELM'D in depths of woe,
   Upon the Tree of scorn
Hangs the Redeemer of mankind,
   With racking anguish torn.
See how the nails those hands
   And feet so tender rend ;
See down His *face*, and neck, and breast
   His sacred Blood descend.

O hear that last loud cry
  Which pierced His Mother's heart,
Ere into GOD the FATHER's hands
  He bade His soul depart.

Earth hears, and trembling quakes
  Around that tree of pain ;
The rocks are rent ; the graves are burst ;
  The veil is rent in twain.

Shall man alone be mute ?
  Have we no griefs, or fears ?
Come, old and young, come, all mankind,
  And bathe those feet in tears.

Come, fall before His Cross
  Who shed for us His Blood,
Who died, the victim of pure love,
  To make us sons of GOD.

JESU, all praise to Thee,
  Our joy and endless rest ;
Be Thou our guide while pilgrims here,
  Our crown amid the blest.   Amen.

113   *He was wounded for our transgressions.*

Prome vocem, mens, canoram.

NOW, my soul, thy voice upraising,
    Tell in sweet and mournful strain
How the Crucified, enduring
  Grief, and wounds, and dying pain,
Of His love was freely offer'd,
  Sinless was for sinners slain.

PASSIONTIDE.

Scourged with unrelenting fury,
　　Our iniquities He bore ;
By His livid stripes He heals us,
　　Raises us to stand once more,
All our bruises gently soothing,
　　Binding up the bleeding sore.

See ! His hands and feet are fasten'd ;
　　So He makes His people free ;
Not a wound whence Blood is flowing
　　But a fount of grace shall be ;
And the very nails which nail Him
　　Nail us also to the Tree.

Through His heart the spear is driven,
　　Though His foes have seen Him die ;
Blood and water thence are streaming
　　In a tide of mystery,—
Water from our guilt to cleanse us,
　　Blood to win us crowns on high.

Jesu, may those precious fountains
　　Drink to thirsting souls afford ;
Let them be our cup and healing,
　　And hereafter our reward :
So a ransom'd world shall ever
　　Praise Thee, its redeeming Lord.　　Amen.

14　　*Jesus Christ openly set forth crucified.*
　　Attolle paulum lumina.

O SINNER, for a little space
　　Lift up thine eyes, discerning
How terrible a thing is sin,
　　And so to wisdom turning.
Upon the Crucified One look,
And thou shalt read, as in a book,
　　What well is worth thy learning.

PASSIONTIDE.

Look on His head, that bleeding head,
  With crown of thorns surrounded ;
Look on His sacred hands and feet
  Which piercing nails have wounded ;
See every limb with scourges rent ;
On Him, the just, the innocent,
  What malice hath abounded !

'Tis not alone those tender limbs
  With so much pain are aching ;
For the ingratitude of man
  His heart within is breaking.
Oh, fearful was the chastisement
The Son of Mary underwent,
  The place of sinners taking.

No man has any sorrow borne
  Like unto that affliction,
When Jesus for our sake endured
  His people's contradiction ;
Beyond imagination were
The sufferings He will'd to bear
  In that dread crucifixion.

Now mark, O man, and ponder well
  Sin's awful condemnation.
For whom were all those wounds endured ?
  To purchase thy salvation.
Had Jesus never bled and died,
Then what could thee and all betide
  But fiery reprobation ?

Flee therefore, sinner, flee from sin
  And Satan's wiles ensnaring ;
Flee from those everlasting flames
  For evil ones preparing.
O thank thy Saviour, and entreat
To rest hereafter at His feet,
  The life eternal sharing.   Amen.

15 *Thou wast slain, and hast redeemed us to God by thy blood.*

Ira justa Conditoris.

HE Who once in righteous vengeance
   Whelm'd the world beneath the flood,
Once again in mercy cleansed it
  With His own most precious Blood,
Coming from His throne on high
On the painful Cross to die.

Oh the wisdom of th' Eternal !
  Oh the depth of love divine !
Oh the sweetness of that mercy
  Which in JESUS CHRIST did shine !
We were sinners doom'd to die ;
JESUS paid the penalty.

When before the Judge we tremble,
  Conscious of His broken laws,
May the Blood of His atonement
  Cry aloud, and plead our cause,
Bid our guilty terrors cease,
Be our pardon and our peace.

Prince and Author of salvation,
  LORD of majesty supreme,
JESU, praise to Thee be given
  By the world Thou didst redeem ;
Glory to the FATHER be
And the SPIRIT One with Thee. Amen.

16 *Peace through the blood of his cross.*

In passione Domini.

IN the LORD's atoning grief
  Be our rest and sweet relief ;
Store we deep in heart's recess
All the shame and bitterness,—

Thorns, and cross, and nails, and lance,
Wounds, our rich inheritance,
Vinegar, and gall, and reed,
And the cry His soul that freed.

May these all our spirits fill,
And with love's devotion thrill ;
In our souls plant virtue's root,
And mature its glorious fruit.

Crucified ! we Thee adore ;
Thee with all our hearts implore,
Us with all Thy Saints unite
In the realms of heav'nly light.

CHRIST, by coward hands betray'd,
CHRIST, for us a captive made,
CHRIST, upon the bitter Tree
Slain for man, be praise to Thee.   Amen.

117   *We love him, because he first loved us.*

O Deus, ego amo te.

MY GOD, I love Thee ; not because
I hope for heav'n thereby,
Nor yet because who love Thee not
Are lost eternally.

Thou, O my JESUS, Thou didst me
Upon the Cross embrace ;
For me didst bear the nails and spear,
And manifold disgrace,

And griefs and torments numberless,
And sweat of agony ;
Yea, death itself ; and all for one
Who was Thine enemy.

Then why, most loving JESU CHRIST,
  Should I not love Thee well,
Not for the sake of winning heav'n,
  Or of escaping hell ;

Not from the hope of gaining aught,
  Not seeking a reward ;
But as Thyself hast lovèd me,
  O ever-loving LORD ?

So do I love Thee, and will love,
  Who such a love hast show'd,
Only because Thou art my King,
  Because Thou art my GOD. Amen.

118 *Come unto me, all ye that labour and are heavy-laden,*
and I will give you rest.

Quicumque certum quæritis.

ALL ye who seek for sure relief
  In trouble and distress,
Whatever sorrow vex the mind,
  Or guilt the soul oppress,

JESUS, Who gave Himself for you
  Upon the Cross to die,
Opens to you His sacred heart ;
  O to that heart draw nigh.

Ye hear how kindly He invites ;
  Ye hear His words so blest ;
"All ye that labour come to Me,
  And I will give you rest."

O JESUS, joy of Saints on high,
  Thou hope of sinners here,
Attracted by *those* loving words
  To Thee we lift our prayer.

Wash Thou our wounds in that dear Blood
  Which from Thy heart doth flow ;
A new and contrite heart on all
  Who cry to Thee bestow. Amen.

119   *The precious blood of Christ.*

Viva ! Viva ! Gesù.

GLORY be to JESUS,
  Who, in bitter pains,
Pour'd for me the life-blood
  From His sacred veins.

Grace and life eternal
  In that Blood I find ;
Blest be His compassion
  Infinitely kind.

Blest through endless ages
  Be the precious stream
Which from death eternal
  Did the world redeem.

Abel's blood for vengeance
  Pleaded to the skies ;
But the Blood of JESUS
  For our pardon cries.

Oft as it is sprinkled
  On our guilty hearts,
Satan in confusion
  Terror-struck departs.

Oft as earth exulting
  Wafts its praise on high,
Angel-hosts rejoicing
  Make their glad reply.

Lift ye then your voices ;
  Swell the mighty flood ;
Louder still and louder
  Praise the precious Blood. Amen.

PASSIONTIDE.

120 *What things were gain to me, those I counted loss for Christ.*

WHEN I survey the wondrous Cross
    On which the Prince of glory died,
My richest gain I count but loss,
And pour contempt on all my pride.

Forbid it, LORD, that I should boast
Save in the Cross of CHRIST my GOD ;
All the vain things that charm me most,
I sacrifice them to His Blood.

See from His head, His hands, His feet,
Sorrow and love flow mingled down ;
Did e'er such love and sorrow meet,
Or thorns compose so rich a crown ?

Were the whole realm of nature mine,
That were an offering far too small ;
Love so amazing, so divine,
Demands my soul, my life, my all.

To CHRIST, Who won for sinners grace
By bitter grief and anguish sore,
Be praise from all the ransom'd race
For ever and for evermore.   Amen.

121 *Unto you therefore which believe he is precious.*

SWEET the moments, rich in blessing,
    Which before the Cross I spend,
Life, and health, and peace possessing
    From the sinner's dying Friend.
Here I rest, for ever viewing
    Mercy pour'd in streams of Blood ;
Precious drops, my soul bedewing,
    Plead and claim my peace with GOD.
Truly blessèd is the station,
    Low before His Cross to lie,
Whilst I see divine compassion
    Beaming from His dying eye.

LORD, in ceaseless contemplation
    Fix my thankful heart on Thee,
Till I taste Thy full salvation,
    And Thine unveil'd glory see.   Amen.

122   *Who loved me, and gave himself for me.*

O Haupt voll Blut und Wunden.

O SACRED head, surrounded
    By crown of piercing thorn !
O bleeding head, so wounded,
    So shamed, and put to scorn !
Death's pallid hue comes o'er Thee,
    The glow of life decays,
Yet Angel-hosts adore Thee,
    And tremble as they gaze.

Thy comeliness and vigour
    Is wither'd up and gone,
And in Thy wasted figure
    I see death drawing on.
O agony and dying !
    O love to sinners free !
JESU, all grace supplying,
    Turn Thou Thy face on me.

In this Thy bitter Passion,
    Good Shepherd, think of me
With Thy most sweet compassion,
    Unworthy though I be :
Beneath Thy Cross abiding
    For ever would I rest,
In Thy dear love confiding,
    And with Thy presence blest.   Amen.

123 *Forasmuch then as Christ hath suffered in the flesh
arm yourselves likewise with the same mind.*

MY LORD, my Master, at Thy feet adoring,
    I see Thee bow'd beneath Thy load of woe
For me, a sinner, is Thy life-blood pouring :
    For Thee, my SAVIOUR, scarce my tears will flow

PASSIONTIDE.

Thine own disciple to the Jews has sold Thee,
 With friendship's kiss and loyal word he came ;
How oft of faithful love my lips have told Thee,
 While Thou hast seen my falsehood and my
 shame !

With taunts and scoffs they mock what seems Thy
 weakness,
 With blows and outrage adding pain to pain ;
Thou art unmoved and steadfast in Thy meekness ;
 When I am wrong'd, how quickly I complain !

My LORD, my SAVIOUR, when I see Thee wearing
 Upon Thy bleeding brow the crown of thorn,
Shall I for pleasure live, or shrink from bearing
 Whate'er may be my lot of pain or scorn ?

O victim of Thy love ! O pangs most healing !
 O saving death ! O fruitful agonies !
I pray Thee, CHRIST, before Thee humbly kneeling,
 For ever keep Thy Cross before mine eyes.
                                        Amen.

124 *Ye shall leave me alone: and yet I am not alone,
 because the Father is with me.'*

ALONE Thou trodd'st the winepress, and alone
 Through the dark valley went Thy toil-worn
 feet,
Betray'd, denied, deserted by Thine own,
 The agony, the shame, the death to meet.

Alone, yet not alone ; ev'n on the Tree,
 Whence, 'mid the darkness, rang the awful cry,
"Why, O My GOD, hast Thou forsaken Me ?"
 Thy GOD was there, Thy FATHER very nigh.

PASSIONTIDE.

O LORD of Life, when heavily doth press
 The load which each of us, alone, must bear ;
When 'midst the crowd our utter loneliness
 Drifts on the soul the shadow of despair ;

When friendship fails,—the nearest earthly love
 Knows little of our heart's deep bitterness ;
When all seems dark, within, around, above,
 And Satan whispers,"Ye are comfortless ;"

And in the last, the loneliest, hour of life,
 When past and future whelm the soul in fear ;
Grant us in Thee, amid, above, the strife,
 Our FATHER'S arms to feel, His voice to hear.
Amen.

125   *Weep not for me, but weep for yourselves.*

WEEP not for Him Who onward bears
 His Cross to Calvary ;
He does not ask man's pitying tears,
 Who wills for man to die.

The awful sorrow of His face,
 The bowing of His frame,
Come not from torture or disgrace ;
 He fears not cross or shame.

There is a deeper pang of grief,
 An agony unknown,
In which His love finds no relief ;
 He bears it all alone.

He sees the souls for whom He dies
 Yet clinging to their sin,
And heirs of mansions in the skies
 Who will not enter in.

O may I in Thy sorrow share,
 And mourn that sins of mine
Should ever wound with grief or care
 That loving heart of Thine.   Amen.

126 *Remembering mine affliction and my misery, the wormwood and the gall.*

GO to dark Gethsemane,
  Ye that feel the Tempter's power,
Your Redeemer's conflict see,
  Watch with Him one bitter hour ;
Turn not from His griefs away,
Learn of JESUS CHRIST to pray.

Follow to the judgment-hall,
  View the LORD of life arraign'd ;
Oh the wormwood and the gall !
  Oh the pangs His soul sustain'd !
Shun not suffering, shame, or loss ;
Learn of Him to bear the cross.

Calvary's mournful mountain climb ;
  There, adoring at His feet,
Mark that miracle of time,—
  GOD'S own sacrifice complete ;
" It is finish'd," hear Him cry ;
Learn of JESUS CHRIST to die.   Amen.

127 *Is it nothing to you, all ye that pass by? Behold, and see if there be any sorrow like unto my sorrow.*

SEE the destined day arise !
  See, a willing sacrifice,
JESUS, to redeem our loss,
Hangs upon the shameful Cross !

JESU, who but Thou had borne,
Lifted on that Tree of scorn,
Every pang and bitter throe,
Finishing Thy life of woe?

Who but Thou had dared to drain,
Steep'd in gall, that cup of pain,
And with tender Body bear
Thorns, *and nails*, and piercing spear?

Thence the cleansing water flow'd,
Mingled from Thy side with Blood,—
Sign to all attesting eyes
Of the finish'd sacrifice.

Holy JESU, grant us grace
In that sacrifice to place
All our trust for life renew'd,
Pardon'd sin, and promised good.   Amen.

The following Hymns are also suitable:
342 To CHRIST, the Prince of peace.
448 LORD, as to Thy dear Cross we flee.
452 O Saviour, may we never rest.
604 My GOD! my GOD! and can it be.
610 O my Saviour, lifted.

128   *They crucified him.*

GOOD FRIDAY.

O COME and mourn with me awhile ;
   O come ye to the Saviour's side ;
O come, together let us mourn ;
JESUS, our LORD, is crucified.

Have we no tears to shed for Him,
While soldiers scoff and Jews deride ?
Ah ! look how patiently He hangs ;
JESUS, our LORD, is crucified.

How fast His hands and feet are nail'd ;
His throat with parching thirst is dried ;
His failing eyes are dimm'd with Blood ;
JESUS, our LORD, is crucified.

Seven times He spake, seven words of love ;
And all three hours His silence cried
For mercy on the souls of men ;
JESUS, our LORD, is crucified.

O love of GOD, O sin of man,
In this dread act your strength is tried ;
And victory remains with love,
For LOVE Himself is crucified.

(108)

O break, O break, hard heart of mine !
Thy weak self-love and guilty pride
Betray'd and slew thy GOD and King :
And LOVE Himself is crucified.

A broken heart, a fount of tears,
Ask, and they will not be denied ;
LORD JESUS, may we love and weep
Since Thou for us art crucified.   Amen.

129 *Father, forgive them, for they know not what they do.*

O WORD of pity, for our pardon pleading,
  Breathed in the hour of loneliness and pain ;
O voice, which through the ages interceding
  Calls us to fellowship with GOD again.

O word of comfort, through the silence stealing,
  As the dread act of sacrifice began ;
O infinite compassion, still revealing
  The infinite forgiveness won for man.

O word of hope to raise us nearer heaven,
  When courage fails us and when faith is dim ;
The souls for whom CHRIST prays to CHRIST are
    given,
  To find their pardon and their joy in Him.

O Intercessor, Who art ever living
  To plead for dying souls that they may live,
Teach us to know our sin which needs forgiving,
  Teach us to know the love which can forgive.
                                    Amen.

130 *Father, forgive them, for they know not what they do.*

" FORGIVE them, O My FATHER,
    They know not what they do :"
The Saviour spake in anguish,
    As the sharp nails went through.

For me was that compassion,
  For me that tender care ;
I need His wide forgiveness
  As much as any there.

It was my pride and hardness
  That hung Him on the Tree ;
Those cruel nails, O Saviour,
  Were driven in by me.

And often I have slighted
  Thy gentle voice that chid ;
Forgive me too, LORD JESUS ;
  I knew not what I did.

O depth of sweet compassion !
  O love divine and true !
Save Thou the souls that slight Thee,
  And know not what they do.   Amen.

131 *Verily I say unto thee, To-day shalt thou be with m
     in paradise.*

"LORD, when Thy Kingdom comes, remembe
    me ;"
Thus spake the dying lips to dying ears ;
O faith, which in that darkest hour could see
The promised glory of the far-off years !

No kingly sign declares that glory now,
No ray of hope lights up that awful hour ;
A thorny crown surrounds the bleeding brow,
The hands are stretch'd in weakness, not in power

Hark ! through the gloom the dying Saviour saith
"Thou too shalt rest in Paradise to-day ;"
O words of love to answer words of faith !
O words of hope for those who live to pray !

LORD, when with dying lips my prayer is said,
Grant that in faith Thy kingdom I may see ;
And, thinking on Thy Cross and bleeding head,
May breathe my parting words, " Remember me."

Remember me, but not my shame or sin ;
Thy cleansing Blood hath wash'd them all away ;
Thy precious Death for me did pardon win ;
Thy Blood redeem'd me in that awful day.

Remember me ; and, ere I pass away,
Speak Thou th' assuring word that sets us free,
And make Thy promise to my heart, " To-day
Thou too shalt rest in Paradise with Me."   Amen.

132 *Woman, behold thy son ... Behold thy mother.*
Stabat Mater dolorosa.

AT the Cross her station keeping,
    Stood the mournful Mother weeping,
      Where He hung, the dying LORD ;
For her soul of joy bereavèd,
Bow'd with anguish, deeply grievèd,
      Felt the sharp and piercing sword.

Oh, how sad and sore distressèd
In that hour the Mother blessèd
      Of the sole-begotten One ;
With a mother's keen affliction
Looking on the crucifixion
      Of her ever-glorious Son !

Who upon that Mother gazing,
In her anguish so amazing,
      Born of woman, would not weep ?
Who, of CHRIST's dear Mother thinking, ·
While her Son that cup is drinking,
      Would *not share her* sorrows deep ?

She beheld His tribulation
For the sins of every nation,
　Saw Him scourged and led to death,
All His comfort from Him taken,
And His soul by God forsaken,
　Till He yielded up His breath.

O good JESU, let me borrow
Something of Thy Mother's sorrow,
　JESU, LORD, Redeemer kind ;
That my heart fresh ardour gaining,
And a purer love attaining,
　May with Thee acceptance find.　Amen.

133 *My God, my God, why hast thou forsaken me ?*

THRONED upon the awful Tree,
　King of grief, I watch with Thee ;
Darkness veils Thine anguish'd face,
None its lines of woe can trace,
None can tell what pangs unknown
Hold Thee silent and alone ;

Silent through those three dread hours
Wrestling with the evil powers,
Left alone with human sin,
Gloom around Thee and within,
Till th' appointed time is nigh,
Till the LAMB of GOD may die.

Hark that cry that peals aloud
Upward through the whelming cloud !
He, the FATHER's only SON,
He, the CHRIST, th' anointed One,
He doth ask Him—even He—
"Why hast Thou forsaken Me ?"

LORD, should fear and anguish roll
Darkly o'er my sinful soul,
Thou, Who once wast thus bereft
That Thine own might ne'er be left,
Teach me by that bitter cry
In the gloom to know Thee nigh.   Amen.

134   *I thirst.*

O PERFECT GOD, Thy love
     As perfect Man did share
Here upon earth each form of ill
     Thy fellow-men must bear.

Now from the Tree of scorn
     We hear Thy voice again ;
Thou Who didst take our mortal flesh,
     Hast felt our mortal pain.

Thy Body suffers thirst,
     Parch'd are Thy lips and dry :
How poor the offering man can bring
     Thy thirst to satisfy !

O Saviour, by Thy thirst
     Borne on the Cross of shame,
Grant us in all our sufferings here
     To glorify Thy Name ;

That through each pain and grief
     Our souls may onward move
To gain more likeness to Thy life,
     More knowledge of Thy love.   Amen.

135   *It is finished.*

O PERFECT life of love !
     All, all is finish'd now ;
All that He left His throne above
     To do for us below.

PASSIONTIDE.

No work is left undone
Of all the FATHER will'd ;
His toils and sorrows, one by one,
The Scriptures have fulfill'd.

No pain that we can share
But He has felt its smart ;
All forms of human grief and care
Have pierced that tender heart.

And on His thorn-crown'd head,
And on His sinless soul,
Our sins in all their guilt were laid,
That He might make us whole.

In perfect love He dies :
For me He dies, for me :
O all-atoning Sacrifice,
I cling by faith to Thee.

In every time of need,
Before the judgment-throne,
Thy work, O LAMB of GOD, I plead,
Thy merits, not my own. Amen.

136 *Father, into thy hands I commend my spirit.*

THE lifelong task was done,
    The world's redemption won ;
The mighty Labourer turn'd Him to His rest.
Not forced by mightier foes,
    By His own act He goes,—
Lays down His own life when it seems Him be

With hands extended wide
    He bow'd Himself and died,
Like that strong man who smote the Philistine
He cried aloud with might,
    And leapt into the light,
Which for the godly in the darkness shines.

Death still was unexplored ;
But for the dying LORD
In one glad thought its terrors found an end ;
The FATHER'S love was there ;
And, " FATHER," was His prayer,
"Into Thy hands My spirit I commend."

E'en unto death our Guide,
Thou, LORD, for all hast tried,
And proved, the greatness of the FATHER'S power.
When Thou hast published
Thy Gospel to the dead,
The third day ushers in Thy glorious hour. Amen.

137 *In Paradise.*

FROM THE EVENING OF GOOD FRIDAY TO EASTER DAY.

IT is finish'd ! Blessèd JESUS,
 Thou hast breathed Thy latest sigh,
Teaching us the sons of Adam
 How the SON of GOD can die.

Lifeless lies the piercèd Body,
 Resting in its rocky bed ;
Thou 'hast left the Cross of anguish
 For the mansions of the dead.

In the hidden realms of darkness
 Shines a light unseen before,
When the LORD of dead and living .
 Enters at the lowly door.

Lo ! in spirit, rich in mercy
 Comes He from the world above,
Preaching to the souls in prison
 Tidings of His dying love.

Lo ! the heav'nly light around Him,
 As He draws His people near ;
All amazed they come rejoicing
 At *the gracious* words they hear.

Patriarch and Priest and Prophet
    Gather round Him as He stands,
In adoring faith and gladness
    Hearing of the piercèd hands.

There in lowliest joy and wonder
    Stands the robber by His side,
Reaping now the blessèd promise
    Spoken by the Crucified.

JESUS, LORD of our salvation,
    Let Thy mercy rest on me ;
Grant me too, when life is finish'd,
    Rest in Paradise with Thee.   Amen.

138 *And when Joseph had taken the body, he wrapped i
a clean linen cloth, and laid it in his own new t
which he had hewn out in the rock. . . . And t
was Mary Magdalene, and the other Mary, sit
over against the sepulchre.*

RESTING from His work to-day
    In the tomb the Saviour lay ;
Still He slept, from head to feet
Shrouded in the winding-sheet,
Lying in the rock alone,
Hidden by the sealèd stone.

Late at even there was seen
Watching long the Magdalene ;
Early, ere the break of day,
Sorrowful she took her way
To the holy garden glade,
Where her buried LORD was laid.

So with Thee, till life shall end,
I would solemn vigil spend ;
Let me hew Thee, LORD, a shrine
In this rocky heart of mine,
Where in pure embalmèd cell
None but Thou may ever dwell.

Myrrh and spices will I bring,
True affection's offering ;
Close the door from sight and sound
Of the busy world around ;
And in patient watch remain
Till my LORD appear again.   Amen.

139 *Mary Magdalene and Mary the mother of Joses beheld
where he was laid.*

BY Jesus' grave on either hand,
While night is brooding o'er the land,
The sad and silent mourners stand.

At last the weary life is o'er,
The agony and conflict sore
Of Him Who all our sufferings bore.

Deep in the rock's sepulchral shade
The LORD, by Whom the worlds were made,
The Saviour of mankind, is laid.

O hearts bereaved and sore distress'd,
Here is for you a place of rest,
Here leave your griefs on JESUS' breast.
                                    Amen.

The following Hymns are also suitable:
291 With CHRIST we share a mystic grave.
386 They whose course on earth is o'er.
387 Let saints on earth in concert sing.

EASTER.

140 *O death, where is thy sting ? O grave, where is thy
victory ?*

Chorus novæ Jerusalem.

YE choirs of new Jerusalem,
    Your sweetest notes employ,
The Paschal victory to hymn
In strains of holy joy.

For Judah's Lion bursts His chains,
  Crushing the serpent's head,
And cries aloud through death's domains
  To wake th' imprison'd dead.
Devouring depths of hell their prey
  At His command restore ;
His ransom'd hosts pursue their way
  Where JESUS goes before.
Triumphant in His glory now,
  To Him all power is given ;
To Him in one communion bow
  All saints in earth and heaven.
While we, His soldiers, praise our King,
  His mercy we implore,
Within His palace bright to bring
  And keep us evermore.
All glory to the FATHER be,
  Alllglory to the SON,
All glory, HOLY GHOST, to Thee,
  While endless ages run.   Alleluia !   Amen.

141 *O death, where is thy sting ? O grave, where is thy*
    victory ?

Chorus novæ Jerusalem.

UP, new Jerusalem, and sing
  The sweet new song of CHRIST thy King ;
In sober joy thy children call
To keep the Paschal festival.
To-day th' unconquer'd Lion's tread
Hath crush'd the ancient serpent's head ;
With living voice the Victor cries,
And makes the waiting dead to rise.
The jaws of hell must now restore
The prey it had devour'd before ;
And following Him Who set them free
The captives leave captivity.

He triumphs glorious with His train,
And worthy of His wide domain
Joins in one commonwealth of love
Our earthly home and heav'n above.

Let us, His soldiers, while we sing,
In lowliness beseech our King
To grant us in His palace bright
A station 'midst the ranks of light.

Through ages that no limit see
To GOD on high all glory be ;
All honour to the FATHER, SON,
And HOLY GHOST be ever done.   Amen.

42 *The Lord is King, and hath put on glorious apparel.*

Aurora lucis rutilat.

LIGHT'S glittering morn bedecks the sky ;
　　Heav'n thunders forth its victor-cry ;
The glad earth shouts her triumph high,
And groaning hell makes wild reply ;

While He, the King, the mighty King,
Despoiling death of all its sting,
And trampling down the powers of night,
Brings forth His ransom'd Saints to light.

His tomb of late the threefold guard
Of watch and stone and seal had barr'd ;
But now, in pomp of triumph high,
He comes from death to victory.

The days of mourning now are past ;
The pains of hell are loosed at last ;
An Angel robed *in light* hath said,
"*The LORD is risen* from the dead."

EASTER.

Th' Apostles' hearts were full of pain
For their dear LORD so lately slain,
By rebel servants doom'd to die
A death of cruel agony.

With gentle voice the Angel gave
The women tidings at the grave ;
" Fear not, the LORD ye soon shall see ;
He goes before to Galilee."

Then, hastening on their eager way
The joyful tidings to convey,
Their LORD they met, their living LORD,
And falling at His feet adored.

Th' Eleven, when they hear, with speed
To Galilee forthwith proceed,
That there once more they may behold
The LORD's dear face, as He foretold.

PART 3.

That Easter-tide with joy was bright,
The sun shone out with fairer light,
When, to their longing eyes restored,
Th' Apostles saw their risen LORD,

He bade them see His hands, His side,
Where yet the glorious wounds abide,
The tokens true which made it plain
Their LORD indeed was risen again.

JESU, the King of gentleness,
Do Thou our hearts and souls possess,
That we may give Thee all our days
The loving tribute of our praise.

EASTER.

The following may be sung at the end of any Part:

O LORD of all, with us abide
In this our joyful Easter-tide ;
From every weapon death can wield
Thine own redeem'd for ever shield.

All praise be Thine, O risen LORD,
From death to endless life restored ;
All praise to GOD the FATHER be
And HOLY GHOST eternally.   Amen.

43 *Christ our passover is sacrificed for us ; therefore let us keep the feast.*

Ad cenam Agni providi.

THE LAMB's high banquet call'd to share,
Array'd in garments white and fair,
The Red Sea past, we fain would sing
To JESUS our triumphant King.

Upon the altar of the Cross
His Body hath redeem'd our loss :
And tasting of His precious Blood
In Him we live anew to GOD.

Protected in the Paschal night
From the destroying Angel's might,
By strength of hand our hosts go free
From Pharaoh's ruthless tyranny.

Now CHRIST our Passover is slain,
The LAMB of GOD without a stain ;
His flesh, the true unleaven'd Bread,
For us is freely offerèd.

O all-sufficient Sacrifice,
Beneath Thee Satan vanquish'd lies ;
Thy captive *people are* set free,
And crowns of life restored by Thee.

EASTER.

CHRIST rises conqueror from the grave,
From death returning, strong to save ;
His own right hand the tyrant chains,
And Paradise for man regains.

O LORD of all, with us abide
In this our joyful Easter-tide ;
From every weapon death can wield
Thine own redeem'd for ever shield.

All praise be Thine, O risen LORD,
From death to endless life restored ;
All praise to GOD the FATHER be,
And HOLY GHOST eternally.   Amen.

144　　*This is the day which the Lord hath made.*
Salve, festa dies.

HAIL, festal day, whose glory never ends :
　　Now hell is vanquish'd, CHRIST to heav'n
　　ascends.

All nature with new births of beauty gay
Acknowledges her LORD's return to-day.
　　　　　　Hail, festal day, &c.

The Crucified is King ; creation's prayer
To its Creator rises everywhere.
　　　　　　Hail, festal day, &c.

Let what Thou promisedst, fair Power, be done ;
The third day shines ; arise, O buried One.
　　　　　　Hail, festal day, &c.

It cannot be that Joseph's sepulchre
Should keep the whole world's Ransom prisoner.
　　　　　　Hail, festal day, &c.

No rock of stone His passage can withstand,
Who gathers all the world within His hand.
　　　　　　Hail, festal day, &c.

EASTER.

Leave to the grave Thy grave-clothes; let them fall:
Without Thee we have naught, and with Thee all.
Hail, festal day, &c.

Thou gavest life, and dost endure the grave;
Thou tread'st the way of death, from death to save.
Hail, festal day, &c.

Bring back the day,—Thy dying made it night,—
That ages in Thy face may see the light.
Hail, festal day, &c.

Thy rescued are like sand beside the sea,
And where their SAVIOUR goes, they follow free.
Hail, festal day, &c.

The law of death has ceased the world to blight,
And darkness quails before the face of light.
Hail, festal day, &c.

145 *Buried with him in baptism, wherein also ye are risen with him through the faith of the operation of God, who hath raised him from the dead.*

Rex sempiterne cælitum.

O CHRIST, the heav'ns' Eternal King,
   Creator, unto Thee we sing,
With GOD the FATHER ever One,
Co-equal, co-eternal SON.

Thy hand, when first the world began,
Made in Thine own pure image man,
And link'd to fleshly form of earth
A living soul of heav'nly birth.

And when the envy of the foe
Had marr'd Thy noblest work below,
Thou didst our ruin'd state repair
By *deigning flesh* Thyself to wear.

(123)

EASTER.

Once of a Virgin born to save,
And now new-born from death's dark grave,
O Christ, Thou bidd'st us rise with Thee
From death to immortality.

Eternal Shepherd, Thou art wont
To cleanse Thy people at the font,
That mystic bath, that grave of sin,
Where ransom'd souls new life begin.

Divine Redeemer, Thou didst deign
To bear for us the Cross of pain,
And give for us the lavish price
Of Thine own Blood in sacrifice.

O Lord of all, with us abide
In this our joyful Easter-tide;
From every weapon death can wield
Thine own redeem'd for ever shield.

All praise be Thine, O risen Lord,
From death to endless life restored;
All praise to God the Father be
And Holy Ghost eternally.   Amen.

146 *This is the day which the Lord hath made; we will
rejoice and be glad in it.*
O filii et filiæ.

ALLELUIA ! Alleluia ! Alleluia !
O sons and daughters, let us sing !
The King of heav'n, the glorious King,
O'er death to-day rose triumphing.
                              Alleluia !

That Easter morn, at break of day,
The faithful women went their way
Their spices o'er the dead to lay.
                              Alleluia !

An Angel clad in white they see,
Who sat, and spake unto the three,
"The Lord is risen again," said he.
                              Alleluia !

(124)

That night th' Apostles met in fear ;
Amidst them did the LORD appear,
And said, " My peace be on all here."
                    Alleluia !

When Didymus the tidings heard,
How they had seen the risen LORD,
He doubted the disciples' word.
                    Alleluia !

" My piercèd side, O Thomas, see ;
Behold My hands, My feet," saith He ;
" Not faithless, but believing be."
                    Alleluia !

No longer Thomas then denied ;
He saw the feet, the hands, the side ;
" My LORD, my GOD," straightway he cried.
                    Alleluia !

Blessèd are they who have not seen,
And yet whose faith hath constant been ;
Life everlasting they shall win.
                    Alleluia !

On this most holy day of days,
Our hearts and voices, LORD, we raise
To Thee in jubilee and praise.
                    Alleluia !   Amen.

147 _Thanks be to God, which giveth us the victory._
Cedant justi signa luctus.

FAR be sorrow, tears, and sighing !
  Waves are calming, storms are dying ;
  Moses hath o'erpass'd the sea,
  Israel's captive hosts are free ;
Life by death slew death and saved us,
In His Blood the LAMB hath lavèd us,
  Clothing us with victory.

JESUS CHRIST from death hath risen,
Lo ! His Godhead bursts the prison,
   While His Manhood passes free,
   Vanquishing our misery.
Rise we free from condemnation
Through His self-humiliation ;
   Ours is now the victory.

Vain the foe's despair and madness !
See the dayspring of our gladness !
   Slaves no more of Satan we ;
   Children, by the SON set free ;
Rise, for Life with death hath striven,
All the snares of hell are riven ;
   Rise and claim the victory.   Amen.

148 *O sing unto the Lord a new song ; for he hath done marvellous things.*

Finita jam sunt prælia.

ALLELUIA ! ALLELUIA ! ALLELUIA !
   The strife is o'er, the battle done ;
Now is the Victor's triumph won ;
Now be the song of praise begun.
          Alleluia !

Death's mightiest powers have done their worst,
And JESUS hath His foes dispersed ;
Let shouts of praise and joy outburst.
          Alleluia !

On the third morn He rose again
Glorious in majesty to reign ;
O let us swell the joyful strain.
          Alleluia !

He closed the yawning gates of hell ;
The bars from heav'n's high portals fell ;
Let songs of praise His triumph tell.
          Alleluia !

LORD, by the stripes which wounded Thee,
From death's dread sting Thy servants free,
That we may live, and sing to Thee.
Alleluia! Amen.

49 *Sing ye to the Lord, for he hath triumphed gloriously.*

AT the LAMB's high feast we sing
　　Praise to our victorious King,
Who hath wash'd us in the tide
Flowing from His piercèd side;
Praise we Him Whose love divine
Gives His sacred Blood for wine,
Gives His Body for the feast,
CHRIST the victim, CHRIST the priest.

Where the Paschal blood is pour'd,
Death's dark Angel sheathes his sword;
Israel's hosts triumphant go
Through the wave that drowns the foe.
Praise we CHRIST, Whose Blood was shed,
Paschal victim, Paschal bread;
With sincerity and love
Eat we manna from above.

Mighty Victim from the sky,
Hell's fierce powers beneath Thee lie;
Thou hast conquer'd in the fight,
Thou hast brought us life and light;
Now no more can death appal,
Now no more the grave enthral;
Thou hast open'd Paradise,
And in Thee Thy Saints shall rise.

Easter triumph, Easter joy,
Sin alone can this destroy;
From sin's power *do* Thou set free
Souls new-born, O LORD, in Thee.
(127)

Hymns of glory and of praise,
Risen LORD, to Thee we raise ;
Holy FATHER, praise to Thee,
With the SPIRIT, ever be.   Amen.

150   *Jesus met them, saying, All hail.*

'Αναστάσεως ἡμέρα.

THE Day of Resurrection !
  Earth, tell it out abroad ;
The Passover of gladness,
  The Passover of GOD !
From death to life eternal,
  From earth unto the sky,
Our GOD hath brought us over
  With hymns of victory.

Our hearts be pure from evil,
  That we may see aright
The LORD in rays eternal
  Of resurrection-light ;
And, listening to His accents,
  May hear so calm and plain
His own " All hail," and, hearing,
  May raise the victor strain.

Now let the heav'ns be joyful,
  And earth her song begin,
The round world keep high triumph,
  And all that is therein ;
Let all things seen and unseen
  Their notes of gladness blend,
For CHRIST the LORD is risen,
  Our Joy that hath no end.   Amen.

Lo, the winter is past.

Ἄισωμεν πάντες λαοί.

COME, ye faithful, raise the strain
 Of triumphant gladness ;
God hath brought His Israel
 Into joy from sadness ;
Loosed from Pharaoh's bitter yoke
 Jacob's sons and daughters ;
Led them with unmoisten'd foot
 Through the Red Sea waters.

'Tis the spring of souls to-day ;
 Christ hath burst His prison,
And from three days' sleep in death
 Like a sun hath risen ;
All the winter of our sins,
 Long and dark, is flying
From His light, to Whom we give
 Laud and praise undying.

Now the Queen of seasons, bright
 With the Day of splendour,
With the royal Feast of feasts,
 Comes its joy to render ;
Comes to glad Jerusalem,
 Who with true affection
Welcomes in unwearied strains
 Jesu's resurrection.

Alleluia now to Thee,
 Christ, our King immortal,
Who hast pass'd the gates of death
 And the tomb's seal'd portal ; .
Who, though never door unclose,
 In th' assembly standing,
Breathest on Thy friends the peace
 Past all understanding. Amen.

152 *The Lord is risen indeed.*

JESUS CHRIST is risen to-day, Alleluia !
Our triumphant holy day, Alleluia !
Who did once, upon the Cross, Alleluia !
Suffer to redeem our loss. Alleluia !

Hymns of práise then let us sing Alleluia !
Unto CHRIST, our heav'nly King, Alleluia !
Who endured the Cross and grave, Alleluia !
Sinners to redeem and save. Alleluia !

But the pains that He endured Alleluia !
Our salvation have procured ; Alleluia !
Now above the sky He's King, Alleluia !
Where the Angels ever sing. Alleluia ! Amen.

153 *If Christ be not raised, your faith is vain, ye are yet in your sins.*

LIFT your glad voices in triumph on high,
For JESUS hath risen, and man cannot die.
Vain were the terrors that gather'd around Him,
And short the dominion of death and the grave :
He burst from the fetters of darkness that bound
Him,
Resplendent in glory to live and to save.
Loud was the chorus of angels on high,
The Saviour hath risen, and man shall not die.

Glory to GOD, in full anthems of joy ;
The being He gave us death cannot destroy ;
Sad were the life we must part with to-morrow,
If tears were our birthright and death were our
end ;

But JESUS hath cheer'd the dark valley of sorrow,
  And bade us, immortal, to heaven ascend.
Lift, then, your voices in triumph on high,
For JESUS hath risen, and man shall not die. Amen.

154 *Now is Christ risen from the dead, and become the first-fruits of them that slept.*

ALLELUIA ! Alleluia !
    Hearts to heav'n and voices raise ;
Sing to GOD a hymn of gladness,
  Sing to GOD a hymn of praise ;
He Who on the Cross a victim
  For the world's salvation bled,
JESUS CHRIST, the King of glory,
  Now is risen from the dead.

CHRIST is risen, CHRIST the first-fruits
  Of the holy harvest field,
Which will all its full abundance
  At His second coming yield ;
Then the golden ears of harvest
  Will their heads before Him wave,
Ripen'd by His glorious sunshine
  From the furrows of the grave.

CHRIST is risen, we are risen ;
  Shed upon us heav'nly grace,
Rain, and dew, and gleams of glory
  From the brightness of Thy face ;
That we, with our hearts in heaven,
  Here on earth may fruitful be,
And by Angel-hands be gather'd,
  And be ever, LORD, with Thee.

Alleluia ! Alleluia !
  Glory be to GOD on high ;
Alleluia to the Saviour,
  Who hath gain'd the victory ;
Alleluia to the SPIRIT,
  Fount of love and sanctity ;
Alleluia ! Alleluia !
  To the TRIUNE Majesty.   Amen.

155   *The first-begotten of the dead.*

COME, see the place where JESUS lay,
    And hear Angelic watchers say,
" He lives, Who once was slain :
Why seek the living 'midst the dead ?
Remember how the Saviour said
    That He would rise again."

O joyful sound ! O glorious hour,
When by His own almighty power
    He rose, and left the grave !
Now let our songs His triumph tell,
Who burst the bands of death and hell,
    And ever lives to save.

The First-begotten of the dead,
For us He rose, our glorious Head,
    Immortal life to bring ;
What though the saints like Him shall die,
They share their Leader's victory,
    And triumph with their King.

No more they tremble at the grave,
For JESUS will their spirits save,
    And raise their slumbering dust :
O risen LORD, in Thee we live,
To Thee our ransom'd souls we give,
    To Thee our bodies trust.   Amen.

EASTER.

6 *I am he that liveth, and was dead; and, behold, I am, alive for evermore, Amen; and have the keys of hell and of death.*

Jesus lebt.

JESUS lives ! thy terrors now
  Can no more, O Death, appal us :
JESUS lives ! by this we know
  Thou, O grave, canst not enthral us.
                Alleluia !

JESUS lives ! henceforth is death
  But the gate of life immortal ;
This shall calm our trembling breath,
  When we pass its gloomy portal.
                Alleluia !

JESUS lives ! for us He died ;
  Then, alone to JESUS living,
Pure in heart may we abide,
  Glory to our Saviour giving.
                Alleluia !

JESUS lives ! our hearts know well
  Nought from us His love shall sever ;
Life, nor death, nor powers of hell
  Tear us from His keeping ever.
                Alleluia !

JESUS lives ! to Him the throne
  Over all the world is given ;
May we go where He is gone,
  Rest and reign with Him in heaven.
                Alleluia ! Amen.

7 *When I awake up after thy likeness, I shall be satisfied with it.*

ON the Resurrection morning
  Soul and body meet again ;
No more sorrow, no more weeping,
                No more pain !

EASTER.

Here awhile they must be parted,
　And the flesh its Sabbath keep,
Waiting in a holy stillness,
　　　　　Wrapt in sleep.

For a while the wearied body
　Lies with feet toward the morn ;
Till the last and brightest Easter
　　　　　Day be born.

But the soul in contemplation
　Utters earnest prayer and strong,
Bursting at the Resurrection
　　　　　Into song.

Soul and body reunited
　Thenceforth nothing shall divide,
Waking up in CHRIST's own likeness
　　　　　Satisfied.

Oh the beauty, Oh the gladness
　Of that Resurrection day,
Which shall not through endless ages
　　　　　Pass away !

On that happy Easter morning
　All the graves their dead restore ;
Father, sister, child, and mother
　　　　　Meet once more.

To that brightest of all meetings
　Bring us, JESU CHRIST, at last,
By Thy Cross, through death and judgment,
　　　　　Holding fast.　Amen.

158　　　*Being seen of them forty days.*

FORTY days of Easter-tide
　　Thou didst commune with Thine own ;
Now by glimpses, LORD, *descried,*
　Handled now and proved and known ;—

EASTER.

Known, Most Merciful, yet veil'd;
    Else before the awful sight
Surely heart and flesh had fail'd,
    Smitten with exceeding light.

Risen Master, fain would we,
    Sharing those unearthly days,
Morn and eve, on shore and sea,
    Watch Thy movements, mark Thy ways ;—

Catch by faith each glad surprise
    Of Thy footstep drawing nigh,
Hear Thy sudden greeting rise—
    "Peace be to you ! It is I ;"—

Secrets of Thy kingdom learn,
    Read the vision open spread,
Feel Thy word within us burn,
    Know Thee in the broken Bread.

So Thy glory's skirts beside
    Gently led from grace to grace,
We Thy coming may abide,
    And adore Thee face to face.   Amen.

59   *The song of Moses . . . and the song of the Lamb.*

THE foe behind, the deep before,
    Our hosts have dared and pass'd the sea ;
And Pharaoh's warriors strew the shore,
    And Israel's ransom'd tribes are free.

Lift up, lift up your voices now !
The whole wide world rejoices now ;
The LORD hath triumph'd gloriously !
The LORD *shall reign* victoriously !

EASTER.

Happy morrow,
Turning sorrow
Into peace and mirth !
Bondage ending,
Love descending
  O'er the earth.

Seals assuring,
Guards securing,
 Watch His earthly prison ;
Seals are shatter'd,
Guards are scatter'd ;—
  CHRIST is risen !

No longer must the mourners weep,
  Nor call departed Christians dead ;
For death is hallow'd into sleep,
  And every grave becomes a bed.

Now once more
Eden's door
Open stands to mortal eyes ;
For CHRIST hath risen, and man shall rise.

Now at last,
Old things past,
Hope, and joy, and peace begin :
For CHRIST hath won, and man shall win.

It is not exile, rest on high ;
  It is not sadness, peace from strife ;
To fall asleep is not to die ;
  To dwell with CHRIST is better life.

Where our banner leads us
  We may safely go ;
Where our Chief precedes us
  We may face the foe.

EASTER.

His right arm is o'er us,
   He our Guide will be :
CHRIST hath gone before us,
   Christians, follow ye ! .

Lift up, lift up your voices now !
The whole wide world rejoices now ;
The LORD hath triumph'd gloriously !
The LORD shall reign victoriously ! Amen.

*My beloved spake and said unto me, Rise up, my love,
my fair one, and come away. For, lo, the winter is
past, the rain is over and gone; the flowers appear on
the earth; the time of the singing of birds is come,
and the voice of the turtle is heard in our land.*

O VOICE of the Belovèd,
   The Bride hath heard Thee say,—
"Rise up, My love, My fair one,
   Arise and come away.
For lo, 'tis past, the winter,
   The winter of thy year ;
The rain is past and over,
   The flowers on earth appear.

"And now the time of singing
   Is come for every bird ;
And over all the country
   The turtle dove is heard :
The fig her green fruit ripens,
   The vines are in their bloom ;
Arise and smell their fragrance,
   My love, My fair one, come !"

Yea, LORD ! Thy Passion over,
   We know this life of ours
Hath pass'd from death and winter
   To leaves and budding flowers :

No more Thy rain of weeping
In drear Gethsemane ;
No more the clouds and darkness,
That veil'd Thy bitter Tree.

Our Easter Sun is risen !
And yet we slumber long,
And need Thy Dove's sweet pleading
To waken prayer and song.
Oh breathe upon our deadness,
Oh shine upon our gloom ;
LORD, let us feel Thy presence,
And rise and live and bloom.   Amen.

161   *Risen with him.*

THE LORD is risen indeed :
Now is His work perform'd ;
Now is the mighty Captive freed,
And death's strong castle storm'd.

The LORD is risen indeed ;
Then hell has lost his prey ;
With Him is risen the ransom'd seed
To reign in endless day.

The LORD is risen indeed ;
He lives to die no more ;
He lives, the sinner's cause to plead,
Whose curse and shame He bore.

The LORD is risen indeed ;
Attending Angels, hear !
Up to the courts of heav'n with speed
The joyful tidings bear.

Then take your golden lyres,
And strike each cheerful chord ;
Join, all ye bright celestial choirs,
To sing our risen LORD.   Amen.

EASTER.

Christus ist erstanden.

CHRIST the LORD is risen again ;
   CHRIST hath broken every chain ;
Hark ! Angelic voices cry,
Singing evermore on high,
          Alleluia !

He Who gave for us His life,
Who for us endured the strife,
Is our Paschal LAMB to-day ;
We too sing for joy, and say
          Alleluia !

He Who bore all pain and loss
Comfortless upon the Cross,
Lives in glory now on high,
Pleads for us, and hears our cry.
          Alleluia !

He Who slumber'd in the grave,
Is exalted now to save ;
Now through Christendom it rings
That the LAMB is King of kings.
          Alleluia !

Now He bids us speak the word
How the lost may be restored,
How the penitent forgiven,
How we too may enter heaven.
          Alleluia !

Thou, our Paschal LAMB indeed,
CHRIST, Thy ransom'd people feed :
Take our sins and guilt away,
Let us sing by night and day
          Alleluia ! Amen.

163 *When thou liest down, thou shalt not be afraid*
thou shalt lie down, and thy sleep shall be sweet

Jesu Salvator sæculi.

FOR A LATE EVENING SERVICE.

JESU, the world's redeeming LORD,
   The FATHER'S co-eternal WORD,
Of Light invisible true Light,
Thine Israel's Keeper day and night ;

Our great Creator and our Guide,
Who times and seasons dost divide,
Refresh to-night with quiet rest
Our limbs by daily toil oppress'd :

That while in this frail house of clay
A little longer here we stay,
Our weary flesh may take its sleep,
Our souls in CHRIST their vigils keep.

We pray Thee, while we dwell below,
Preserve us from our ghostly foe ;
That he may ne'er victorious be
O'er those so dearly bought by Thee.

O LORD of all, with us abide
In this our joyful Easter-tide ;
From every weapon death can wield
Thine own redeem'd for ever shield.

All praise be Thine, O risen LORD,
From death to endless life restored ;
All praise to GOD the FATHER be
And HOLY GHOST eternally.   Amen.

The following Hymns are suitable for this season
   37 Again the LORD'S own day is here.
   343 Come, let us join our cheerful songs.
   351 Come, ye faithful, raise the anthem.
   380 Light's abode, celestial Salem.
   421 The King of love my Shepherd is.

164 *The earth is the Lord's, and the fulness thereof.*

O THRONED, O crown'd with all renown,
   Since Thou the earth hast trod,
Thou reignest, and by Thee come down ·
   Henceforth the gifts of GOD.
By Thee the suns of space, that burn
   Unspent, their watches hold ;
The hosts that turn, and still return,
   Are sway'd, and poised, and · roll'd.

The powers of earth, for all her ills,
   An endless treasure yield ;
The precious things of th' ancient hills,
   Forest, and fruitful field.
Thine is the health, and Thine the wealth,
   ˙ That in our halls abound ;
And Thine the beauty and the joy
   With which the years are crown'd. ·

And as, when ebb'd the flood, our sires
   Kneel'd on the mountain sod,
While o'er the new world's altar fires
   Shone out the Bow of GOD ;
And sweetly fell the peaceful spell—
   Word that shall aye avail—
" Summer and winter shall not cease,
   Seed time nor harvest fail ; "—

Thus in their change let frost and heat
   And winds and dews be given ;
All fostering power, all influence sweet,
   Breathe from the bounteous heaven.
Attemper fair with gentle air
   The sunshine and the rain,
That kindly earth with timely birth
   May *yield her fruits* again ;

(141)

That we may feed Thy poor aright,
  And, gathering round Thy throne,
Here in the holy Angels' sight
  Repay Thee of Thine own.
For so our sires in olden time
  Spared neither gold nor gear,
Nor precious wood, nor hewen stone,
  Thy sacred shrines to rear.

For there to give the second birth
  In mysteries and signs,
The face of CHRIST o'er all the earth
  On kneeling myriads shines.
And if so fair beyond compare
  Thine earthly houses be,
In how great grace shall we Thy face
  In Thine own palace see ! Amen.

165 *The eyes of all wait upon thee, O Lord; and t*
givest them their meat in due season.

LORD, in Thy Name Thy servants plead
  And Thou hast sworn to hear ;
Thine is the harvest, Thine the seed,
  The fresh and fading year.

Our hope, when autumn winds blew wild,
  We trusted, LORD, with Thee :
And still, now spring has on us smiled,
  We wait on Thy decree.

The former and the latter rain,
  The summer sun and air,
The green ear, and the golden grain,
  All Thine, are ours by prayer.

Thine too by right, and ours by grace,
  The wondrous growth unseen,
The hopes that soothe, the fears that brace,
  The love that shines serene

So grant the precious things brought forth
  By sun and moon below,
That Thee in Thy new heav'n and earth
We never may forgo. Amen.

166   *The eternal God is thy refuge.*

ETERNAL GOD, we look to Thee,
  To Thee for help we fly ;
Thine eye alone our wants can see,
  Thy hand alone supply.

LORD, let Thy fear within us dwell,
  Thy love our footsteps guide :
That love will all vain love expel ;
  That fear, all fear beside.

Not what we wish, but w at we want,
  O let Thy grace supplyḥ
The good, unask'd, in mercy grant ;
  The ill, though ask'd, deny. Amen.

This Hymn may also be sung at other seasons.

The following Hymns are also suitable for this season :
  419 O GOD of Jacob, by Whose hand.
  455 LORD, when we bend before Thy throne.
  489 JESUS, LORD of life and glory.
  636 Litany for the Rogation Days.
  640 Litany of Intercession. No. 1
  641 Litany of Intercession. No. 2.

ASCENSIONTIDE.

167 *All power is given unto me in heaven and in earth.*

Æterne rex altissime.

O THOU Eternal King most High,
  Whose Blood has brought salvation nigh,
The bonds of death are burst by Thee,
And grace has won the victory.
Ascending to the FATHER's throne
Thou tak'st the kingdom as Thine own ;
Thy days of mortal weakness o'er,
All *power is Thine* for evermore.

Nurse in Thine arms Thy people cleansed from stain,
And bear to God a gift made pure again.
> Hail, festal day, &c.

One wreath receive for Thine own works on high,
Another for Thy people's victory.
> Hail, festal day, &c.

O Saviour Christ, Thou art God's only Son,
Creator and Redeemer both in one.
> Hail, festal day, &c.

As ancient as Thy Father and not less,
By Thee the world arose from nothingness.
> Hail, festal day, &c.

Thou, seeing all men crush'd beneath the ban,
Didst put on manhood to deliver man.
> Hail, festal day, &c.

170 *By his own blood he entered in once into the holy place.*
Opus peregisti tuum.

THY work on earth, O Christ, is done,
Thy victory over death is won ;
Ascend, and claim again on high
Thy glory left for us to die.

A radiant cloud is now Thy car,
And earth lies stretch'd beneath Thee far ;
Ten thousand thousands round Thee sing,
And share the triumph of their King.

The Angel-host enraptured waits :
Wide open stand th' eternal gates :
O God and Man ! the Father's throne
Henceforth is evermore Thine own.

Our Advocate, our great High Priest,
Our Peacemaker, Thou enterest
To offer there the precious Blood
Thy love shed once upon the Rood.

From thence the Church, Thy chosen Bride,
With countless graces beautified,
Through all her members draws from Thee
Her hidden life of sanctity.

Where Thou, O CHRIST, the Head, art gone,
Thou callest us to follow on ;
O may Thy sacred footsteps be
The road by which we come to Thee.

All praise from every heart and tongue
To Thee, ascended LORD, be sung ;
All praise to GOD the FATHER be,
And HOLY GHOST eternally.   Amen.

1 *To him that overcometh will I grant to sit with me in my throne, even as I also overcame, and am set down with my Father in his throne.*

THE Head that once was crown'd with
   Is crown'd with glory now :   [thorns,
A royal diadem adorns
   The mighty Victor's brow.

The highest place that heav'n affords
   Is His, is His by right,
The King of kings and LORD of lords,
   And heav'n's eternal Light ;

The Joy of all who dwell above,
   The Joy of all below,
To whom He manifests His love,
   And grants His Name to know.

To them the Cross, with all its shame,
   With all its grace, is given :
Their name an everlasting name,
   Their joy the joy of heaven.

They suffer with their LORD below,
  They reign with Him above ;
Their profit and their joy to know
  The mystery of His love.

The Cross He bore is life and health,
  Though shame and death to Him ;
His people's hope, His people's wealth,
  Their everlasting theme. Amen.

172 *Lift up your heads, O ye gates, and be ye lift up, ye everlasting doors ; and the king of glory shall come in.*

HAIL the day that sees Him rise Alleluia !
  To His throne above the skies ; Alleluia !
CHRIST, the LAMB for sinners given, Alleluia !
Enters now the highest heaven. Alleluia !

There for Him high triumph waits ; Alleluia !
Lift your heads, eternal gates ; Alleluia !
He hath conquer'd death and sin ; Alleluia !
Take the King of glory in. Alleluia !

Lo'! the heav'n its LORD receives, Alleluia !
Yet He loves the earth He leaves : Alleluia !
Though returning to His throne, Alleluia !
Still He calls mankind His own. Alleluia !

See ! He lifts His hands above ; Alleluia !
See ! He shows the prints of love : Alleluia !
Hark ! His gracious lips bestow Alleluia !
Blessings on His Church below. Alleluia !

Still for us He intercedes ; Alleluia !
His prevailing death He pleads ; Alleluia !
Near Himself prepares our place, Alleluia !
Harbinger of human race. Alleluia !

LORD, though parted from our sight, Alleluia !
High above yon azure height, Alleluia !
Grant our hearts may thither rise, Alleluia !
Following Thee above the skies. Alleluia ! **Amen.**

(148)

ASCENSIONTIDE.

73 *Thou art gone up on high, thou hast led captivity captive, and received gifts for men.*

PART 1.

SEE the Conqueror mounts in triumph,
　　See the King in royal state
Riding on the clouds His chariot
　　To His heav'nly palace gate ;
Hark ! the choirs of Angel voices
　　Joyful Alleluias sing,
And the portals high are lifted
　　To receive their heav'nly King.

Who is this that comes in glory,
　　With the trump of jubilee ?
LORD of battles, GOD of armies,
　　He has gain'd the victory ;
He Who on the Cross did suffer,
　　He Who from the grave arose,
He has vanquish'd sin and Satan,
　　He by death has spoil'd His foes.

While He lifts His hands in blessing,
　　He is parted from His friends ;
While their eager eyes behold Him,
　　He upon the clouds ascends ;
He who walk'd with GOD, and pleased Him,
　　Preaching truth and doom to come,
He, our Enoch, is translated
　　To His everlasting home.

Now our heav'nly Aaron enters,
　　With His Blood, within the veil ;
Joshua now is come to Canaan,
　　And the kings before Him quail ;
Now He plants the tribes of Israel
　　In their promised resting-place ;
Now our great Elijah offers
　　Double portion of His grace.

(149)

F 2

ASCENSIONTIDE.

Thou hast raised our human nature
  In the clouds to God's right hand ;
There we sit in heav'nly places,
  There with Thee in glory stand ;
Jesus reigns, adored by Angels ;
  Man with God is on the throne ;
Mighty Lord, in Thine Ascension
We by faith behold our own.

Part 2.

Holy Ghost, Illuminator,
  Shed Thy beams upon our eyes,
Help us to look up with Stephen,
  And to see beyond the skies,
Where the Son of Man in glory
  Standing is at God's right hand,
Beckoning on His Martyr army,
  Succouring His faithful band ;

See Him, Who is gone before us,
  Heav'nly mansions to prepare,
See Him, Who is ever pleading
  For us with prevailing prayer,
See Him, Who with sound of trumpet
  And with His Angelic train,
Summoning the world to judgment,
  On the clouds will come again.

Raise us up from earth to heaven,
  Give us wings of faith and love,
Gales of holy aspirations
  Wafting us to realms above ;
That, with hearts and minds uplifted,
  We with Christ our Lord may dwell
Where He sits enthroned in glory
  In His heav'nly citadel.

ASCENSIONTIDE.

So at last, when He appeareth,
 We from out our graves may spring,
With our youth renew'd like eagles,
 Flocking round our heav'nly King,
Caught up on the clouds of heaven,
 And may meet Him in the air,
Rise to realms where He is reigning,
 And may reign for ever there.

following Doxology may be sung at the end of either Part:

Glory be to GOD the FATHER ;
 Glory be to GOD the SON,
Dying, risen, ascending for us,
 Who the heav'nly realm has won ;
Glory to the HOLY SPIRIT ;
 To ONE GOD in Persons THREE ;
Glory both in earth and heaven,
 Glory, endless glory, be. Amen.

₂ second part of this Hymn may be used in Whitsuntide.

4   *Who is gone into heaven.*

THOU art gone up on high,
 To mansions in the skies,
And round Thy throne unceasingly
 The songs of praise arise ;
But we are lingering here
 With sin and care oppress'd ;
LORD, send Thy promised Comforter,
 And lead us to our rest.

Thou art gone up on high ;
 But Thou didst first come down,
Through earth's most bitter misery
 To pass unto Thy crown ;
And girt with griefs and fears
 Our onward course must be ;
But only let that path of tears
 Lead us at last to Thee.

Thou art gone up on high ;
　But Thou shalt come again,
With all the bright ones of the sky
　· Attendant in Thy train.
LORD, by Thy saving power
　So make us live and die,
That we may stand in that dread hour
　At Thy right hand on high.　Amen.

175 *Knowest thou that the Lord will take away thy master*
from thy head to-day ?

KNOW ye the LORD doth take away
　　Your Master from your head to-day ?
Yea, we know it ; yet we raise
Joyous strains of hope and praise !
He is gone, but not before
All His earthly work is o'er.
　　　　　　　　　　Alleluia !

Know ye the LORD doth take away
Your Master from your head to-day ?
　　Yea, we know it ; stand afar ;
　　Mark His bright triumphal car,
　　Mighty end of mighty deeds,
　　Clouds His chariot, winds His steeds !
　　　　　　　　　　Alleluia !

Know ye the LORD doth take away
Your Master from your head to-day ?
　　Yea, we know it ; ere He left,
　　Jordan's stream in twain was cleft :
　　With that glorious act in view,
　　We shall one day cleave it too !

ASCENSIONTIDE.

Know ye the LORD doth take away
Your Master from your head to-day ?
    Yea, we know it ; wondrous love
    Bids Him seek His home above :
    He hath said 'tis better so ;
    See His mantle dropt below.
                Alleluia !

Know ye the LORD doth take away
Your Master from your head to-day ?
    Yea, we know it ; lo ! we trace
    Plenteous portions of His grace,
    Sent to all whose hearts can soar
    Whither He has gone before.
                Alleluia !

Know ye the LORD doth take away
Your Master from your head to-day ?
    Yea, we know it ; search would fail,
    If ye pass'd through mount and vale ;
    Earth contains Him not, though wide :
    Seek Him at His FATHER's side.
            Alleluia !   Amen.

76 *Who . . . when he had by himself purged our sins, sat down on the right hand of the Majesty on high.*

Jesu nostra redemptio.

FOR A LATE EVENING SERVICE.

JESU, our Hope, our heart's Desire,
    Maker and GOD of all,
WORD in the latter days made Flesh,
    Redeemer from the Fall ;

How vast the mercy and the love,
    Which laid our sins on Thee,
And led *Thee to a cruel death*,
    To set Thy people free !

ASCENSIONTIDE.

But now the bonds of death are burst ;
  The ransom has been paid ;
And Thou art on Thy FATHER's throne
  In majesty array'd.

Oh may Thy mighty love prevail
  Our sinful souls to spare !
Oh may we stand around Thy throne,
  And see Thy glory there !

JESU, our only joy be Thou,
  As Thou our prize wilt be ;
In Thee be all our glory now
  And through eternity.

All praise to Thee Who art gone up
  Triumphantly to heaven ;
All praise to GOD the FATHER's Name
  And HOLY GHOST be given.   Amen.

The following Hymns are suitable for this season :

WHITSUN EVEN.

177 *If I go not away, the Comforter will not come unt*
you; but if I depart, I will send him unto you.

Supreme rector cælitum.

RULER of the hosts of light,
  Death hath yielded to Thy might,
And Thy Blood hath mark'd a road
Which will lead us back to GOD.

From Thy dwelling-place above,
From Thy FATHER's throne of love,
With Thy look of mercy bless
Those without Thee comfortless.

WHITSUN EVEN.

Bitter were Thy throes on earth,
Giving to the Church her birth
From the spear-wound open'd wide
In Thine own life-giving side.

Now in glory Thou dost reign
Won by all Thy toil and pain ;
Thence the promised Gift confer,
Send to us the Comforter.

JESU, praise to Thee be given
With the FATHER high in heaven ;
HOLY SPIRIT, praise to Thee
Now and through eternity.   Amen.

WHITSUNTIDE.

78 *And when the day of Pentecost was fully come, they were all with one accord in one place.*

Jam Christus astra ascenderat.

NOW CHRIST above the starry floor
    Had enter'd where He was before,
The FATHER's promised Gift to claim,
And send the SPIRIT in His Name.

The solemn time was drawing nigh,
Full charged with heav'nly mystery,
That week of weeks which brought the feast
That spoke of ancient bonds released.

When the third hour shone all around,
There came a rushing mighty sound,
Which told the Apostles at their prayer
That He was come, that GOD was there.

Forth from the FATHER's light it came,
That beautiful and kindly flame,
And fill'd and kindled with the word
Those *hearts so loyal to* their LORD.

WHITSUNTIDE.

Of old in every hallow'd breast
Thou camest in Thy grace to rest ;
O grant us now from sin release,
And in our time, good LORD, give peace.
Praise we the FATHER and the SON,
And HOLY SPIRIT with Them One :
And may the SON on us bestow
The gifts that from the SPIRIT flow. Amen.

179   *I will pour out my Spirit upon all flesh.*

Beata nobis gaudia.

OH joy ! because the circling year
    Hath brought our day of blessing here,
The day when first the light divine
Upon the Church began to shine.

Like unto quivering tongues of flame
Upon each one the SPIRIT came,—
Tongues, that the earth might hear their call,
And fire, that love might burn in all.

Thus wondrously were spread abroad
To all the wondrous works of GOD ;
In every tribe's familiar tone
The glorious marvel was made known.

While harden'd scoffers vainly jeer'd,
The listening strangers heard and fear'd ;
They knew the prophet's word fulfill'd,
And own'd the work which GOD had will'd.

Of old in every hallow'd breast
Thou camest in Thy grace to rest ;
O grant us now from sin release,
And in our time, good LORD, give peace.
Praise we the FATHER and the SON,
And HOLY SPIRIT with Them One :
And may the SON on us bestow
The gifts that from the SPIRIT flow. Amen.

80 *The Comforter, which is the Holy Ghost.*

Veni Creator Spiritus.

COME, HOLY GHOST, our souls inspire,
   And lighten with celestial fire ;
Thou the anointing SPIRIT art,
Who dost Thy sevenfold gifts impart.
Thy blessèd unction from above
Is comfort, life, and fire of love ;
Enable with perpetual light
The dulness of our blinded sight :
Anoint and cheer our soilèd face
With the abundance of Thy grace ;
Keep far our foes, give peace at home ;
Where Thou art Guide no ill can come.
Teach us to know the FATHER, SON,
And Thee, of Both, to be but One ;
That through the ages all along
This may be our endless song,
Praise to Thy eternal merit,
FATHER, SON, and HOLY SPIRIT.   Amen.

.81 *The Comforter, which is the Holy Ghost.*

Veni Creator Spiritus.

COME, HOLY GHOST, Creator Blest,
   Vouchsafe within our souls to rest ;
Come with Thy grace and heav'nly aid,
And fill the hearts which Thou hast made.
To Thee, the Comforter, we cry,
To Thee, the Gift of GOD most High,
The Fount of life, the Fire of love,
The soul's Anointing from above.
The sevenfold gifts of grace are Thine,
O Finger of the Hand Divine ;
True promise *of the* FATHER Thou,
Who dost the tongue with speech endow.

Thy light to every thought impart,
And shed Thy love in every heart;
The weakness of our mortal state
With deathless might invigorate.

Drive far away our ghostly foe,
And Thine abiding peace bestow;
If Thou be our preventing Guide,
No evil can our steps betide.

Make Thou to us the FATHER known;
Teach us th' Eternal SON to own,
And Thee, Whose Name we ever bless,
Of Both the SPIRIT to confess.

Praise we the FATHER and the SON,
And HOLY SPIRIT with Them One:
And may the SON on us bestow
The gifts that from the SPIRIT flow. Ame

182 *This is the day which the Lord hath made.*
Salve, festa dies.

HAIL, festal day, of never-dying fame,
When first upon the Church the SPIR
came.

Now takes the sun through heav'n a higher trac
'Twixt leaving ocean's bed and coming back.
Hail, festal day, &c.

He moves through liquid air and shoots his rays
And makes short nights between the lengtheni
days.
Hail, festal day, &c.

Far depths of cloudless sky are bared to sight;
The clear stars tell their story of delight.
Hail, festal day, &c.

WHITSUNTIDE.

The merry country offers all her store,
Now spring has brought its yearly wealth o
more.
        Hail, festal day, &c.
White gleam the hawthorn bushes as we pass,
And green and tall grows up the waving grass.
        Hail, festal day, &c.
Day after day fresh flowers like stars arise,
And all the turf breaks into laughing eyes.
        Hail, festal day, &c.

183   *The spirit of the Lord filleth the world.*
    Almum flamen, vita mundi.
BOUNTEOUS Spirit, ever shedding
    Life the world to fill !
Swarms the fruitful earth o'erspreading,
Shoals their ocean pathway threading,
    Own Thy quickening thrill :
Author of each creature's birth,
Life of life beneath the earth,
Everywhere, O Spirit blest,
Thou art motion, Thou art rest.
*Come, Creator ! come bestowing
    All Thy sevenfold dower !
Come, the face of earth renewing,
Peace and wealth around Thee strewing,
    Rich in soothing power.
Comforter ! what joy Thou art
To the blest and faithful heart ;
To the plots that hell doth lay
Bringing uttermost dismay.
O'er the waters of creation
    Moved Thy wings divine ;
When the world, to animation
Waking 'neath Thy visitation,
    Teem'd with powers benign :

WHITSUNTIDE.

Thou didst man to being call,
Didst restore him from his fall,
Pouring, like the latter rain,
Grace to quicken him again.

Thine the Gospel voices, crying
    As with trumpet clear ;
Till the world, in darkness lying,
Rose from deathly sleep, descrying
    Bliss and glory near.
Man, to reach that prize reveal'd,
Arm'd with Thee as with a shield,
Strengthen'd with Thy might within,
Quells the prince of death and sin.

*Lowliest homage now before Thee
    Let the ransom'd pay,
For Thy wondrous gifts implore Thee,
In Thy holiness adore Thee,
    While in love they pray :
Holy ! Holy ! we repeat,
Kneeling at Thy mercy-seat ;
To a Father's pity show
All the story of our woe.

Fount of grace for every nation,
    Refuge of the soul !
Strengthen Thou each new creation,
With the waters of salvation
    Make the guilty whole :
Rule on earth the powers that be ;
Give us priests inspired of Thee ;
Through Thy holy Church increase
Purest unity and peace.

*Purge and sanctify us wholly
    From the leaven of ill ;
Save from Satan's grasp unholy ;
To a living faith and lowly
    Join a strenuous will ;

Till the olden zeal return,
And with mutual love we burn;
Till in peace, no more to roam,
All the flock be gather'd home.   Amen.

These verses can be omitted.

4 *When thou lettest thy breath go forth they shall be
made, and thou shalt renew the face of the earth.*

Veni Sancte Spiritus.

COME, Thou HOLY SPIRIT, come;
  And from Thy celestial home
Shed a ray of light divine;
Come, Thou Father of the poor,
Come, Thou source of all our store,
  Come, within our bosoms shine:

Thou of comforters the best,
Thou the soul's most welcome guest,
  Sweet refreshment here below;
In our labour rest most sweet,
Grateful coolness in the heat,
  Solace in the midst of woe.

O most blessèd Light divine,
Shine within these hearts of Thine,
  And our inmost being fill;
Where Thou art not, man hath naught,
Nothing good in deed or thought,
  Nothing free from taint of ill.

Heal our wounds; our strength renew;
On our dryness pour Thy dew;
  Wash the stains of guilt away:
Bend the stubborn heart and will;
Melt the frozen, warm the chill;
  Guide the steps that go astray.

(161)

WHITSUNTIDE.

On the faithful, who adore
And confess Thee, evermore
  In Thy sevenfold gifts descend :
Give them virtue's sure reward ;
Give them Thy salvation, LORD ;
  Give them joys that never end. Amen.

185 *And suddenly there came a sound from heaven, as of a rushing mighty wind.*

WHEN GOD of old came down from heaven,
  In power and wrath He came ;
Before His feet the clouds were riven,
  Half darkness and half flame :

But when He came the second time,
  He came in power and love ;
Softer than gale at morning prime
  Hover'd His holy Dove.

The fires, that rush'd on Sinai down
  In sudden torrents dread,
Now gently light, a glorious crown,
  On every sainted head.

And as on Israel's awe-struck ear
  The voice exceeding loud,
The trump, that Angels quake to hear,
  Thrill'd from the deep, dark cloud ;

So, when the SPIRIT of our GOD
  Came down His flock to find,
A voice from heav'n was heard abroad,
  A rushing, mighty wind.

It fills the Church of GOD ; it fills
  The sinful world around ;
Only in stubborn hearts and wills
  No place for it is found.

(162)

'ome, LORD ; come, Wisdom, Love and Power ;
  Open our ears to hear ;
,et us not miss th' accepted hour ;
  Save, LORD, by love or fear.   Amen.

6 *And the same day there were added unto them about
  three thousand souls.*

SPIRIT of mercy, truth, and love,
    Shed Thy sweet influence from above ;
And still from age to age convey
The wonders of this sacred day.

In every clime, by every tongue,
Be GOD's surpassing glory sung ;
Through all the listening earth be taught
The acts our ris'n Redeemer wrought.

Unfailing Comfort, heav'nly Guide,
Still o'er Thy Holy Church preside ;
Still let mankind Thy blessings prove,
SPIRIT of mercy, truth, and love.   Amen.

7 *If I go not away, the Comforter will not come unto
  you ; but if I depart, I will send him unto you.*

OUR Blest Redeemer, ere He breathed
    His tender last farewell,
A Guide, a Comforter, bequeath'd
    With us to dwell.

He came sweet influence to impart,
    A gracious willing Guest,
While He can find one humble heart
    Wherein to rest.

And His that gentle voice we hear,
    Soft as the breath of even,
That checks each fault, that calms each fear,
    And *speaks of heaven.*

(163)

WHITSUNTIDE.

And every virtue we possess,
    And every victory won,
And every thought of holiness,
    Are His alone.

SPIRIT of purity and grace,
    Our weakness, pitying, see:
O make our hearts Thy dwelling-place,
    And meet for Thee.   Amen.

The following Hymns are suitable for this season:
173 Part 2. HOLY GHOST, Illuminator.
356 O HOLY SPIRIT, LORD of grace.
359 LORD GOD the HOLY GHOST.
360 Come, HOLY SPIRIT, come.
361 Come, gracious SPIRIT, heav'nly Dove.,
362 O HOLY GHOST, Thy people bless.
363 Gracious SPIRIT, HOLY GHOST.
365 Come to our poor nature's night.
399 Come, HOLY GHOST, our hearts inspire.
449 Breathe on me, Breath of GOD.
454 Awake, O LORD, as in the time of old.
525 O SPIRIT of the living GOD.
637 Litany of the HOLY GHOST.

TRINITY SUNDAY.

188 *I am Alpha and Omega, the beginning and the
ending . . . the first and the last.*

Adesto, sancta Trinitas.

BE near us, Holy TRINITY,
    One GOD of equal majesty !
All things that are on Thee depend,
Who art beginning without end.

The myriad armies of the sky
Praise, worship, tell Thy Name most high
This triple frame—earth, air, and sea—
Doth bless Thee everlastingly.

We also come, Thy servants all,
And at Thy feet adoring fall :
O join the vows and prayers we bring
With those high hymns the Angels sing.

TRINITY SUNDAY.

Thee we confess one Light to be,
Thee, we adore, co-equal THREE ;
Alpha and Omega, we cry,
And all things having breath reply,—

Praise to the FATHER, made of none,
Praise to His sole-begotten SON,
Praise to the HOLY SPIRIT be,—
Eternal Godhead, ONE in THREE ! Amen.

189 *Praise our God, all ye his servants, and ye that fear him, both small and great.*

O Pater sancte.

FATHER most Holy, merciful and loving,
     JESU, Redeemer, ever to be worshipp'd,
Life-giving SPIRIT, Comforter most gracious,
          GOD everlasting.

Three in a wondrous unity unbroken,
One perfect Godhead, love that never faileth,
Light of the Angels, succour of the needy,
          Hope of all living ;

All Thy creation serveth its Creator,
Thee every creature praiseth without ceasing ;
We too would sing Thee psalms of true devotion ;
          Hear, we beseech Thee.

Lord GOD Almighty, unto Thee be glory,
One in Three Persons, over all exalted ;
Thine, as is meet, be honour, praise, and blessing
          Now and for ever.   Amen.

O *And one cried unto another, and said, Holy, Holy, Holy is the Lord of Hosts.*

Ave, colenda Trinitas.

ALL hail, adorèd TRINITY ;
     All hail, Eternal UNITY ;
O GOD the FATHER, GOD the SON,
And GOD the SPIRIT, ever ONE.

(165)

TRINITY SUNDAY.

To Thee upon this festal day
We offer here our thankful lay :
O let our work accepted be,
That wholesome work of praising Thee.

THREE Persons praise we evermore,
ONE only GOD our hearts adore ;
In Thy sure mercy ever kind
May we our strong protection find.

O TRINITY ! O UNITY !
Be present as we worship Thee ;
Amid the songs that Angels sing
Accept the tribute that we bring.   Amen.

The following Hymns are suitable for this Festival :

36 O TRINITY, most blessèd Light.
308 Holy, Holy, Holy ! LORD GOD Almighty !
309 Sound aloud Jehovah's praises.
310 Bright the vision that delighted.
311 THREE in ONE, and ONE in THREE.
312 FATHER, of heav'n, Whose love profound.
325 Glory to GOD, all the heavens are telling.

SAINTS' DAYS.

191 *He ordained twelve . . . that he might send them forth to preach, and to have power to heal sicknesses.*

Exultet cælum laudibus.

FOR APOSTLES.

LET all on earth their voices raise,
Re-echoing heav'n's triumphant praise
To Him, Who gave th' Apostles grace
To run on earth their glorious race.

Thou, at Whose word they bore the light
Of Gospel truth o'er heathen night,
To us that heav'nly light impart,
To glad our eyes and cheer our heart.

Thou, at Whose will to them was given
To bind and loose in earth and heaven,
Our chains unbind, our sins undo,
And in our hearts Thy grace renew. .

(166)

Thou, in Whose might they spake the word
Which cured disease and health restored,
To us its healing power prolong,
Support the weak, confirm the strong.

And when the thrones are set on high,
And judgment's awful hour draws nigh,
Then, LORD, with them pronounce us blest,
And take us to Thine endless rest.   Amen.

92 *And the wall of the city had twelve foundations, and
in them the names of the twelve Apostles of the Lamb.*

Æterna Christi munera.

FOR APOSTLES.

TH' eternal gifts of CHRIST the King,
  The Apostles' glory, let us sing ;
And all with hearts of gladness raise
Due hymns of thankful love and praise.

For they the Church's Princes are,
Triumphant leaders in the war,
The heav'nly King's own warrior band,
True lights to lighten every land.

Theirs was the steadfast faith of Saints,
The hope that never yields nor faints,
The love of CHRIST in perfect glow,
That lay the prince of this world low.

In them the FATHER's glory shone,
In them the SPIRIT's will was done,
The SON Himself exults in them ;
Joy fills the new Jerusalem.

To Thee, Redeemer, now we cry,
That Thou wouldst join with them on high
Thy servants, who this grace implore,
For *ever and for* evermore.   Amen.

193 *We preach not ourselves, but Christ Jesus the Lord.*

Supreme, quales, Arbiter.

FOR APOSTLES.

DISPOSER Supreme, and Judge of the earth,
Who choosest for Thine the weak and the
poor ;
To frail earthen vessels and things of no worth
Entrusting Thy riches which aye shall endure ;

Those vessels soon fail, though full of Thy light,
And at Thy decree are broken and gone ;
Thence brightly appeareth Thy truth in its might,
As through the clouds riven the lightnings have
shone.

Like clouds are they borne to do Thy great will,
And swift as the winds about the world go ;
The WORD with His wisdom their spirits doth fill ;
They thunder, they lighten, the waters o'erflow.

Their sound goeth forth, "CHRIST JESUS the
LORD ; "
Then Satan doth fear, his citadels fall :
As when the dread trumpets went forth at Thy
word,
And one long blast shatter'd the Canaanite's wall.

O loud be their trump, and stirring their sound,
To rouse us, O LORD, from slumber of sin ;
The lights Thou hast kindled in darkness around,
O may they awaken our spirits within.

All honour and praise, dominion and might,
To GOD, THREE in ONE, eternally be,
Who round us hath shed His own marvellous light,
And call'd us from darkness His glory to see.
Amen.

4 *He chose twelve, whom also he named Apostles.*

Stola regni laureatus.

FOR APOSTLES.

IN royal robes of splendour,
　　Before the great King's feet,
The Princes of His Kingdom,
　　The crown'd Apostles, meet ;
To Him their songs adoring
　　With heart and tongue they bring,
Pure hearts and mighty voices—
　　E'en as the Angels sing.

This Order sheds its lustre
　　O'er all the human race ;
ᴧ court of righteous judgment,
　　The Rock of Gospel grace :—
Rock of His Church, for ages
　　Elected and foreknown ;
Whose glorious Master-Builder
　　Is Head and Corner-Stone.

These are the famous heralds
　　Who, pledged to want and loss,
Proclaim'd the war of suffering,
　　The glory of the Cross.
Day unto day shows knowledge ;
　　Night unto night gives speech ;
So these to earth's four corners
　　Their wondrous Gospel preach.

CHRIST'S burden light they proffer,
　　His easy yoke proclaim ;
The seed of life they scatter,
　　That all may own His Name.
The earth brought forth and budded,
　　Where'er their ploughshare ran,
And fruits of increase follow'd
　　The faith of GOD made Man.

(169)

These are the sure foundation
  On which the temple stands ;
The living stones compacting
  That house not made with hands ;
The gates by which man enters
  Jerusalem the new ;
The bond which knits together
  The Gentile and the Jew.

Let error flee before them,
  Let truth extend her sway ;
Let dread of final judgment
  To faith and love give way ;
That, loosed from our offences,
  We then may number'd be
Among Thy Saints in glory,
  Around the throne with Thee.   Amen.

195   *Ye also shall sit upon twelve thrones, judging th*
        twelve tribes of Israel.

Cælestis aulæ principes.

FOR APOSTLES.

CAPTAINS of the saintly band,
  Lights who lighten every land,
Princes who with JESUS dwell,
Judges of His Israel.

On the nations sunk in night
Ye have shed the Gospel light ;
Falsehood flies before the day ;
Truth is shining on our way.

Not by warrior's spear and sword,
Not by art of human word,
Preaching but the Cross of shame,
Rebel hearts for CHRIST ye tame.

Earth, that long in sin and pain
Groan'd in Satan's deadly chain,
Now to serve its GOD is free
In the law of liberty.

Distant lands with one acclaim
Tell the honour of your name,
Who, wherever man has trod,
Teach the mysteries of GOD.

Glory to the THREE in ONE
While eternal ages run,
Who from deepest shades of night
Call'd us to His glorious light.   Amen.

96 *Behold upon the mountains the feet of him that bringeth good tidings, that publisheth peace.*

Christi perennes nuntii.

FOR EVANGELISTS.

YE deathless messengers of CHRIST,
   Who bear to every place
The unveil'd mysteries of GOD,
   The Gospel of His grace,

The things in type and shadow dim
   By holy prophets seen
In all the light of day ye saw
   With not a cloud between.

What CHRIST, true Man, divinely wrought,
   What GOD in Manhood bore,
Ye wrote, as GOD inspired, in words
   That live for evermore.

Although in space and time apart,
   One SPIRIT moved your will;
We in your sacred pages hear
   That SPIRIT speaking still.

To GOD, the Blessèd THREE in ONE,
   Be glory, praise, and might,
Who call'd us *from* the shades of death
   To His own glorious light.   Amen.

197	*They four had one likeness.*

Plausu chorus lætabundo.

FOR EVANGELISTS.

COME sing, ye choirs exultant,
    Those messengers of GOD,
Through whom the living Gospels
    Came sounding all abroad !
They spake, and lo ! salvation
    Stream'd forth and banish'd night ;
Up rose the sun of glory
    To flood the world with light.

He chose them, our Good Shepherd,
    And, tending evermore
His flock through earth's four quarters,
    In wisdom made them four ;
One charter for all nations
    The Lawgiver decreed ;
And by four penmen utter'd
    One glorious title-deed.

In one harmonious witness
    The chosen four combine,
While each his own commission
    Fulfils in every line ;
As, in the Prophet's vision,
    From out the amber flame
In form of visage diverse
    Four living creatures came.

Lo, these the wingèd chariots,
    That bring Emmanuel nigh ;
The golden staves uplifting
    The ark of GOD on high ;
And these the fourfold river
    Of Paradise above,
Whence flow for all the nations
    New mysteries of love.

Four-square on this foundation
　The Church of CHRIST remains,
A house to stand unshaken
　By floods or winds or rains.
O glorious happy portion
　In this safe home to be,
By GOD, true Man, united
　With GOD eternally ! Amen.

98 *And a river went out of Eden to water the garden : and
from thence it was parted, and became into four heads.*

Jucundare, plebs fidelis.

FOR EVANGELISTS.

COME, pure hearts, in sweetest measure
　Sing of those who spread the treasure
In the holy Gospels shrined ;
Blessèd tidings of salvation,
Peace on earth their proclamation,
　Love from GOD to lost mankind.

See the rivers four that gladden
With their streams the better Eden
　Planted by our LORD most dear ;
CHRIST the Fountain, these the waters :
Drink, O Sion's sons and daughters,
　Drink and find salvation here.

O that we Thy truth confessing,
And Thy holy word possessing,
　JESU, may Thy love adore ;
Unto Thee our voices raising,
Thee with all Thy ransom'd praising
　Ever and for evermore. Amen.

99 *How beautiful upon the mountains are the feet of him
that . . . publisheth salvation.*

FOR EVANGELISTS.

HOW beauteous are their feet,
　Who stand on Sion's hill ;
Who bring salvation on their tongues
And words *of peace* instil.

(173)

How happy are our ears
That hear this joyful sound,·
Which kings and prophets waited for,
And sought, but never found !

How blessèd are our eyes
That see this heav'nly light !
Prophets and kings desired it long,
But died without the sight.

The LORD makes bare His arm
Through all the earth abroad ;
Let every nation now behold
Their Saviour and their GOD.   Amen.

200 *Blessed is the man that endureth temptation, ſo
when he is tried he shall receive the crown of life.*

Deus, tuorum militum.

FOR MARTYRS.

O GOD, Thy soldiers' faithful LORD,
  Their portion, and their great reward,
From all transgressions set us free
Who sing Thy Martyr's victory.

By wisdom taught he learn'd to know
The vanity of all below,
The fleeting joys of earth disdain'd,
And everlasting glory gain'd.

His painful course he bravely ran,
In deadly conflict play'd the man ;
For Thee he pour'd his life away,
With Thee he lives in endless day.

We therefore pray Thee, LORD of love,
Regard us from Thy throne above ;
On this Thy Martyr's triumph-day
Wash every stain of sin away.

SAINTS' DAYS.

All praise to God the FATHER be,
All praise, Eternal SON, to Thee,
Whom with the SPIRIT we adore,
For ever and for evermore.   Amen.

1 *Who through faith and patience inherit the promises.*
Sanctorum meritis inclyta gaudia.
FOR MARTYRS.

THE triumphs of the Saints,
The toils they bravely bore,
The love that never faints,
Their glory evermore,—
For these the Church to-day
Pours forth her joyous lay ;
What victors wear so rich a bay ?

This clinging world of ill
Them and their works abhorr'd ;
Its withering flowers still
They spurn'd with one accord ;
They knew them shortlived all,
How soon they fade and fall,
And follow'd, JESU, at Thy call.

What tongue may here declare,
Fancy or thought descry,
The joys Thou dost prepare
For these Thy Saints on high ?
Empurpled in the flood
Of their victorious blood,
They won the laurel from their GOD.

O LORD most High, we pray,
Stretch forth Thy mighty arm
To put our sins away
And shelter us from harm ;
O give Thy servants peace,
From guilt and pain release ;
Our praise to Thee shall never cease.
Amen.

202 *Others were tortured, not accepting deliverance, that they might obtain a better resurrection.*

Æterna Christi munera.

FOR MARTYRS.

TH' eternal gifts of CHRIST the King,
    The Martyrs' triumphs let us sing,
And all with hearts of gladness raise
Due hymns of thankful love and praise.

The world its terrors urged in vain;
They reck'd not of the body's pain :
One step, and holy death made sure
The life that ever shall endure.

The flame might scorch, the knife lay bare,
And savage beasts their members tear ;
But naught their constancy could shake
For that eternal kingdom's sake.

To Thee, Redeemer, now we cry,
That Thou wouldst join with them on high
Thy servants, who this grace implore,
For ever and for evermore.   Amen.

203 *They were stoned, they were sawn asunder, were tempted, were slain with the sword; . . . being destitute, afflicted, tormented; of whom the world was not worthy.*

O beata beatorum.

FOR MARTYRS.

BLESSÈD feasts of blessèd Martyrs,
    Holy days of holy men,
With affection's recollections
    Greet we your return again.

Worthy deeds they wrought and wonders,
    Worthy of the Name they bore ;
We with meetest praise and sweetest
    Honour them for evermore.

Faith ne'er alter'd, hope ne'er falter'd,
   Love of JESUS fill'd their heart ;
Thus they glorious and victorious
   Bravely bore the Martyr's part.

Rack'd with torments, haled to slaughter,
   Fire, and axe, and murderous sword,
Chains and prison, foes' derision,
   They endured for CHRIST the LORD.

So they pass'd through pain and sorrow,
   Till they sank in death to rest ;
Earth's rejected, GOD's elected,
   Gain'd the portion of the blest.

By contempt of worldly pleasures,
   And by deeds of valour done,
They have reach'd the land of Angels,
   And with them are knit in one.

Made co-heirs with CHRIST in glory,
   His celestial bliss they share :
May they now before Him bending
   Help us onward by their prayer ;

That, this weary life completed,
   And its fleeting trials past,
We may win eternal glory .
   In our FATHER's home at last.   Amen.

204 *Blessed are they which are persecuted for righteousness'*
   sake ; for theirs is the kingdom of heaven.

        Τῶν ἱερῶν ἀθλοφόρων.

FOR MARTYRS.

L ET our choir new anthems raise,
   Wake the song of gladness :
GOD Himself to joy and praise
   Turns the Martyrs' sadness :

Bright the day that won their crown,
  Open'd heav'n's high portal,
As they laid the mortal down
  To put on th' immortal.
Never flinch'd they from the flame,
  From the torture never ;
Vain the foeman's sharpest aim,
  Satan's worst endeavour :
For by faith they saw the land
  Deck'd in all its glory,
Where triumphant now they stand
  With the victor's story.
Faith they had that knew no shame,
  Love that could not languish ;
And eternal hope o'ercame
  Momentary anguish.
He Who trod the self-same road,
  Death and hell defeated,
Wherefore those their sufferings show'd
  Calvary repeated.
Up and follow, Christian men !
  Press through toil and sorrow ;
Scorn the night of fear, and then,
  Oh the glorious morrow !
Who will venture on the strife ?
  Blest who first begin it ;
Who will grasp the land of life ?
  Warriors, up and win it ! Amen.

205 *It is good, being put to death by men, to look for ho,*
    from God to be raised again by him.

Ex quo salus mortalium.

FOR MARTYRS.

OUR LORD the path of suffering trod,
  And since His Blood for man hath flow'(
'Tis meet that man should yield to GOD
  The life he owed. Alleluia.

No shame to own the Crucified,—
  Nay, 'tis our immortality
That we confess our GOD Who died,
    And for Him die. Alleluia.

Fill'd with this thought, with patient smile
  All threats the Martyr doth withstand,
Fights, LORD, Thy cause, and leans the while
    Upon Thine hand. Alleluia.

Beholding his predestined crown,
  Into death's arms he willing goes ;
Dying, he conquers death ; o'erthrown,
    O'erthrows his foes. Alleluia.

LORD, make us Thine own soldiers true,
  Grant us brave faith, a spirit pure,
That for Thy Name, Thy Cross in view,
    We may endure. Alleluia.

Eternal FATHER of the WORD,
  Eternal WORD, we Thee adore,
Eternal SPIRIT, GOD and LORD,
    For evermore. Alleluia. Amen.

206 *I reckon that the sufferings of this present time are not worthy to be compared with the glory which shall be revealed in us.*

FOR MARTYRS.

OH, what, if we are CHRIST's,
  Is earthly shame or loss ?
Bright shall the crown of glory be
  When we have borne the cross.

Keen was the trial once,
  Bitter the cup of woe,
When martyr'd Saints, baptized in blood,
  CHRIST's sufferings shared below :

(179)   G

Bright is their glory now,
Boundless their joy above,
Where, on the bosom of their GOD,
They rest in perfect love.

LORD, may that grace be ours,
Like them in faith to bear
All that of sorrow, grief, or pain
May be our portion here ;

Enough if Thou at last
The word of blessing give,
And let us rest beneath Thy feet,
Where Saints and Angels live.

All glory, LORD, to Thee,
Whom heav'n and earth adore ;
To FATHER, SON, and HOLY GHOST,
One GOD for evermore.   Amen.

207 *Whosoever therefore shall confess me before men, I
will I confess also before my Father which is
heaven.*

Non parta solo sanguine.

FOR A CONFESSOR.

NOT by the Martyr's death alone
The Saints their crown in heav'n have wo
There is a triumph robe on high
For bloodless fields of victory.

What though Thy servant did not feel
The cross, or flame, or torturing wheel,
Yet daily to the world he died ;
His flesh, through grace, he crucified.

What though nor chain, nor scourging sore,
Nor cruel beasts his members tore,
In perfect love to Thee, O CHRIST,
His life was daily sacrificed.

O LORD, to us Thy grace supply,
That we through life may learn to die,
And thus, when life's brief day is o'er,
May live with Thee for evermore.

O Fount of sanctity and love,
O perfect Rest of Saints above,
All praise, all glory be to Thee
Both now and through eternity.   Amen.

8 *He gave some . . . . pastors and teachers.*

FOR A DOCTOR.

JESU, for the beacon-light
    By Thy holy Doctors given,
When the mists of error's night
    Gather'd o'er the path to heaven,
For the witness that they bare
    To the truth they learn'd of Thee,
For the glory that they share,
    Let our praise accepted be.

In Jerusalem below
    They were workmen at Thy call ;
Each with one hand met the foe,
    With the other built the wall ;
Watchmen on the mountain set,
    Scribes instructed in Thy word,
Menders of the Gospel net
    For the service of the LORD.

Like Thy learnèd sons of yore,
    JESU, may our teachers still
Know and guard Thy sacred lore
    With brave heart and patient skill ;
In these latter days of strife
    Keep, O keep them true to Thee,
Till beside the well of life
    Light in Thine own light they see.   Amen.

209 *I have fought the good fight, I have finished my course, I have kept the faith.*

Jesu, Redemptor omnium.

FOR A BISHOP.

O THOU Whose all-redeeming might
   Crowns every chief in faith's good fight,
In mercy bend Thine ear to-day
And hear us, JESU, while we pray.

In faithful strife for Thy dear Name
Thy servant earn'd the saintly fame,
And pious hearts with praise revere
His memory from year to year.

Earth's fleeting joys he counted naught,
For higher, truer joys he sought ;
And with the Angels round Thy throne
Unfailing treasures are his own.

O grant that we, most gracious GOD,
May follow in the steps he trod,
And, aided by his prayers, may gain
The cleansing of our guilty stain.

To Thee, O CHRIST, our loving King,
All glory, praise and thanks we bring ;
Whom with the FATHER we adore
And HOLY GHOST for evermore.   Amen.

210 *The memory of the just is blessed.*

FOR A BISHOP.

O SHEPHERD of the sheep,
   High Priest of things to come,
Who didst in grace Thy servant keep,
   And take him safely home ;

   Accept our song of praise
   For all his holy care,
His zeal unquench'd through length of **days,**
   The trials that he bare.

Chief of Thy faithful band,
  He held himself the least,
Though Thy dread keys were in his hand,
  O everlasting Priest.
  So, trusting in Thy might,
  He won a fair renown ;
So, waxing valiant in the fight,
  He trod the lion down ;
  Then render'd up to Thee
  The charge Thy love had given ;
And when Thou comest he shall see
  Thy face in highest heaven.
  On all our Bishops pour
  The SPIRIT of Thy grace ;
That, as he won the palm of yore,
  So they may run their race ;
  That, when this life is done,
  They may with him adore
The ever Blessèd THREE in ONE,
  In bliss for evermore. Amen.

11   *My beloved is mine, and I am his.*

FOR A VIRGIN.

O LAMB of GOD, Whose love divine
  Draws virgin souls to follow Thee,
And bids them earthly joys resign
  If so they may Thy beauty see ;
The Saint of whom we sing to-day
  Was faithful to Thy loving call,
And, casting other hopes away,
  Took Thee to be her GOD, her All.
To Thee she yielded up her will,
  Her heart was drawn to Thine above ;
Content if Thou wouldst deign to fill
  Thine handmaid with Thy perfect love.

Beneath Thy Cross she loved to stand,
  Like Mary in Thy dying hour,
That blessings from Thy piercèd hand
  Might clothe her with undying power ;

With power to win the crown of light
  For virgin-souls laid up on high,
And ready keep her lamp at night
  To hail the Bridegroom drawing nigh.

And surely Thou at last didst come
  To end the sorrows of Thy bride,
And bear her to Thy peaceful home
  With Thee for ever to abide.

All glory, JESU, for the grace
  That drew Thy Saint to follow Thee :
O grant us in Thy love a place
  Both now and through eternity. Amen.

212 *Thy name is as ointment poured forth, therefore d*
the virgins love thee.

Jesu, corona virginum.

FOR A VIRGIN.

O JESU, Thou the Virgins' Crown,
  Thy gracious ear to us bow down,
Born of that Virgin whom alone
The Mother and the Maid we own.

Amongst the lilies Thou dost feed,
By virgin choirs accompanied ;
In Thee, their Bridegroom and their LORD,
They find their plentiful reward.

And wheresoe'er Thy footsteps wend,
The Virgins still with praise attend ;
Rejoicing after Thee they throng,
And pour for Thee their sweetest song.

'O gracious LORD, we Thee implore
Thy grace into our minds to pour ;
From all defilement keep us free,
And pure in heart to follow Thee.

All praise to GOD the FATHER be,
All praise, Eternal SON, to Thee,
Whom with the SPIRIT we adore,
For ever and for evermore. Amen.

3   *And they glorified God in me.*

FOR SAINTS' DAYS IN GENERAL.

FOR Thy dear Saint, O LORD,
   Who strove in Thee to live,
Who follow'd Thee, obey'd, adored,
   Our grateful hymn receive.

For Thy dear Saint, O LORD,
   Who strove in Thee to die,
And found in Thee a full reward,
   Accept our thankful cry.

Thine earthly members fit
   To join Thy Saints above,
In one communion ever knit,
   One fellowship of love.

JESU, Thy Name we bless,
   And humbly pray that we
May follow them in holiness,
   Who lived and died for Thee.

All might, all praise, be Thine,
   FATHER, co-equal SON,
And SPIRIT, Bond of love divine,
   While endless ages run. Amen.

214 *These are they which came out of great tribulation, and have washed their robes, and made them white in the blood of the Lamb.*

HOW bright these glorious spirits shine !
  Whence all their white array ?
How came they to the blissful seats
  Of everlasting day ?

Lo ! these are they from sufferings great
  Who came to realms of light,
And in the Blood of CHRIST have wash'd
  Those robes that shine so bright.

Now with triumphal palms they stand
  Before the throne on high,
And serve the GOD they love amidst
  The glories of the sky.

Hunger and thirst are felt no more,
  Nor suns with scorching ray ;
GOD is their sun, Whose cheering beams
  Diffuse eternal day.

The LAMB, Which dwells amidst the throne,
  Shall o'er them still preside,
Feed them with nourishment divine,
  And all their footsteps guide.

Midst pastures green He'll lead His flock,
  Where living streams appear ;
And GOD the LORD from every eye
  Shall wipe off every tear.

To FATHER, SON, and HOLY GHOST,
  The GOD Whom we adore,
Be glory, as it was, is now,
  And shall be evermore. Amen.

215 *What are these which are arrayed in white robes?*
and whence came they?

Wer sind die vor Gottes Throne.

WHO are these like stars appearing,
 These, before GOD's throne who stand?
Each a golden crown is wearing;
 Who are all this glorious band?
  Alleluia, hark! they sing,
  Praising loud their heavenly King.

Who are these in dazzling brightness,
 Clothed in GOD's own righteousness?
These, whose robes of purest whiteness
 Shall their lustre still possess,
  Still untouch'd by time's rude hand;
  Whence came all this glorious band?

These are they who have contended
 For their SAVIOUR's honour long,
Wrestling on till life was ended,
 Following not the sinful throng;
  These, who well the fight sustain'd,
  Triumph by the LAMB have gain'd.

These are they whose hearts were riven,
 Sore with woe and anguish tried,
Who in prayer full oft have striven
 With the GOD they glorified;
  Now, their painful conflict o'er,
  GOD has bid them weep no more.

These, th' ALMIGHTY contemplating,
 Did as priests before Him stand,
Soul and body always waiting
 Day and night at His command:
  Now in GOD's most holy place
  Blest *they stand* before His face.   Amen.

216 *After this I beheld, and lo, a great multitude, which*
no man could number, of all nations, and kindreds,
and people, and tongues, stood before the throne, and
before the Lamb, clothed with white robes, and palms
in their hands.

HARK ! the sound of holy voices,
   Chanting at the crystal sea,
Alleluia, Alleluia,
   Alleluia, LORD, to Thee :
Multitude which none can number,
   Like the stars in glory, stands
Clothed in white apparel, holding
   Palms of victory in their hands.

Patriarch, and holy Prophet,
   Who prepared the way of CHRIST,
King, Apostle, Saint, Confessor,
   Martyr, and Evangelist,
Saintly Maiden, godly Matron,
   Widows who have watch'd to prayer,
Join'd in holy concert, singing
   To the LORD of all, are there.

They have come from tribulation,
   And have wash'd their robes in Blood,
Wash'd them in the Blood of JESUS ;
   Tried they were, and firm they stood ;
Mock'd, imprison'd, stoned, tormented,
   Sawn asunder, slain with sword,
They have conquer'd death and Satan
   By the might of CHRIST the LORD.

Marching with Thy Cross their banner,
   They have triumph'd following
Thee, the Captain of salvation,
   Thee, their Saviour and their King ;
Gladly, LORD, with Thee they suffer'd ;
   Gladly, LORD, with Thee they died,
And by death to life immortal
   They were born, and glorified.

Now they reign in heavenly glory,
  Now they walk in golden light,
Now they drink, as from a river,
  Holy bliss and infinite ;
Love and peace they taste for ever,
  And all truth and knowledge see
In the Beatific Vision
  Of the Blessèd TRINITY.

GOD of GOD, the One-begotten,
  LIGHT of LIGHT, Emmanuel,
In whose Body join'd together
  All the Saints for ever dwell ;
Pour upon us of Thy fulness,
  That we may for evermore
GOD the FATHER, GOD the SON, and
  GOD the HOLY GHOST adore.   Amen.

17 *Fight the good fight of faith, lay hold on eternal life.*

THE SON of GOD goes forth to war,
  A kingly crown to gain ;
His blood-red banner streams afar !
  Who follows in His train ?
Who best can drink his cup of woe,
  Triumphant over pain,
Who patient bears his cross below,
  He follows in His train.

The Martyr first, whose eagle eye
  Could pierce beyond the grave ;
Who saw his Master in the sky,
  And call'd on Him to save.
Like Him, with pardon on his tongue
  In midst of mortal pain,
He pray'd for them that did the wrong ;
  Who follows in his train ?

(189)

A glorious band, the chosen few
  On whom the SPIRIT came, .
Twelve valiant Saints, their hope they knew,
  And mock'd the cross and flame.
They met the tyrant's brandish'd steel,
  The lion's gory mane,
They bow'd their necks, the death to feel ;
  Who follows in their train ?

A noble army, men and boys,
  The matron and the maid,
Around the Saviour's throne rejoice
  In robes of light array'd.   ‘
They climb'd the steep ascent of heaven
  Through peril, toil, and pain ;
O GOD, to us may grace be given
  To follow in their train.   Amen.

218 *Therefore are they before the throne of God, and*
  serve him day and night in his temple.

LO ! round the throne, a glorious band,
  The Saints in countless myriads stand,
Of every tongue redeem'd to GOD,
Array'd in garments wash'd in Blood.

Through tribulation great they came ;
They bore the cross, despised the shame ;
From all their labours now they rest,
In GOD's eternal glory blest.

They see their Saviour face to face,
And sing the triumphs of His grace ;
Him day and night they ceaseless praise,
To Him the loud thanksgiving raise :

"Worthy the LAMB, for sinners slain,
Through endless years to live and reign ;
Thou hast redeem'd us by Thy Blood,
And made us kings and priests to GOD."

O may we tread the sacred road
That Saints and holy Martyrs trod;
Wage to the end the glorious strife,
And win, like them, a crown of life. Amen.

219 *Clothed with white robes, and palms in their hands.*

PALMS of glory, raiment bright,
　Crowns that never fade away,
Gird and deck the Saints in light,
Priests, and kings, and conquerors they.

Yet the conquerors bring their palms
To the LAMB amidst the throne,
And proclaim in joyful psalms
Victory through His Cross alone.

Kings their crowns for harps resign,
Crying, as they strike the chords,
"Take the Kingdom, it is Thine,
King of kings, and Lord of lords."

Round the altar priests confess,
If their robes are white as snow,
'Twas the Saviour's righteousness,
And His Blood, that made them so.

They were mortal too like us;
O when we like them must die,
May our souls translated thus
Triumph, reign, and shine on high.　Amen.

220 *Compassed about with so great a cloud of witnesses.*

FOR all the Saints who from their labours rest,
　Who Thee by faith before the world confess'd,
Thy Name, O JESU, be for ever bless'd.
　　　　　　　　Alleluia!

SAINTS' DAYS.

Thou wast their Rock, their Fortress, and their
    Might;
Thou, LORD, their Captain in the well-fought
    fight;
Thou in the darkness still their one true Light.
                Alleluia!

O may Thy soldiers, faithful, true, and bold,
Fight as the Saints who nobly fought of old,
And win, with them, the victor's crown of gold.
                Alleluia!

O blest communion! fellowship divine!
We fight, as they did, 'neath the holy sign;
And all are one in Thee, for all are Thine.
                Alleluia!

And when the strife is fierce, the warfare long,
Steals on the ear the distant triumph-song,
And hearts are brave again, and arms are strong.
                Alleluia!

The golden evening brightens in the west;
Soon, soon to faithful warriors comes their rest;
Sweet is the calm of Paradise the blest.
                Alleluia!

But lo! there breaks a yet more glorious day;
The Saints triumphant rise in bright array:
The King of glory passes on His way.
                Alleluia!

From earth's wide bounds, from ocean's farthest
    coast,
Through gates of pearl streams in the countless
    host,
Singing to FATHER, SON, and HOLY GHOST
                Alleluia! Amen.

21 *That they may rest from their labours.*

THE Saints of GOD ! their conflict past,
And life's long battle won at last,
No more they need the shield or sword ;
They cast them down before their LORD :
O happy Saints ! for ever blest,
At JESUS' feet how safe your rest !

The Saints of GOD ! their wanderings done,
No more their weary course they run,
No more they faint, no more they fall,
No foes oppress, no fears appal :
O happy Saints ! for ever blest,
In that dear home how sweet your rest !

The Saints of GOD ! life's voyage o'er,
Safe landed on that blissful shore,
No stormy tempests now they dread,
No roaring billows lift their head :
O happy Saints ! for ever blest,
In that calm haven of your rest !

The Saints of GOD their vigil keep
While yet their mortal bodies sleep,
Till from the dust they too shall rise
And soar triumphant to the skies :
O happy Saints ! rejoice and sing ;
He quickly comes, your LORD and King.

O GOD of Saints, to Thee we cry ;
O SAVIOUR, plead for us on high ;
O HOLY GHOST, our Guide and Friend,
Grant us Thy grace till life shall end ;
That with all Saints our rest may be
In that bright Paradise with Thee.   Amen.

The following Hymns are also suitable for Saints' Days :

413 Soldiers, who are CHRIST'S below.
414 O happy band of pilgrims.

THE BLESSED VIRGIN MARY.

222 *Hail, thou that art highly favoured, the Lord is with thee: blessed art thou among women.*

Quem terra, pontus, æthera.

THE GOD, Whom earth, and sea, and sky
Adore, and laud, and magnify,
Who governs all the threefold frame,
To birth as Child of Mary came.

Beneath th' o'ershadowing of grace,
A maiden lent a dwelling-place
To that dread LORD, Whom night and day
The sun and moon and all obey.

O blessèd Mother, blessèd Maid,
Thou art the ark wherein was laid
The high Artificer Whose hand
The round world in its hollow spann'd.

Bless'd in the word that Gabriel brought,
The HOLY GHOST within her wrought
To fashion for a human birth
The long Desired of all the earth.

O glorious above woman-kind,
More high than any star hath shined,
Thy Maker, Who His work foreknew,
His nurture from thy bosom drew.

All that was lost by woful Eve
Thy beauteous Offspring did retrieve ;
That mourners might regain the height,
Heav'n made of thee its window bright.

Thou wast the great King's entrance door,
Light's gate, through which the sunbeams pour
Ye ransom'd nations, hail with mirth
Life through the Virgin brought to earth.

O LORD, the Virgin-born, to Thee
Eternal praise and glory be,
Whom with the FATHER we adore
And HOLY GHOST for evermore.   Amen.

Mary, the mother of Jesus.

SHALL we not love thee, Mother dear,
  Whom JESUS loves so well,
And to His glory, year by year,
  Thy joy and honour tell?

Bound with the curse of sin and shame
  We helpless sinners lay,
Until in tender love He came
  To bear the curse away.

And thee He chose from whom to take
  True flesh His Flesh to be,
In it to suffer for our sake,
  By it to make us free.

Thy Babe He lay upon thy breast,
  To thee He turn'd for food ;
Thy gentle nursing soothed to rest
  Th' Incarnate SON of GOD.

O wondrous depth of grace divine
  That He should bend so low !
And, Mary, oh, what joy 'twas thine
  In His dear love to know ;

Joy to be Mother of the LORD—
  And thine the truer bliss,
In every thought, and deed, and word
  To be for ever His.

And as He loves thee, Mother dear,
  We too will love thee well,
And to His glory, year by year,
  Thy joy and honour tell.

JESU, the Virgin's Holy Son,
  We praise Thee and adore,
Who art with GOD the FATHER One
  And SPIRIT evermore.   Amen.

THE BLESSED VIRGIN MARY.

224 *Blessed is the womb that bare thee, and the paps which thou hast sucked.*

VIRGIN-BORN, we bow before Thee ;
    Blessèd was the womb that bore Thee ;
       Mary, Mother meek and mild,
       Blessèd was she in her Child.

Blessèd was the breast that fed Thee ;
Blessèd was the hand that led Thee ;
       Blessèd was the parent's eye
       That watch'd Thy slumbering infancy.

Blessèd she by all creation,
Who brought forth the world's salvation,
       And blessèd they—for ever blest,
       Who love Thee most and serve Thee best.

Virgin-born, we bow before Thee :
Blessèd was the womb that bore Thee ;
       Mary, Mother meek and mild,
       Blessèd was she in her Child. Amen.

SAINT ANDREW'S DAY.

225 *One of the two which . . . followed him was Andrew.*

JESUS calls us ; o'er the tumult
    Of our life's wild restless sea
Day by day His sweet voice soundeth,
    Saying, " Christian, follow Me : "

As of old Saint Andrew heard it
    By the Galilean lake,
Turn'd from home, and toil, and kindred,
    Leaving all for His dear sake.

JESUS calls us from the worship
    Of the vain world's golden store,
From each idol that would keep us,
    Saying, " Christian, love Me more."

In our joys and in our sorrows,
  Days of toil and hours of ease,
Still He calls, in cares and pleasures,
  "Christian, love Me more than these."
JESUS calls us : by Thy mercies,
  Saviour, make us hear Thy call,
Give our hearts to Thine obedience,
  Serve and love Thee best of all.   Amen.

SAINT THOMAS THE APOSTLE.

226   *Be not faithless, but believing.*

HOW oft, O LORD, Thy face hath shone
  On doubting souls whose wills were true !
Thou CHRIST of Cephas and of John,
  Thou art the CHRIST of Thomas too.

He loved Thee well, and calmly said,
  "Come, let us go, and die with Him : "
Yet when Thine Easter-news was spread,
  'Mid all its light his eyes were dim.

His brethren's word he would not take,
  But craved to touch those hands of Thine :
The bruisèd reed Thou didst not break ;
  He saw, and hail'd his LORD Divine.

He saw Thee risen ; at once he rose
  To full belief's unclouded height ;
And still through his confession flows
  To Christian souls Thy life and light.

O Saviour, make Thy presence known
  To all who doubt Thy word and Thee ;
And teach them in that word alone
  To find the truth that sets them free.

And we who know how true Thou art,
  And Thee as GOD and LORD adore,
Give us, we pray, a loyal heart,
  To *trust and love* Thee more and more.   Amen.

THE CONVERSION OF SAINT PAUL.

227 *Benjamin shall ravin as a wolf; in the morning shall devour the prey, and at night he shall divide the spoil.*

Quæ gloriosum tanta cælis evocat.

LORD, from out Thy glorious skies,
　Where Thy palace lies,
What cause constraining in Thine eyes
　Brings Thee again to earth ?
That Thou, the Judge of endless doom,
Again should as a Saviour come,—
　What foe doth call Thee forth ?

With defying mien and tread
　Hastes a warrior dread ;
Afar the trembling flock is fled :
　What hand can succour lend ?
With suppliant gaze beseechingly
Their eyes look up ; but from the sky
　No pitying form doth bend.

Forth hath gone one awful sound,
　And the world is bound,
With Saul laid suppliant on the ground :
　At morn went forth to slay
The ravening wolf of Benjamin,
But with the sheep, when eve comes in,
　He shall divide the prey.

Through all climes GOD's glory plant !
　Through all ages chant !
Sing praise and honour jubilant
　As is and aye hath been !
All worship, all dominion,
To Him Who all things holds in one,
　The Triune GOD unseen !　Amen.

28 *I obtained mercy because I did it ignorantly, in unbelief.*

LORD, Who fulfillest thus anew
   Thine own blest dying prayer,
That they who know not what they do,
   May in Thy ransom share :

When foes Thy Church's power defy,
   Or slight Thy sacred word,
Or Thee, true GOD and Man, deny,
   Grant them conversion, LORD.

Grant that the light may round them shine,
   That, set from error free,
They in Thy word the truth divine,
   Thee in Thy Church, may see ;

That so when our brief time is done
   We may with them adore
The FATHER and co-equal SON
   And SPIRIT evermore.   Amen.

HE PRESENTATION OF CHRIST IN THE TEMPLE,
COMMONLY CALLED
HE PURIFICATION OF SAINT MARY THE VIRGIN.

29 *The Lord, whom ye seek, shall suddenly come to his temple.*

Templi sacratas pande, Sion, fores.

O SION, open wide thy gates,
   Let shadows disappear ;
A Priest and Victim, both in one,
   The Truth Himself is here.

No more the simple flock shall bleed ;
   Behold, the FATHER's SON
His temple enters, soon Himself
   For sinners to atone.

THE PRESENTATION OF CHRIST IN THE TEMPLE.

Conscious of hidden Deity,
  The lowly Virgin brings
Her new-born Babe, with those young do
  Her humble offerings.

There waiting Simeon sees at last
  The Saviour long desired,
And Anna welcomes Israel's Hope,
  With holy rapture fired.

But silent stood the Mother blest
  Of the yet silent WORD,
And, pondering in her steadfast heart,
  With speechless praise adored.

All glory to the FATHER be,
  All glory to the SON,
All glory, HOLY GHOST, to Thee,
  While endless ages run. Amen.

230 *They brought him to Jerusalem to present him*
*   Lord.*

HAIL to the LORD Who comes,
  Comes to His temple gate !
Not with His Angel host,
  Not in His Kingly state ;
No shouts proclaim Him nigh,
  No crowds His coming wait ;

But borne upon the throne
  Of Mary's gentle breast,
Watch'd by her duteous love,
  In her fond arms at rest ;
Thus to His FATHER's house
  He comes, the heavenly Guest.

PRESENTATION OF CHRIST IN THE TEMPLE.

There Joseph at her side
   In reverent wonder stands ;
And, fill'd with holy joy,
   Old Simeon in his hands
Takes up the promised Child,
   The glory of all lands.

Hail to the great First-born,
   Whose ransom-price they pay !
The Son before all worlds,
   The Child of man to-day,
That He might ransom us
   Who still in bondage lay.

O Light of all the earth,
   Thy people wait for Thee !
Come to Thy temples here,
   That we from sin set free
Before Thy Father's face
   May all presented be !   Amen.

The following Hymn is suitable:

445 Bless'd are the pure in heart.

SAINT MATTHIAS'S DAY.

*And they gave forth their lots: and the lot fell upon
Matthias; and he was numbered with the eleven
apostles.*

BISHOP of the souls of men,
   When the foeman's step is nigh,
When the wolf lays wait by night
   For the lambs continually,
Watch, O Lord, about us keep,
Guard us, Shepherd of the sheep.

SAINT MATTHIAS'S DAY.

When the hireling flees away,
  Caring only for his gold,
And the gate unguarded stands
  At the entrance to the fold,
Stand, O LORD, Thy flock before,
Thou the Guardian, Thou the Door.

LORD, Whose guiding finger ruled
  In the casting of the lot,
That Thy Church might fill the throne
  Of the lost Iscariot,
In our trouble ever thus
Stand, good Master, nigh to us.

When the Saints their order take
  In the new Jerusalem,
And Matthias stands elect,
  Give us part and lot with him,
Where in Thine own dwelling-place
We may witness face to face.   Amen.

THE ANNUNCIATION OF THE BLESSED VIRGIN MARY.

232 *Behold, a virgin shall be with child, and shall bring forth a son, and they shall call his name Emmanuel, which being interpreted is, God with us.*

PRAISE we the LORD this day,
    This day so long foretold,
Whose promise shone with cheering ray
  On waiting saints of old.

The Prophet gave the sign
  For faithful men to read ;
A Virgin, born of David's line,
  Shall bear the promised Seed.

3 ANNUNCIATION OF THE B. V. MARY.

3 ANNUNCIATION OF THE B. V. MARY.

Ask not how this should be,
But worship and adore,
Like her, whom GOD's own majesty
Came down to shadow o'er.

Meekly she bow'd her head
To hear the gracious word,
Mary, the pure and lowly Maid,
The favour'd of the LORD.

Blessèd shall be her name
In all the Church on earth,
Through whom that wondrous mercy came,
The Incarnate Saviour's birth.

JESU, the Virgin's Son,
We praise Thee and adore,
Who art with GOD the FATHER One
And SPIRIT evermore.   Amen.

The following Hymns are also suitable:

335 From highest heav'n th' Eternal SON.
336 O Love, how deep! how broad! how high!
337 Praise to the Holiest in the height.

SAINT MARK'S DAY.

The Hymns for Evangelists are suitable.

SAINT PHILIP AND SAINT JAMES'S DAY.

The Hymns for Apostles are suitable; also
344 Thou art the Way ; by Thee alone.

SAINT BARNABAS THE APOSTLE.

3 *Joses, who by the apostles was surnamed Barnabas,
which is, being interpreted, The son of consolation.*

SON of GOD, our Captain of salvation,
 Thyself by suffering school'd to human grief,
bless Thee for Thy sons of consolation,
ho follow *in the steps of* Thee their Chief ;

(203)

SAINT BARNABAS THE APOSTLE.

Those whom Thy SPIRIT's dread vocation severs
 To lead the vanguard of Thy conquering host;
Whose toilsome years are spent in brave endeavour
 To bear Thy saving Name from coast to coast

Those whose bright faith makes feeble heart
 grow stronger,
 And sends fresh warriors to the great campaign
Bids the lone convert feel estranged no longer,
 And wins the sunder'd to be one again ;

And all true helpers, patient, kind, and skilful,
 Who shed Thy light across our darken'd earth,
Counsel the doubting, and restrain the wilful,
 Soothe the sick bed, and share the children
 mirth.

Such was Thy Levite, strong in self-oblation
 To cast his all at Thine Apostles' feet; [nation
He whose new name, through every Christian
 From age to age our thankful strains repeat.

Thus, LORD, Thy Barnabas in memory keeping,
 Still be Thy Church's watchword, "Comfort ye ;
Till in our FATHER'S house shall end our weeping
 And all our wants be satisfied in Thee.   Amen

SAINT JOHN BAPTIST'S DAY.

234 *Repent ye, for the kingdom of heaven is at hand.*
Nunc suis tandem novus e latebris.

LO ! from the desert homes,
 Where he hath hid so long,
The new Elijah comes,
 In sternest wisdom strong ;
 The voice that cries
 Of CHRIST from high,
 And judgment nigh
From rending skies.

(204)

SAINT JOHN BAPTIST'S DAY.

Your GOD e'en now doth stand
  At heaven's opening door ;
His fan is in His hand,
  And He will purge His floor ;
    The wheat He claims
      And with Him stows ;
      The chaff He throws
    To quenchless flames.

Ye haughty mountains, bow
  Your sky-aspiring heads ;
Ye valleys, hiding low,
  Lift up your gentle meads ;
    Make His way plain
      Your King before ;
      For evermore
    He comes to reign.

May thy dread voice around,
  Thou harbinger of light,
On our dull ears still sound,
  Lest here we sleep in night,
    Till judgment come,
      And on our path
      The LAMB'S dread wrath
    Shall burst in doom.

O GOD, with love's sweet might
  Who dost anoint and arm
CHRIST'S soldier for the fight
  With grace that shields from harm,
    Thrice-blessèd THREE,
      Heav'n's endless days
      Shall sing Thy praise
    Eternally. Amen.

SAINT JOHN BAPTIST'S DAY.

235 *Behold I will send my messenger, and he shall prepa
the way before me.*

Præcursor altus luminis.

THE high forerunner of the morn,
The herald of the WORD, is born ;
Be glad, true hearts, and never fail
With joy and praise his light to hail.

His lofty name of John was given
By Gabriel sent down from heaven,
Who told before with utterance true
The glorious deeds that he should do.

John, still unborn, yet gave his sign
Of witness to the Light Divine ;
And all his life of wondrous fame
Was spent in perfecting the same.

No greater, since creation's morn,
Was ever yet of woman born
Than John, by acts of wondrous might
Extoll'd to more than prophet's height.

But why should mortal accents raise
The theme of John the Baptist's praise ;
Of whom, before his course was run,
Thus spake the FATHER to the SON :—

" Behold, I send My messenger,
The way Thou goest to prepare ;
Before Thy rising face to run,
Like morning star before the sun." Ame

The following Hymn is suitable :
49 On Jordan's bank the Baptist's cry.
(206)

SAINT PETER THE APOSTLE.

36 *Jesus said unto them, Come ye after me, and I will make you to become fishers of men.*

CREATOR of the rolling flood,
On Whom Thy people hope alone,
Who cam'st by water and by blood,
For man's offences to atone :—

Who from the labours of the deep
Didst set Thy servant Peter free,
To feed on earth Thy chosen sheep,
And build an endless Church to Thee :—

Grant us, devoid of worldly care,
And leaning on Thy bounteous hand,
To seek Thy help in humble prayer,
And on Thy sacred rock to stand ;

And when, our livelong toil to crown,
Thy call shall set the spirit free,
To cast with joy our burden down,
And rise, O LORD, and follow Thee ! Amen.

The following Hymn is also suitable:
466 Forsaken once, and thrice denied.

SAINT JAMES THE APOSTLE.

37 *Jesus said, Are ye able to drink of the cup that I shall drink of, and to be baptized with the baptism that I am baptized with ? They say unto him, We are able.*

TWO brothers freely cast their lot
With David's royal Son ;
The cost of conquest counting not,
They deem the battle won.

Brothers in heart, they hope to gain
An undivided joy,
That man may one with man remain,
As boy was one with boy.

CHRIST heard ; and will'd that James should
First prey of Satan's rage ;   [fall
John linger out his fellows all,
And die in bloodless age.

SAINT JAMES THE APOSTLE.

Now they join hands once more above
  Before the Conqueror's throne ;
Thus GOD grants prayer ; but in His love
  Makes times and ways His own.

All glory to the FATHER be,
  All glory to the SON,
All glory, HOLY GHOST, to Thee
  While endless ages run.   Amen.

SAINT BARTHOLOMEW THE APOSTLE.
The Hymns for Apostles are suitable.

SAINT MATTHEW THE APOSTLE.

238   *Matthew, the publican.*

HE sat to watch o'er customs paid,
    A man of scorn'd and hardening trade ;
Alike the symbol and the tool
Of foreign masters' hated rule.

But grace within his breast had stirr'd ;
There needed but the timely word ;
It came, true LORD of souls, from Thee,
That royal summons, "Follow Me."

Enough, when Thou wert passing by,
To hear Thy voice, to meet Thine eye :
He rose, responsive to the call,
And left his task, his gains, his all.

O wise exchange ! with these to part,
And lay up treasure in Thy heart ;
With twofold crown of light to shine
Amid Thy servants' foremost line !

Come, Saviour, as in days of old ;
Pass where the world has strongest hold,
And faithless care and selfish greed
Are thorns that choke the holy seed.

Who keep Thy gifts, O bid them claim
The steward's, not the owner's name ;
Who yield all up for Thy dear sake,
Let them of Matthew's wealth partake. Amen.

The Hymns for Apostles and for Evangelists are suitable.

SAINT MICHAEL AND ALL ANGELS.

39   *Michael . . . the great prince.*
    Tibi, Christe, splendor Patris.

THEE, O CHRIST, the FATHER's splendour,
    Life and virtue of the heart,
In the presence of the Angels
    Sing we now with tuneful art,
Meetly in alternate chorus
    Bearing our responsive part.

LORD, we praise with veneration
    All Thine armies of the sky ;
Chiefly him, the first and foremost
    Of celestial chivalry,
Michael, who in princely virtue
    Cast the devil from on high.

By whose watchful care repelling,
    King of everlasting grace,
Every ghostly adversary,
    All things evil, all things base,
Grant us of Thine only goodness
    In Thy Paradise a place.

Laud and honour to the FATHER,
    Laud and honour to the SON,
Laud and honour to the SPIRIT,
    Ever THREE, and ever ONE,
Consubstantial, Co-eternal,
    While unending ages run. Amen.

240 *There was war in heaven; Michael and his ange*
fought against the dragon; and the dragon foug
and his angels, and prevailed not.

Christe, qui sedes Olympo.

CHRIST, the highest heav'ns enthrone Thee
 Equal of the FATHER's might ;
Spirits pure with trembling own Thee,
 GOD of GOD, and LIGHT of LIGHT ;
Thee 'mid Angel hosts we sing,
Thee their Maker and their King.

All who circling round adore Thee,
 All who bow before Thy throne,
Burn with flaming zeal before Thee,
 Thy behests to carry down ;
To and fro, 'twixt earth and heaven,
Speed they each on errands given.

First of all those legions glorious,
 Michael waves his sword of flame,
Who in heavenly war victorious
 Did the dragon's fierceness tame ;
Who with might invincible
Thrust the rebel down to hell.

"Who like GOD," th' Archangel shouted ;
 This the word that peal'd on high
When th' apostate armies routed
 Fell tumultuous from the sky ;
GOD, by Whom they cast them down,
Gave the triumph and the crown.

Strong to aid the sick and dying,
 At our prayer they swiftly fly,
Help divine and strength supplying
 For the mortal agony :
Souls released from earthly care
Safe to Paradise they bear.

SAINT MICHAEL AND ALL ANGELS.

To the FATHER praise be given
  By th' unfallen Angel-host,
Who in His great war have striven
  With the legions of the lost ;
Equal praise in highest heaven
  To the SON and HOLY GHOST. Amen.

241 *When the morning stars sang together, and all the sons of God shouted for joy.*

Φωστῆρες τῆς ἀΰλου.

STARS of the morning, so gloriously bright,
  Fill'd with celestial virtue and light,
These that, where night never followeth day,
Praise the Thrice-Holy One ever and aye :

These are Thy ministers, these dost Thou own,
LORD GOD of Sabaoth, nearest Thy throne ;
These are Thy messengers, these dost Thou send,
Help of the helpless ones ! man to defend.

These keep the guard amid Salem's dear bowers,
Thrones, Principalities, Virtues, and Powers,
Where, with the Living Ones, mystical Four,
Cherubim, Seraphim bow and adore.

Then, when the earth was first poised in mid space,
Then, when the planets first sped on their race,
Then, when were ended the six days' employ,
Then all the Sons of GOD shouted for joy.

Still let them succour us ; still let them fight,
LORD of Angelic hosts, battling for right ;
Till, where their anthems they ceaselessly pour,
We with the *Angels* may bow and adore. Amen.

H

242 *O praise the Lord, all ye his hosts: ye servants of hi*
that do his pleasure.

PRAISE to GOD Who reigns above,
   Binding earth and heav'n in love ;
All the armies of the sky
Worship His dread sovereignty.

Seraphim His praises sing,
Cherubim on fourfold wing,
Thrones, Dominions, Princes, Powers,
Marshall'd Might that never cowers.

Speeds the Archangel from His face,
Bearing messages of grace ;
Angel hosts His word fulfil,
Ruling nature by His will.

Yet on man they joy to wait,
All that bright celestial state,
For in man their LORD they see,
CHRIST, the Incarnate DEITY.

On the throne their LORD Who died
Sits in Manhood glorified ;
Where His people faint below,
Angels count it joy to go.

Oh the depths of joy divine
Thrilling through those Orders nine,
When the lost are found again,
When the banish'd come to reign !

Now in faith, in hope, in love,
We will join the choirs above,
Praising, with the heav'nly host,
FATHER, SON, and HOLY GHOST.   Amen.

SAINT MICHAEL AND ALL ANGELS.

243 *Are they not all ministering spirits, sent forth to minister for them who shall be heirs of salvation?*

THEY come, GOD's messengers of love,
They come from heav'nly realms above,
From homes of never-fading light,
From blissful mansions ever bright.

They come to watch around us here,
To soothe our sorrow, calm our fear :
Ye heav'nly guides, speed not away,
GOD willeth you with us to stay.

But chiefly at its journey's end
'Tis yours the spirit to befriend,
And whisper to the willing heart,
"O Christian soul, in peace depart."

Blest JESU, Thou Whose groans and tears
Have sanctified frail nature's fears,
To earth in bitter sorrow weigh'd,
Thou didst not scorn Thine Angel's aid ;

An Angel guard to us supply,
When on the bed of death we lie ;
And by Thine own almighty power
O shield us in the last dread hour.

To GOD the FATHER, GOD the SON,
And GOD the SPIRIT, THREE in ONE,
From all above and all below
Let joyful praise unceasing flow.   Amen.

The Hymns on the Ministry of Angels may be sung at other times.

The following Hymns are also suitable :
574 Around the throne of GOD a band.
625 There was joy in heav'n.

SAINT LUKE THE EVANGELIST.
The Hymns for Evangelists are suitable.

SAINT SIMON AND SAINT JUDE, APOSTLES.
The Hymns for Apostles are suitable.

244 *And the city had no need of the sun, neither or moon, to shine in it; for the glory of God did li it, and the Lamb is the light thereof.*

Cælestis O Jerusalem.

O HEAVENLY Jerusalem,
　　Of everlasting halls,
Thrice blessèd are the people
　　Thou storest in thy walls.

Thou art the golden mansion,
　　Where Saints for ever sing,
The seat of GOD's own chosen,
　　The palace of the King.

There GOD for ever sitteth,
　　Himself of all the Crown ;
The LAMB the Light that shineth
　　And never goeth down.

Nought to this seat approacheth
　　Their sweet peace to molest ;
They sing their GOD for ever,
　　Nor day nor night they rest.

Sure hope doth thither lead us,
　　Our longings thither bend ;
No short-lived toil shall daunt us
　　For joys that cannot end.

To CHRIST, the Sun that lightens
　　His Church above, below,
To FATHER, and to SPIRIT,
　　All things created bow.　Amen.

245　　*The marriage of the Lamb is come.*

Sponsa Christi, quæ per orbem.

BRIDE of CHRIST, whose glorious war
　　Here on earth hath never rest,
Lift thy voice, and tell the triumphs
Of the holy and the blest :

ALL SAINTS' DAY.

Joyous be the day we hallow,
    Feast of all the Saints on high,
Earth and heav'n together blending
    In one solemn harmony.

First the blessèd Virgin-Mother,
    Reunited to her Son,
With the ministering Angels
    Who the will of GOD have done ;
John the herald, CHRIST'S forerunner,
    Head of the prophetic throng,
Seer and Patriarch responsive
    Unto Psalmist in their song.

Princes of the great assembly
    Throned on their tribunal high,
Lo, the Twelve in kindly judgment
    All the sons of Israel try ;
Lo, the Martyrs, robed in crimson,
    Sign of life-blood freely spent,
Finding life, because they lost it,
    Dwell in undisturb'd content.

All the saintly host who witness'd
    Good confessions for His sake—
Deacon, Priest, the world renouncing,
    Of their Master's joy partake ;
Virgins to the LAMB devoted,
    Following with steadfast love,
Bring their lilies and their roses
    To the marriage feast above.

All, their happy lot fulfilling,
    GOD Omnipotent proclaim ;
Holy, Holy, Holy, crying,
    Glory to His Holy Name !
So may GOD in mercy grant us
    Here to serve in holiness,
Till He call us to the portion
    Which His Saints in light possess.   Amen.

ALL SAINTS' DAY.

246 *Now we see through a glass, darkly; but then face t face: now I know in part; but then shall I know even as also I am known.*

Quisquis valet numerare.

IF there be that skills to reckon
   All the number of the blest,
He perchance can weigh the gladness
   Of the everlasting rest,
Which, their earthly exile finish'd,
   They through suffering have possess'd.

Through the vale of lamentation
   Happily and safely past,
Now the years of their affliction
   In their memory they recast,
And the end of all perfection
   They can contemplate at last.

In a glass through types and riddles
   To us now the truth is shown ;
Then serenely, purely, clearly,
   We shall know as we are known,
Fixing our enlighten'd vision
   On the glory of the throne.

There the Trinity of Persons
   Unbeclouded shall we see ;
There the Unity of Essence
   Shall reveal'd in glory be :
While we hail the Threefold Godhead
   And the simple Unity.

Wherefore, man, take heart and courage,
   Whatsoe'er thy present pain ;
Such untold reward through suffering
   It is given thee to attain,
And for ever in His glory
   With the Light of Light to reign.

Laud and honour to the FATHER,
  Laud and honour to the SON,
Laud and honour to the SPIRIT,
  Ever THREE and ever ONE,
Consubstantial, Co-eternal,
  While unending ages run.   Amen.

SAINT GEORGE'S DAY.

47   *The shout of a king is among them.*

JESUS, LORD of our salvation,
  For Thy warrior, bold and true,
Now accept our thankful praises,
  And our strength do Thou renew,
That, like George, with courage dauntless
We may all our foes subdue.

Blazon'd on our country's banner,
  England bears the true knight's sign ;
LORD, our fatherland empower,
  That, endued with strength divine, .
She may evermore with courage
  Bear the standard that is Thine.

Fill her youth with manly spirit,
  Patient, self-restrain'd, and pure,
Of Thy cause the ready champions,
  Never flinching to endure
Hardness for the Name of JESUS ;
  So their triumph shall be sure.

Teach her manhood to confess Thee
  As the Master, LORD, and King ;
All their powers consecrated
  To Thy service may men bring,
And of loyal speech and action
  Make to Thee an offering.

SAINT GEORGE'S DAY.

JESUS, LORD, Thou mighty Victor,
    Thy all-glorious Name we praise ;
Thou art with us, GOD Almighty ;
    'Midst our ranks Thy shout we raise ;
Where Thy kingly war-cry soundeth,
    Lead us on through all our days.   Amen.

SAINT MARY MAGDALENE.

248 *Mary Magdalene, out of whom he had cast seven devils.*

Summi Parentis unice.

SON of the Highest, deign to cast
    On us a pitying eye,
Thou Who repentant Magdalene
    Didst call to joys on high.

Thy long-lost coin is stored at length
    In treasure-house divine,
And from the mire Thy jewel cleansed
    Doth now the stars outshine.

JESU, the balm of every wound,
    The sinner's only stay,
Grant us, like her, the gift of tears,
    And wash our sins away.

Absolve us by Thy gracious word,
    Fulfil us with Thy love,
And guide us through the storms of life
    To perfect rest above.

All praise, all glory be to Thee,
    O everlasting LORD,
Whose mercy doth our souls forgive,
    Whose bounty doth reward.   Amen.

(218)

49 *Jesus was transfigured before them.*

Cælestis formam gloriæ.

O WONDROUS type, O vision fair
Of glory that the Church shall share,
Which CHRIST upon the mountain shows,
Where brighter than the sun He glows !

From age to age the tale declare,
How with the three disciples there,
Where Moses and Elias meet,
The LORD holds converse high and sweet.

The Law and Prophets there have place,
The chosen witnesses of grace ;
The FATHER's voice from out the cloud
Proclaims His Only SON aloud.

With shining face and bright array,
CHRIST deigns to manifest to-day
What glory shall to faith be given
When we enjoy our GOD in heaven.

And Christian hearts are raised on high
By that great vision's mystery,
For which in thankful strains we raise
On this glad day the voice of praise.

O FATHER, with th' Eternal SON
And HOLY SPIRIT ever One,
Vouchsafe to bring us by Thy grace
To see Thy glory face to face.   Amen.

50 *With him on the holy mount.*

FOR ever we would gaze on Thee,
O LORD, upon the mount ;
With Moses and Elias see
That *light from light's own Fount* ;

For ever with the chosen three
   Would stand upon that height,
And in that blessèd company
   Be plunged in pure delight.

For ever would we train the ear
   To that celestial voice ;
In Thee, the SON of GOD, so near,
   For evermore rejoice.

Here would we pitch our constant tent,
   For ever here abide ;
And dwell in peace and full content,
   Dear Master, at Thy side.

But no ! not yet to man 'tis given
   To rest upon that height ;
'Tis but a passing glimpse of heaven ;
   We must descend and fight.

Beneath the mount is toil and pain ;
   O CHRIST, Thy strength impart,
Till we, transfigured too, shall reign
   For ever where Thou art.   Amen.

251   *Lord, it is good for us to be here.*

'TIS good, LORD, to be here !
   Thy glory fills the night ;
Thy face and garments, like the sun,
   Shine with unborrow'd light.

'Tis good, LORD, to be here ;
   Thy beauty to behold,
Where Moses and Elijah stand,
   Thy messengers of old.

Fulfiller of the past !
   Promise of things to be !
We hail Thy Body glorified,
   And our redemption see.

THE TRANSFIGURATION.

Before we taste of death,
We see Thy Kingdom come ;
We fain would hold the vision bright,
And make this hill our home.

'Tis good, LORD, to be here !
Yet we may not remain ;
But since Thou bidst us leave the mount
Come with us to the plain.   Amen.

The following Hymn is also suitable:
380 Light's abode, celestial Salem.

THE NAME OF JESUS.

252   *Thy name is as ointment poured forth.*

Jesu dulcis memoria.

JESU ! the very thought is sweet ;
In that dear Name all heart-joys meet :
But oh ! than honey sweeter far
The glimpses of His Presence are.

No word is sung more sweet than this,
No sound is heard more full of bliss,
No thought brings sweeter comfort nigh
Than JESUS, SON of GOD most high.

JESU, the hope of souls forlorn,
How good to them for sin that mourn !
To them that seek Thee, oh how kind !
But what art Thou to them that find ?

No tongue of mortal can express,
No pen can write the blessedness,
He only who hath proved it knows
What bliss from love of JESUS flows.

O JESU, King of wondrous might !
O Victor, glorious from the fight !
Sweetness that may not be express'd
And altogether loveliest !

THE NAME OF JESUS.

Abide with us, O LORD, to-day,
Fulfil us with Thy grace, we pray ;
And with Thine own true sweetness feed
Our souls from sin and darkness freed.   An

The following Hymns are also suitable:
338 To the Name of our salvation.
341 Conquering kings their titles take.

THE DEDICATION OF A CHURCH.

253 *I John saw the holy city, new Jerusalem, coming d*
from God out of heaven, prepared as a bride ado
for her husband.

Urbs beata Jerusalem.

BLESSÈD city, heavenly Salem,
   Vision dear of peace and love,
Who of living stones art builded
   In the height of heav'n above,
And by Angel hands apparell'd
   As a bride dost earthward move ;

Out of heav'n from GOD descending,
   New and ready to be wed,
To thy LORD, Whose love espoused thee,
   Fair adorn'd shalt thou be led ;
All thy streets and all thy bulwarks
   Of pure gold are fashionèd.

Bright thy gates of pearl are shining ;
   They are open evermore ;
And their well-earn'd rest attaining
   Thither faithful souls do soar,
Who for CHRIST'S dear Name in this wo
   Pain and tribulation bore.

Many a blow and biting sculpture
   Polish'd well those stones elect,
In their places now compacted
   By the heavenly Architect,
*N*evermore to leave the temple
   Which with them the LORD hath deck

THE DEDICATION OF A CHURCH.

CHRIST is made the sure Foundation,
　CHRIST the Head and Corner-stone,
Chosen of the LORD, and binding
　All the fabric into one ;
Holy Sion stands for ever
　By her trust in Him alone.

All that dedicated city,
　Dearly loved of GOD on high,
In exultant jubilation
　Pours perpetual melody,
GOD the ONE in THREE extolling
　In glad hymns eternally.

To this temple, where we call Thee,
　Come, O LORD of hosts, to-day ;
With Thy wonted loving-kindness
　Hear Thy servants, as they pray ;
And Thy fullest benediction
　Shed within its walls alway.

Here vouchsafe to all Thy servants
　What they ask of Thee to gain ;
What they gain from Thee, for ever
　With the Blessèd to retain ;
And hereafter in Thy glory
　Evermore with Thee to reign.

The following may be sung at the end of either Part:

Laud and honour to the FATHER,
　Laud and honour to the SON,
Laud and honour to the SPIRIT,
　Ever THREE, and ever ONE,
Consubstantial, Co-eternal,
　While *unending* ages run.　Amen.

THE DEDICATION OF A CHURCH.

254 *Their bodies are buried in peace: but their name liveth for evermore.*

IN REMEMBRANCE OF PAST WORSHIPPERS.

IN our day of thanksgiving one psalm let us offer,
 For the Saints who before us have found their
  reward ;
When the shadow of death fell upon them, we
 sorrow'd,
 But now we rejoice that they rest in the LORD.

In the morning of life, and at noon, and at even,
 He call'd them away from our worship below ;
But not till His love, at the font and the altar,
 Had girt them with grace for the way they
  should go.

These stones that have echoed their praises are holy,
 And dear is the ground where their feet have
  once trod ;
Yet here they confess'd they were strangers and
 pilgrims,
 And still they were seeking the city of GOD.

Sing praise, then, for all who here sought and here
 found Him,
 Whose journey is ended, whose perils are past ;
They believed in the Light ; and its glory is round
 them,
 Where the clouds of earth's sorrow are lifted at
  last.   Amen.

255 *This is the day which the Lord hath made.*
Salve, festa dies.

HAIL, festal day, for ever sanctified,
 When CHRIST is married to the Church,
  His Bride.
This is GOD's Court, the place of peace and rest ;
The poor with Solomon's own wealth are blest.
The Son of David, GOD and Man, doth come
To knit us to Him in this Mother-home.

(224)

Ye are the company of heav'n below,
If ye will keep the faith which makes you so.
Here new Jerusalem descends all bright
In angel raiment from the world of light.
Faith, by the mystic laver, doth possess
This guerdon from the King of righteousness.
Here stands the tower of David ; hither run
And find the pledge of realms beyond the sun.
This is the ark of Noah ; safe within,
Believers ride the flood, and harbour win.
Lo, this is Jacob's ladder ; here 'tis given
By faith and godly life to climb to heaven.

Hail, festal day, &c.

256   *This is none other but the house of God.*

Patris æterni suboles coæva.

O WORD of God above,
  Who fillest all in all,
Hallow this house with Thy sure love,
  And bless our Festival.

Here rise the sacred springs
  That wash the sinner white ;
And here the Lord's anointing brings
  The gift of seven-fold might.

Here Christ to faithful hearts
  His Body gives for food ;
The Lamb of God Himself imparts
  The Chalice of His Blood.

Here guilty souls that pine
  May health and pardon win :
The Judge acquits, and grace divine
  Restores the dead in sin.

Yea, God enthroned on high
  Here also dwells to bless,
Here trains adoring souls that sigh
  His mansions to possess.

THE DEDICATION OF A CHURCH.

Against this holy home
Rude tempests harmless beat,
And Satan's angels fiercely come
But to endure defeat.

All might, all praise be Thine,
FATHER, Co-equal SON,
And SPIRIT, Bond of love divine,
While endless ages run.　Amen.

The following Hymns are suitable:

366 Glorious things of thee are spoken.
367 The Church's one foundation.
379 Jerusalem the golden.
388 O GOD of hosts, the mighty LORD.
389 Pleasant are Thy courts above.
390 CHRIST is our corner-stone.
391 Lo! GOD is here! let us adore.
392 JESUS, where'er Thy people meet.
393 Great Shepherd of Thy people, hear.
394 Hosanna to the living LORD!
395 We love the place, O GOD.

LAYING THE FOUNDATION STONE OF A CHURCH.

257 *The glory of Lebanon shall come unto thee, the fir tree, the pine tree, and the box together, to beautify the place of my sanctuary.*

O LORD of hosts, Whose glory fills
　　The bounds of the eternal hills,
And yet vouchsafes, in Christian lands,
To dwell in temples made with hands ;

Grant that all we, who here to-day
Rejoicing this foundation lay,
May be in very deed Thine own,
Built on the precious Corner-stone.

Endue the creatures with Thy grace,
That shall adorn Thy dwelling-place ;
The beauty of the oak and pine,
The gold and silver, make them Thine.

To Thee they all belong ; to Thee
The treasures of the earth and sea ;
And when we bring them to Thy throne,
We but present Thee with Thine own.

The heads that guide endue with skill,
The hands that work preserve from ill,
That we, who these foundations lay,
May raise the topstone in its day.

Both now and ever, LORD, protect
The temple of Thine own elect ;
Be Thou in them, and they in Thee,
O Ever-blessèd TRINITY !   Amen.

THE RESTORATION OF A CHURCH.

58 *Jesus Christ . . . in whom all the building fitly*
framed together groweth unto an holy temple in the
Lord; in whom ye also are builded together for an
habitation of God through the Spirit.

O beata Jerusalem.

MEET it is to tell thy glory, O Jerusalem the
blest ;   [joyful rest,
ᴧpirits of the just made perfect find in thee their
ᴧnd the seal of thy renewal shineth by the King's
behest.

Ⅴe in awe behold thy glory, mother of a goodly
band ;
Ⅴho hast peace in all the borders of thy ever-
joyous land ;
ᴧamps of holiness rekindled in thy courts of
worship stand.

ᴧnd this Church again made glorious, firm and
stable, fair and bright,   [the height,
Ⅼow doth wear a holier likeness of that temple in
'or her star that set aforetime shines to-day with
wonted light.

Here, we pray, be present with us, mighty Bt
  Holy LORD ;
To our rite of dedication graciously Thy
  accord,
And Thyself the Consecrator evermore be
  adored.

As a temple to Thine honour, us, Thy ser·
  deign to bless,
That our hearts and all our members may be
  in holiness ;
Since Thy Name is named upon us, let our]
  that Name confess.

Ever lit and ever honour'd be the altar of our
Ever worthily replenish'd with the gifts His]
  bring,
Evermore the benediction of His peace inhel

Here ourselves as Thy true altars consecra
  Judge most High,
By Thy grace for Thy true service heart and
  sanctify ;
From Thy throne to us descending let the
  GHOST draw nigh.

So in every generation, O most Holy]
  in ONE,   [
Let the glory of Thy greatness here be mag
And let everlasting honour to Thy chan
  Name be done.   Amen.

259 *We are the servants of the God of heaven and
and build the house that was builded these
years ago.*

L IFT the strain of high thanksgiving
  Tread with songs the hallow'd wa,
Praise our fathers' GOD for mercies
  New to us their sons to-day :

THE RESTORATION OF A CHURCH.

Here they built for Him a dwelling,
   Served Him here in ages past,
Fix'd it for His sure possession,
   Holy ground, while time shall last.

When the years had wrought their changes,
   He, our own unchanging GOD,
Thought on this His habitation,
   Look'd on His decay'd abode ;
Heard our prayers, and help'd our counsels,
   Bless'd the silver and the gold,
Till once more His house is standing
   Firm and stately as of old.

Entering then Thy gates with praises,
   LORD, be ours Thine Israel's prayer ;
"Rise into Thy place of resting,
   Show Thy promised Presence there ! "
Let the gracious word be spoken
   Here, as once on Sion's height,
"This shall be My rest for ever,
   This My dwelling of delight."

Fill this latter house with glory
   Greater than the former knew ;
Clothe with righteousness its priesthood,
   Guide its choir to reverence true ;
Let Thy Holy One's anointing
   Here its sevenfold blessing shed ;
Spread for us the heavenly banquet,
   Satisfy Thy poor with Bread.

Praise to Thee, Almighty FATHER,
   Praise to Thee, Eternal SON,
Praise to Thee, all-quickening SPIRIT,
   Ever blessèd THREE in ONE ;
Threefold Power and Grace and Wisdom,
   Moulding out of sinful clay
Living stones for that true temple
   Which *shall never* know decay.   Amen.

260 *The cup of blessing which we bless, is it not the communion of the blood of Christ? The bread which we break, is it not the communion of the body of Christ?*

Pange, lingua, gloriosi Corporis mysterium.

NOW, my tongue, the mystery telling
  Of the glorious Body sing,
And the Blood, all price excelling,
  Which the Gentiles' LORD and King,
Once on earth amongst us dwelling,
  Shed for this world's ransoming.

Virgin-born, He condescended
  To be given to our need,
Here His stay with men extended,
  While He sow'd the word's good seed,
Then His patient sojourn ended
  With a wondrous act indeed.

That last night, at supper lying,
  'Mid the Twelve, His chosen band,
JESUS, with the Law complying,
  Keeps the feast its rites demand;
Then, more precious food supplying,
  Gives Himself with His own hand.

WORD-made-Flesh true bread He maketh
  By His word His Flesh to be;
Wine His Blood; which whoso taketh
  Must from earthly thoughts be free;
Faith alone, where sight forsaketh,
  Shows true hearts the mystery.

PART 2.

Therefore we, before Him bending,
  This great Sacrament revere;
Types and shadows have their ending,
  For the better rite is here;
Faith, our outward sense befriending,
  Makes the inward vision clear.

Glory let us give and blessing
  To the FATHER and the SON,
Honour, thanks, and praise addressing,
  While eternal ages run,
His co-equal might confessing
  Who from Both with Both is One.   Amen.

61 *As the living Father hath sent me, and I lire by the
Father; so he that eateth me, even he shall lire by me.*

Verbum supernum prodiens.

THE Heav'nly WORD proceeding forth,
  Yet leaving not the FATHER'S side,
Went forth unto His work on earth
Until He reach'd life's eventide.

By false disciple to be given
To foemen for His death athirst,
Himself, the Bread of Life from heaven,
He gave to His disciples first.

He gave Himself in either kind,
His precious Flesh, His precious Blood ;
In love's own fulness thus design'd
Of the whole man to be the Food.

By birth their fellow-man was He ;
Their Meat, when sitting at the board ;
He died, their Ransomer to be ;
He ever reigns, their great Reward.

PART 2.
O saving Victim, opening wide
The gate of heav'n to man below,
Our foes press on from every side,
Thine aid supply, Thy strength bestow.

All praise and thanks to Thee ascend
For evermore, Blest ONE in THREE ;
O grant us life that shall not end
In our true native land with Thee.   Amen.

HOLY COMMUNION.

262 *I love them that love me; and those that seek me*
shall find me.

IN PREPARATION FOR COMMUNION.

WE pray Thee, heav'nly FATHER,
　To hear us in Thy love,
And pour upon Thy children
　The unction from above;
That so in love abiding,
　From all defilement free,
We may in pureness offer
　Our Eucharist to Thee.

Be Thou our Guide and Helper,
　O JESU CHRIST, we pray;
So may we well approach Thee,
　If Thou wilt be the Way:
Thou, very Truth, hast promised
　To help us in our strife,
Food of the weary pilgrim,
　Eternal Source of life.

And Thou, Creator SPIRIT,
　Look on us, we are Thine;
Renew in us Thy graces,
　Upon our darkness shine;
That, with Thy benediction
　Upon our souls outpour'd,
We may receive in gladness
　The Body of the LORD.

O TRINITY of Persons!
　O UNITY most High!
To Thy tremendous worship
　With trembling we draw nigh:
Unworthy in our weakness,
　On Thee our hope is stay'd,
And bless'd by Thy forgiveness
　We will not be afraid. Amen.

163 *Forasmuch then as the children are partakers of flesh and blood, he likewise took part of the same, that through death he might destroy him that had the power of death.*

FOR A PROCESSION.

CHRISTIANS, sing the Incarnation
    Of th' Eternal SON of GOD,
Who, to save us, took our nature,
    Soul and body, flesh and blood:
GOD, He saw man's cruel bondage,
    Who in death's dark dungeon lay;
MAN, He came to fight man's battle,
    And for man He won the day.
      Alleluia, Alleluia
        To th' Incarnate SON of GOD,
      Who for man as Man hath conquer'd
      In our own true flesh and blood.

King of kings and Lord of Angels,
    He put off His glory-crown,
Had a stable-cave for palace,
    And a manger for His throne;
Helpless lay, to Whom creation
    All its life and being owed,
And the lowly Hebrew Maiden
    Was the Mother of her GOD.
      Alleluia, Alleluia
        To th' Incarnate SON of GOD,
      Who conceal'd His dazzling GODHEAD
      'Neath the veil of flesh and blood.

Through a life of lowly labour
    He on earth was pleased to dwell,
All our want and sorrow sharing;
    GOD with us, EMMANUEL:
Yet a dearer, closer union
    JESUS in His love would frame;
He, the Passover fulfilling,
    Gave Himself as Paschal Lamb.

HOLY COMMUNION.

Alleluia, Alleluia
    To th' Incarnate SON of GOD,
Who the heavenly gifts bequeath'd us
    Of His own true Flesh and Blood.

Then, by man refused and hated,
    GOD for man vouchsafed to die,
Love divine its depth revealing
    On the heights of Calvary ;
Through His dying the dominion
    From the tyrant death was torn,
When its Victim rose its Victor
    On the Resurrection morn.
    Alleluia, Alleluia
        To th' Incarnate SON of GOD,
    Who through His eternal SPIRIT
        Offers His own Flesh and Blood.

Forty days of mystic converse
    Lived on earth the Risen One,
Speaking of His earthly kingdom,
    Ere He sought His heavenly throne :
Then, His latest words a blessing,
    He ascended up on high,
And through rank on rank of Angels
    Captive led captivity.
    Alleluia, Alleluia
        To th' Incarnate SON of GOD,
    Who the Holiest place hath enter'd
        In our flesh and by His Blood.

Now upon the golden altar,
    In the midst before the throne,
Incense of His intercession
    He is offering for His own.
And on earth at all His altars
    His true Presence we adore,
And His Sacrifice is pleaded,
    Yea, till time shall be no more.

Alleluia, Alleluia
　To th' Incarnate SON of GOD,
Who, abiding Priest for ever,
　Still imparts His Flesh and Blood.

Then, adored in highest heaven,
　We shall see the Virgin's Son,
All creation bow'd before Him,
　MAN upon th' eternal throne :
Where, like sound of many waters
　In one ever rising flood,
Myriad voices hymn His triumph,
　Victim, Priest, Incarnate GOD.
　　Worthy He all praise and blessing
　　Who, by dying, death o'ercame :
　　Glory be to GOD for ever !
　　Alleluia to the LAMB ! Amen.

64   *Look upon the face of thine anointed.*

AT THE OFFERTORY.

ALMIGHTY FATHER, LORD most High,
　Who madest all, Who fillest all,
Thy Name we praise and magnify,
For all our needs on Thee we call.

We offer to Thee of Thine own
Ourselves and all that we can bring,
In Bread and Cup before Thee shown,
Our universal offering.

All that we have we bring to Thee,
Yet all is naught when all is done,
Save that in it Thy love can see
The sacrifice of Thy dear SON.

By His command in Bread and Cup
His Body and His Blood we plead ;
What on the Cross He offer'd up
Is *here our Sacrifice* indeed.

For all Thy gifts of life and grace,
Here we Thy servants humbly pray
That Thou would'st look upon the face
Of Thine anointed SON to-day.   Amen.

265   *It is the spirit that quickeneth.*
BEFORE THE CONSECRATION.

LOOK down upon us, GOD of grace,
    And send from Thy most holy place
The quickening SPIRIT all Divine
On us, and on this bread and wine.

O may His overshadowing
Make now for us this bread we bring
The Body of Thy SON our LORD,
This cup His Blood for sinners pour'd.   Amen.

266   *Jesus said unto them, I am the bread of life.*
Adoro Te devote, latens Deitas.
DURING THE COMMUNION.

THEE we adore, O hidden Saviour, Thee,
    Who in Thy Sacrament dost deign to be ;
Both flesh and spirit at Thy presence fail,
Yet here Thy presence we devoutly hail.

O blest memorial of our dying LORD !
Thou Living Bread, Who life dost here afford !
O may our souls for ever live by Thee,
And Thou to us for ever precious be.

Fountain of goodness, JESU, LORD, and GOD,
Cleanse us, unclean, with Thy most cleansing Blood;
Make us in Thee devoutly to believe,
In Thee to hope, to Thee in love to cleave.

O CHRIST, Whom now beneath a veil we see,
May what we thirst for soon our portion be,
There in the glory of Thy dwelling-place
To gaze on Thee unveil'd, and see Thy face.
                                    Amen.

HOLY COMMUNION.

267 *In every place incense shall be offered unto my name, and a pure offering.*

DURING THE COMMUNION.

AND now, O FATHER, mindful of the love
    That bought us, once for all, on Calvary's
      Tree,
And having with us Him that pleads above,
  We here present, we here spread forth to Thee
That only Offering perfect in Thine eyes,
The one true, pure, immortal Sacrifice.

Look, FATHER, look on His anointed face,
  And only look on us as found in Him ;
Look not on our misusings of Thy grace,
  Our prayer so languid, and our faith so dim :
For lo ! between our sins and their reward
We set the Passion of Thy SON our LORD.

And then for those, our dearest and our best,
  By this prevailing presence we appeal ;
O fold them closer to Thy mercy's breast,
  O do Thine utmost for their souls' true weal ;
From tainting mischief keep them white and clear,
And crown Thy gifts with strength to persevere.

And so we come ; O draw us to Thy feet,
  Most patient Saviour, Who canst love us still ;
And by this Food, so awful and so sweet,
  Deliver us from every touch of ill :
In Thine own service make us glad and free,
And grant us never more to part with Thee.
                        Amen.

268   *The body and blood of the Lord.*

DURING THE COMMUNION.

HAIL, Body true, of Mary born, and in the
    manger laid,
That once with thorn and scourging torn wast on
  the Cross display'd,

HOLY COMMUNION.

That every eye might there descry th' uplifted
    Sacrifice,
Which once for all to GOD on high paid our
    redemption's price !

Hail, precious Blood, by true descent drawn from
    our own first sire,
Yet innocent of that fell taint which fills our veins
    with fire,
Once from the side of Him that died for love of
    us His kin
Drain'd, an atonement to provide and wash away
    our sin !

Still Thou art there amidst us, LORD, unchangeably
    the same,
When at Thy board with one accord Thy promises
    we claim ;
But in the way Thou com'st to-day the forms of
    bread and wine
Conceal the presence they convey, both Human
    and Divine.

How glorious is that Body now, throned on the
    throne of heaven !
The Angels bow, and marvel how to us on earth
    'tis given ;
Oh to discern what splendours burn within these
    veils of His,—
That faith could into vision turn, and see Him as
    He is !

How mighty is the Blood that ran for sinful
    nature's needs !
It broke the ban, it rescued man ; it lives, and
    speaks, and pleads ;
And all who sup from this blest Cup in faith and
    hope and love,
Shall prove that death is swallow'd up in richer
    life above. Amen.

HOLY COMMUNION.

69 *Wisdom saith . . . Come, eat of my bread, and drink of the wine which I have mingled.*

Sancti, venite, Christi Corpus sumite.

DURING THE COMMUNION.

DRAW nigh and take the Body of the LORD,
    And drink the holy Blood for you outpour'd.
By that pure Body and that holy Blood
Saved and refresh'd, we render thanks to GOD.
Salvation's Giver, CHRIST, the Only SON,
By His dear Cross and Blood the world hath won.
Offer'd was He for greatest and for least,
Himself the Victim, and Himself the Priest.
Victims were offer'd by the law of old,
Which in a type this heav'nly mystery told.
He, Lord of light, and Saviour of our race,
Hath given to His saints a wondrous grace.
Approach ye then with faithful hearts sincere,
And take the safeguard of salvation here.
He, that His saints in this world rules and shields,
To all believers life eternal yields ;
He feeds the hungry with the Bread of heaven,
And living streams to those who thirst are given.
Alpha and Omega, to Whom shall bow
All nations at the Doom, is with us now.   Amen.

70   *Thanks be to God for his unspeakable gift.*

O Jesu, sode Jesu, dig.

AFTER COMMUNION.

O JESU, Blessèd LORD, to Thee
    My heartfelt thanks for ever be,
Who hast so lovingly bestow'd
On me Thy Body and Thy Blood.
Break forth, my soul, for joy, and say,
What wealth is come to me to-day !
My SAVIOUR dwells within me now ;
How blest am I ! how good art Thou ! Amen.

(239)

271 *He that eateth me, even he shall live by me.*

AFTER COMMUNION.

JESU, gentlest Saviour,
   Thou art in us now,
Fill us with Thy goodness
   Till our hearts o'erflow.

Nature cannot hold Thee,
   Heav'n is all too strait
For Thine endless glory
   And Thy royal state.

Yet the hearts of children
   Hold what worlds can not,
And the GOD of wonders
   Loves the lowly spot.

Oh, how can we thank Thee
   For a gift like this,
Gift that truly maketh
   Heav'n's eternal bliss?

Multiply our graces,
   Chiefly love and fear,
And, dear LORD, the chiefest,
   Grace to persevere.

JESU, gentlest Saviour,
   Thou art in us now,
Fill us with Thy goodness
   Till our hearts o'erflow.   Amen.

272 *They took knowledge of them that they had been with Jesus.*

AFTER COMMUNION.

O CHRIST, our GOD, Who with Thine own hast been,
Our spirits cleave to Thee, the Friend unseen.

Vouchsafe that all who on Thy bounty feed
May heed Thy love, and prize Thy gifts indeed.

Make every heart that is Thy dwelling-place
A water'd garden fill'd with fruits of grace.

Each holy purpose help us to fulfil ;
Increase our faith to feed upon Thee still.

Illuminate our minds, that we may see
In all around us holy signs of Thee ;

And may such witness in our lives appear,
That all may know Thou hast been with us here.

O grant us peace, that by Thy peace possess'd,
Thy life within us we may manifest.

So shall we pass our days in holy fear,
In joyful consciousness that Thou art near.

So shalt Thou be for ever, loving LORD,
Our Shield and our exceeding great Reward.
Amen.

273   *He shall feed his flock like a shepherd.*

Bone Pastor, Panis vere.

FOR GENERAL USE.

O TRUE Bread, Good Shepherd, tend us,
     JESU, of Thy love befriend us,
Thou refresh us, Thou defend us,
Let Thy goodness here attend us
     Till the land of life we see.

Thou Who all things canst and knowest,
Who such food on earth bestowest,
Make us, where Thy face Thou showest,
'Midst Thy saints, though 'least and lowest,
     Guests and fellow heirs with Thee.
Amen.

274 *He that eateth my flesh and drinketh my blood, dwelleth in me, and I in him.*

O esca viatorum.

O FOOD that weary pilgrims love,
O Bread of Angel-hosts above,
O Manna of the Saints,
The hungry soul would feed on Thee ;
Ne'er may the heart unsolaced be
Which for Thy sweetness faints.

O Fount of love, O cleansing Tide,
Which from the Saviour's piercèd side
And sacred heart dost flow,
Be ours to drink at Thy pure rill,
Which only can our spirits fill,
And all we need, bestow.

LORD JESU, Whom, by power divine
Now hid beneath the outward sign,
We worship and adore,
Grant, when the veil away is roll'd,
With open face we may behold
Thyself for evermore.   Amen.

275 *Verily thou art a God that hidest thyself, O God of Israel, the Saviour.*

L ORD, enthroned in heav'nly splendour,
First begotten from the dead,
Thou alone, our strong Defender,
Liftest up Thy people's head ;
Alleluia,
JESU, true and living Bread !

Here for faith's discernment praying,
Lest we fail to know Thee now,
Here our deepest homage paying,
We in loving rev'rence bow ;
Alleluia,
Thou art here, we ask not how.

HOLY COMMUNION.

Now though lowliest form do veil Thee
　　As of old in Bethlehem,
Angels in Thy mystery hail Thee ;
　　We in worship join with them ;
　　　　Alleluia,
　　　Branch and Flower of Jesse's stem.

Paschal LAMB, Thine Offering finish'd
　　Once for all when Thou wast slain,
In its fulness undiminish'd
　　Shall for evermore remain,
　　　　Alleluia,
　　　Cleansing souls from every stain.

Great High Priest of our profession,
　　Through the veil Thou wentest in,
By Thy mighty intercession
　　Grace and peace for us to win ;
　　　　Alleluia,
　　Only Sacrifice for sin.

Life-imparting heav'nly Manna,
　　Smitten Rock with streaming side,
Heav'n and earth with one Hosanna,
　　Worship Thee, the LAMB that died,
　　　　Alleluia,
　　　Risen, ascended, glorified !　Amen.

76　*The blood of sprinkling, which speaketh.*

VICTIM Divine, Thy grace we claim
　　While thus Thy precious death we show ;
Once offer'd up, a spotless Lamb,
In Thy great temple here below,
Thou didst for all mankind atone,
And standest *now before* the throne.

Thou standest in the holiest place,
As now for guilty sinners slain ;
Thy Blood of sprinkling speaks and prays
All-prevalent for helpless man ;
Thy Blood is still our ransom found,
And spreads salvation all around.

God still respects Thy sacrifice,
Its savour sweet doth always please ;
The Offering smokes through earth and skies,
Diffusing life and joy and peace ;
To these Thy lower courts it comes,
And fills them with divine perfumes.

We need not now go up to heaven
To bring the long-sought Saviour down ;
Thou art to all that seek Thee given,
Thou dost e'en now Thy banquet crown :
To every faithful soul appear,
And show Thy real presence here.   Amen.

277   *This do in remembrance of me.*

BREAD of heav'n, on Thee we feed,
   For Thy Flesh is meat indeed ;
Ever may our souls be fed
With this true and living Bread,
Day by day with strength supplied
Through the life of Him Who died.

Vine of heav'n, Thy Blood supplies
This blest cup of sacrifice ;
Lord, Thy wounds our healing give ;
To Thy Cross we look and live :
Jesus, may we ever be
Grafted, rooted, built in Thee.   Amen.

278 *The Lord's table.*

AUTHOR of life divine,
 Who hast a table spread;
Furnish'd with mystic Wine
And everlasting Bread,
Preserve the life Thyself hast given,
And feed and train us up for heaven.

Our needy souls sustain
 With fresh supplies of love,
Till all Thy life we gain,
 And all Thy fulness prove,
And, strengthen'd by Thy perfect grace,
Behold without a veil Thy face. Amen.

279 *We being many are one bread, and one body, for we
are all partakers of that one bread.*

THOU Who at Thy first Eucharist didst pray
 That all Thy Church might be for ever one,
Grant us at every Eucharist to say
 With longing heart and soul, " Thy will be done."
O may we all one Bread, one Body be,
Through this blest Sacrament of unity.

For all Thy Church, O LORD, we intercede ;
 Make Thou our sad divisions soon to cease ;
Draw us the nearer each to each, we plead,
 By drawing all to Thee, O Prince of peace ;
Thus may we all one Bread, one Body be,
Through this blest Sacrament of unity.

We pra Thee too for wand'rers from Thy fold ;
 O bring them back, good Shepherd of the sheep,
Back to the faith which Saints believed of old,
 Back to the Church which still that faith doth
Soon may we all *one Bread,* one Body be, [keep ;
*Through this blest Sacra*ment of unity.

So, LORD, at length when Sacraments shall cease,
  May we be one with all Thy Church above,
One with Thy Saints in one unbroken peace,
  One with Thy Saints in one unbounded love :
More blessèd still, in peace and love to be
One with the TRINITY in UNITY.   Amen.

280   *Come, for all things are now ready.*

MY GOD, and is Thy table spread,
    And doth Thy cup with love o'erflow ?
Thither be all Thy children led,
And let them all Thy sweetness know.

Hail, sacred feast, which JESUS makes,
Rich banquet of His Flesh and Blood !
Thrice happy he who here partakes
That sacred stream, that heav'nly food.

Why are its dainties all in vain
Before unwilling hearts display'd ?
Was not for them the Victim slain ?
Are they forbid the children's Bread ?

O let Thy table honour'd be,
And furnish'd well with joyful guests ;
And may each soul salvation see,
That here its sacred pledges tastes.

Revive Thy dying Churches, LORD ;
Bid all our drooping graces live ;
*And more that energy afford
A Saviour's Blood alone can give.*   Amen.

HOLY COMMUNION.

1 *My flesh is meat indeed, and my blood is drink indeed..*

O GOD, unseen yet ever near,
   Thy presence may we feel,
And thus inspired with holy fear
   Before Thine altar kneel.

Here may Thy faithful people know
   The blessings of Thy love,
The streams that through the desert flow,
   The manna from above.

We come, obedient to Thy word,
   To feast on heavenly food ;
Our meat the Body of the LORD,
   Our drink His precious Blood.

Thus may we all Thy word obey,
   For we, O GOD, are Thine,
And go rejoicing on our way,
   Renew'd with strength divine.   Amen.

2   *A lamb as it had been slain.*

O THOU, before the world began,
   Ordain'd a sacrifice for man,
And by th' Eternal SPIRIT made
An Offering in the sinner's stead ;
Our everlasting Priest art Thou,
Pleading Thy death for sinners now.

Thy Offering still continues new
Before the righteous FATHER'S view ;
Thyself the LAMB for ever slain,
Thy Priesthood doth unchanged remain ;
Thy years, O GOD, can never fail,
Nor Thy *blest work* within the veil.

O that our faith may never move,
But stand unshaken as Thy love !
Sure evidence of things unseen,
Now let it pass the years between,
And view Thee bleeding on the Tree,—
My LORD, my GOD, Who dies for me. Amen.

283   *An high priest over the house of God.*

ONCE, only once, and once for all,
His precious life He gave ;
Before the Cross our spirits fall,
And own it strong to save.

"One offering, single and complete,"
With lips and heart we say ;
But what He never can repeat
He shows forth day by day.

For, as the priest of Aaron's line
Within the holiest stood,
And sprinkled all the mercy-shrine
With sacrificial blood ;

So He, Who once atonement wrought,
Our Priest of endless power,
Presents Himself for those He bought
In that dark noontide hour.

His Manhood pleads where now it lives
On heav'n's eternal throne,
And where in mystic rite He gives
Its presence to His own.

And so we show Thy death, O LORD,
Till Thou again appear,
And feel, when we approach Thy board,
We have an altar here. Amen.

84   *Thou art a priest for ever.*

ALLELUIA ! sing to JESUS !
  His the sceptre, His the throne ;
Alleluia ! His the triumph,
  His the victory alone :
Hark ! the songs of peaceful Sion
  Thunder like a mighty flood ;
JESUS out of every nation
  Hath redeem'd us by His Blood.

Alleluia ! not as orphans
  Are we left in sorrow now ;
 Alleluia ! He is near us,
  Faith believes, nor questions how ;
Though the cloud from sight received Him
  When the forty days were o'er,
Shall our hearts forget His promise,
  "I am with you evermore ?"

Alleluia ! Bread of Angels,
  Thou on earth our Food, our Stay ;
Alleluia ! here the sinful
  Flee to Thee from day to day ;
Intercessor, Friend of sinners,
  Earth's Redeemer, plead for me,
Where the songs of all the sinless
  Sweep across the crystal sea.

Alleluia ! King Eternal,
  Thee the LORD of lords we own ;
Alleluia ! born of Mary,
  Earth Thy footstool, heav'n Thy throne :
Thou within the veil hast enter'd,
  Robed in flesh, our great High Priest ;
Thou on earth both Priest and Victim
  In *the Eucharistic* Feast.

HOLY COMMUNION.

Alleluia ! sing to JESUS !
  His the sceptre, His the throne ;
Alleluia ! His the triumph,
  His the victory alone ;
Hark ! the songs of peaceful Sion
  Thunder like a mighty flood ;
JESUS out of every nation
  Hath redeem'd us by His Blood.   Amen

285 *My soul thirsteth for thee, my flesh also longeth afte*
               thee.

I HUNGER and I thirst,
  JESU, my manna be ;
Ye living waters, burst
Out of the rock for me.

Thou bruised and broken Bread,
My life-long wants supply ;
As living souls are fed,
O feed me, or I die.

Thou true life-giving Vine,
Let me Thy sweetness prove ;
Renew my life with Thine,
Refresh my soul with love.

Rough paths my feet have trod
Since first their course began ;
Feed me, Thou Bread of GOD ;
Help me, Thou Son of Man.

For still the desert lies
My thirsting soul before ;
O living waters, rise
Within me evermore. Amen.

HOLY COMMUNION.

86 *The centurion answered and said, Lord, I am not worthy that thou shouldest come under my roof; but speak the word only, and my servant shall be healed.*

I AM not worthy, Holy LORD,
 That Thou shouldst come to me ;
Speak but the word ; one gracious word
 Can set the sinner free.

I am not worthy ; cold and bare
 The lodging of my soul ;
How canst Thou deign to enter there ?
 LORD, speak, and make me whole.

I am not worthy ; yet, my GOD,
 How can I say Thee nay ;
Thee, Who didst give Thy Flesh and Blood
 My ransom-price to pay ?

O come ! in this sweet morning hour
 Feed me with food divine ;
And fill with all Thy love and power
 This worthless heart of mine.   Amen.

The following Hymns are suitable:

119 Glory be to JESUS.
252 JESU ! the very thought is sweet.
421 The King of love my Shepherd is.
461 Not for our sins alone.
468 Behold the LAMB of GOD !
478 As pants the hart for cooling streams.
484 JESU, grant me this, I pray.
483 JESU, Lover of my soul.
492 JESU, Thou Joy of loving hearts !
493 JESU, the very thought of Thee.
495 O Love, Who formedst me to wear.
496 Hark, my soul ! it is the LORD.
498 Love Divine, all loves excelling.
499 JESU, my LORD, my GOD, my All.
638 *Litany of the Blessed Sacrament.*

HOLY BAPTISM.

287 *Ask, and it shall be given you: seek, and ye shall find: knock, and it shall be opened unto you.*

O Vaterherz, das erd, und Himmel schuf.

O FATHER, Thou Who hast creáted all
 In wisest love, we pray,
Look on this babe, who at Thy grácious call
 Is entering on life's way ;
Bend o'er *him* in *his* nothingness,
Thine image on *his* soul impress ;
  O FATHER, hear !

O SON of GOD, Who diedst for ús, behold,
 We bring our child to Thee ;
Thou tender Shepherd, take *him* tó Thy fold,
 Thine own for aye to be ;
Defend *him* through this earthly strife,
And lead *him* in Thy way of life,
  O SON of GOD !

O HOLY GHOST, Who broodedst ó'er the wave,
 Descend upon this child ;
Give *him* undying life, *his* spírit lave
 With waters undefiled ;
Grant *him* from earliest years to be
Thy learner apt, a home for Thee,
  O HOLY GHOST !

O TRIUNE GOD, what Thou commánd'st is done ;
 We speak, but Thine the might ;
This child hath scarce yet seen our éarthly sun,
 O pour on *him* Thy light,
In faith and hope, in joy and love,
Thou Sun of all below, above,
  O TRIUNE GOD ! Amen.

(252)

HOLY BAPTISM.

38 *Baptizing them in the name of the Father, and of the Son, and of the Holy Ghost.*

O FATHER, bless the children
　　Brought hither to Thy gate ;
Lift up their fallen nature,
　　Restore their lost estate ;
Renew Thine image in them,
　　And own them, by this sign,
Thy very sons and daughters,
　　New born of birth divine.

O JESU LORD, receive them ;
　　Thy loving arms of old
Were open'd wide to welcome
　　The children to Thy fold ;
Let these, with Thee now dying
　　And rising from the dead,
Henceforth be living members
　　Of Thee, their living Head.

O HOLY SPIRIT, keep them ;
　　Dwell with them to the last,
Till all the fight is ended,
　　And all the storms are past.
Renew the gift baptismal
　　From strength to strength, till each
The troublous waves o'ercoming,
　　The land of life shall reach.

O FATHER, SON, and SPIRIT,
　　O Wisdom, Love, and Power,
We wait the promised blessing
　　In this accepted hour !
We name upon the children
　　The threefold Name divine ;
Receive them, cleanse them, own them,
　　And keep them ever Thine.　　Amen.

HOLY BAPTISM.

Chosen to be a soldier.

GRANT to this child the inward grace,
  While we the outward sign impart,
The Cross we on *his* forehead trace
  Do Thou engrave upon *his* heart.

May it *his* pride and glory be,
  Beneath Thy banner fair unfurl'd,
To march to certain victory
  O'er sin, o'er Satan, o'er the world.   Amen.

290 *Be not thou therefore ashamed of the testimony of our*
Lord.

IN token that thou shalt not fear
  CHRIST crucified to own,
We print the Cross upon thee here,
  And stamp thee His alone.

In token that thou shalt not blush
  To glory in His Name,
We blazon here upon thy front
  His glory and His shame.

In token that thou shalt not flinch
  CHRIST's quarrel to maintain,
But 'neath His banner manfully
  Firm at thy post remain ;

In token that thou too shalt tread
  The path He travell'd by,
Endure the cross, despise the shame,
  And sit thee down on high ;

Thus outwardly and visibly
  We seal thee for His own ;
And may the brow that wears His Cross
  Hereafter share His crown.   Amen.

This Hymn may also be sung when a child who has been
  privately baptized is received into the congregation ; and
  at the baptism of an adult.

291 *Buried with him in baptism, wherein also ye are risen with him.*

WITH CHRIST we share a mystic grave,
    With CHRIST we buried lie;
But 'tis not in the darksome cave
    By mournful Calvary.

The pure and bright baptismal flood
    Entombs our nature's stain :
New creatures from the cleansing wave
    With CHRIST we rise again.

Thrice blest, if through this world of sin
    And lust and selfish care
Our resurrection mantle white
    And undefiled we wear.

Thrice blest, if through the gate of death,
    Glorious at last and free,
We to our joyful rising pass,
    O risen LORD, with Thee. Amen.

292 *If any man be in Christ, he is a new creature.*

FOR AN ADULT.

FATHER, SON, and HOLY GHOST, in solemn
    power come down,   [crown :
Present with Thy heav'nly host Thine ordinance to
See a sinful child of earth; bless to *him* the
    cleansing flood ;
Plunge *him* by a second birth into the depths of GOD.

Let the promised inward grace accompany the sign,
On *his* new-born soul impress the character divine ;
FATHER, all Thy love reveal ; JESUS, all Thy Name
    impart ;
HOLY GHOST, renew, and dwell for ever in *his* heart.
                        Amen.

The following Hymns are suitable for use at a Baptism :
    572 CHRIST, Who once amongst us.
    573 *Loving* Shepherd of Thy sheep.

CONFIRMATION.

293 *Then laid they their hands on them, and they received the Holy Ghost.*

BEFORE THE CONFIRMATION.

BEHOLD us, LORD, before Thee met,
  Whom each bright Angel serves and fears,
Who on Thy throne rememberest yet
  Thy spotless Boyhood's quiet years ;
Whose feet the hills of Nazareth trod,
Who art true Man and perfect GOD.

To Thee we look, in Thee confide,
  Our help is in Thine own dear Name ;
For who on JESUS e'er relied,
  And found not JESUS still the same ?
Thus far Thy love our souls hath brought :
O stablish well what Thou hast wrought.

The seed of our baptismal life,
  O living WORD, by Thee was sown ;
So, where Thy soldiers wage their strife,
  Our post we take, our vows we own,.
And ask, in Thine appointed way,
Confirm us in Thy grace to-day.

We need Thee more than tongue can speak,
  'Mid foes that well might cast us down ;
But thousands, once as young and weak,
  Have fought the fight, and won the crown ;
We ask the help that bore them through ;
We trust the Faithful and the True.

So bless us with the gift complete
  By hands of Thy chief pastors given,—
That awful presence kind and sweet
  Which comes in sevenfold might from heaven ;
Eternal CHRIST, to Thee we bow,
Give us Thy SPIRIT here and now.   Amen.

CONFIRMATION.

294 *With my whole heart have I sought thee; O let me not go wrong out of thy commandments.*

MY GOD, accept my heart this day,
  And make it always Thine,
That I from Thee no more may stray,
  No more from Thee decline.

Before the Cross of Him Who died,
  Behold, I prostrate fall ;
Let every sin be crucified,
  And CHRIST be all in all.

Anoint me with Thy SPIRIT's grace,
  And seal me for Thine own ;
That I may see Thy glorious face,
  And worship near Thy throne.

Let every thought, and work, and word
  To Thee be ever given ;
Then life shall be Thy service, LORD,
  And death the gate of heaven.

All glory to the FATHER be,
  All glory to the SON,
All glory, HOLY GHOST, to Thee,
  While endless ages run.   Amen.

295 *Wist ye not that I must be about my Father's business?*

LORD, Who while yet a boy wast found
  Within Thy FATHER's house of prayer,
While listening sages all around
  Wonder'd what child of GOD were there.

Then wentest forth, and yet again
  Wast subject unto earthly rule,
Learning through years of toil and pain
  Thy *guileless* mind and heart to school ;

CONFIRMATION.

So here Thy children at Thy shrine
   Await in faith and hope and love
The Finger of the Hand divine,
   Thine own anointing from above.

As they to Thee their souls uplift
   Obedient to Thy dread commands,
So seal them with Thy SPIRIT's gift
   Through touch of Apostolic hands.

Then send them forth to do Thy will
   With single-hearted trust in Thee,
Thee their sure Guide through good and ill,
   Their Joy to all eternity.   Amen.

296   *Take unto you the whole armour of God.*

AFTER THE CONFIRMATION.

ONCE pledged by the Cross,
   As children of GOD,
To tread in the steps
   Your Captain has trod,
Now, seal'd by the SPIRIT
   Of Wisdom and Might,
Go forward, CHRIST's soldiers,
   Go forward and fight !

Your weapons of war
   Are sent from above,
The SPIRIT's good sword,
   The breastplate of love ;
Your feet with the Gospel
   Of peace be well shod ;
Put on the whole armour,
   The armour of GOD.

Full well do ye know
   The foe must be met,
Full well do ye feel
   That Satan has set

His powers of darkness
   In battle array ;
But those who are for you
   Are stronger than they.
The fight may be long,
   But triumph is sure,
And rest comes at last
   To those who endure ;
The rest that remaineth,
   The victory won,
And—dearer than all things—
. Your Captain's " Well done."
Then, on to the fight
   'Gainst sin and the world,
Stand fast in His strength,
   His banner unfurl'd ;
And, seal'd by the SPIRIT
   Of Wisdom and Might,
Go forward, CHRIST's soldiers,
   Go forward and fight ! Amen.

7 *And they shall be mine, saith the Lord of hosts, in
that day when I make up my jewels.*

THINE for ever ! GOD of love,
   Hear us from Thy throne above ;
Thine for ever may we be
Here and in eternity.

Thine for ever ! Oh, how blest
They who find in Thee their rest !
Saviour, Guardian, heav'nly Friend,
O defend us to the end.

Thine for ever ! LORD of life,
Shield us through our earthly strife ;
Thou the Life, the Truth, the Way,
Guide *us to* the realms of day.

CONFIRMATION.

Thine for ever ! Shepherd, keep
These Thy frail and trembling sheep ;
Safe alone beneath Thy care,
Let us all Thy goodness share.

Thine for ever ; Thou our Guide,
All our wants by Thee supplied,
All our sins by Thee forgiven,
Lead us, LORD, from earth to heaven. Amen.

The following Hymns are also suitable :

177 Ruler of the hosts of light.
180 Come, HOLY GHOST, our souls inspire.
181 Come, HOLY GHOST, Creator Blest.
184 Come, Thou HOLY SPIRIT, come.
187 Our Blest Redeemer, ere He breathed.
402 O FATHER, we would thank Thee.
412 Oft in danger, oft in woe.
413 Soldiers, who are CHRIST'S below.
433 Ye servants of the LORD.
436 Stand up !—stand up for JESUS !
437 Soldiers of CHRIST, arise.
446 O Light, Whose beams illumine all.
487 O JESUS, I have promised.
619 Fight the good fight with all thy might.

HOLY MATRIMONY.

298 *A threefold cord is not quickly broken.*

THE voice that breathed o'er Eden,
    That earliest wedding day,
The primal marriage blessing,
    It hath not pass'd away :

Still in the pure espousal
    Of Christian man and maid
The HOLY THREE are with us,
    The threefold grace is said,

For dower of blessèd children,
    For love and faith's sweet sake,
For high mysterious union
    Which naught on earth may break.

(260)

HOLY MATRIMONY.

Be present, awful FATHER,
  To give away this bride,
As Eve Thou gav'st to Adam
  Out of his own pierced side ;

Be present, SON of Mary,
  To join their loving hands,
As Thou didst bind two natures
  In Thine eternal bands ;

Be present, Holiest SPIRIT,
  To bless them as they kneel,
As Thou for CHRIST, the Bridegroom,
  The heav'nly Spouse dost seal.

O spread Thy pure wing o'er them,
  Let no ill power find place,
When onward to Thine altar
  The hallow'd path they trace,

To cast their crowns before Thee
  In perfect sacrifice,
Till to the home of gladness
  With CHRIST'S own Bride they rise.
                          Amen.

9 *Both Jesus was called, and his disciples, to the*
       marriage.

HOW welcome was the call,
      And sweet the festal lay,
When JESUS deign'd in Cana's hall
  To bless the marriage day !

His gracious power divine
  The water vessels knew ;
And plenteous was the mystic wine
  The wondering servants drew.

O LORD of life and love,
  Come Thou again to-day ;
And bring a blessing from above
  That *ne'er shall pass away.*

(261)

O bless now, as of old,
The bridegroom and the bride ;
Bless with the holier stream that flow'd
Forth from Thy piercèd side.

Before Thine altar-throne
This mercy we implore ;
As Thou dost knit them, Lord, in one,
So bless them evermore.   Amen.

300 *The Lord do so to me and more also, if aught but
death part thee and me.*

O PERFECT Love, all human thought tran-
scending,
Lowly we kneel in prayer before Thy throne,
That theirs may be the love which knows no
ending,
Whom Thou for evermore dost join in one.

O perfect Life, be Thou their full assurance
Of tender charity and steadfast faith,
Of patient hope, and quiet brave endurance,
With childlike trust that fears nor pain nor death.

Grant them the joy which brightens earthly
sorrow,   [strife ;
Grant them the peace which calms all earthly
And to life's day the glorious unknown morrow
That dawns upon eternal love and life.   Amen.

301 *Except the Lord build the house, their labour is but
lost that build it.*

O FATHER all creating,
Whose wisdom, love, and power
First bound two lives together
In Eden's primal hour,
To-day to these Thy children
Thine earliest gifts renew,—
A home by Thee made happy,
A love by Thee kept true.

HOLY MATRIMONY.

O Saviour, Guest most bounteous
　　Of old in Galilee,
Vouchsafe to-day Thy presence
　　With these who call on Thee ;
Their store of earthly gladness
　　Transform to heavenly wine, ·
And teach them, in the tasting,
　　To know the gift is Thine.

O Spirit of the Father,
　　Breathe on them from above,
·So mighty in Thy pureness,
　　So tender in Thy love ;
That guarded by Thy presence,
　　From sin and strife kept free,
Their lives may own Thy guidance,
　　Their hearts be ruled by Thee.

Except Thou build it, Father,
　　The house is built in vain ;
Except Thou, Saviour, bless it,
　　The joy will turn to pain ;
But naught can break the marriage
　　Of hearts in Thee made one,
And love Thy Spirit hallows
　　Is endless love begun.　Amen.

BURIAL OF THE DEAD.

2　　　　*He cometh to judge the earth.*
　　　　Dies iræ, dies illa.

DAY of wrath ! O day of mourning !
　　See fulfill'd the prophets' warning—
Heav'n and earth in ashes burning !
Oh, what fear man's bosom rendeth,
When *from heav'n the Judge descendeth,*
On Whose sentence all dependeth !

BURIAL OF THE DEAD.

Wondrous sound the trumpet flingeth,
Through earth's sepulchres it ringeth,
All before the throne it bringeth.
Death is struck, and nature quaking,
All creation is awaking,
To its Judge an answer making.

Lo! the book exactly worded,
Wherein all hath been recorded;
Thence shall judgment be awarded.
When the Judge His seat attaineth,
And each hidden deed arraigneth,
Nothing unavenged remaineth.

What shall I, frail man, be pleading,
Who for me be interceding,
When the just are mercy needing?
King of majesty tremendous,
Who dost free salvation send us,
Fount of pity, then befriend us!

Think, good JESU! my salvation
Caused Thy wondrous Incarnation;
Leave me not to reprobation.
Faint and weary Thou hast sought me,
On the Cross of suffering bought me;
Shall such grace be vainly brought me?

Righteous Judge! for sin's pollution
Grant Thy gift of absolution,
Ere that day of retribution.
Guilty, now I pour my moaning,
All my shame with anguish owning;
Spare, O GOD, Thy suppliant groaning.

From that sinful woman shriven,
From the dying thief forgiven,
Thou to me a hope hast given.
Worthless are my prayers and sighing,
Yet, good LORD, in grace complying,
Rescue me from fires undying.

BURIAL OF THE DEAD.

With Thy favour'd sheep O place me,
Nor among the goats abase me,
But to Thy right hand upraise me.
While the wicked are confounded,
Doom'd to flames of woe unbounded,
Call me with Thy Saints surrounded.

Low I kneel, with heart submission,
Crush'd to ashes in contrition ;
Help me in my last condition.

Ah ! that day of tears and mourning !
From the dust of earth returning
Man for judgment must prepare him ;
Spare, O GOD, in mercy spare him !
LORD, all-pitying, JESU Blest,
Grant them Thine eternal rest.   Amen.

03 *The souls of the righteous are in the hand of God,
and there shall no torment touch them.*

NOW the labourer's task is o'er ;
    Now the battle day is past ;
Now upon the farther shore
    Lands the voyager at last.
FATHER, in Thy gracious keeping
Leave we now Thy servant sleeping.

There the tears of earth are dried ;
    There its hidden things are clear ;
There the work of life is tried
    By a juster Judge than here.
FATHER, in Thy gracious keeping
Leave we now Thy servant sleeping.

There the sinful souls, that turn
    To the Cross their dying eyes,
All the love of CHRIST shall learn
    At His feet in Paradise.
FATHER, in Thy gracious keeping
Leave we now Thy servant sleeping.

BURIAL OF THE DEAD.

There no more the powers of hell
    Can prevail to mar their peace ;
CHRIST the LORD shall guard them well,
    He Who died for their release.
FATHER, in Thy gracious keeping
Leave we now Thy servant sleeping.

"Earth to earth, and dust to dust,"
    Calmly now the words we say,
Leaving *him* to sleep in trust
    Till the Resurrection-day.
FATHER, in Thy gracious keeping
Leave we now Thy servant sleeping. Amen.

At sea the following should be sung instead of the last verse:

Laid in ocean's quiet bed,
    Calmly now the words we say,
"Till the sea gives up her dead,"
    Till the Resurrection-day,
FATHER, in Thy gracious keeping
Leave we now Thy servant sleeping. Amen.

304 *It was said unto them, that they should rest yet for a little season.*

O LORD, to Whom the spirits live
    Of all the faithful pass'd away,
Unto their path that brightness give
    Which shineth to the perfect day.
O LAMB of GOD, Redeemer blest,
Grant them eternal light and rest.

Bless Thou the dead which die in Thee ;
    As Thou hast given them release,
So quicken them Thy face to see,
    And give them everlasting peace.
      O LAMB of GOD, &c.

In Thy green, pleasant pastures feed
 The sheep which Thou hast summon'd hence ;
And by the still, cool waters lead
 Thy flock in loving providence.
   O LAMB of GOD, &c.

How long, O Holy LORD, how long
 Must we and they expectant wait
To hear the gladsome bridal song,
 To see Thee in Thy royal state ?
   O LAMB of GOD, &c.

O hearken, Saviour, to their cry,
 O rend the heavens and come down,
Make up Thy jewels speedily,
 And set them in Thy golden crown.
   O LAMB of GOD, &c.

Direct us with Thine arm of might,
 And bring us, perfected with them,
To dwell within Thy city bright,
 The heavenly Jerusalem.
   O LAMB of GOD, &c. Amen.

305 *My soul was precious in thine eyes this day.*

FATHER, SON, and HOLY SPIRIT,
 At this dear one's grave,
Hear us pleading for Thy mercy,
 Hear, and save.

Loving FATHER, look in pity,
 While in prayer we bend ;
Into Thine own hands *his* spirit
 We commend.

Loving Saviour, dear Redeemer,
 Judge, Who judgest right,
May this soul, we pray, be precious
 In Thy sight.

Thou hast to the suffering body
  Granted sweet release;
May the soul, in Thy safe keeping,
  Rest in peace.
Grant *him* to behold Thy goodness,
  Set *him* near Thy side
From all stain of earth's defilement
  Purified.
FATHER, by Thy quickening SPIRIT,
  To this mortal clay
Grant a joyful resurrection
  In that day. Amen.

306   *Jesus called a little child unto him.*

FOR A CHILD.

FATHER, Who hast gather'd
  This dear child to rest,
Unto Thee we yield *him*,
  Sure Thou knowest best.

Thou, O LORD, Who gavest,
  Dost Thine own reclaim:
Thou, O LORD, hast taken—
  Blessèd still Thy Name!

Thine by right creative,
  By redemption Thine,
By regeneration
  And the holy sign.

Thou Who didst endow *him*
  With baptismal grace,
Now in love hast brought *him*
  To behold Thy face.

Safe from all earth's sorrow,
  Safe from all its pains,
Now this child of Adam
  Paradise regains:

Safe from all temptation,
  Safe from fear of sin,
Through the Blood of sprinkling
  Holy, bright, and clean.

Lay we this dear body
  In the earth to sleep,
His sweet soul commending
  Unto Thee to keep :—

Looking for the dawning
  Of that deathless day,
When all earthly shadows
  Shall have fled away.

Only grant us, FATHER,
  Courage in our strife,
And with *him* a portion
  In unending life.   Amen.

307   *They are in peace.*

Guter Hirt, Du hast gestillt.

FOR A CHILD.

TENDER Shepherd, Thou hast still'd
    Now Thy little lamb's brief weeping;
Oh how peaceful, pale, and mild,
  In its narrow bed 'tis sleeping,
      And no sigh of anguish sore
      Heaves that little bosom more.

In a world of pain and care,
  LORD, Thou wouldst no longer leave *him;*
To Thy meadows bright and fair
  Lovingly Thou dost receive *him;*
      Clothed in robes of spotless white
      Now *he* dwells with Thee in light.

(269)

BURIAL OF THE DEAD.

Ah, LORD JESU, grant that we
  There may live where *he* is living,
And the blissful pastures see
  That *his* heavenly food are giving :
    Lost awhile our treasured love,
    Gain'd for ever, safe above.   Amen.

The following Hymns are also suitable:

156 JESUS lives ! thy terrors now.
157 On the Resurrection morning.
159 The foe behind, the deep before.
244 O heavenly Jerusalem.
376 Brief life is here our portion.
381 Oh, what the joy and the glory must be.
387 Let saints on earth in concert sing.
425 My GOD, my FATHER, while I stray.
428 A few more years shall roll.
429 Days and moments quickly flying.
430 Sunset and evening star.
467 Rock of ages, cleft for me.
473 O let him whose sorrow.
490 When our heads are bow'd with woe.

GENERAL HYMNS.

308 *They rest not day and night, saying, Holy, holy, holy,
Lord God Almighty, which was, and is, and is to
come.*

HOLY, Holy, Holy ! LORD GOD Almighty !
  Early in the morning our song shall rise to
    Thee :
Holy, Holy, Holy ! Merciful and Mighty !
  GOD in Three Persons, Blessèd TRINITY !

Holy, Holy, Holy ! all the Saints adore Thee,
  Casting down their golden crowns around the
    glassy sea ;
Cherubim and Seraphim falling down before Thee,
Which wert, and art, and evermore shalt be.

oly, Holy, Holy ! though the darkness hide Thee,
Though the eye of sinful man Thy glory may
  not see,
ly Thou art Holy, there is none beside Thee
Perfect in power, in love, and purity.

oly, Holy, Holy ! LORD GOD Almighty !
All Thy works shall praise Thy Name, in earth,
  and sky, and sea :
oly, Holy, Holy ! Merciful and Mighty !
GOD in Three Persons, Blessèd TRINITY ! Amen.

09   *Hallowed be thy name.*

SOUND aloud Jehovah's praises ;
    Tell abroad the awful Name ;
Heav'n the ceaseless anthem raises,
    Let the earth her GOD proclaim,—
GOD, the hope of every nation,
GOD, the source of consolation,
    Holy, blessèd TRINITY !

This the Name from ancient ages
    Hidden in its dazzling light ;
This the Name that kings and sages
    Pray'd and strove to know aright,
Through GOD's wondrous Incarnation
Now reveal'd the world's salvation,
    Ever blessèd TRINITY !

Into this great Name and holy
    We all tribes and tongues baptize ;
Thus the Highest owns the lowly,
    Homeward, heav'nward, bids them rise,
Gathers them from every nation,
Bids them *join in* adoration
    Of the blessèd TRINITY !

In this Name the heart rejoices,
    Pouring forth its secret prayer ;
In this Name we lift our voices,
    And our common faith declare,
Off'ring praise and supplication,
And the thankful life's oblation,
      To the blessèd TRINITY !

Still Thy Name o'er earth and ocean
    Shall be carried, " GOD is Love,"
Whisper'd by the heart's devotion,
    Echo'd by the choirs above,
Hallow'd through all worlds for ever,
LORD, of life the only Giver,
      Blessèd, glorious TRINITY ! Amen.

310 *And one cried unto another, and said, Holy, Holy,
Holy, is the Lord of hosts; the whole earth is full of
his glory.*

BRIGHT the vision that delighted
    Once the sight of Judah's seer ;
Sweet the countless tongues united
    To entrance the prophet's ear.

Round the LORD in glory seated
    Cherubim and Seraphim
Fill'd His temple, and repeated
    Each to each th' alternate hymn ;

" LORD, Thy glory fills the heaven ;
    Earth is with its fulness stored ;
Unto Thee be glory given,
    Holy, Holy, Holy, LORD."

Heav'n is still with glory ringing,
    Earth takes up the Angels' cry,
" Holy, Holy, Holy,"—singing,
    " LORD of hosts, The LORD most High."

With His seraph train before Him,
  With His holy Church below,
Thus unite we to adore Him,
  Bid we thus our anthem flow;

"LORD, Thy glory fills the heaven;
  Earth is with its fulness stored;
Unto Thee be glory given,
  Holy, Holy, Holy, LORD." Amen.

11   *Sing unto the Lord, and praise his name.*

THREE in ONE, and ONE in THREE,
  Ruler of the earth and sea,
Hear us, while we lift to Thee
  Holy chant and psalm.

Light of lights ! with morning-shine
Lift on us Thy Light divine ;
And let charity benign
  Breathe on us her balm.

Light of lights ! when falls the even,
Let it close on sin forgiven ;
Fold us in the peace of heaven ;
  Shed a holy calm.

THREE in ONE and ONE in THREE,
Dimly here we worship Thee ;
With the Saints hereafter we
  Hope to bear the palm. Amen.

12   *Let us therefore come boldly unto the throne of grace,*
that we may obtain mercy, and find grace to help in
time of need.

FATHER, of heav'n, Whose love profound
  A ransom for our souls hath found,
Before Thy throne we sinners bend,
To us Thy *pardoning love* extend.

Almighty Son, Incarnate Word,
Our Prophet, Priest, Redeemer, Lord,
Before Thy throne we sinners bend,
To us Thy saving grace extend.
Eternal Spirit, by Whose breath
The soul is raised from sin and death,
Before Thy throne we sinners bend,
To us Thy quickening power extend.
Thrice Holy ! Father, Spirit, Son ;
Mysterious Godhead, Three in One,
Before Thy throne we sinners bend,
Grace, pardon, life to us extend.   Amen.

313 *The grace of our Lord Jesus Christ, and the love*
God, and the communion of the Holy Ghost be wi
you all.

MAY the grace of Christ our Saviour,
   And the Father's boundless love,
With the Holy Spirit's favour,
   Rest upon us from above.
Thus may we abide in union
   With each other and the Lord,
And possess, in sweet communion,
   Joys which earth cannot afford.   Amen.

314   *Lo, these are parts of his ways.*

HAIL, Father, Whose creating call
   Unnumber'd worlds attend ;
Who art in all and over all,
   Thyself both Source and End :
In light unsearchable enthroned
   Whom Angels dimly see,
The Fountain of the Godhead own'd,
   First-named among the Three.
From Thee, through an eternal Now,
   Springs Thy co-equal Son ;
An everlasting Father Thou,
   Ere time began to run.

Not quite display'd to worlds above,
  Nor quite on earth conceal'd,
By wondrous, unexhausted love
  To mortal man reveal'd ;

When Nature's outworn robe shall be
  Exchanged for new attire,
And earth, which rose at Thy decree,
  Dissolve before Thy fire ;

Thy Name, O God, be still adored
  Through ages without end,
Whom none but Thine essential Word
  And Spirit comprehend.   Amen.

5   *Stand up and bless the Lord your God.*

STAND up, and bless the Lord,
  Ye people of His choice ;
Stand up, and bless the Lord your God
  With heart, and soul, and voice.

Though high above all praise,
  Above all blessing high,
Who would not fear His holy Name,
  And laud and magnify ?

Oh, for the living flame
  From His own altar brought,
To touch our lips, our minds inspire,
  And wing to heav'n our thought.

God is our strength and song,
  And His salvation ours ;
Then be His love in Christ proclaim'd
  With all our ransom'd powers.

Stand up, and bless the Lord,
  The Lord your God adore ;
Stand up, and bless His glorious Name
  Henceforth for evermore.   Amen.

316   *O be joyful in the Lord, all ye lands.*

ALL people that on earth do dwell,
     Sing to the LORD with cheerful voice ;
Him serve with fear, His praise forth tell,
Come ye before Him, and rejoice.

The LORD, ye know, is GOD indeed ;
Without our aid He did us make ;
We are His folk, He doth us feed,
And for His sheep He doth us take.

O enter then His gates with praise,
Approach with joy His courts unto ;
Praise, laud, and bless His Name always, .
For it is seemly so to do.

For why, the LORD our GOD is good ;
His mercy is for ever sure ;
His truth at all times firmly stood,
And shall from age to age endure.

To FATHER, SON, and HOLY GHOST,
The GOD Whom heav'n and earth adore,
From men and from the Angel-host
Be praise and glory evermore.   Amen.

317   *O be joyful in the Lord, all ye lands.*

BEFORE JEHOVAH'S awful throne,
     Ye nations, bow with sacred joy ;
Know that the LORD is GOD alone ;
He can create, and He destroy.

His sov'reign power, without our aid,
Made us of clay, and form'd us men ;
And when like wand'ring sheep we stray'd,
He brought us to His fold again.

We'll crowd Thy gates with thankful songs ;
High as the heav'ns our voices raise ;
And earth, with her ten thousand tongues,
Shall fill Thy courts with sounding praise.

Wide as the world is Thy command ;
Vast as eternity Thy love ;
Firm as a rock Thy truth shall stand,
When rolling years shall cease to move.

Amen.

18 *His name only is excellent, and his praise above heaven and earth.*

LET all the world in every corner sing,
My GOD and King !
The heav'ns are not too high,
His praise may thither fly ;
The earth is not too low,
His praises there may grow.
Let all the world in every corner sing,
My GOD and King !

Let all the world in every corner sing,
My GOD and King !
The Church with psalms must shout,
No door can keep them out ;
But above all the heart
Must bear the longest part.
Let all the world in every corner sing,
My GOD and King ! Amen.

19 *When I laid the foundations of the earth . . . when the morning stars sang together, and all the sons of God shouted for joy.*

SONGS of praise the Angels sang,
Heaven with Alleluias rang,
When creation was begun,
When GOD *spake* and it was done.

(277)

K 2

Songs of praise awoke the morn
When the Prince of peace was born ;
Songs of praise arose when He
Captive led captivity.

Heav'n and earth must pass away,
Songs of praise shall crown that day ;
GOD will make new heav'ns and earth,
Songs of praise shall hail their birth.

And will man alone be dumb
Till that glorious kingdom come ?
No, the Church delights to raise
Psalms and hymns and songs of praise.

Saints below, with heart and voice,
Still in songs of praise rejoice ;
Learning here, by faith and love,
Songs of praise to sing above.

Hymns of glory, songs of praise,
FATHER, unto Thee we raise,
JESU, glory unto Thee,
With the SPIRIT, ever be.   Amen.

320 *This glorious and fearful name, the Lord thy God.*

GLORIOUS is Thy Name, O LORD !
   Heav'n and earth with one accord
Tell Thy greatness, part reveal'd,
But the larger part conceal'd.
    How shall we poor sinners dare
    Seek Thy face in praise and prayer ?

Fearful is Thy Name, O LORD !
Dread Thy voice, and sharp Thy sword ;
Thunders roll around Thy path :
None can stand before Thy wrath !
    How shall trembling sinners dare
    Lift their voice in praise and prayer ?

Yet with all Thy wondrous might,
Far beyond our mortal sight,
Perfect wisdom, boundless powers,
Thou, O glorious GOD ! art ours.
So, though fill'd with awe, we dare
Name Thy Name in praise and prayer.

Since, to save a world undone,
Thou didst give Thine only SON,
All Thy greatness, LORD most High,
Brings Thee to our hearts more nigh.
Thus in faith and hope we dare
Claim Thy love in praise and prayer.
Amen.

1 *Thus saith the high and lofty One that inhabiteth eternity, whose name is Holy: I dwell in the high and holy place, with him also that is of a contrite and humble spirit.*

MY GOD, how wonderful Thou art,
Thy majesty how bright,
How beautiful Thy mercy-seat,
In depths of burning light !

How dread are Thine eternal years,
O everlasting LORD,
By prostrate spirits day and night
Incessantly adored !

How wonderful, how beautiful,
The sight of Thee must be,
Thine endless wisdom, boundless power,
And awful purity !

Oh, how I fear Thee, Living GOD,
With deepest, tenderest fears,
And worship Thee with trembling hope,
And penitential tears !

Yet I may love Thee too, O LORD,
 Almighty as Thou art,
For Thou hast stoop'd to ask of me
 `The love of my poor heart.

No earthly father loves like Thee,
 No mother, e'er so mild,
Bears and forbears as Thou hast done
 With me Thy sinful child.

FATHER of JESUS, love's reward,
 What rapture will it be
Prostrate before Thy throne to lie,
 And gaze and gaze on Thee. Amen.

322 *How unsearchable are his judgments.*

LORD, my weak thought in vain would climb
 To search the starry vault profound ;
In vain would wing her flight sublime,
 To find creation's utmost bound.

But weaker yet that thought must prove
 To search Thy great eternal plan,—
Thy sovereign counsels, born of love
 Long ages ere the world began.

When my dim reason would demand
 Why that, or this, Thou dost ordain,
By some vast deep I seem to stand,
 Whose secrets I must ask in vain.

When doubts disturb my troubled breast
 And all is dark as night to me,
Here, as on solid rock, I rest,
 That so it seemeth good to Thee.

Be this my joy, that evermore
 Thou rulest all things at Thy will ;
Thy sovereign wisdom I adore,
 And calmly, sweetly, trust Thee still. Amen.

323 *I am the Lord; I change not.*

LORD GOD ! by Whom all change is wrought,
  By Whom new things to birth are brought,
In Whom no change is known :
Whate'er Thou dost, whate'er Thou art,
Thy people still in Thee have part ;
  Still, still Thou art our own.

Ancient of Days ! we dwell in Thee ;
Out of Thine own eternity
  Our peace and joy are wrought :
We rest in our eternal GOD,
And make secure and sweet abode
  With Thee Who changest not.

Each stedfast promise we possess ;
Thine everlasting truth we bless,
  Thine everlasting love :
Th' unfailing Helper close we clasp,
The everlasting arms we grasp,
  Nor from the refuge move.

In Thee we rise, in Thee we rest ;
We stay at home, we go in quest,
  Still Thou art our abode ;
As rapture swells, the wonder grows
Full on us new life still flows
  From our unchanging GOD.   Amen.

The Lord God omnipotent reigneth.

LET all the world rejoice,
  The great Jehovah reigns,
The thunders are His awful voice,
  Our life His will ordains ;
    The glories of His Name
The lightnings, floods, and hail proclaim.

He rules by sea and land,
  All space His word obeys,
He holds the oceans in His hand,
  And mighty mountains weighs;
  Unequall'd and alone
In majesty He fills His throne.

The universe He made
  By His prevailing might;
The earth's foundations deep He laid
  And scatter'd ancient night;
  All heav'n, and earth, and sea
Proclaim'd His awful majesty.

When the bright orb of day
  First gleam'd with ruddy light;
When first the moon, with silver ray,
  March'd up the vault of night;
  And stars bedeck'd the skies
That seem'd creation's thousand eyes;

And earth's fair form was seen
  With flowers and blossoms drest;
And trees, and fields, and meadows green
  Adorn'd her youthful breast,
  Hung out in boundless space
Amid the ocean's cool embrace;

Glad was the Angel throng
  To see His might prevail;
And loud they sung a joyful song
  This universe to hail,
  While yet in youth it stood;
The Maker, too, pronounced it good.

But this fair world shall die,
  The creature of a day;
In ashes and in ruins lie,
  Its glory pass'd away;

Again this mighty earth
Shall be as ere it came to birth.

Soon shall the day be o'er
Of yonder brilliant sun,
And he shall set to rise no more,
His race of glory run ;
From heaven's vault all soon
Shall fade the stars, and yon pale moon.

But ever fix'd, the throne
Of the Eternal One
Shall stand, when time and space are gone,
Unequall'd and alone ;
New worlds to make at will,
And His own wise designs fulfil.   Amen.

5   *The heavens declare the glory of God.*

GLORY to GOD, all the heavens are telling,
   Glory to GOD, in the earth and the sky,
Glory to GOD, the loud anthem is swelling,
         Glory to GOD.
GOD in Three persons transcendent, supernal,
GOD the most Mighty, most Holy, most High,
GOD uncreated Creator eternal—
         Glory to GOD.

GOD the all-present, all-seeing, all-giving,
GOD on Whom all things for ever depend,
GOD ever loving, and GOD ever living—
         Glory to GOD.
GOD the great FATHER, Upholder, Defender,
GOD the REDEEMER, our Saviour, and Friend,
GOD the Blest SPIRIT, the patient, the tender.
         Glory to GOD.   Amen.

(283)

GENERAL HYMNS.

326 *Praise the Lord, O my soul: O Lord my God, thou art become exceeding glorious; thou art clothed with majesty and honour.*

O WORSHIP the King,
   All-glorious above;
O gratefully sing
   His power and His love;
Our Shield and Defender,
   The Ancient of days,
Pavilion'd in splendour,
   And girded with praise.

O tell of His might,
   O sing of His grace,
Whose robe is the light,
   Whose canopy space;
His chariots of wrath
   The deep thunder clouds form,
And dark is His path
   On the wings of the storm.

The earth with its store
   Of wonders untold,
Almighty, Thy power
   Hath founded of old;
Hath stablish'd it fast
   By a changeless decree,
And round it hath cast,
   Like a mantle, the sea.

Thy bountiful care
   What tongue can recite?
It breathes in the air,
   It shines in the light;
It streams from the hills,
   It descends to the plain,
And sweetly distils
   In the dew and the rain.

Frail children of dust,
  And feeble as frail,
In Thee do we trust,
  Nor find Thee to fail ;
Thy mercies how tender !
  How firm to the end !
Our Maker, Defender,
  Redeemer, and Friend.

O measureless Might,
  Ineffable Love,
While Angels delight
  To hymn Thee above,
Thy humbler creation,
  Though feeble their lays,
With true adoration
  Shall sing to Thy praise. Amen.

327 *O praise the Lord of heaven, praise him in the height.*

PRAISE the LORD ! ye heav'ns, adore Him,
  Praise Him, Angels, in the height ;
Sun and moon, rejoice before Him,
  Praise Him, all ye stars and light :
Praise the LORD ! for He hath spoken,
  Worlds His mighty voice obey'd ;
Laws, which never shall be broken,
  For their guidance He hath made.

Praise the LORD ! for He is glorious ;
  Never shall His promise fail ;
God hath made His Saints victorious,
  Sin and death shall not prevail.
Praise the GOD of our salvation ;
  Hosts on high, His power proclaim ;
Heav'n and earth, and all creation,
  Laud and magnify His Name ! Amen.

328   *All thy works praise thee, O Lord.*

Cantemus cuncti melodum.

THE strain upraise of joy and praise, Alleluia !

To the glory of their King
Let the ransom'd people sing   Alleluia !

And the choirs that dwell on high
Swell the chorus in the sky,   Alleluia !

Ye, through the fields of Paradise that roam,
Ye blessèd ones, repeat through that bright home
                    Alleluia !

Ye planets glittering on your heavenly way,
Ye shining constellations, join and say   Alleluia !

Ye clouds that onward sweep,
Ye winds on pinions light,
Ye thunders, echoing loud and deep,
Ye lightnings, wildly bright,
In sweet consent unite your   Alleluia !

Ye floods and ocean billows,
Ye storms and winter snow,
Ye days of cloudless beauty,
Hoar frost and summer glow,
Ye groves that wave in spring,
And glorious forests, sing   Alleluia !

First let the birds, with painted plumage gay,
Exalt their great Creator's praise, and say Alleluia !

Then let the beasts of earth, with varying strain,
Join in creation's hymn, and cry again   Alleluia !

Here let the mountains thunder forth sonorous
                    Alleluia !

There let the valleys sing in gentler chorus
                    Alleluia !

Thou jubilant abyss of ocean, cry   Alleluia !

Ye tracts of earth and continents, reply   Alleluia !

To GOD, Who all creation made,
The frequent hymn be duly paid,   Alleluia !

This is the strain, the eternal strain, the LORD of
     all things loves,   Alleluia !

This is the song, the heavenly song, that CHRIST
     Himself approves,   Alleluia !

Wherefore we sing, both heart and voice awaking,
                   Alleluia !

And children's voices echo, answer making,
                   Alleluia !

Now from all men be out-pour'd
Alleluia to the LORD ;
With Alleluia evermore
The SON and SPIRIT we adore.
Praise be done to the THREE in ONE.
     Alleluia ! Alleluia ! Alleluia ! Amen.

329 *All thy works praise thee, O Lord; and thy saints
     give thanks unto thee.*

LORD GOD ! our praise we give
     For lake, and sea, and mountain ;
The power by which we live
     Flows freely from Thy fountain ;
     Like dew at morn and eve,
       Thou enterest every heart
     Of those who will receive,
       Thy blessing to impart.

With dawn and sunset light
     Thy glory Thou preparest ;
By wind and storm Thy might,
     Thy *love by* calm, declarest ;

The rainbows Thou dost bend
　Speak peace to us afar ;
At night-time Thou canst send
　A word from every star.

On earth, in heav'n above,
　One anthem life is singing ;
The creatures as they rove,
　The bird in beauty winging,
　　The wave with rhythmic call,
　　The music of the wind,
　　The lake, the waterfall,
　　　Praise one Creator's mind.

Shall we, whom GOD has made
　Than Angels little lower,
Not join the homage paid
　And hymn th' almighty power,
　　Till hearts have all confess'd
　　This truth with lips sincere,
　　That he alone can rest
　　　Who finds GOD everywhere? Amen

330 *The earth is full of the goodness of the Lord.*

A LMIGHTY FATHER of all things that be,
　　Our life, our work, we consecrate to Thee :
Whose heav'ns declare Thy glory from above,
Whose earth below is witness to Thy love.

For well we know this weary, soilèd earth
Is yet Thine own by right of its new birth ;
Since that great Cross uprear'd on Calvary
Redeem'd it from its fault and shame to Thee.

Thine still the changeful beauty of the hills,
The purple valleys fleck'd with silver rills,
The ocean glistening 'neath the golden rays,
They all are Thine, and voiceless speak Thy praise.

Thou dost the strength to workman's arm impart,
From Thee the skill'd musician's mystic art,
The grace of poet's pen or painter's hand
To teach the loveliness of sea and land.

Then grant us, LORD, in all things Thee to own,
To dwell within the shadow of Thy throne;
To speak and work, to think, and live, and move,
Reflecting Thy own nature, which is love.

That so, by CHRIST redeem'd from sin and shame,
And hallow'd by Thy SPIRIT's cleansing flame,
Ourselves, our work, and all our powers may be
A sacrifice acceptable to Thee.   Amen.

331 *The invisible things of him from the creation of the world are clearly seen, being understood by the things that are made.*

THERE is a book, who runs may read,
    Which heav'nly truth imparts,
And all the lore its scholars need,
    Pure eyes and Christian hearts.

The works of GOD above, below,
    Within us and around,
Are pages in that book, to show
    How GOD Himself is found.

The glorious sky, embracing all,
    Is like the Maker's love,
Wherewith encompass'd, great and small
    In peace and order move.

* The Moon above, the Church below,
    A wondrous race they run;
But all their radiance, all their glow,
    Each borrows of its Sun.

* The Saviour lends the light and heat
    That crown His holy hill;
The Saints, like stars, around His seat
    Perform their courses still.

GENERAL HYMNS.

* The Saints above are stars in heaven—
    What are the Saints on earth ?
Like trees they stand whom GOD has given,
    Our Eden's happy birth.

* Faith is their fix'd unswerving root,
    Hope their unfading flower,
Fair deeds of charity their fruit,
    The glory of their bower.

The dew of heav'n is like Thy grace,
    It steals in silence down ;
But where it lights, the favour'd place
    By richest fruits is known.

One Name, above all glorious names,
    With its ten thousand tongues
The everlasting sea proclaims,
    Echoing Angelic songs.

The raging fire, the roaring wind,
    Thy boundless power display :
But in the gentler breeze we find
    Thy SPIRIT'S viewless way.

Two worlds are ours : 'tis only sin
    Forbids us to descry
The mystic heav'n and earth within,
    Plain as the sea and sky.

Thou Who hast given me eyes to see
    And love this sight so fair,
Give me a heart to find out Thee,
    And read Thee everywhere.   Amen.

* *These verses can be omitted.*

332 *O send out thy light and thy truth that they may lead me.*

GIVE light, O LORD, that we may learn
  The way that leads to Thee,
That where our hearts true joys discern,
    Our life may be.

Give light, O LORD, that we may know
  Thy one unchanging truth,
And follow, all our days below,
    Our Guide in youth.

Give light, O LORD, that we may see
  Where wisdom bids beware,
And turn our doubting minds to Thee
    In faithful prayer.

Give light, O LORD, that we may look
  Beneath, around, above,
And learn from nature's living book
    Thy power and love.

Give light, O LORD, that we may read
  All signs that Thou art near,
And, while we live, in word and deed
    Thy Name revere.

Give light, O. LORD, that we may trace
  In trial, pain, and loss,
In poorest lot, and lowest place,
    A Saviour's Cross.

Give light, O LORD, that we may see
  A home beyond the sky,
Where all who live in CHRIST with Thee
    Shall never die.   Amen.

333 *Every good gift and every perfect gift is from above.*

FOR the beauty of the earth,
   For the beauty of the skies,
For the love which from our birth
   Over and around us lies,
Lord of all, to Thee we raise
This our grateful hymn of praise.

For the beauty of each hour
   Of the day and of the night,
Hill and vale, and tree and flower,
   Sun and moon and stars of light,
Lord of all, to Thee we raise
This our grateful hymn of praise.

For the joy of human love,
   Brother, sister, parent, child,
Friends on earth, and friends above,
   Pleasures pure and undefiled,
Lord of all, to Thee we raise
This our grateful hymn of praise.

For each perfect gift of Thine
   To our race so freely given,
Graces human and divine,
   Flowers of earth and buds of heaven,
Lord of all, to Thee we raise
This our grateful hymn of praise.   Amen.

334 *Thou, O Lord, art our Father; . . . thy name is
from everlasting.*

ALMIGHTY Father, Unoriginate,
   Whom no man hath seen ever, nor can see ;
Who reignest Bless'd and Only Potentate,
   Light unapproachable encircling Thee :
Almighty Father, hallow'd be Thy Name,
Who ever art, unchangeably the same.

Thou lovest us, else had we never been :
    Before we were, in ages long ago,
Thy love had us and all our want foreseen,
    Creating us that we Thy love might know.
Yea, FATHER, Thou, in Whom we live and move,
Hast loved us with an everlasting love.

Thou madest man immortal at the first,
    An image of Thine own eternity ;
And when he fell from life, through sin accurst,
    And lost his right to the life-giving tree,
Thy love, unconquer'd, would to him restore
His life ennobled and for evermore.

Such was Thy love, Thou didst not even spare
    Thy Best-beloved, but gav'st Him for us all ;
To live that human life beyond compare,
    And dying, by His death retrieve our fall.
In Him Thy love unbounded we behold,
For, giving Him, Thou canst not aught withhold.

Thou knowest what we are, how frail and blind,
    Thou still rememb'rest that we are but dust :
Like as a father pitieth, Thou art kind,
    Thy justice kindness and Thy kindness just.
Then hear Thy children's prayer from heav'n Thy
      throne,
FATHER, Thy kingdom come ; Thy will be done.
                          Amen.

335 *Worthy is the Lamb that was slain to receive power,*
and riches, and wisdom, and strength, and honour,
and glory, and blessing.

FROM highest heav'n th' Eternal SON,
    With GOD the FATHER ever One,
Came down to suffer and to die ;
For love of sinful man He bore
Our human griefs and troubles sore,
    Our load of guilt and misery.

Rejoice, ye Saints of GOD, and praise
The LAMB Who died, His flock to raise
   From sin and everlasting woe ;
With Angels round the throne above
O tell the wonders of His love,
   The joys that from His mercy flow.

In darkest shades of night we lay,
Without a beam to guide our way,
   Or hope of aught beyond the grave ;
But He has brought us life and light,
And open'd heaven to our sight,
   And lives for ever strong to save.

Rejoice, ye Saints of GOD, rejoice ;
Sing out, and praise with cheerful voice
   The LAMB Whom heav'n and earth adore ;
To Him Who gave His only SON,
To GOD the SPIRIT, with Them One,
   Be praise and glory evermore.　Amen.

336　*The love of Christ which passeth knowledge.*
O amor quam ecstaticus.

O LOVE, how deep ! how broad ! how high !
   It fills the heart with ecstasy,
That GOD, the SON of GOD, should take
Our mortal form for mortals' sake.

He sent no Angel to our race
Of higher or of lower place,
But wore the robe of human frame
Himself, and to this lost world came.

For us He was baptized, and bore
His holy fast, and hunger'd sore ;
For us temptations sharp He knew ;
For us the tempter overthrew.

For us He pray'd, for us He taught,
For us His daily works He wrought,
By words, and signs, and actions, thus
Still seeking not Himself but us.

For us to wicked men betray'd,
Scourged, mock'd, in purple robe array'd,
He bore the shameful Cross and death ;
For us at length gave up His breath.

For us He rose from death again,
For us He went on high to reign,
For us He sent His SPIRIT here
To guide, to strengthen, and to cheer.

To Him Whose boundless love has won
Salvation for us through His SON,
To GOD the FATHER, glory be
Both now and through eternity. Amen.

37 *The second man is the Lord from heaven.*

PRAISE to the Holiest in the height,
   And in the depth be praise,
In all His words most wonderful,
   Most sure in all His ways.

O loving wisdom of our GOD !
   When all was sin and shame,
A second Adam to the fight
   And to the rescue came.

O wisest love ! that flesh and blood,
   Which did in Adam fail,
Should strive afresh against the foe,
   Should strive and should prevail ;

And that a higher gift than grace
   Should flesh and blood refine,
GOD's presence and His very Self,
   And Essence all-divine.

O generous love ! that He Who smote
   In Man for man the foe,
The double agony in Man
   `For man should* undergo ;

And in the garden secretly,
　　And on the Cross on high,
Should teach His brethren, and inspire
　　To suffer and to die.
Praise to the Holiest in the height,
　　And in the depth be praise,
In all His words most wonderful,
　　Most sure in all His ways.　Amen.

338 *There is none other name under heaven given ame*
men whereby we must be saved.

Gloriosi Salvatoris.

TO the Name of our salvation
　　Laud and honour let us pay,
Which for many a generation
　　Hid in GOD'S foreknowledge lay,
But with holy exultation
　　We may sing aloud to-day.

JESUS is the Name we treasure,
　　Name beyond what words can tell ;
Name of gladness, Name of pleasure,
　　Ear and heart delighting well ;
Name of sweetness passing measure,
　　Saving us from sin and hell.

'Tis the Name for adoration,
　　Name for songs of victory,
Name for holy meditation
　　In this vale of misery,
Name for joyful veneration
　　By the citizens on high.

'Tis the Name that whoso preacheth
　　Speaks like music to the ear ;
Who in prayer this Name beseecheth
　　Sweetest comfort findeth near ;
Who its perfect wisdom reacheth
　　Heav'nly joy possesseth here.

JESUS is the Name prevailing
  Over every name by right;
At this Name, in terror quailing,
  Powers of hell are put to flight:
GOD, in mercy never failing,
  Saves us by this Name of might.

Therefore we in love adoring
  This most blessèd Name revere,
Holy JESU, Thee imploring
  So to write it in us here,
That hereafter heavenward soaring
  We may sing with Angels there.   Amen.

39 *In the beginning was the Word, and the Word was
with God, and the Word was God. All things were
made by him.*

JESUS is GOD : the solid earth,
  The ocean broad and bright,
The countless stars, like golden dust,
  That strew the skies at night,
The wheeling storm, the dreadful fire,
  The pleasant wholesome air,
The summer's sun, the winter's frost,
  His own creations were.

JESUS is GOD : the glorious bands
  Of golden Angels sing
Songs of adoring praise to Him,
  Their Maker and their King.
He was true GOD in Bethlehem's crib,
  On Calvary's Cross true GOD ;
He, Who in heav'n Eternal reign'd,
  In time on earth abode.

JESUS is GOD : let sorrow come,
  And pain, and every ill,
All are worth while, for all are means
  His glory to fulfil ;

Worth while a thousand years of earth
  To speak one little word,
If by that "I believe" we own
  The GODHEAD of our LORD. Amen.

340 *Blessed are they that have not seen, and yet have*
  believed.

WE saw Thee not when Thou didst come
    To this poor world of sin and death,
Nor e'er beheld Thy cottage-home
  In that despisèd Nazareth ;
But we believe Thy footsteps trod
Its streets and plains, Thou SON of GOD.

We did not see Thee lifted high
  Amid that wild and savage crew,
Nor heard Thy meek, imploring cry,
  "Forgive, they know not what they do ;"
Yet we believe the deed was done,
Which shook the earth and veil'd the sun.

We stood not by the empty tomb
  Where late Thy sacred Body lay,
Nor sat within that upper room,
  Nor met Thee in the open way ;
But we believe that Angels said,
"Why seek the living with the dead ?"

We did not mark the chosen few,
  When Thou didst through the clouds ascend,
First lift to heav'n their wondering view,
  Then to the earth all prostrate bend ;
Yet we believe that mortal eyes
Beheld that journey to the skies.

And now that Thou dost reign on high,
  And thence Thy waiting people bless,
No ray of glory from the sky
  Doth shine upon our wilderness ;
But we believe Thy faithful word,
And watch for our returning LORD. Amen.

11 *Thou shalt call his name JESUS, for he shall save his people from their sins.*

Victis sibi cognomina.

CONQUERING kings their titles take
From the foes they captive make :
JESUS, by a nobler deed,
From the thousands He hath freed.

Yes : none other name is given
Unto mortals under heaven,
Which can make the dead arise,
And exalt them to the skies.

That which CHRIST so hardly wrought,
That which He so dearly bought,
That salvation, brethren, say,
Shall we madly cast away ?

Rather gladly for that Name
Bear the cross, endure the shame ;
Joyfully for Him to die
Is not death but victory.

JESU, Who dost condescend
To be call'd the sinner's Friend,
Hear us, as to Thee we pray,
Glorying in Thy Name to-day.

Glory to the FATHER be,
Glory, Holy SON, to Thee,
Glory to the HOLY GHOST,
From the Saints and Angel-host.   Amen.

12 *The everlasting Father, the Prince of peace.*

Summi parentis filio.

TO CHRIST, the Prince of peace,
And SON of GOD most High,
The Father of the world to come,
We lift our joyful cry.

Deep in His heart for us
The wound of love He bore,
That love which He enkindles still
In hearts that Him adore.

O JESU, Victim Blest,
What else but love divine
Could Thee constrain to open thus
That sacred heart of Thine ?

O wondrous Fount of love,
O Well of waters free,
O heav'nly Flame, refining Fire,
O burning Charity !

Hide us in Thy dear heart,
JESU, our Saviour Blest,
So shall we find Thy plenteous grace,
And heav'n's eternal rest.   Amen.

343 *I heard the voice of many angels . . . saying, . . .*
Worthy is the Lamb that was slain to receive power,
and riches, and wisdom, and strength, and honour,
and glory, and blessing.

COME, let us join our cheerful songs
With Angels round the throne ;
Ten thousand thousand are their tongues,
But all their joys are one.

" Worthy the LAMB that died," they cry,
" To be exalted thus ; "
" Worthy the LAMB," our lips reply,
" For He was slain for us."

JESUS is worthy to receive
Honour and power divine ;
And blessings more than we can give
Be, LORD, for ever Thine.

Let all creation join in one
To bless the sacred Name
Of Him that sits upon the throne,
And to adore the LAMB.   Amen.

344 *Jesus saith unto him, I am the way, the truth, and the life.*

THOU art the Way ; by Thee alone
  From sin and death we flee :
And he who would the FATHER seek
  Must seek Him, LORD, by Thee.

Thou art the Truth ; Thy word alone
  True wisdom can impart ;
Thou only canst inform the mind,
  And purify the heart.

Thou art the Life ; the rending tomb
  Proclaims Thy conquering arm ;
And those who put their trust in Thee
  Nor death nor hell shall harm.

Thou art the Way, the Truth, the Life,
  Grant us that Way to know,
That Truth to keep, that Life to win,
  Whose joys eternal flow.   Amen.

345 *We have a great high priest, that is passed into the heavens . . . Let us therefore come boldly unto the throne of grace.*

WHERE high the heav'nly temple stands,
  The house of GOD not made with hands,
A great High-Priest our nature wears,
The Guardian of mankind appears.

He Who for men their Surety stood,
And pour'd on earth His precious Blood,
Pursues in heav'n His mighty plan,
The Saviour and the Friend of man.

Though now ascended up on high,
He bends on earth a brother's eye ;
Partaker of the human name,
He *knows the frailty* of our frame.

Our fellow Sufferer yet retains
A fellow-feeling of our pains,
And still remembers in the skies
His tears, His agonies, and cries.

In every pang that rends the heart
The Man of Sorrows had a part ;
He sympathizes with our grief,
And to the sufferer sends relief.

With boldness therefore at the throne
Let us make all our sorrows known,
And ask the aid of heav'nly power
To help us in the evil hour.   Amen.

346 *Rejoice in the Lord alway, and again I say, rejoice.*

REJOICE, the LORD is King,
 Your LORD and King adore ;
Mortals, give thanks and sing,
 And triumph evermore :
Lift up your heart, lift up your voice ;
Rejoice, again I say, rejoice.

JESUS, the Saviour, reigns,
 The GOD of truth and love :
When He had purged our stains,
 He took His seat above :
Lift up your heart, lift up your voice ;
Rejoice, again I say, rejoice.

His Kingdom cannot fail ;
 He rules o'er earth and heaven ;
The keys of death and hell
 Are to our JESUS given :
Lift up your heart, lift up your voice ;
Rejoice, again I say, rejoice.

He sits at GOD's right hand
  Till all His foes submit,
And bow to His command,
  And fall beneath His feet :
Lift up your heart, lift up your voice ;
Rejoice, again I say, rejoice. Amen.

47 *Wherefore God also hath highly exalted him, and given him a name which is above every name: that at the name of Jesus every knee should bow.*

AT the Name of JESUS
  Every knee shall bow,
Every tongue confess Him
  King of glory now ;
'Tis the FATHER's pleasure
  We should call Him LORD,
Who from the beginning
  Was the mighty WORD.

At His voice creation
  Sprang at once to sight,
All the Angel faces,
  All the hosts of light,
Thrones and Dominations,
  Stars upon their way,
All the heav'nly Orders,
  In their great array.

Humbled for a season,
  To receive a Name
From the lips of sinners
  Unto whom He came,
Faithfully He bore it
  Spotless to the last,
Brought it back victorious
  When from death He pass'd :

Bore it up triumphant
　　With its human light,
Through all ranks of creatures,
　　To the central height,
To the throne of GODHEAD,
　　To the FATHER's breast ;
Fill'd it with the glory
　　Of that perfect rest.

Name Him, brothers, name Him,
　　With love as strong as death,
But with awe and wonder,
　　And with bated breath ;
He is GOD the Saviour,
　　He is CHRIST the LORD,
Ever to be worshipp'd,
　　Trusted, and adored.

In your hearts enthrone Him ;
　　There let Him subdue
All that is not holy,
　　All that is not true :
Crown Him as your Captain
　　In temptation's hour ;
Let His will enfold you
　　In its light and power.

Brothers, this LORD JESUS
　　Shall return again,
With His FATHER's glory,
　　With His Angel train ;
For all wreaths of empire
　　Meet upon His brow
And our hearts confess Him
　　King of glory now.　　Amen.

348 *Sing ye to the Lord, for he hath triumphed gloriously.*

PRAISE the LORD through every nation ;
   His holy arm hath wrought salvation ;
  Exalt Him on His FATHER'S throne ;
Praise your King, ye Christian legions,
Who now prepares in heav'nly regions
  Unfailing mansions for His own :
    With voice and minstrelsy
    Extol His majesty :
      Alleluia !
His praise shall sound all nature round,
Where'er the race of man is found.

GOD with GOD dominion sharing,
And Man with man our image bearing,
  Gentile and Jew to Him are given :
Praise your Saviour, ransom'd sinners,
Of life, through Him, immortal winners ;
  No longer heirs of earth, but heaven.
    O beatific sight
    To view His face in light :
      Alleluia !
And, while we see, transform'd to be
From bliss to bliss eternally.

JESU, LORD, our Captain glorious,
O'er sin, and death, and hell victorious,
  Wisdom and might to Thee belong :
We confess, proclaim, adore Thee,
We bow the knee, we fall before Thee,
  Thy love henceforth shall be our song :
    The cross meanwhile we bear,
    The crown ere long to wear.
      Alleluia !
Thy reign extend world without end,
Let praise *from all* to Thee ascend. Amen.

349 *And on his head were many crowns.*

CROWN Him with many crowns,
The LAMB upon His throne ;
Hark ! how the heav'nly anthem drowns
All music but its own :
Awake, my soul, and sing
Of Him Who died for thee,
And hail Him as thy matchless King
Through all eternity.

Crown Him the Virgin's Son,
The GOD Incarnate born,
Whose arm those crimson trophies won
Which now His brow adorn :
Fruit of the mystic Rose,
As of that Rose the Stem ;
The Root whence mercy ever flows,
The Babe of Bethlehem.

Crown Him the LORD of love :
Behold His hands and side,
Those wounds yet visible above
In beauty glorified :
No Angel in the sky
Can fully bear that sight,
But downward bends his burning eye
At mysteries so bright.

Crown Him the LORD of peace,
Whose power a sceptre sways
From pole to pole, that wars may cease,
And all be prayer and praise :
His reign shall know no end,
And round His piercèd feet
Fair flowers of Paradise extend
Their fragrance ever sweet.

Crown Him the LORD of years,
The Potentate of time,
Creator of the rolling spheres,
Ineffably sublime :
All hail, Redeemer, hail !
For Thou hast died for me ;
Thy praise shall never, never fail
Throughout eternity.   Amen.

50   *King of kings, and Lord of lords.*

ALL hail the power of JESUS' Name :
Let Angels prostrate fall ;
Bring forth the royal diadem
And crown Him LORD of all.

Crown Him, ye morning stars of light,
Who fix'd this floating ball ;
Now hail the Strength of Israel's might,
And crown Him LORD of all.

Crown Him, ye Martyrs of your GOD,
Who from His altar call ;
Extol the Stem-of-Jesse's Rod,
And crown Him LORD of all.

Ye seed of Israel's chosen race,
Ye ransom'd of the fall,
Hail Him Who saves you by His grace,
And crown Him LORD of all.

Hail Him, ye heirs of David's line,
Whom David LORD did call,
The GOD Incarnate, Man Divine,
And crown Him LORD of all.

Sinners, whose love can ne'er forget
The wormwood and the gall,
Go spread your trophies at His feet,
And *crown Him* LORD of all.

Let every tribe and every tongue
Before Him prostrate fall,
And shout in universal song
The crownèd LORD of all.   Amen.

351 *The four beasts and four and twenty elders fell down
before the Lamb, having every one of them harps,
and golden vials full of odours, which are the
prayers of saints.*

COME, ye faithful, raise the anthem,
Cleave the skies with shouts of praise;
Sing to Him Who found the ransom,
Ancient of eternal days,
GOD of GOD, the WORD Incarnate,
Whom the heav'n of heav'n obeys.

Ere He raised the lofty mountains,
Form'd the seas, or built the sky,
Love eternal, free, and boundless,
Moved the LORD of life to die,
Fore-ordain'd the Prince of princes
For the throne of Calvary.

There, for us and our redemption,
See Him all His life-blood pour!
There He wins our full salvation,
Dies that we may die no more;
Then, arising, lives for ever,
Reigning where He was before.

High on yon celestial mountains
Stands His sapphire throne, all bright,
Where unceasing Alleluias
They upraise, the sons of light;
Sion's people tell His praises,
Victor after hard-won fight.

Bring your harps, and bring your incense,
  Sweep the string and sound the lay ;
Let the earth proclaim His wonders,
  King of that celestial day ;
He the LAMB once slain is worthy,
  Who was dead, and lives for aye.

Laud and honour to the FATHER,
  Laud and honour to the SON,
Laud and honour to the SPIRIT,
  Ever THREE and ever ONE,
Consubstantial, Co-eternal,
  While unending ages run.   Amen.

52 *He . . . saith, Surely I come quickly.   Amen.   Even
so, come, Lord Jesus.*

THOU art coming, O my Saviour,
    Thou art coming, O my King,
In Thy beauty all-resplendent,
In Thy glory all-transcendent ;
  Well may we rejoice and sing ;
Coming ! In the opening east
  Herald brightness slowly swells ;
Coming ! O my glorious Priest,
  Hear we not Thy golden bells ?

Thou art coming, Thou art coming ;
  We shall meet Thee on Thy way,
We shall see Thee, we shall know Thee,
We shall bless Thee, we shall show Thee
  All our hearts could never say ;
What an anthem that will be,
  Music rapturously sweet,
Pouring out our love to Thee
  At *Thine own all-glorious* feet.

Thou art coming ; at Thy table
  We are witnesses for this ;
While remembering hearts Thou meetest
In communion clearest, sweetest,
  Earnest of our coming bliss,
Showing not Thy death alone,
  And Thy love exceeding great,
But Thy coming, and Thy throne,
  All for which we long and wait.

Oh the joy to see Thee reigning,
  Thee, my own belovèd LORD !
Every tongue Thy Name confessing,
Worship, honour, glory, blessing
  Brought to Thee with one accord,
Thee, my Master and my Friend,
  Vindicated and enthroned,
Unto earth's remotest end
  Glorified, adored, and own'd !   Amen.

353 *God shall wipe away all tears from their eyes.*

TEN thousand times ten thousand,
  In sparkling raiment bright,
The armies of the ransom'd Saints
  Throng up the steeps of light :
'Tis finish'd ! all is finish'd,
  Their fight with death and sin ;
Fling open wide the golden gates,
  And let the victors in.

What rush of Alleluias
  Fills all the earth and sky !
What ringing of a thousand harps
  Proclaims the triumph nigh !
O day, for which creation
  And all its tribes were made !
O joy, for all the former woes
  A thousand-fold repaid !

Oh, then what raptured greetings
  On Canaan's happy shore,
What knitting sever'd friendships up,
  Where partings are no more !
Then eyes with joy shall sparkle
  That brimm'd with tears of late ;
Orphans no longer fatherless,
  Nor widows desolate.

Bring near Thy great salvation,
  Thou LAMB for sinners slain,
Fill up the roll of Thine elect,
  Then take Thy power and reign :
Appear, Desire of nations ;
  Thine exiles long for home ;
Show in the heav'ns Thy promised sign ;
  Thou Prince and Saviour, come.   Amen.

54 *Take ye heed, watch and pray ; for ye know not when*
the time is.

THOU Judge of quick and dead,
  Before Whose bar severe
With holy joy, or guilty dread,
  We all shall soon appear ;

  Our waken'd souls prepare
  For that tremendous day,
And fill us now with watchful care,
  And stir us up to pray ;

  To pray, and wait that hour,
  The awful hour unknown,
When, robed in majesty and power,
  Thou shalt from heav'n come down,

  Th' immortal SON of Man,
  To judge the human race,
With all Thy FATHER's dazzling train,
  With all Thy glorious grace.

To sober earthly joys,
To quicken holy fears,
For ever let th' Archangel's voice
Be sounding in our ears ;

The solemn midnight cry,
" Ye dead, the Judge is come !
Arise, and meet Him in the sky,
And meet your instant doom !"

O may we thus be found
Obedient to His word,
Attentive to the trumpet's sound,
And looking for our LORD.

O may we thus insure
Our lot among the blest,
And watch a moment to secure
An everlasting rest.   Amen.

.

355 *The day of the Lord will come as a thief in the night.*

THAT day of wrath, that dreadful day
When heav'n and earth shall pass away
What power shall be the sinner's stay ?
How shall he meet that dreadful day ?

When, shrivelling like a parchèd scroll,
The flaming heav'ns together roll ;
When louder yet, and yet more dread,
Swells the high trump that wakes the dead ;

Oh, on that day, that wrathful day,
When man to judgment wakes from clay,
Be Thou, O CHRIST, the sinner's stay,
Though heav'n and earth shall pass away.
                              Amen.

56 *The communion of the Holy Ghost.*

O fons amoris, Spiritus.

O HOLY SPIRIT, LORD of grace,
　Eternal Fount of love,
Inflame, we pray, out inmost hearts
　With fire from heav'n above.

As Thou in bond of love dost join
　The FATHER and the SON,
So fill us all with mutual love
　And knit our hearts in one.

All glory to the FATHER be,
　All glory to the SON,
All glory, HOLY GHOST, to Thee,
　While endless ages run.　Amen.

57 *He is faithful.*

TO Thee, O Comforter Divine,
　For all Thy grace and power benign,
　　Sing we Alleluia !

To Thee, Whose faithful love had place
In GOD's great covenant of grace,
　　Sing we Alleluia !

To Thee, Whose faithful voice doth win
The wandering from the ways of sin,
　　Sing we Alleluia !

To Thee, Whose faithful power doth heal,
Enlighten, sanctify, and seal,
　　Sing we Alleluia !

To Thee, Whose faithful truth is shown
By every promise made our own,
　　Sing we Alleluia !

To Thee, our Teacher and our Friend,
Our faithful Leader to the end,
　　Sing we Alleluia !

GENERAL HYMNS.

To Thee, by JESUS CHRIST sent down,
Of all His gifts the sum and crown,
    Sing we Alleluia !

To Thee, Who art with GOD the SON
And GOD the FATHER ever One,
    Sing we Alleluia ! Amen.

358 *And he shewed me a pure river of water of life, clear
as crystal, proceeding out of the throne of God and
of the Lamb.*

A LIVING stream, as crystal clear,
    Welling from out the throne
Of GOD and of the LAMB on high,
    The LORD to man hath shown.

This stream doth water Paradise ;
    It makes the Angels sing :
One precious drop within the heart
    Is of all joy the spring :

Joy passing speech, of glory full,
    But stored where none may know,
As manna hid in dewy heaven,
    As pearls in ocean low.

Eye hath not seen, nor ear hath heard,
    Nor to man's heart hath come,
What for those loving Thee in truth
    Thou hast in love's own home.

But by His SPIRIT He to us
    The secret doth reveal :
Faith sees and hears : but O for wings
    That we might taste, and feel ;

Wings like a dove to waft us on
    High o'er the flood of sin !
LORD of the Ark, put forth Thine hand,
    And take Thy wanderers in.

O praise the FATHER, praise the SON,
The LAMB for sinners given,
And HOLY GHOST, through Whom alone
Our hearts are raised to heaven.   Amen.

59 *When they had prayed, the place was shaken where they were assembled together, and they were all filled with the Holy Ghost.*

LORD GOD the HOLY GHOST,
In this accepted hour,
As on the day of Pentecost,
O come in all Thy power.

Like mighty rushing wind
Upon the waves beneath,
Move with one impulse every mind,
One soul, one feeling breathe :

The young, the old inspire
With wisdom from above ;
And give us hearts and tongues of fire,
To pray and praise and love.

SPIRIT of light, explore
And chase our gloom away,
With lustre shining more and more
Unto the perfect day.

SPIRIT of truth, be Thou
In life and death our Guide ;
O SPIRIT of adoption, now
May we be sanctified.   Amen.

30 *When he is come he will convince the world of sin.*

COME, HOLY SPIRIT, come,
Let Thy bright beams arise ;
Dispel the sorrow from our minds,
The darkness from our eyes.

Convince us of our sin,
Then lead to JESU's Blood ;
And to our wond'ring view reveal
The secret love of GOD.

Revive our drooping faith,
Our doubts and fears remove,
And kindle in our breasts the flame
Of never-dying love.

Cheer our desponding hearts,
Thou heav'nly Paraclete ;
Give us to lie with humble hope
At our Redeemer's feet.

'Tis Thine to cleanse the heart,
To sanctify the soul,
To pour fresh life through every part,
And new create the whole.

Dwell, therefore, in our hearts,
Our minds from bondage free ;
Then we shall know, and praise, and love
The FATHER, SON, and Thee. Amen.

361 *As many as are led by the Spirit of God, they are the sons of God.*

COME, gracious SPIRIT, heav'nly Dove,
  With light and comfort from above ;
Be Thou our Guardian, Thou our Guide,
O'er every thought and step preside.

The light of truth to us display,
And make us know and love Thy way ;
Plant holy fear in every heart,
That we from GOD may ne'er depart.

Lead us to CHRIST, the living Way,
Nor let us from His pastures stray ;
Lead us to holiness, the road
That we must take to dwell with GOD.

(316)

Lead us to heav'n, that we may share
Fulness of joy for ever there ;
Lead us to GOD, our final rest,
To be with Him for ever blest.   Amen.

62 *Awake, O north wind; and come, thou south; blow upon my garden, that the spices thereof may flow out.*

O HOLY GHOST, Thy people bless,
   Who long to feel Thy might,
And fain would grow in holiness
   As children of the light.

To Thee we bring, Who art the LORD,
   Ourselves to be Thy throne ;
Let every thought, and deed, and word
   Thy pure dominion own.

Life-giving SPIRIT, o'er us move,
   As on the formless deep ;
Give life and order, light and love,
   Where now is death or sleep.

Great Gift of our ascended King,
   His saving truth reveal ;
Our tongues inspire His praise to sing,
   Our hearts His love to feel.

True Wind of heav'n, from south or north,
   For joy or chastening, blow ;
The garden-spices shall spring forth
   If Thou wilt bid them flow.

O HOLY GHOST, of sevenfold might,
   All graces come from Thee ;
Grant us to know and serve aright
   ONE GOD in Persons THREE.   Amen.

363 *And now abideth faith, hope, charity, these three; but the greatest of these is charity.*

GRACIOUS Spirit, Holy Ghost,
 Taught by Thee, we covet most
Of Thy gifts at Pentecost,
 Holy, heav'nly love.

Love is kind, and suffers long,
Love is meek, and thinks no wrong,
Love than death itself more strong;
 Therefore give us love.

Prophecy will fade away,
Melting in the light of day;
Love will ever with us stay;
 Therefore give us love.

Faith will vanish into sight;
Hope be emptied in delight;
Love in heav'n will shine more bright;
 Therefore give us love.

Faith and hope and love we see
Joining hand in hand agree;
But the greatest of the three,
 And the best, is love.

From the overshadowing
Of Thy gold and silver wing
Shed on us, who to Thee sing,
 Holy, heav'nly love.   Amen.

364   *Spring up, O well: sing ye unto it.*

HOLY Spirit, Truth divine,
 Dawn upon this soul of mine;
Voice of God, and inward Light,
Wake my spirit, clear my sight.

Holy Spirit, Love divine,
Glow within this heart of mine ;
Kindle every high desire ;
Perish self in Thy pure fire.

Holy Spirit, Power divine,
Fill and nerve this will of mine ;
By Thee may I strongly live,
Bravely bear, and nobly strive.

Holy Spirit, Law divine,
Reign within this soul of mine ;
Be my law, and I shall be
Firmly bound, for ever free.

Holy Spirit, Peace divine,
Still this restless heart of mine ;
Speak to calm this tossing sea,
Stay'd in Thy tranquillity.

Holy Spirit, Joy divine,
Gladden Thou this heart of mine ;
In the desert ways I sing,—
Spring, O Well, for ever spring.   Amen.

365   *The Spirit also helpeth our infirmities.*

COME to our poor nature's night
  With Thy blessèd inward light,
Holy Ghost the Infinite,
        Comforter Divine.

We are sinful,—cleanse us, Lord ;
Sick and faint,—Thy strength afford ;
Lost, until by Thee restored,
        Comforter Divine.

Orphan are our souls and poor,—
· Give us, from Thy heav'nly store,
Faith, love, joy for evermore,
        Comforter Divine.

Like the dew Thy peace distil ;
Guide, subdue our wayward will,
Things of CHRIST unfolding still,
   Comforter Divine.

In us, for us, intercede,
And with voiceless groaning plead
Our unutterable need,
   Comforter Divine.

Earnest of our bliss on high,
Seal of immortality,
In us "Abba, Father," cry,
   Comforter Divine.

Search for us the depths of GOD ;
Bear us up the starry road,
To the height of Thine abode,
   Comforter Divine. Amen.

366 *Glorious things are spoken of thee, thou city of God.*

GLORIOUS things of thee are spoken,
 Zion, city of our GOD ;
He Whose word cannot be broken
 Form'd thee for His own abode.
On the Rock of ages founded,
 What can shake thy sure repose ?
With salvation's walls surrounded,
 Thou may'st smile at all thy foes.

See, the streams of living waters,
 Springing from eternal love,
Well supply thy sons and daughters,
 And all fear of want remove.
Who can faint while such a river
 Ever flows their thirst to assuage ;
Grace, which like the LORD the Giver,
 Never fails from age to age ?

Round each habitation hovering,
　See the cloud and fire appear,
For a glory and a covering—
　Showing that the LORD is near.
Thus they march, the pillar leading,
　Light by night and shade by day;
Daily on the manna feeding
　Which He gives them when they pray.

Saviour, since of Zion's city
　I, through grace, a member am,
Let the world deride or pity,
　I will glory in Thy Name.
Fading is the world's best p eas e,
　All its boasted pomp and bhowr;
Solid joys and lasting treasure
　None but Zion's children know.　Amen.

17 *Other foundation can no man lay than that is laid,*
which is Jesus Christ.

THE Church's one foundation
　Is JESUS CHRIST, her LORD;
She is His new creation
　By water and the Word:
From heav'n He came and sought her,
　To be His holy Bride;
With His own Blood He bought her,
　And for her life He died.

Elect from every nation,
　Yet one o'er all the earth,
Her charter of salvation
　One LORD, one Faith, one Birth,
One holy Name she blesses,
　Partakes one holy Food,
And to one hope she presses
　With every grace endued.

Though with a scornful wonder
　　Men see her sore opprest,
By schisms rent asunder,
　　By heresies distrest,
Yet Saints their watch are keeping,
　　Their cry goes up, " How long ? "
And soon the night of weeping
　　Shall be the morn of song.

'Mid toil, and tribulation,
　　And tumult of her war,
She waits the consummation
　　Of peace for evermore ;
Till with the vision glorious
　　Her longing eyes are blest,
And the great Church victorious
　　Shall be the Church at rest.

Yet she on earth hath union
　　With GOD the THREE in ONE,
And mystic sweet communion
　　With those whose rest is won :
O happy ones and holy !
　　LORD, give us grace that we,
Like them the meek and lowly,
　　On high may dwell with Thee.　Amen.

368 *God is in the midst of her, therefore shall she not be removed; God shall help her, and that right early.*

ROUND the Sacred City gather
　　Egypt, Edom, Babylon ;
All the warring hosts of error,
　　Sworn against her, move as one :
Vain the leaguer ! her foundations
　　Are upon the holy hills,
And the love of the Eternal
　　All her stately temple fills.

Get thee, watchman, to the rampart !
  Gird thee, warrior, with thy sword !
Be ye strong as ye remember
  That amidst you is the LORD :
Like the night mists from the valley,
  These shall vanish one by one,
Egypt's malice, Edom's envy,
  And the hate of Babylon.

But be true, ye sons and daughters,
  Lest the peril be within ;
Watch to prayer, lest, while ye slumber,
  Stealthy foemen enter in :
Safe the mother and the children,
  If their will and love be strong,
While their loyal hearts go singing
  Prayer and praise for battle song.

Church of CHRIST ! upon thy banner,
  Lo, His Passion's awful sign ;
By that seal of His Redemption
  Thou art His, and He is thine :
From the depth of His Atonement
  Flows thy sacramental tide :
From the height of His Ascension
  Flows the grace which is thy guide.

GOD the SPIRIT dwells within thee,
  His Society divine,
His the living word thou keepest,
  His thy apostolic line.
Ancient prayer and song liturgic,
  Creeds that change not to the end,
As His gift we have received them,
  As His charge we will defend.

Alleluia, Alleluia,
  To the FATHER, SPIRIT, SON,
In Whose will the Church at warfare
  With the Church at rest is one ;

O quickly come, true Life of all ;
  For death is mighty all around ;
On every home his shadows fall,
  On every heart his mark is found :
O quickly come : for grief and pain
Can never cloud Thy glorious reign.

O quickly come, sure Light of all,
  For gloomy night broods o'er our way,
And weakly souls begin to fall
  With weary watching for the day :
O quickly come : for round Thy throne
No eye is blind, no night is known. Amen.

372 *God be merciful unto us, and bless us; and shew us*
the light of his countenance.

GOD of mercy, GOD of grace,
  Show the brightness of Thy face ;
Shine upon us, Saviour, shine,
Fill Thy Church with light divine ;
And Thy saving health extend
Unto earth's remotest end.

Let the people praise Thee, LORD ;
Be by all that live adored ;
Let the nations shout and sing
Glory to their Saviour King ;
At Thy feet their tribute pay,
And Thy holy will obey.

Let the people praise Thee, LORD ;
Earth shall then her fruits afford ;
GOD to man His blessing give,
Man to GOD devoted live ;
All below, and all above,
One in joy, and light, and love. **Amen.**

573 *The kingdoms of this world are become the kingdoms of our Lord and of his Christ; and he shall reign for ever and ever.*

JESUS shall reign where'er the sun
    Doth his successive journeys run ;
His kingdom stretch from shore to shore,
Till moons shall wax and wane no more.

People and realms of every tongue
Dwell on His love with sweetest song,
And infant voices shall proclaim
Their early blessings on His Name.

Blessings abound where'er He reigns ;
The prisoner leaps to lose his chains ;
The weary find eternal rest,
And all the sons of want are blest.

Let every creature rise and bring
Peculiar honours to our King ;
Angels descend with songs again,
And earth repeat the long Amen.   Amen.

574 *All the earth shall be filled with his majesty.*

HAIL to the LORD's Anointed,
    Great David's greater Son !
Hail, in the time appointed,
    His reign on earth begun !
He comes to break oppression,
    To set the captive free,
To take away transgression,
    And rule in equity.
He comes with succour speedy
    To those who suffer wrong ;
To help the poor and needy,
    And bid the weak be strong ;
To give them songs for sighing,
    Their darkness turn to light,
Whose souls, condemn'd and dying,
    Were precious in His sight.

He shall come down like showers
  Upon the fruitful earth,
And joy and hope, like flowers,
  Spring in His path to birth :
Before Him on the mountains
  Shall peace, the herald, go ;
Of righteousness the fountains
  From hill to valley flow.

Kings shall fall down before Him,
  And gold and incense bring ;
All nations shall adore Him,
  His praise all people sing ;
To Him shall prayer unceasing
  And daily vows ascend ;
His kingdom still increasing,
  A kingdom without end.

O'er every foe victorious,
  He on His throne shall rest,
From age to age more glorious,
  All-blessing and all-blest :
The tide of time shall never
  His covenant remove ;
His Name shall stand for ever ;
  That Name to us is Love.   Amen.

375 *When shall I come to appear before the presence of God*

JERUSALEM, my happy home,
  Name ever dear to me,
When shall my labours have an end ?
  Thy joys when shall I see ?

When shall t ese eyes thy heav'n-built walls
  And pearly gates behold ?
Thy bulwarks with salvation strong,.
  And streets of shining gold ?

Apostles, Martyrs, Prophets, there
　Around my Saviour stand ;
And all I love in CHRIST below
　Will join the glorious band.

Jerusalem, my happy home,
　When shall I come to thee ?
When shall my labours have an end ?
　Thy joys when shall I see ?

O CHRIST, do Thou my soul prepare
　For that bright home of love,
That I may see Thee and adore,
　With all Thy Saints above.　Amen.

6 *Here have we no continuing city, but we seek one to come.*

Hic breve vivitur.

BRIEF life is here our portion ;
　Brief sorrow, short-lived care ;
The life that knows no ending,
　The tearless life, is there.

O happy retribution !
　Short toil, eternal rest ;
For mortals and for sinners
　A mansion with the blest !

And now we fight the battle,
　But then shall wear the crown
Of full and everlasting
　And passionless renown ;

And now we watch and struggle,
　And now we live in hope,
And Sion in her anguish
　With Babylon must cope ;

But He Whom now we trust in
　Shall then be seen and known ;
And they that know and see Him
　Shall have Him for their own.

The morning shall awaken,
  The shadows shall decay,
And each true-hearted servant
  Shall shine as doth the day.

There grief is turn'd to pleasure,
  Such pleasure as below
No human voice can utter,
  No human heart can know.

There GOD, our King and Portion,
  In fulness of His grace,
Shall we behold for ever,
  And worship face to face.

O sweet and blessèd country,
  The home of GOD's elect !
O sweet and blessèd country
  That eager hearts expect !

JESU, in mercy bring us
  To that dear land of rest ;
Who art, with GOD the FATHER
  And SPIRIT, ever Blest.   Amen.

377 *The nations of them which are saved shall walk in
the light of it.*

Hora novissima.

THE world is very evil,
  The times are waxing late ;
Be sober and keep vigil,
  The Judge is at the gate,—
The Judge Who comes in mercy,
  The Judge Who comes with might,
Who comes to end the evil,
  Who comes to crown the right.

GENERAL HYMNS.

Arise, arise, good Christian,
   Let right to wrong succeed ;
Let penitential sorrow
   To heav'nly gladness lead,
To light that has no evening,
   That knows nor moon nor sun,
The light so new and golden,
   The light that is but one.

O home of fadeless splendour,
   Of flowers that bear no thorn,
Where they shall dwell as children
   Who here as exiles mourn ;
'Midst power that knows no limit,
   Where knowledge has no bound,
The Beatific Vision
   Shall glad the Saints around.

Strive, man, to win that glory ;
   Toil, man, to gain that light ;
Send hope before to grasp it,
   Till hope be lost in sight.
Exult, O dust and ashes,
   The LORD shall be thy part,
His only, His for ever
   Thou shalt be and thou art.

O sweet and blessèd country,
   The home of GOD's elect !
O sweet and blessèd country
   That eager hearts expect !
JESU, in mercy bring us
   To that dear land of rest ;
Who art, with GOD the FATHER
   And SPIRIT, ever Blest.   Amen.

378 *A better country, that is, an heavenly.*

O bona patria.

FOR thee, O dear, dear country,
　Mine eyes their vigils keep ;
For very love, beholding
　Thy happy name, they weep.
The mention of thy glory
　Is unction to the breast,
And medicine in sickness,
　And love, and life, and rest.

O one, O only mansion !
　O Paradise of joy !
Where tears are ever banish'd,
　And smiles have no alloy ;
The LAMB is all thy splendour ;
　The Crucified thy praise ;
His laud and benediction
　Thy ransom'd people raise.

With jasper glow thy bulwarks,
　Thy streets with emeralds blaze ;
The sardius and the topaz
　Unite in thee their rays ;
Thine ageless walls are bonded
　With amethyst unpriced ;
The Saints build up thy fabric,
　And the corner-stone is CHRIST.

Thou hast no shore, fair ocean !
　Thou hast no time, bright day !
Dear fountain of refreshment
　To pilgrims far away !
Upon the Rock of ages
　They raise thy holy tower ;
Thine is the victor's laurel,
　And thine the golden dower.

O sweet and blessèd country,
  The home of GOD's elect !
O sweet and blessèd country
  That eager hearts expect !
JESU, in mercy bring us
  To that dear land of rest ;
Who art, with GOD the FATHER
  And SPIRIT, ever Blest.   Amen.

'9   *And the city was pure gold.*

Urbs Sion aurea.

JERUSALEM the golden,
  With milk and honey blest,
Beneath thy contemplation
  Sink heart and voice opprest.
I know not, oh, I know not
  What joys await us there,
What radiancy of glory,
  What bliss beyond compare.

They stand, those halls of Sion,
  All jubilant with song,
And bright with many an Angel,
  And all the Martyr throng ;
The Prince is ever in them,
  The daylight is serene,
The pastures of the blessèd
  Are deck'd in glorious sheen.

There is the throne of David ;
  And there, from care released,
The shout of them that triumph,
  The song of them that feast ;
And they who with their Leader
  Have conquer'd in the fight,
For ever and for ever
  Are clad in robes of white.

(833)

O sweet and blessèd country,
  The home of GOD's elect !
O sweet and blessèd country
  That eager hearts expect !
JESU, in mercy bring us
  To that dear land of rest ;
Who art, with GOD the FATHER
  And SPIRIT, ever Blest. Amen.

380 *The Lord shall be unto thee an everlasting light, and
      thy God thy glory.*

Jerusalem luminosa.

LIGHT'S abode, celestial Salem,
  Vision whence true peace doth spring,
Brighter than the heart can fancy,
  Mansion of the Highest King ;
Oh, how glorious are the praises
  Which of thee the prophets sing !

There for ever and for ever
  Alleluia is out-pour'd ;
For unending, for unbroken
  Is the feast-day of the LORD ;
All is pure and all is holy
  That within thy walls is stored.

There no cloud nor passing vapour
  Dims the brightness of the air ;
Endless noon-day, glorious noon-day,
  From the Sun of suns is there ;
There no night brings rest from labour,
  For unknown are toil and care.

Oh, how glorious and resplendent,
  Fragile body, shalt thou be,
When endued with so much beauty,
  Full of health, and strong, and free,
Full of vigour, full of pleasure
  That shall last eternally !

Now with gladness, now with courage,
  Bear the burden on thee laid,
That hereafter these thy labours
  May with endless gifts be paid,
And in everlasting glory
  Thou with brightness be array'd.

Laud and honour to the FATHER,
  Laud and honour to the SON,
Laud and honour to the SPIRIT,
  Ever THREE and ever ONE,
Consubstantial, Co-eternal,
  While unending ages run. Amen.

381 *There remaineth therefore a rest to the people of God.*
   O quanta qualia sunt illa sabbata.

OH, what the joy and the glory must be,
  Those endless sabbaths the blessèd ones see ;
Crown for the valiant, to weary ones rest ;
GOD shall be all and in all ever Blest.

What are the Monarch, His court, and His throne ?
What are the peace and the joy that they own ?
O that the blest ones, who in it have share,
All that they feel could as fully declare !

Truly Jerusalem name we that shore,
Vision of peace, that brings joy evermore ;
Wish and fulfilment can sever'd be ne'er,
Nor the thing pray'd for come short of the prayer.

There, where no troubles distraction can bring,
We the sweet anthems of Sion shall sing,
While for Thy grace, LORD, their voices of praise
Thy blessèd people eternally raise.

There dawns no sabbath, no sabbath is o'er,
Those sabbath-keepers have one evermore ;
One and unending is that triumph-song
Which *to the Angels* and us shall belong.

Now in the meanwhile, with hearts raised on high,
We for that country must yearn and must sigh,
Seeking Jerusalem, dear native land,
Through our long exile on Babylon's strand.

Low before Him with our praises we fall,   [all ;
Of Whom, and through Whom, and to Whom are
Praise to the FATHER, and praise to the SON,
Praise to the SPIRIT, with Them ever One. Amen.

382   *Our conversation is in heaven.*

JERUSALEM on high
    My song and city is,
My home whene'er I die,
    The centre of my bliss :
        O happy place !
        When shall I be,
        My GOD, with Thee,
    To see Thy face ?

There dwells my LORD, my King,
    Judged here unfit to live ;
There Angels to Him sing,
    And lowly homage give :
        O happy place !
        When shall I be,
        My GOD, with Thee,
    To see Thy face ?

The Patriarchs of old
    There from their travels cease ;
The Prophets there behold
    Their long'd-for Prince of peace :
        O happy place !
        When shall I be,
        My GOD, with Thee,
    To see Thy face ?

The Lamb's Apostles there
　I might with joy behold,
The harpers I might hear
　Harping on harps of gold :
　　O happy place !
　　　When shall I be,
　　　My God, with Thee,
　　To see Thy face ?

The bleeding Martyrs, they
　Within those courts are found,
Clothèd in pure array,
　Their scars with glory crown'd :
　　O happy place !
　　　When shall I be,
　　　My God, with Thee,
　　To see Thy face ?

Ah ! woe is me that I
　In Kedar's tents here stay ;
No place like that on high ;
　Lord, thither guide my way :
　　O happy place !
　　　When shall I be,
　　　My God, with Thee,
　　To see Thy face ?　Amen.

383　　*And all her streets shall say, Alleluia.*

Alleluia piis edite laudibus.

SING Alleluia forth in duteous praise,
　Ye citizens of heav'n ; O sweetly raise
　　An endless Alleluia.

Ye Powers who stand before th' Eternal Light,
In hymning choirs re-echo to the height
　　An endless Alleluia.

The Holy City shall take up your strain,
And with glad songs resounding wake again
   An endless Alleluia.

In blissful antiphons ye thus rejoice
To render to the LORD with thankful voice
   An endless Alleluia.

Ye who have gain'd at length your palms in bliss,
Victorious ones, your chant shall still be this,
   An endless Alleluia.

There, in one grand acclaim, for ever ring
The strains which tell the honour of your King,
   An endless Alleluia.

This is sweet rest for weary ones brought back,
This is glad food and drink which ne'er shall lack,
   An endless Alleluia ;

While Thee, by Whom were all things made, we
 praise
For ever, and tell out in sweetest lays
   An endless Alleluia.

Almighty CHRIST, to Thee our voices sing
Glory for evermore ; to Thee we bring
   An endless Alleluia. Amen.

384 *There remaineth therefore a rest to the people of God.*

THERE is a blessèd home
  Beyond this land of woe,
Where trials never come,
 Nor tears of sorrow flow ;
Where faith is lost in sight,
 And patient hope is crown'd,
And everlasting light
 Its glory throws around.

There is a land of peace,
 Good Angels know it well ;
Glad songs that never cease
 Within its portals swell ;

Around its glorious throne
　Ten thousand Saints adore
CHRIST, with the FATHER One
　And SPIRIT, evermore.

O joy all joys beyond,
　To see the LAMB Who died,
And count each sacred wound
　In hands, and feet, and side ;
To give to Him the praise
　Of every triumph won,
And sing through endless days
　The great things He hath done.

Look up, ye saints of GOD,
　Nor fear to tread below
The path your Saviour trod
　Of daily toil and woe ;
Wait but a little while
　In uncomplaining love,
His own most gracious smile
　Shall welcome you above.　Amen.

385 *For now they desire a better country, that is a heavenly.*

THERE is a land of pure delight,
　Where Saints immortal reign ;
Infinite day excludes the night,
　And pleasures banish pain.
There everlasting spring abides,
　And never-withering flowers ;
Death, like a narrow sea, divides
　That heav'nly land from ours.

Sweet fields beyond the swelling flood
　Stand dress'd in living green ;
So to the *Jews old* Canaan stood,
　While Jordan roll'd between.

But timorous mortals start and shrink
  To cross the narrow sea,
And linger shivering on the brink,
  And fear to launch away.

O could we make our doubts remove,
  Those gloomy doubts that rise,
And see the Canaan that we love
  With unbeclouded eyes :
Could we but climb where Moses stood,
  And view the landscape o'er,
Not Jordan's stream, nor death's cold flood,
  Should fright us from the shore.   Amen.

386 *That whether we wake or sleep, we should live together*
with him.

THEY whose course on earth is o'er,
  Think they of their brethren more ?
They before the throne who bow,
Feel they for their brethren now ?

We, by enemies distrest—
They in Paradise at rest ;
We the captives—they the freed—
We and they are one indeed.

One in all we seek or shun,
One—because our LORD is One ;
One in heart and one in love—
We below, and they above.

Those whom many a land divides,
Many mountains, many tides,
Have they with each other part,
Fellowship of heart with heart ?

Each to each may be unknown,
Wide apart their lots be thrown ;
Differing tongues their lips may speak,
One be strong, and one be weak ;—

Yet in Sacrament and prayer
Each with other hath a share ;
Hath a share in tear and sigh,
Watch, and fast, and litany.

Saints departed even thus
Hold communion still with us ;
Still with us, beyond the veil
Praising, pleading without fail.

With them still our hearts we raise,
Share their work and join their praise,
Rend'ring worship, thanks, and love
To the TRINITY above.   Amen.

387 *Of whom the whole family in heaven and earth is named.*

LET saints on earth in concert sing
   With those whose work is done ;
For all the servants of our King
   Both quick and dead are one.

One family, we dwell in Him,
   One Church, above, beneath ;
Though now divided by the stream,
   The narrow stream of death.

One army of the living GOD,
   To His command we bow ;
Part of His host hath cross'd the flood,
   And part is crossing now.

E'en now to their eternal home
   There pass some spirits blest,
While others to the margin come,
   Waiting their call to rest.

JESU, be Thou our constant Guide ;
   Then, when the word is given,
Bid Jordan's narrow stream divide,
   And show the path to heaven.   Amen.

388 *O how amiable are thy dwellings, thou Lord of hosts.*

O GOD of hosts, the mighty LORD,
　　How lovely is the place
Where Thou, enthroned in glory, show'st
　　The brightness of Thy face !

My longing soul faints with desire
　　To view Thy blest abode ;
My panting heart and flesh cry out
　　For Thee the living GOD.

For in Thy courts one single day
　　'Tis better to attend,
Than, LORD, in any place besides
　　A thousand days to spend.

O LORD of hosts, my King and GOD,
　　How highly blest are they
Who in Thy temple always dwell,
　　And there Thy praise display !

To FATHER, SON, and HOLY GHOST,
　　The GOD Whom we adore,
Be glory, as it was, is now,
　　And shall be evermore.　Amen.

389 *O how amiable are thy dwellings, thou Lord of hosts.*

PLEASANT are Thy courts above
　　In the land of light and love ;
Pleasant are Thy courts below
In this land of sin and woe :
Oh, my spirit longs and faints
For the converse of Thy Saints,
For the brightness of Thy face,
For Thy fulness, GOD of grace.

Happy birds that sing and fly
Round Thy altars, O most High ;
Happier souls that find a rest
In a heav'nly FATHER'S breast ;
Like the wandering dove that found
No repose on earth around,
They can to their ark repair,
And enjoy it ever there.

Happy souls, their praises flow
Even in this vale of woe ;
Waters in the desert rise,
Manna feeds them from the skies ;
On they go from strength to strength,
Till they reach Thy throne at length,
At Thy feet adoring fall,
Who hast led them safe through all.

LORD, be mine this prize to win,
Guide me through a world of sin,
Keep me by Thy saving grace,
Give me at Thy side a place ;
Sun and Shield alike Thou art,
Guide and guard my erring heart ;
Grace and glory flow from Thee ;
Shower, O shower them, LORD, on me.

Amen.

390 *The Lord said unto him, . . . I have hallowed this house . . . to put my name there for ever, and mine eyes and mine heart shall be there perpetually.*

Angulare fundamentum.

CHRIST is our corner-stone,
    On Him alone we build ;
With His true Saints alone
    The courts of heav'n are fill'd :
        On His great love
            Our hopes we place
            Of present grace
        And joys above.

Oh, then with hymns of praise
　These hallow'd courts shall ring ;
Our voices we will raise
　The THREE in ONE to sing ;
　　And thus proclaim
　　　In joyful song,
　　　Both loud and long,
　　That glorious Name.

Here, gracious GOD, do Thou
　For evermore draw nigh ;
Accept each faithful vow,
　And mark each suppliant sigh ;
　　In copious shower
　　　On all who pray
　　　Each holy day
　　Thy blessings pour.

Here may we gain from heaven
　The grace which we implore ;
And may that grace, once given,
　Be with us evermore,
　　Until that day
　　　When all the blest
　　　To endless rest
　　Are call'd away.　Amen.

391 *The Lord is in this place . . . how dreadful is this*
　　　　　　place.　　　　　・

Gott ist gegenwärtig!

L O ! GOD is here ! let us adore,
　And own how dreadful is this place !
Let all within us feel His power,
　And silent bow before His face ;
Who know His power, His grace who prove,
Serve Him with awe, with reverence love.

(344)

Lo! God is here! Him day and night
  The united choirs of Angels sing;
To Him, enthroned above all height,
  The hosts of heav'n their praises bring;
Disdain not, Lord, our meaner song,
Who praise Thee with a falt'ring tongue.

Being of beings! may our praise
  Thy courts with grateful fragrance fill;
Still may we stand before Thy face,
  Still hear and do Thy sovereign will;
To Thee may all our thoughts arise
A true and ceaseless sacrifice. Amen.

392 *In all places where I record my name, I will come*
*   unto thee, and I will bless thee.*

JESUS, where'er Thy people meet,
  There they behold Thy mercy-seat;
Where'er they seek Thee, Thou art found,
And every place is hallow'd ground.

For Thou, within no walls confined,
Inhabitest the humble mind;
Such ever bring Thee where they come,
And going, take Thee to their home.

Great Shepherd of Thy chosen few,
Thy former mercies here renew;
Here to our waiting hearts proclaim
The sweetness of Thy saving Name.

Here may we prove the power of prayer,
To strengthen faith and sweeten care,
To teach our faint desires to rise,
And bring all heav'n before our eyes.

Lord, we are few, but Thou art near,
Nor short Thine arm, nor deaf Thine ear;
O rend the heav'ns, come quickly down,
And *make a thousand* hearts Thine own. Amen

393 *I will give you assured peace in this place.*

GREAT Shepherd of Thy people, hear,
   Thy presence now display ;
As Thou hast given a place for prayer,
   So give us hearts to pray.

Within these walls let holy peace,
   And love, and concord dwell ;
Here give the troubled conscience ease,
   The wounded spirit heal.

May we in faith receive Thy word,
   In faith present our prayers,
And in the presence of our LORD
   Unbosom all our cares.

The hearing ear, the seeing eye,
   The contrite heart bestow :
And shine upon us from on high,
   That we in grace may grow.   Amen.

394   *Hosanna in the highest.*

HOSANNA to the living LORD !
   Hosanna to the Incarnate WORD !
To CHRIST, Creator, Saviour, King,
Let earth, let heav'n Hosanna sing,
     Hosanna in the highest !

O Saviour, with protecting care
Abide in this Thy house of prayer,
Where we Thy parting promise claim,
Assembled in Thy sacred Name.
     Hosanna in the highest !

But, chiefest, in our cleansèd breast,
ETERNAL, bid Thy SPIRIT rest ;
And make our secret soul to be
A temple pure and worthy Thee.
     Hosanna in the highest !

To God the Father, God the Son,
And God the Spirit, Three in One,
Be honour, praise, and glory given
By all on earth and all in heaven.
Hosanna in the highest!
Amen.

5 *Lord, I have loved the habitation of thy house; and
the place where thine honour dwelleth.*

WE love the place, O God,
Wherein Thine honour dwells;
The joy of Thine abode
All earthly joys excels.

We love the house of prayer,
Wherein Thy servants meet;
And Thou, O Lord, art there
Thy chosen flock to greet.

We love the sacred font;
For there the Holy Dove
To pour is ever wont
His blessing from above.

We love Thine altar, Lord;
Oh, what on earth so dear?
For there, in faith adored,
We find Thy presence near.

We love the word of life,
The word that tells of peace,
Of comfort in the strife,
And joys that never cease.

We love to sing below
For mercies freely given;
But, oh, we long to know
The triumph-song of heaven.

Lord Jesus, give us grace
On earth to love Thee more,
In heav'n *to* see Thy face,
And with Thy Saints adore. Amen.

396 *Thy word is tried to the uttermost; and thy servant loveth it.*

CHURCH of the living GOD,
  Pillar and ground of truth,
Keep the old paths the fathers trod
  In thy illumined youth.

Lo, in thy bosom lies
  The touchstone for the age ;
Seducing error shrinks and dies
  At light from yonder page.

Woe if thou spurn a line
  By wilfulness enticed,
Or with the truth of GOD entwine
  The frauds of Antichrist.

Once to the saints was given
  All blessèd gospel lore ;
There, written down in words from heaven,
  Thou hast it evermore.

Fear not, though doubts abound
  And scoffing tongues deride ;
Love of GOD'S word finds surer ground
  When to the utmost tried.

Toil at thy sacred text ;
  More fruitful grows the field ;
Each generation for the next
  Prepares a richer yield.

GOD'S SPIRIT in the Church
  Still lives unspent, untired,
Inspiring hearts that fain would search
  The truths Himself inspired.

Move, HOLY GHOST, with might
  Amongst us as of old ;
Dispel the falsehood, and unite
  In true faith the true fold. Amen.

97 *Thy word is a lantern unto my feet, and a light unto my paths.*

LORD, Thy word abideth,
  And our footsteps guideth ;
Who its truth believeth
Light and joy receiveth.

When our foes are near us,
Then Thy word doth cheer us,
Word of consolation,
Message of salvation.

When the storms are o'er us,
And dark clouds before us,
Then its light directeth,
And our way protecteth.

Who can tell the pleasure,
Who recount the treasure,
By Thy word imparted
To the simple-hearted ?

Word of mercy, giving
Succour to the living ;
Word of life, supplying
Comfort to the dying !

O that we discerning
Its most holy learning,
LORD, may love and fear Thee,
Evermore be near Thee.   Amen.

98   *O how sweet are thy words.*

FATHER of mercies, in Thy word
  What endless glory shines !
For ever be Thy Name adored
  For these celestial lines.
Here may the blind and hungry come,
  And light and food receive ;
Here shall the lowliest guest have room,
  And taste and see and live.

Here springs of consolation rise
  To cheer the fainting mind,
And thirsting souls receive supplies,
  And sweet refreshment find. .

Here the Redeemer's welcome voice
  Spreads heav'nly peace around,
And life and everlasting joys
  Attend the blissful sound.

O may these heav'nly pages be
  My ever dear delight,
And still new beauties may I see,
  And still increasing light.

Divine Instructor, gracious LORD,
  Be Thou for ever near ;
Teach me to love Thy sacred word,
  And view my Saviour here.   Amen.

399 *Holy men of God spake as they were moved by the
          Holy Ghost.*

COME, HOLY GHOST, our hearts inspire,
  Let us Thy influence prove,
Source of the old prophetic fire,
  Fountain of life and love.

Come, HOLY GHOST, for moved by Thee
  The prophets wrote and spoke ;
Unlock the truth, Thyself the Key,
  Unseal the sacred book.

GOD through Himself we then shall know,
  If Thou within us shine,
And sound, with all Thy saints below,
  The depths of love divine.   Amen.

00 *Who led his people through the wilderness; for his mercy endureth for ever.*

O PRAISE our great and gracious LORD
   And call upon His Name ;
To strains of joy tune every chord ;
   His mighty acts proclaim ;
Tell how He led His chosen race
   To Canaan's promised land ;
Tell how His covenant of grace
   Unchanged shall ever stand.

He gave the shadowing cloud by day,
   The moving fire by night ;
To guide His Israel on their way,
   He made their darkness light ;
And have not we a sure retreat,
   A Saviour ever nigh,
The same clear light to guide our feet,
   The Day-spring from on high ?

We too have Manna from above,
   The Bread that came from heaven ;
To us the same kind hand of love
   Hath living waters given.
A Rock we have, from whence the spring
   In rich abundance flows ;
That Rock is CHRIST, our Priest, our King,
   Who life and health bestows.

O may we prize this blessèd food,
   And trust our heav'nly Guide ;
So shall we find death's fearful flood
   Serene as Jordan's tide,
And safely reach that happy shore,
   The land of peace and rest,
Where Angels worship and adore,
   In GOD's own presence blest. Amen.

401 *Praise the Lord, O my soul; and all that is within me praise his holy name.*

PRAISE, my soul, the King of heaven,
　　To His feet thy tribute bring;
Ransom'd, heal'd, restored, forgiven,
　　Evermore His praises sing;
　　　　Alleluia! Alleluia!
　　Praise the everlasting King.

Praise Him for His grace and favour
　　To our fathers in distress;
Praise Him still the same as ever,
　　Slow to chide, and swift to bless;
　　　　Alleluia! Alleluia!
　　Glorious in His faithfulness.

Father-like, He tends and spares us,
　　Well our feeble frame He knows;
In His hands He gently bears us;
　　Rescues us from all our foes;
　　　　Alleluia! Alleluia!
　　Widely yet His mercy flows.

Angels in the height, adore Him;
　　Ye behold Him face to face;
Saints triumphant, bow before Him,
　　Gather'd in from every race;
　　　　Alleluia! Alleluia!
　　Praise with us the GOD of grace.　Amen.

402 *Behold, what manner of love the Father hath bestowed upon us, that we should be called the sons of God.*

O FATHER, we would thank Thee
　　For all Thy love has given,
Our present joy of sonship,
　　Our future joy in heaven;
The life which sin had blighted
　　So wondrously restored
By our mysterious union
　　With JESUS CHRIST our LORD;

Rich gifts of life and gladness,—
  A new and heav'nly birth,
Baptismal waters flowing
  To cleanse the sons of earth ;
The strength in which to follow
  The steps that JESUS trod ;
And love beyond all knowledge
  Which calls us sons of GOD.

O mercy all abundant
  Bestow'd on us to-day !
O hope of future glory
  Which fadeth not away !
By GOD's great love begotten
  To living hope and sure,
May we at CHRIST's appearing
  Be pure as He is pure.

For all Thy gifts, O FATHER,
  Our hymns of praise arise,—
The love which calls us children,
  The hope which purifies ;
The grace by which we offer
  A service glad and free ;
The earnest of perfection,
  Of fuller life with Thee.   Amen.

403 *Lord, thou hast been our refuge from one generation*
to another.

O GOD, our help in ages past,
    Our hope for years to come,
Our shelter from the stormy blast,
  And our eternal home ;

Beneath the shadow of Thy throne
  Thy Saints have dwelt secure ;
Sufficient is Thine arm alone,
  And our defence is sure.

Before the hills in order stood,
  Or earth received her frame,
From everlasting Thou art GOD,
  To endless years the Same.

A thousand ages in Thy sight
  Are like an evening gone,
Short as the watch that ends the night
  Before the rising sun.

Time, like an ever-rolling stream,
  Bears all its sons away ;
They fly forgotten, as a dream
  Dies at the opening day.

O GOD, our help in ages past,
  Our hope for years to come,
Be Thou our guard while troubles last,
  And our eternal home.   Amen.

404   *The multitude of his mercies.*

WHEN all Thy mercies, O my GOD,
  My rising soul surveys,
Transported with the view, I'm lost
  In wonder, love, and praise.

Unnumber'd comforts to my soul
  Thy tender care bestow'd,
Before my infant heart conceived
  From Whom those comforts flow'd.

When in the slippery paths of youth
  With heedless steps I ran,
Thine arm unseen convey'd me safe,
  And led me up to man.

Through every period of my life
  Thy goodness I'll pursue,
And after death in distant worlds
  The glorious theme renew.

(354)

Through all eternity to Thee
 A joyful song I'll raise ;
But oh ! eternity's too short
 To utter all Thy praise.   Amen.

105 *I will alway give thanks unto the Lord: his praise*
 shall ever be in my mouth.

THROUGH all the changing scenes of life,
 In trouble and in joy,
The praises of my GOD shall still
 My heart and tongue employ.

O magnify the LORD with me,
 With me exalt His Name ;
When in distress to Him I call'd,
 He to my rescue came.

The hosts of GOD encamp around
 The dwellings of the just ;
Deliverance He affords to all
 Who on His succour trust.

O make but trial of His love,
 Experience will decide
How blest are they, and only they,
 Who in His truth confide.

Fear Him, ye saints, and you will then
 Have nothing else to fear ;
Make you His service your delight,
 Your wants shall be His care.

To FATHER, SON, and HOLY GHOST,
 The GOD Whom we adore,
Be glory, as it was, is now,
 And shall be evermore.   Amen.

(355)

406 *O that men would therefore praise the Lord for his goodness.*

Sei Lob und Ehr' dem höchsten Gut.

SING praise to God Who reigns above,
  The God of all creation,
The God of power, the God of love,
  The God of our salvation ;
With healing balm my soul He fills,
And every faithless murmur stills ;
  To God all praise and glory.

The Angel-host, O King of kings,
  Thy praise for ever telling,
In earth and sky all living things
  Beneath Thy shadow dwelling,
Adore the wisdom which could span
And power which form'd creation's plan :
  To God all praise and glory.

What God's almighty power hath made
  His gracious mercy keepeth ;
By morning glow or evening shade
  His watchful eye ne'er sleepeth ;
Within the kingdom of His might
Lo ! all is just, and all is right ;
  To God all praise and glory.

The Lord is never far away,
  But, through all grief distressing,
An ever-present help and stay,
  Our peace and joy and blessing ;
As with a mother's tender hand,
He leads His own, His chosen band ;
  To God all praise and glory.

Thus all my toilsome way along
 I sing aloud Thy praises,
That men may hear the grateful song
 My voice unwearied raises :
  Be joyful in the LORD, my heart ;
  Both soul and body bear your part ;
   To GOD all praise and glory. Amen.

107 *Thou hast made heaven . . . the earth . . . the sea,
and all that is in them, and thou preservest them all,
and the host of heaven worshippeth thee.*

Lobe den Herrn.

PRAISE to the LORD, the Almighty, the King
 of creation ;
) my soul, praise Him, for He is thy health and
 salvation ;
  All ye who hear
  Now to His temple draw near,
oining in glad adoration.

'raise to the LORD, Who o'er all things so wondrously reigneth,
hieldeth thee gently from harm, or when fainting
 sustaineth :
  Hast thou not seen
  How thy heart's wishes have been
tranted in what He ordaineth ?

'raise to the LORD, Who doth prosper thy work
 and defend thee,
urely His goodness and mercy shall daily attend
 thee ;
  Ponder anew
  What the Almighty can do,
f to the *end He befriend* thee. Amen.

408 *Praise the Lord from the heavens. Praise the L
from the earth.*

YE holy Angels bright,
  Who wait at GOD's right hand.
Or through the realms of light
  Fly at your LORD's command,
    Assist our song,
      Or else the theme
      Too high doth seem
    For mortal tongue.

Ye blessèd souls at rest,
  Who ran this earthly race,
And now, from sin released,
  Behold your FATHER's face,
    His praises sound,
      As in His light
      With sweet delight
    Ye do abound.

Ye saints, who toil below,
  Adore your heav'nly King,
And onward as ye go
  Some joyful anthem sing ;
    Take what He gives
      And praise Him still,
      Through good and ill,
    Who ever lives !

My soul, bear thou thy part,
  Triumph in GOD above,
And with a well-tuned heart
  Sing thou the songs of love !
    Let all thy days
      Till life shall end,
      Whate'er He send,
    Be fill'd with praise. Amen.

9 *What I do thou knowest not now; but thou shalt know hereafter.*

GOD moves in a mysterious way
   His wonders to perform ;
He plants His footsteps in the sea,
   And rides upon the storm.

Deep in unfathomable mines
   Of never-failing skill
He treasures up His bright designs,
   And works His sovereign will.

Ye fearful saints, fresh courage take ;
   The clouds ye so much dread
Are big with mercy, and shall break
   In blessings on your head.

Judge not the LORD by feeble sense,
   But trust Him for His grace ;
Behind a frowning providence
   He hides a smiling face.

His purposes will ripen fast,
   Unfolding every hour ;
The bud may have a bitter taste,
   But sweet will be the flower.

Blind unbelief is sure to err,
   And scan His work in vain ;
GOD is His own interpreter,
   And He will make it plain.   Amen.

10 *Put thou thy trust in the Lord, and be doing good.*

PUT thou thy trust in GOD,
   In duty's path go on ;
Walk in His strength with faith and hope,
   So shall *thy* work be done.

Commit thy ways to Him,
Thy works into His hands,
And rest on His unchanging word,
Who heav'n and earth commands.

Though years on years roll on,
His covenant shall endure;
Though clouds and darkness hide His path,
The promised grace is sure.

Through waves, and clouds, and storms,
His power will clear thy way:
Wait thou His time, the darkest night
Shall end in brightest day. Amen.

411 *The ransomed of the Lord shall return, and come to
Zion with songs.*

CHILDREN of the heav'nly King,
As ye journey, sweetly sing;
Sing your Saviour's worthy praise,
Glorious in His works and ways.

We are travelling home to GOD
In the way the fathers trod;
They are happy now, and we
Soon their happiness shall see.

Lift your eyes, ye sons of light,
Sion's city is in sight;
There our endless home shall be,
There our LORD we soon shall see.

Fear not, brethren; joyful stand
On the borders of your land;
JESUS CHRIST, your FATHER'S SON,
Bids you undismay'd go on.

LORD, obedient we would go,
Gladly leaving all below;
Only Thou our Leader be,
And we still will follow Thee. Amen.

GENERAL HYMNS.

2 *Fight the good fight of faith, lay hold on eternal life.*

OFT in danger, oft in woe,
  Onward, Christians, onward go;
Bear the toil, maintain the strife,
Strengthen'd with the Bread of Life!

Onward, Christians, onward go,
Join the war, and face the foe;
Faint not! much doth yet remain,
Dreary is the long campaign.

Let not sorrow dim your eye,
Soon shall every tear be dry;
Let not fears your course impede,
Great your strength, if great your need.

Let your drooping hearts be glad;
March in heav'nly armour clad;
Fight, nor think the battle long,
Soon shall victory wake your song.

Onward then in battle move;
More than conquerors ye shall prove;
Though opposed by many a foe,
Christian soldiers, onward go!

Hymns of glory and of praise,
FATHER, unto Thee we raise:
Holy JESUS, praise to Thee
With the SPIRIT ever be.   Amen.

3   *To him that overcometh.*
       Pugnate, Christi milites.

SOLDIERS, who are CHRIST'S below,
  Strong in faith resist the foe:
Boundless is the pledged reward
Unto them who serve the LORD.

'Tis no palm of fading leaves
That the conqueror's hand receives ;
Joys are his, serene and pure,
Light that ever shall endure.

For the souls that overcome
Waits the beauteous heav'nly home,
Where the Blessèd evermore
Tread, on high, the starry floor.

Passing soon and little worth
Are the things that tempt on earth ;
Heav'nward lift thy soul's regard ;
GOD Himself is thy reward.

FATHER, Who the crown dost give,
SAVIOUR, by Whose death we live,
SPIRIT, Who our hearts dost raise,
THREE in ONE, Thy Name we   aise.

pr Ame

414   *The fellowship of his sufferings.*

O HAPPY band of pilgrims,
   If onward ye will tread
With JESUS as your fellow
   To JESUS as your Head !

O happy if ye labour
   As JESUS did for men :
O happy if ye hunger
   As JESUS hunger'd then !

The Cross that JESUS carried
   He carried as your due :
The Crown that JESUS weareth,
   He weareth it for you.

The trials that beset you,
   The sorrows ye endure,
The manifold temptations
   That death alone can cure,

What are they but His jewels
    Of right celestial worth?
What are they but the ladder
    Set up to heav'n on earth?
The faith by which ye see Him,
    The hope in which ye yearn,
The love that through all troubles
    To Him alone will turn,
What are they but the couriers
    To lead you to His sight?
What are they but the foregleams
    Of uncreated Light?
O happy band of pilgrims,
    Look upward to the skies,
Where such a light affliction
    Shall win so great a prize.   Amen.

:15   *If God be for us, who can be against us?*

WHEREFORE, faint and fearful ever,
    Do we yet our fears belie?
Oft sore stricken, still endeavour,
    Oft brought low, still look on high?
        GOD is for us;
    GOD our Helper still is nigh.

He Who suns and worlds upholdeth,
    Lends us His upholding hand;
He the ages Who unfoldeth,
    Doth our times and ways command.
        GOD is for us;
    In His strength and stay we stand.

Hard the fight with flesh and devil,
    Dread the might of inbred sin;
How can we encounter evil
    Strong without and strong within?
        GOD is for us;
    He *will help* and we shall win.

(363)

'Gainst oppression forth He sends us,
  His the cause of truth and right ;
With His own great host He blends us,
  Lending us of His own might.
     GOD is for us ;
  Brings to happy end the fight.

Onward, upward, doth He beckon,
  Onward, upward, would we press,
As His own our burdens reckon,
  As our own His strength possess.
     GOD is for us ;
  GOD, our Helper, still we bless.   Amen.

416   *God is our hope and strength.*

Ein' feste Burg.

GOD is a stronghold and a tower,
  A help that never faileth,
A covering shield, a sword of power,
  When Satan's host assaileth.
    In vain our crafty foe
    Still strives to work us woe,
    Still lurks and lies in wait
    With more than earthly hate ;
We will not faint, nor tremble.

Frail sinners are we ;—nought remains
  For hope or consolation,
Save in His strength Whom GOD ordains
  Our Captain of salvation.
    Yes, JESUS CHRIST alone
    The LORD of hosts we own,
    GOD ere the world began,
    The Word-made-flesh for man,
Still conquering, and to conquer.

Though fiercely strive the hosts of ill
  Within us, and around us,
With fiendish strength, and fiendish skill,
  Yet ne'er may they confound us.
      Man's night of dark despair,
      When storm-clouds fill the air,
      Is GOD's triumphal hour,
      The noonday of His power ;
  One word, and He prevaileth.

Our FATHER's truth abideth sure ;
  CHRIST, our Redeemer, liveth ;
For us He pleads His offering pure,
  To us His SPIRIT giveth.
      Though dear ones pass away,
      Though strength and life decay,
      Yet loss shall be our gain,
      For GOD doth still remain
Our All-in-all for ever.   Amen.

417 *And the apostles said unto the Lord, Increase our*
faith.

OH for a faith that will not shrink,
  Though press'd by many a foe ;
That will not tremble on the brink
  Of poverty or woe ;
That will not murmur nor complain
  Beneath the chastening rod ;
But in the hour of grief or pain
  Can lean upon its GOD ;

A faith that shines more bright and clear
  When tempests rage without ;
That when in danger knows no fear,
  In darkness feels no doubt :
A faith that keeps the narrow way
  Till life's last spark is fled,
And with a pure and heav'nly ray
  Lights up the dying bed.

Lord, give me such a faith as this,
 And then, whate'er may come,
I taste e'en now the hallow'd bliss
 Of an eternal home.   Amen.

418 *Jabez called on the God of Israel, saying, Oh that
thou wouldest bless me indeed . . . and that thine
hand might be with me, and that thou wouldest keep
me from evil . . . And God granted him that which
he requested.*

FATHER, whate'er of earthly bliss
 Thy sovereign will denies,
Accepted at Thy throne of grace
 Let this petition rise :—

Give me a calm and thankful heart,
 From every murmur free ;
The blessings of Thy grace impart,
 And let me live to Thee.

Let the sweet hope that Thou art mine
 My path of life attend ;
Thy presence through my journey shine,
 And crown my journey's end.   Amen.

419 *Jacob vowed a vow, saying, If God will be with me,
and will keep me in this way that I go, and will give
me bread to eat, and raiment to put on, so that I
come again to my father's house in peace; then shall
the Lord be my God.*

O GOD of Jacob, by Whose hand
 Thy people still are fed,
Who through this weary pilgrimage
 Hast all our fathers led ;

Our vows, our prayers, we now present
 Before Thy throne of grace ;
God of our fathers, be the God
 Of their succeeding race.

Through each perplexing path of life
   Our wandering footsteps guide ;
Give us each day our daily bread,
   And raiment fit provide.

O spread Thy covering wings around,
   Till all our wanderings cease,
And at our FATHER's loved abode
   Our souls arrive in peace.   Amen.

20   *To me to live is Christ, and to die is gain.*

LORD, it belongs not to my care
   Whether I die or live ;
To love and serve Thee is my share,
   And this Thy grace must give.

If life be long, O make me glad
   The longer to obey ;
If short, no labourer is sad
   To end his toilsome day.

CHRIST leads me through no darker rooms
   Than He went through before ;
And he that to GOD's kingdom comes
   Must enter by this door.

Come, LORD, when grace hath made me meet
   Thy blessèd face to see :
For if Thy work on earth be sweet,
   What will Thy glory be !

Then I shall end my sad complaints
   And weary sinful days,
And join with the triumphant Saints
   That sing my SAVIOUR's praise.

My knowledge of that life is small,
   The eye of faith is dim ;
But 'tis enough that CHRIST knows all,
   And I shall be with Him.   Amen.

421　　　*The Lord is my shepherd.*

THE King of love my Shepherd is,
　Whose goodness faileth never ;
I nothing lack if I am His
　And He is mine for ever.

Where streams of living water flow
　My ransom'd soul He leadeth,
And where the verdant pastures grow
　With food celestial feedeth.

Perverse and foolish oft I stray'd,
　But yet in love He sought me,
And on His shoulder gently laid,
　And home, rejoicing, brought me.

In death's dark vale I fear no ill
　With Thee, dear LORD, beside me ;
Thy rod and staff my comfort still,
　Thy Cross before to guide me.

Thou spread'st a table in my sight ;
　Thy unction grace bestoweth ;
And oh, what transport of delight
　From Thy pure chalice floweth !

And so through all the length of days
　Thy goodness faileth never ;
Good Shepherd, may I sing Thy praise
　Within Thy house for ever.　Amen.

422　*This God is our God for ever and ever; he shall b*
　　　our guide unto death.

GUIDE me, O Thou great Redeemer,
　Pilgrim through this barren land ;
I am weak, but Thou art mighty,
　Hold me with Thy powerful hand ;
　　Bread of heaven,
Feed me now and evermore.

Open now the crystal fountain,
 Whence the healing stream doth flow :
Let the fiery cloudy pillar
 Lead me all my journey through ;
  Strong Deliverer,
Be Thou still my strength and shield.

When I tread the verge of Jordan,
 Bid my anxious fears subside :
Death of death, and hell's Destruction,
 Land me safe on Canaan's side ;
  Songs of praises
I will ever give to Thee.   Amen.

3 *I am the Lord thy God . . . which leadeth thee by*
  the way that thou shouldest go.

LEAD us, heav'nly FATHER, lead us
 O'er the world's tempestuous sea ;
Guard us, guide us, keep us, feed us,
 For we have no help but Thee ;
Yet possessing every blessing,
 If our GOD our FATHER be.

SAVIOUR, breathe forgiveness o'er us,
 All our weakness Thou dost know ;
Thou didst tread this earth before us,
 Thou didst feel its keenest woe ;
Lone and dreary, faint and weary,
 Through the desert Thou didst go.

SPIRIT of our GOD, descending,
 Fill our hearts with heav'nly joy,
Love with every passion blending,
 Pleasure that can never cloy ;
Thus provided, pardon'd, guided,
 Nothing can our peace destroy.   Amen.

GENERAL HYMNS.

424 *Casting all your care upon him; for he careth for y*

O LORD, how happy should we be
  If we could cast our care on Thee,
If we from self could rest,
And feel at heart that One above,
In perfect wisdom, perfect love,
  Is working for the best.

How far from this our daily life,
So oft disturb'd by anxious strife,
  By sudden wild alarms;
Oh, could we but relinquish all
Our earthly props, and simply fall
  On Thy almighty arms!

Could we but kneel and cast our load,
E'en while we pray, upon our GOD,
  Then rise with lighten'd cheer,
Sure that the FATHER, Who is nigh
To still the famish'd raven's cry,
  Will hear in that we fear.

We cannot trust Him as we should;
So chafes weak nature's restless mood
  To cast its peace away;
But birds and flow'rets round us preach;
All, all the present evil teach
  Sufficient for the day.

LORD, make these faithless hearts of ours
Such lessons learn from birds and flowers;
  Make them from self to cease,
Leave all things to a FATHER's will,
And taste, before Him lying still,
  E'en in affliction, peace. Amen.

GENERAL HYMNS.

Thy will be done.

[T]Y GOD, my FATHER, whíle I stray,
    Far from my home, on lífe's rough way,
each me from my heárt to say,
                "Thy will be done."

ough dark my path, and sád my lot,
, me be still and múrmur not,
breathe the prayer divínely taught,
                "Thy will be done."

at though in lonely gríef I sigh
· friends beloved no lónger nigh,
missive would I stíll reply,
                "Thy will be done."

Thou shouldst call me tó resign
at most I prize, it né'er was mine ;
ly yield Thee whát is Thine ;
            Thy will be done.

, but my fainting heárt be blest
th Thy sweet SPIRIT fór its guest,
  GOD, to Thee I leáve the rest ;
            Thy will be done.

ew my will from dáy to day,
nd it with Thine, and táke away
  that now makes it hárd to say,
                "Thy will be done."
                            Amen.

Not as I will, but as thou wilt.

[T]HY way, not mine, O LORD,
    However dark it be ;
Lead me by Thine own hand,
    Choose out the path for me.

Smooth let it be or rough,
    It will be still the best ;
Winding or straight, it leads
    Right onward to Thy rest.

I dare not choose my lot ;
  I would not if I might ;
Choose Thou for me, my GOD,
  So shall I walk aright.

The kingdom that I seek
  Is Thine, so let the way
That leads to it be Thine,
  Else I must surely stray.

Take Thou my cup, and it
  With joy or sorrow fill,
As best to Thee may seem ;
  Choose Thou my good and ill.

Choose Thou for me my friends,
  My sickness or my health ;
Choose Thou my cares for me,
  My poverty or wealth.

Not mine, not mine the choice
  In things or great or small ;
Be Thou my Guide, my Strength,
  My Wisdom, and my All. Amen.

427 *Here have we no continuing city, but we seek one*
      come.

WE'VE no abiding city here :
  This may distress the worldling's mi
But should not cost the saint a tear,
  Who hopes a better rest to find.

We've no abiding city here ;
  Sad truth, were this to be our home ;
But let the thought our spirits cheer,
  We seek a city yet to come.

We've no abiding city here ;
  We seek a city out of sight ;
Zion its name : the LORD is there :
  It shines with everlasting light.

Zion, Jehovah is her strength ;
  Secure, she smiles at all her foes ;
And weary travellers at length
  Within her sacred walls repose.

O sweet abode of peace and love,
  Where pilgrims freed from toil are bless'd ;
Had I the pinions of a dove,
  I'd fly to thee and be at rest.

But hush, my soul, nor dare repine ;
  The time my GOD appoints is best ;
While here, to do His will be mine,
  And His, to fix my time of rest. Amen.

428   *' The time is short.*

A FEW more years shall roll,
    A few more seasons come,
And we shall be with those that rest
  Asleep within the tomb :
  Then, O my LORD, prepare
  My soul for that great day ;
O wash me in Thy precious Blood,
  And take my sins away.

A few more suns shall set
  O'er these dark hills of time,
And we shall be where suns are not,
  A far serener clime :
  Then, O my LORD, prepare
  My soul for that bright day ;
O wash me in Thy precious Blood,
  And take my sins away.

A few more storms shall beat
  On this wild rocky shore,
And we shall be where tempests cease,
  And surges swell no more :

Then, O my LORD, prepare
My soul for that calm day ;
O wash me in Thy precious Blood,
And take my sins away.

A few more struggles here,
A few more partings o'er,
A few more toils, a few more tears,
And we shall weep no more :
Then, O my LORD, prepare
My soul for that blest day ;
O wash me in Thy precious Blood,
And take my sins away.

'Tis but a little while
And He shall come again,
Who died that we might live, Who lives
That we with Him may reign :
Then, O my LORD, prepare
My soul for that glad day ;
O wash me in Thy precious Blood,
And take my sins away.   Amen.

429   *So soon passeth it away, and we are gone.*
PART 1.

DAYS and moments quickly flying
Blend the living with the dead ;
Soon will you and I be lying
Each within our narrow bed.

Soon our souls to GOD Who gave them
Will have sped their rapid flight :
Able now by grace to save them,
Oh, that while we can we might !

JESU, infinite Redeemer,
Maker of this mighty frame,
Teach, O teach us to remember
What we are, and whence we came ;

Whence we came, and whither wending ;
  Soon we must through darkness go,
To inherit bliss unending,
  Or eternity of woe.

O by Thy power grant, LORD, that we
At our last hour fall not from Thee ;
Saved by Thy grace, Thine may we be
All through the days of eternity.   Amen.

PART 2.

As a shadow life is fleeting ;
  As a vapour, so it flies ;
For the bygone years retreating
  Pardon grant, and make us wise,—

Wise that we our days may number,
  Strive and wrestle with our sin,
Stay not in our work, nor slumber,
  Till Thy holy rest we win.

JESU, merciful Redeemer,
  Rouse dead souls to hear Thy voice ;
Wake, O wake each idle dreamer
  Now to make th' eternal choice.

Soon before the Judge all-glorious
  We with all the dead shall stand ;
Saviour, over death victorious,
  Place us then at Thy right hand.

Life passeth soon ; death draweth near :
Keep us, good LORD, till Thou appear,—
With Thee to live, with Thee to die,
With *Thee to reign* through eternity.   Amen.

430 *When thou passest through the waters, I will be with thee.*

SUNSET and evening star,
  And one clear call for me !
And may there be no moaning of the bar,
  When I put out to sea,
But such a tide as moving seems asleep,
  Too full for sound and foam,
When that which drew from out the boundless
    deep
  Turns again home.

Twilight and evening bell,
  And after that the dark !
And may there be no sadness of farewell,
  When I embark :
For, though from out our bourne of time and place
  The flood may bear me far,
I hope to see my Pilot face to face
  When I have crost the bar.

431   *I have set God always before me.*

LORD, be Thy Word my rule,
  In it may I rejoice ;
Thy glory be my aim,
Thy holy will my choice ;
Thy promises my hope ;
Thy providence my guard ;
Thine arm my strong support ;
Thyself my great reward.   Amen.

432 *So then each one of us shall give account of himself to God.*

A CHARGE to keep I have,
  A GOD to glorify,
A never-dying soul to save,
  And fit it for the sky.

To serve the present age,
My calling to fulfil ;
Oh, may it all my powers engage
To do my Master's will.

Arm me with jealous care,
As in Thy sight to live ;
And O Thy servant, LORD, prepare,
A good account to give.

Help me to watch and pray,
And on Thyself rely ;
And let me ne'er my trust betray,
But press to realms on high.   Amen.

33 *Blessed are those servants whom the Lord when he
cometh shall find watching.*

YE servants of the LORD,
Each in his office wait,
Observant of His heav'nly word,
And watchful at His gate.

Let all your lamps be bright,
And trim the golden flame ;
Gird up your loins as in His sight,
For awful is His Name.

Watch ! 'tis your LORD's command,
And while we speak, He's near ;
Mark the first signal of His hand,
And ready all appear.

Oh, happy servant he,
In such a posture found !
He shall his LORD with rapture see,
And be with honour crown'd.

CHRIST shall the banquet spread
With His own royal hand,
And raise that faithful servant's head
Amid th' Angelic band.

All glory, LORD, to Thee,
Whom heav'n and earth adore,
To FATHER, SON, and HOLY GHOST,
One GOD for evermore.   Amen.

434   *Watch and pray.*

" CHRISTIAN ! seek not yet repose,"
   Hear thy guardian Angel say ;
" Thou art in the midst of foes ;
     Watch and pray."

Principalities and powers,
Mustering their unseen array,
Wait for thy unguarded hours :
     Watch and pray.

Gird thy heav'nly armour on,
Wear it ever night and day ;
Ambush'd lies the evil one ;
     Watch and pray.

Hear the victors who o'ercame ;
Still they mark each warrior's way ;
All with one sweet voice exclaim,
     " Watch and pray."

Hear, above all, hear thy LORD,
Him thou lovest to obey ;
Hide within thy heart His word,
     " Watch and pray."

Watch, as if on that alone
Hung the issue of the day ;
Pray, that help may be sent down ;
     Watch and pray.   Amen.

GENERAL HYMNS.

35 *If any man will come after me, let him deny himself,
and take up his cross, and follow me.*

TAKE up thy cross, the Saviour said,
   If thou wouldst My disciple be ;
Deny thyself, the world forsake,
And humbly follow after Me.

Take up thy cross ; let not its weight
Fill thy weak spirit with alarm ;
His strength shall bear thy spirit up,
And brace thy heart, and nerve thine arm.

Take up thy cross, nor heed the shame,
Nor let thy foolish pride rebel ;
Thy LORD for thee the Cross endured,
To save thy soul from death and hell.

Take up thy cross then in His strength,
And calmly every danger brave ;
'Twill guide thee to a better home,
And lead to victory o'er the grave.

Take up thy cross, and follow CHRIST,
Nor think till death to lay it down ;
For only he who bears the cross
May hope to wear the glorious crown.

To Thee, great LORD, the ONE in THREE,
All praise for evermore ascend ;
O grant us in our home to see
The heav'nly life that knows no end.   Amen.

36   *Quit you like men ; be strong.*

STAND up !—stand up for JESUS !
   Ye soldiers of the Cross ;
Lift high His royal banner,
   It must not suffer loss.
From victory unto victory
   His army shall He lead,
Till every foe is vanquish'd,
   And CHRIST is LORD indeed.

(379)

GENERAL HYMNS.

Stand up !—stand up for JESUS !
   The solemn watchword hear ;
If while ye sleep He suffers,
   Away with shame and fear ;
Where'er ye meet with evil,
   Within you or without,
Charge for the GOD of battles,
   And put the foe to rout.

Stand up !—stand up for JESUS !
   The trumpet call obey ;
Forth to the mighty conflict
   In this His glorious day.
Ye that are men now serve Him
   Against unnumber'd foes ;
Let courage rise with danger
   And strength to strength-oppose.

Stand up !—stand up for JESUS !
   Stand in His strength alone ;
The arm of flesh will fail you,
   Ye dare not trust your own.
Put on the Gospel armour,
   Each piece put on with prayer ;
When duty calls or danger,
   Be never wanting there !

Stand up !—stand up for JESUS !
   The strife will not be long ;
This day the noise of battle,
   The next the victor's song.
To him that overcometh,
   A crown of life shall be ;
He with the King of Glory
   Shall reign eternally. Amen.

37   *Put on the whole armour of God.*

SOLDIERS of CHRIST, arise,
   And put your armour on ;
Strong in the strength which GOD supplies,
   Through His Eternal SON ;

Strong in the LORD of hosts,
   And in His mighty power ;
Who in the strength of JESUS trusts
   Is more than conqueror.

Stand then in His great might,
   With all His strength endued ;
And take, to arm you for the fight,
   The panoply of GOD.

From strength to strength go on,
   Wrestle, and fight, and pray ;
Tread all the powers of darkness down,
   And win the well-fought day :

That having all things done,
   And all your conflicts past,
Ye may obtain, through CHRIST alone,
   A crown of joy at last.

JESU, Eternal SON,
   We praise Thee and adore,
Who art with GOD the FATHER One
   And SPIRIT evermore.   Amen.

38 *The voice said, Cry. And he said, What shall I cry?*

THE voice says, Cry ! What shall we cry ?
   " All flesh is grass, and like the flower
Its glories droop, its pleasures die,
   Its *joys but last* one fleeting hour."

The voice says, Cry ! O piteous cry !
  And are there none to help and save ?
Have all that live beneath the sky
  No other prospect but a grave ?

The voice says, Cry ! Yet glorious cry !
  The word of GOD can never fall,
And tells how JESUS, throned on high,
  Holds out eternal life to all.

The voice says, Cry ! Who needs the cry ?
  O brother men ! who needs it not ?
By countless millions, far and nigh,
  'Tis still unheard, despised, forgot.

The voice says, Cry ! What stops the cry ?
  Our greed of wealth, our love of ease,
Our lack of earnest will to try
  Mankind to save, and GOD to please.

The voice says, Cry ! O let us cry !
  Though standing on death's awful brink,
Men feast, they jest, they sell, they buy,
  And cannot see, and will not think.

The voice says, Cry ! LORD, we would cry,
  But of Thy goodness teach us how ;
For fast the hours of mercy fly,
  And, if we cry, it must be now ! Amen.

439 *We are members one of another.*

SON of GOD, Eternal Saviour,
  Source of life and truth and grace,
Son of Man, Whose birth incarnate
  Hallows all our human race,
Thou, our Head, Who, throned in glory,
  For Thine own dost ever plead,
Fill us with Thy love and pity ;
  Heal our wrongs, and help our need.

GENERAL HYMNS.

Bind us all as one together
  In Thy Church's sacred fold,
Weak and healthy, poor and wealthy,
  Sad and joyful, young and old.
Is there want, or pain, or sorrow?
  Make us all the burden share.
Are there spirits crush'd and broken?
  Teach us, LORD, to soothe their care.

As Thou, LORD, hast lived for others,
  So may we for others live;
Freely have Thy gifts been granted,
  Freely may Thy servants give.
Thine the gold and Thine the silver,
  Thine the wealth of land and sea,
We but stewards of Thy bounty,
  Held in solemn trust for Thee.

Come, O CHRIST, and reign among us,
  King of love, and Prince of peace,
Hush the storm of strife and passion,
  Bid its cruel discords cease;
By Thy patient years of toiling,
  By Thy silent hours of pain,
Quench our fever'd thirst of pleasure,
  Shame our selfish greed of gain.

Son of GOD, Eternal Saviour,
  Source of life and truth and grace,
Son of Man, Whose birth incarnate
  Hallows all our human race,
Thou Who prayedst, Thou Who willest
  That Thy people should be one,
Grant, O grant our hope's fruition:
  Here on *earth* Thy will be done. Amen.

GENERAL HYMNS.

440 *Strive for the truth to the death, and the Lord shal*
fight for thee.

O GOD of Truth, Whose living word
　　Upholds whate'er hath breath,
Look down on Thy creation, LORD,
　　Enslaved by sin and death.

Set up Thy standard, LORD, that they
　　Who claim a heav'nly birth
May march with Thee to smite the lies
　　That vex Thy ransom'd earth.

Ah ! would we join that blest array,
　　And follow in the might
Of Him, the Faithful and the True,
　　In raiment clean and white ?

Then, GOD of Truth, for Whom we long—
　　Thou Who wilt hear our prayer—
Do Thine own battle in our hearts,
　　And slay the falsehood there.

Yea, come ! then, tried as in the fire,
　　From every lie set free,
Thy perfect truth shall dwell in us,
　　And we shall live in Thee.　Amen.

441　　　　*Knit together in love.*

　　　Hanc tu colendam, qui tuis.

O FATHER, Who the earth hast given
　　Our place of toil to be,
Knit all within its one wide bound
　　In one true charity.

Strangers and pilgrims here below,
　　We seek a home above,
Where Thou wilt gather in Thine own
　　Who live in holy love.

(384)

Unloving souls, with deeds of ill
　And words of angry strife,
Shall never, LORD, Thy glory see,
　Nor win the heav'nly life.

The earth itself from day to day
　Their burden scarce sustains,
And yearns, in travail, to be free
　From dark corruption's chains.

Yea, we too groan within ourselves,
　And that adoption wait
For which the HOLY SPIRIT'S seal
　Did us predestinate.

Eternal glory be ascribed
　To GOD, the ONE in THREE,
By Whom is pour'd into our hearts
　The grace of charity.　Amen.

42　　　*One hope of your calling.*

Igjennem Nat og Trængsel.

THROUGH the night of doubt and sorrow
　Onward goes the pilgrim band,
Singing songs of expectation,
　Marching to the Promised Land.
Clear before us through the darkness
　Gleams and burns the guiding light;
Brother clasps the hand of brother,
　Stepping fearless through the night.

One the light of GOD's own presence
　O'er His ransom'd people shed,
Chasing far the gloom and terror,
　Brightening all the path we tread:
One the object of our journey,
　One the faith which never tires,
One the earnest looking forward,
　One the hope our GOD inspires:

One the strain that lips of thousands
  Lift as from the heart of one ;
One the conflict, one the peril,
  One the march in GOD begun :
One the gladness of rejoicing
  On the far eternal shore,
Where the One Almighty FATHER
  Reigns in love for evermore.

Onward, therefore, pilgrim brothers,
  Onward with the Cross our aid ;
Bear its shame, and fight its battle,
  Till we rest beneath its shade.
Soon shall come the great awaking,
  Soon the rending of the tomb ;
Then the scattering of all shadows,
  And the end of toil and gloom.   Amen.

443 *One is your Master, even Christ; and all ye are
                brethren.*

BROTHERS, joining hand to hand,
  In one bond united,
Pressing onward to that land
  Where all wrongs are righted :
Let your words and actions be
  Worthy your vocation ;
Chosen of the LORD, and free,
  Heirs of CHRIST's salvation.

CHRIST, the Way, the Truth, the Life,
  Who hath gone before you
Through the turmoil and the strife,
  Holds His banner o'er you ;
All who see the sacred sign
  Press tow'rds heaven's portal,
Fired by hope that is divine,
  Love that is immortal.

They who follow fear no foe,
 Care not who assail them ;
Where the Master leads they go,
 He will never fail them ;
Courage, brothers ! we are one,
 In the love that sought us ;
Soon the warfare shall be done,
 Through the grace He brought us. Amen.

144 *Behold, how good and joyful a thing it is, brethren,*
to dwell together in unity !

O quam juvat fratres, Deus.

O LORD, how joyful 'tis to see
 The brethren join in love to Thee !
On Thee alone their heart relies,
Their only strength Thy grace supplies.

How sweet within Thy holy place
With one accord to sing Thy grace,
Besieging Thine attentive ear
With all the force of fervent prayer !

O may we love the house of GOD,
Of peace and joy the blest abode ;
O may no angry strife destroy
That sacred peace, that holy joy.

The world without may rage, but we
Will only cling more close to Thee,
With hearts to Thee more wholly given,
More wean'd from earth, more fix'd on heaven.

LORD, shower upon us from above
The sacred gift of mutual love ;
Each other's wants may we supply,
And reign together in the sky.

Praise GOD, from Whom all blessings flow,
Praise Him, all creatures here below,
Praise Him above, Angelic host,
Praise FATHER, SON, and HOLY GHOST. Amen.

445 *Blessed are the pure in heart, for they shall see God.*

BLESS'D are the pure in heart,
   For they shall see our GOD ;
The secret of the LORD is theirs,
   Their soul is CHRIST'S abode.

The LORD, Who left the heavens
   Our life and peace to bring,
To dwell in lowliness with men,
   Their Pattern and their King ;

He to the lowly soul
   Doth still Himself impart,
And for His dwelling and His throne
   Chooseth the pure in heart.

LORD, we Thy presence seek ;
   May ours this blessing be ;
Give us a pure and lowly heart,
   A temple meet for Thee.   Amen.

446 *In him was life, and the life was the light of men.*

O LIGHT, Whose beams illumine all
   From twilight dawn to perfect day,
Shine Thou before the shadows fall
   That lead our wandering feet astray :
At morn and eve Thy radiance pour,
That youth may love, and age adore.

O Way, through Whom our souls draw near
   To yon eternal home of peace,
Where perfect love shall cast out fear,
   And earth's vain toil and wandering cease,
In strength or weakness may we see
Our heav'nward path, O LORD, through Thee.

O Truth, before Whose shrine we bow,
  Thou priceless Pearl for all who seek,
To Thee our earliest strength we vow,
  Thy love will bless the pure and meek ;
When dreams or mists beguile our sight,
Turn Thou our darkness into light.

O Life, the well that ever flows
  To slake the thirst of those that faint,
Thy power to bless what Seraph knows ?
  Thy joy supreme what words can paint ?
In earth's last hour of fleeting breath
Be Thou our Conqueror over death.

O Light, O Way, O Truth, O Life,
  O JESU, born mankind to save,
Give Thou Thy peace in deadliest strife,
  Shed Thou Thy calm on stormiest wave ;
Be Thou our hope, our joy, our dread,
LORD of the living and the dead.   Amen.

47 *Now abideth faith, hope, charity, these three; but the
       greatest of these is charity.*

Supreme motor cordium.

GREAT Mover of all hearts, Whose hand
      Doth all the secret springs command
Of human thought and will,
Thou, since the world was made, dost bless
Thy Saints with fruits of holiness,
  Their order to fulfil.

Faith, hope, and love here weave one chain ;
But love alone shall then remain
  When this short day is gone :
O Love, O Truth, O endless Light,
When shall we see Thy Sabbath bright
  With *all our* labours done ?

We sow 'mid perils here and tears ;
There the glad hand the harvest bears,
   Which here in grief hath sown :
Great THREE in ONE, the increase give ;
Thy gifts of grace, by which we live,
   With heav'nly glory crown.   Amen.

448 *Let this mind be in you, which was also in Chri Jesus.*

LORD, as to Thy dear Cross we flee,
   And plead to be forgiven,
So let Thy life our pattern be,
   And form our souls for heaven.

Help us, through good report and ill,
   Our daily cross to bear ;
Like Thee, to do our FATHER's will,
   Our brethren's griefs to share.

Let grace our selfishness expel,
   Our earthliness refine,
And kindness in our bosoms dwell,
   As free and true as Thine.

If joy shall at Thy bidding fly,
   And grief's dark day come on,
We in our turn would meekly cry,
   "FATHER, Thy will be done."

Kept peaceful in the midst of strife,
   Forgiving and forgiven,
O may we lead the pilgrim's life,
   And follow Thee to heaven.   Amen.

449 *The breath of the Almighty hath given me life.*

BREATHE on me, Breath of GOD,
   Fill me with life anew,
That I may love what Thou dost love,
   And do what Thou wouldst do.

Breathe on me, Breath of GOD,
 Until my heart is pure ;
Until with Thee I will one will
 To do and to endure.

Breathe on me, Breath of GOD,
 Till I am wholly Thine ;
Until this earthly part of me
 Glows with Thy fire divine.

Breathe on me, Breath of GOD,
 So shall I never die,
But live with Thee the perfect life
 Of Thine eternity.   Amen.

50 *A perfect heart.*

OH for a heart to praise my GOD,
 A heart from sin set free ;
A heart that's sprinkled with the Blood
 So freely shed for me :

A heart resign'd, submissive, meek,
 My dear Redeemer's throne ;
Where only CHRIST is heard to speak,
 Where JESUS reigns alone :

A humble, lowly, contrite heart,
 Believing, true, and clean,
Which neither life nor death can part
 From Him that dwells within :

A heart in every thought renew'd,
 And full of love divine ;
Perfect, and right, and pure, and good,
 A copy, LORD, of Thine.

Thy nature, gracious LORD, impart,
 Come quickly from above ;
Write Thy new Name upon my heart,
 Thy *new best* Name of Love.   Amen.

451 *The things which are seen are temporal; but the things which are not seen are eternal.*

THE roseate hues of early dawn,
  The brightness of the day,
The crimson of the sunset sky,
  How fast they fade away!
Oh for the pearly gates of heaven,
  Oh for the golden floor,
Oh for the Sun of righteousness
  That setteth nevermore!

The highest hopes we cherish here,
  How fast they tire and faint;
How many a spot defiles the robe
  That wraps an earthly saint!
Oh for a heart that never sins,
  Oh for a soul wash'd white,
Oh for a voice to praise our King,
  Nor weary day or night!

Here faith is ours, and heav'nly hope,
  And grace to lead us higher;
But there are perfectness and peace,
  Beyond our best desire.
O by Thy love and anguish, LORD,
  And by Thy life laid down,
Grant that we fall not from Thy grace,
  Nor cast away our crown.   Amen.

452 *Until Christ be formed in you.*

O SAVIOUR, may we never rest
  Till Thou art form'd within,
Till Thou hast calm'd our troubled breast,
  And crush'd the power of sin.

O may we gaze upon Thy Cross,
  Until the wondrous sight
Makes earthly treasures seem but dross,
  And earthly sorrows light:

Until, released from carnal ties,
  Our spirit upward springs,
And sees true peace above the skies,
  True joy in heav'nly things.

There as we gaze, may we become
  United, LORD, to Thee,
And in a fairer, happier home
  Thy perfect beauty see. Amen.

453 *Thou art about my path, and about my bed, and spiest*
out all my ways.

THOU, LORD, by strictest search hast known
  My rising up and lying down ;
My secret thoughts are known to Thee,
Known long before conceived by me.

Thine eye my bed and path surveys,
My public haunts and private ways ;
Thou know'st what 'tis my lips would vent,
My yet unutter'd word's intent.

Surrounded by Thy power I stand,
On every side I find Thy hand :
O skill, for human reach too high !
Too dazzling bright for mortal eye !

Search, try, O GOD, my thought and heart,
If mischief lurks in any part ;
Correct me where I go astray,
And guide me in Thy perfect way. Amen.

454 *Turn thou us unto thee, O LORD, and we shall be*
turned; renew our days as of old.

AWAKE, O LORD, as in the time of old !
  Come, HOLY SPIRIT, in Thy power and might ;
For lack of Thee our hearts are strangely cold,
  Our *minds* but blindly groping tow'rds the light

Doubts are abroad : make Thou these doubts to
  cease ;
Fears are within : set Thou these fears at rest !
Strife is among us : melt that strife to peace !
  Change marches onward : may all change be
  blest !

Make us to be what we profess to be ;
  Let prayer be prayer, and praise be heart-felt
  praise ;
From unreality, O set us free,
  And let our words be echo'd by our ways.

Turn us, good LORD, and so shall we be turn'd :
  Let every passion grieving Thee be still'd :
Then shall our race be won, our guerdon earn'd,
  Our Master look'd on, and our joy fulfill'd.
                                        Amen.

455 *A broken and contrite heart, O God, shalt thou not
despise.*

LORD, when we bend before Thy throne,
    And our confessions pour,
Teach us to feel the sins we own,
    And hate what we deplore.

Our broken spirits pitying see ;
    True penitence impart ;
Then let a kindling glance from Thee
    Beam hope upon the heart.

When we disclose our wants in prayer,
    May we our wills resign,
And not a thought our bosoms share
    Which is not wholly Thine.

Let faith each meek petition fill,
    And waft it to the skies ;
And teach our hearts 'tis goodness still
    That grants it or denies. Amen.

56 *Thou preparest their heart, and thine ear hearkeneth thereto. .*

LORD, teach us how to pray aright
   With reverence and with fear ;
Though dust and ashes in Thy sight,
   We may, we must draw near.

We perish if we cease from prayer ;
   O grant us power to pray ;
And when to meet Thee we prepare,
   LORD, meet us by the way.

GOD of all grace, we bring to Thee
   A broken contrite heart ;
Give, what Thine eye delights to see,
   Truth in the inward part ;

Faith in the only Sacrifice
   That can for sin atone ;
To cast our hopes, to fix our eyes,
   On CHRIST, on CHRIST alone ;

Patience to watch, and wait, and weep,
   Though mercy long delay ;
Courage our fainting souls to keep,
   And trust Thee though Thou slay.

Give these, and then Thy will be done ;
   Thus, strengthen'd with all might,
We, through Thy SPIRIT and Thy SON,
   Shall pray, and pray aright.   Amen.

57 *I beseech you, brethren, by the mercies of God, that ye present your bodies a living sacrifice, holy, acceptable to God, which is your reasonable service.*

O THOU Who camest from above,
   The fire celestial to impart,
Kindle a flame of sacred love
   On the mean altar of my heart.

There let it for Thy glory burn
    With ever-bright, undying blaze,
And trembling to its source return
    In humble prayer, and fervent praise.

JESUS, confirm my heart's desire
    To work, and speak, and think for Thee ;
Still let me guard the holy fire
    And still stir up the gift in me.

Still let me prove Thy perfect will,
    My acts of faith and love repeat ;
Till death Thy endless mercies seal;
    And make the sacrifice complete.   Amen.

458   *Men ought always to pray, and not to faint.*

WHAT various hindrances we meet
    In coming to the Mercy-seat ;
Yet who, that knows the worth of prayer,
But wishes to be often there ?

Prayer makes the darken'd cloud withdraw,
Prayer climbs the ladder Jacob saw,
Gives exercise to faith and love,
Brings every blessing from above.

Restraining prayer, we cease to fight ;
Prayer makes the Christian's armour bright ;
And Satan trembles when he sees
The weakest saint upon his knees.

When Moses stood with arms spread wide,
Success was found on Israel's side ;
But when through weariness they fail'd,
That moment Amalek prevail'd.

Have we no words ? ah, think again,
Words flow apace when we complain
And fill our fellow-creature's ear
With the sad tale of all our care.

Were half the breath thus vainly spent
To heav'n in supplication sent,
Our cheerful song would oftener be,
" Hear what the LORD hath done for me."

O LORD, increase our faith and love,
That we may all Thy goodness prove,
And gain from Thy exhaustless store
The fruits of prayer for evermore.   Amen.

59 *And he said, I will not let thee go, except thou bless me.*

SHEPHERD Divine, our wants relieve
   In this our evil day ;
To all Thy tempted followers give
   The power to watch and pray.

Long as our fiery trials last,
   Long as the cross we bear,
O let our souls on Thee be cast
   In never-ceasing prayer.

The SPIRIT'S interceding grace
   Give us in faith to claim,
To wrestle till we see Thy face,
   And know Thy hidden Name.

Till Thou Thy perfect love impart,
   Till Thou Thyself bestow,
Be this the cry of every heart,
   " I will not let Thee go."

I will not let Thee go, unless
   Thou tell Thy Name to me,
With all Thy great salvation bless,
   And make me all like Thee.

Then let me on the mountain-top
   Behold Thine open face,
Where faith in sight is swallow'd up,
   And prayer in endless praise.   Amen.

460 *Ask what I shall give thee.*

COME, my soul, thy suit prepare,
  JESUS loves to answer prayer ;
He Himself has bid thee pray,
Therefore will not say thee nay.

Thou art coming to a King,
Large petitions with thee bring ;
For His grace and power are such,
None can ever ask too much.

With my burden I begin ;
LORD, remove this load of sin ;
Let Thy Blood, for sinners spilt,
Set my conscience free from guilt.

LORD, I come to Thee for rest ;
Take possession of my breast ;
There Thy blood-bought right maintain,
And without a rival reign.

While I am a pilgrim here,
Let Thy love my spirit cheer ;
Be my Guide, my Guard, my Friend ;
Lead me to my journey's end.   Amen.

461 *All our righteousnesses are as filthy rags.*

NOT for our sins alone
  Thy mercy, LORD, we sue ;
Let fall Thy pitying glance
  On our devotions too,
What we have done for Thee,
  And what we think to do.

The holiest hours we spend
  In prayer upon our knees,
The times when most we deem
  Our songs of praise will please,
Thou Searcher of all hearts
  Forgiveness pour on these.

And all the gifts we bring,
　And all the vows we make,
And all the acts of love
　We plan for Thy dear sake,
Into Thy pardoning thought,
　O God of mercy, take.

And most, when we, Thy flock,
　Before Thine altar bend,
And strange, bewildering thoughts
　With those sweet moments blend,
By Him Whose death we plead,
　Good Lord, Thy help extend.

Bow down Thine ear and hear !
　Open Thine eyes and see !
Our very love is shame,
　And we must come to Thee
To make it of Thy grace
　What Thou would'st have it be. Amen.

2 *Have mercy upon me, O God, after thy great goodness:
according to the multitude of thy mercies do away
mine offences.*

HAVE mercy, Lord, on me,
　　As Thou wert ever kind ;
Let me, opprest with loads of guilt,
　Thy wonted mercy find.

Wash off my foul offence,
　And cleanse me from my sin ;
For I confess my crime, and see
　How great my guilt has been.

The joy Thy favour gives
　Let me again obtain,
And Thy free Spirit's firm support
　My fainting soul sustain.

We have not fear'd Thee as we ought,
  Nor bow'd beneath Thine awful eye,
Nor guarded deed, and word, and thought,
  Remembering that GOD was nigh.
    LORD, give us faith to know Thee near,
    And grant the grace of holy fear.

We have not loved Thee as we ought,
  Nor cared that we are loved by Thee ;
Thy presence we have coldly sought,
  And feebly long'd Thy face to see.
    LORD, give a pure and loving heart
    To feel and own the love Thou art.

We have not served Thee as we ought,
  Alas ! the duties left undone,—
The work with little fervour wrought,—
  The battles lost, or scarcely won !
    LORD, give the zeal, and give the might,
    For Thee to toil, for Thee to fight.

When shall we know Thee as we ought,
  And fear, and love, and serve aright !
When shall we, out of trial brought,
  Be perfect in the land of light !
    LORD, may we day by day prepare
    To see Thy face, and serve Thee there.
                                    Amen.

466   *Lovest thou me ?*

FORSAKEN once, and thrice denied,
  The risen LORD gave pardon free,
Stood once again at Peter's side,
  And ask'd him, " Lov'st thou Me ? "

How many times with faithless word
Have we denied His holy Name !
How oft forsaken our dear LORD,
  And shrunk when trial came !

Saint Peter, when the cock crew clear,
Went out, and wept his broken faith ;
Strong as a rock through strife and fear,
    He served his LORD till death.

How oft his cowardice of heart
We have without his love sincere,
The sin without the sorrow's smart,
    The shame without the tear !

O oft forsaken, oft denied,
Forgive our shame, wash out our sin ;
Look on us from Thy FATHER's side
    And let that sweet look win.

Hear when we call Thee from the deep,
Still walk beside us on the shore,
Give hands to work, and eyes to weep,
    And hearts to love Thee more.   Amen.

167   *That rock was Christ.*

ROCK of ages, cleft for me,
   Let me hide myself in Thee ;
Let the Water and the Blood,
From Thy riven side which flow'd,
Be of sin the double cure,
Cleanse me from its guilt and power.

Not the labours of my hands
Can fulfil Thy law's demands ;
Could my zeal no respite know,
Could my tears for ever flow,
All for sin could not atone ;
Thou must save, and Thou alone.

Nothing in my hand I bring,
Simply to Thy Cross I cling ;
Naked, come to Thee for dress ;
Helpless, look to Thee for grace ;
Foul, I to the fountain fly ;
Wash me, Saviour, or I die.

While I draw this fleeting breath,
When my eyelids close in death,
When I soar through tracts unknown,
See Thee on Thy judgment throne ;
Rock of ages, cleft for me,
Let me hide myself in Thee.   Amen.

468 *Behold the Lamb of God, which taketh away the s*
of the world.

BEHOLD the LAMB of GOD !
　　O Thou for sinners slain,
Let it not be in vain
　　That Thou hast died :
Thee for my Saviour let me take,
My only refuge let me make
　　Thy piercèd side.

Behold the LAMB of GOD !
Into the sacred flood
Of Thy most precious Blood
　　My soul I cast :
Wash me and make me clean within,
And keep me pure from every sin,
　　Till life be past.

Behold the LAMB of GOD !
All hail, Incarnate WORD,
Thou everlasting LORD,
　　Saviour most Blest ;
Fill us with love that never faints,
Grant us with all Thy blessèd Saints
　　Eternal rest.

Behold the LAMB of GOD !
Worthy is He alone
To sit upon the throne
　　Of GOD above ;
One with the Ancient of all days,
One with the Comforter in praise,
　　All Light, all Love.   Amen.

39 *Jesus, Master, have mercy on us.*

SAVIOUR, when in dust to Thee
Low we bow the adoring knee;
When, repentant, to the skies
Scarce we lift our weeping eyes;
Oh, by all Thy pains and woe
Suffer'd once for man below,
Bending from Thy throne on high,
Hear our solemn litany.

By Thy helpless infant years,
By Thy life of want and tears,
By Thy days of sore distress
In the savage wilderness;
By the dread mysterious hour
Of the insulting tempter's power;
Turn, O, turn a favouring eye;
Hear our solemn litany.

By the sacred griefs that wept
O'er the grave where Lazarus slept;
By the boding tears that flow'd
Over Salem's loved abode;
By the troubled sigh that told
Treachery lurk'd within Thy fold;
From Thy seat above the sky
Hear our solemn litany.

By Thine hour of whelming fear;
By Thine agony of prayer;
By the Cross, the nail, the thorn,
Piercing spear, and torturing scorn;
By the gloom that veil'd the skies
O'er the dreadful Sacrifice;
Listen to our humble cry;
Hear our solemn litany.

By Thy deep expiring groan ;
By the sad sepulchral stone ;
By the vault whose dark abode
Held in vain the rising GOD ;
Oh ! from earth to heav'n restored,
Mighty, re-ascended LORD,
Listen, listen to the cry
Of our solemn litany.   Amen.

470 *I, if I be lifted up from the earth, will draw all m*
unto me.

JESU, meek and lowly,
    Saviour, pure and holy,
On Thy love relying
Hear me humbly crying.

Prince of life and power,
My salvation's tower,
On the Cross I view Thee
Calling sinners to Thee.

There behold me gazing
At the sight amazing ;
Bending low before Thee,
Helpless I adore Thee.

By Thy red wounds streaming,
With Thy Life-Blood gleaming,
Blood for sinners flowing,
Pardon free bestowing ;

By that fount of blessing,
Thy dear love expressing,
All my aching sadness
Turn Thou into gladness.

LORD, in mercy guide me,
Be Thou e'er beside me ;
In Thy ways direct me,
'Neath Thy wings protect me.   Amen

GENERAL HYMNS.

71 *Come unto me, all ye that labour and are heavy laden,*
and I will give you rest.

ART thou weary, art thou languid,
   Art thou sore distrest?
"Come to Me," saith One, "and coming
       Be at rest!"

Hath He marks to lead me to Him,
   If He be my Guide?
"In His feet and hands are wound-prints, .
       And His side."

Hath He diadem as Monarch
   That His brow adorns?
"Yea, a crown, in very surety,
       But of thorns."

If I find Him, if I follow,
   What His guerdon here?
"Many a sorrow, many a labour,
       Many a tear."

If I still hold closely to Him,
   What hath He at last?
"Sorrow vanquish'd, labour ended,
       Jordan past."

If I ask Him to receive me,
   Will He say me nay?
"Not till earth, and not till heaven
       Pass away."

Finding, following, keeping, struggling,
   Is He sure to bless?
"Angels, Martyrs, Prophets, Virgins,
       Answer, Yes!"   Amen.

472 *Him that cometh to me I will in no wise cast out.*

"COME unto Me, ye weary,
    And I will give you rest."
O blessèd voice of JESUS,
    Which comes to hearts opprest ;
It tells of benediction,
    Of pardon, grace, and peace,
Of joy that hath no ending,
    Of love which cannot cease.

"Come unto Me, ye wanderers,
    And I will give you light."
O loving voice of JESUS,
    Which comes to cheer the night ;
Our hearts were fill'd with sadness,
    And we had lost our way ;
But morning brings us gladness,
    And songs the break of day.

"Come unto Me, ye fainting,
    And I will give you life."
O cheering voice of JESUS,
    Which comes to aid our strife ;
The foe is stern and eager,
    The fight is fierce and long ;
But Thou hast made us mighty,
    And stronger than the strong.

"And whosoever cometh,
    I will not cast him out."
O patient love of JESUS,
    Which drives away our doubt ;
Which, though we be unworthy
    Of love so great and free,
Invites us very sinners
    To come, dear LORD, to Thee.   Ame

GENERAL HYMNS.

'3 *Our light affliction, which is but for a moment, worketh for us a far more exceeding and eternal weight of glory.*

Wem in Leidenstagen.

O LET him whose sorrow
    No relief can find,
Trust in GOD, and borrow
    Ease for heart and mind.

Where the mourner weeping
    Sheds the secret tear,
GOD His watch is keeping,
    Though none else be near.

GOD will never leave thee,
    All thy wants He knows,
Feels the pains that grieve thee,
    Sees thy cares and woes.

Raise thine eyes to heaven
    When thy spirits quail,
When, by tempests driven,
    Heart and courage fail.

When in grief we languish,
    He will dry the tear,
Who His children's anguish
    Soothes with succour near.

All our woe and sadness
    In this world below
Balance not the gladness
    We in heav'n shall know.

JESU, Holy Saviour,
    In the realms above
Crown us with Thy favour,
    Fill us with Thy love. Amen.

474 *Whom have I in heaven but thee? and there is none upon earth that I desire in comparison of thee.*

NEARER, my GOD, to Thee,
   Nearer to Thee ;
E'en though it be a cross
   That raiseth me ;
Still all my song shall be,
"Nearer, my GOD, to Thee,
   Nearer to Thee."

Though, like the wanderer,
   The sun gone down,
Darkness comes over me,
   My rest a stone ;
Yet in my dreams I'd be
Nearer, my GOD, to Thee,
   Nearer to Thee.

There let my way appear
   Steps unto heaven,
All that Thou sendest me
   In mercy given,
Angels to beckon me
Nearer, my GOD, to Thee,
   Nearer to Thee.

Then, with my waking thoughts
   Bright with Thy praise,
Out of my stony griefs
   Beth-el I'll raise ;
So by my woes to be
Nearer, my GOD, to Thee,
   Nearer to Thee.   Amen.

475 *God is our hope and strength, a very present help i trouble.*

GOD of our life, to Thee we call,
 Afflicted at Thy feet we fall ;
When the great water-floods prevail,
Leave not our trembling hearts to fail.

Amidst the roaring of the sea
Our souls still hang their hopes on Thee ;
Thy constant love, Thy faithful care,
Alone can save us from despair.

Friend of the friendless and the faint,
Where should we lodge our deep complaint?
Where but with Thee, Whose open door
Invites the helpless and the poor?

Did ever mourner plead with Thee,
And Thou refuse that mourner's plea?
Does not the word still fix'd remain,
That none shall seek Thy face in vain?

Then hear, O LORD, our humble cry,
And bend on us Thy pitying eye :
To Thee their prayer Thy people make :
Hear us, for our Redeemer's sake.   Amen.

:76 *And he arose and rebuked the wind, and said unto
the sea, Peace, be still.*

FIERCE raged the tempest o'er the deep,
   Watch did Thine anxious servants keep,
But Thou wast wrapp'd in guileless sleep,
          Calm and still.

"Save, LORD, we perish," was their cry,
"O save us in our agony !"
Thy word above the storm rose high,
          "Peace, be still."

The wild winds hush'd ; the angry deep
Sank, like a little child, to sleep ;
The sullen billows ceased to leap,
          At Thy will.

So, when our life is clouded o'er,
And storm-winds drift us from the shore,
Say, lest we sink to rise no more,
          "Peace, be still."   Amen.

(411)

477

Lord, help me.

O HELP us, LORD ; each hour of need
　Thy heav'nly succour give ;
Help us in thought, and word, and deed,
　Each hour on earth we live.

O help us, when our spirits bleed
　With contrite anguish sore ;
And when our hearts are cold and dead,
　O help us, LORD, the more.

O help us through the prayer of faith
　More firmly to believe ;
For still the more the servant hath,
　The more shall he receive.

O help us, JESU, from on high,
　We know no help but Thee ;
O help us so to live and die
　As Thine in heav'n to be.　Amen.

478 *Like as the hart desireth the water-brooks, so longeth*
my soul after thee, O God.

AS pants the hart for cooling streams
　When heated in the chase,
So longs my soul, O GOD, for Thee,
　And Thy refreshing grace.
For Thee, my GOD, the living GOD,
　My thirsty soul doth pine :
O when shall I behold Thy face,
　Thou Majesty Divine ?
Why restless, why cast down, my soul ?
　Hope still, and thou shalt sing
The praise of Him Who is thy GOD,
　Thy health's eternal spring.
To FATHER, SON, and HOLY GHOST,
　The GOD Whom we adore,
Be glory, as it was, is now,
　And shall be evermore.　Amen.

479 *Lord, remember me.*

O THOU, from Whom all goodness flows,
  I lift my heart to Thee ;
In all my sorrows, conflicts, woes,
  Good LORD, remember me.

When on my aching burden'd heart
  My sins lie heavily,
Thy pardon grant, Thy peace impart ;
  Good LORD, remember me.

When trials sore obstruct my way,
  And ills I cannot flee,
Then let my strength be as my day ;
  Good LORD, remember me.

If worn with pain, disease, and grief
  This feeble frame should be,
Grant patience, rest, and kind relief ;
  Good LORD, remember me.

And, oh, when in the hour of death
  I bow to Thy decree,
JESU, receive my parting breath ;
  Good LORD, remember me.   Amen.

480 *O look thou upon me, and be merciful unto me.*
Μνώεο Χριστέ.

LORD JESUS, think on me,
  And purge away my sin ;
From earthborn passions set me free,
  And make me pure within.

LORD JESUS, think on me
  With many a care opprest ;
Let me Thy loving servant be,
  And taste Thy promised rest.

LORD JESUS, think on me,
  Nor let me go astray ;
Through darkness and perplexity
  Point Thou the heav'nly way.

Lord Jesus, think on me,
That, when the flood is past,
I may th' eternal Brightness see,
And share Thy joy at last.   Amen.

481 *My soul thirsteth for thee, my flesh also longeth after thee; in a barren and dry land where no water is.*

FAR from my heav'nly home,
    Far from my Father's breast,
Fainting I cry, "Blest Spirit, come,
And speed me to my rest."

My spirit homeward turns,
    And fain would thither flee ;
My heart, O Sion, droops and yearns,
When I remember thee.

To thee, to thee I press,
    A dark and toilsome road ;
When shall I pass the wilderness,
And reach the Saints' abode ?

God of my life, be near ;
    On Thee my hopes I cast ;
O guide me through the desert here,
And bring me home at last.   Amen.

482 *In the day time also he led them with a cloud, and all the night through with a light of fire.*

LEAD, kindly Light, amid th' encircling gloom,
    Lead Thou me on ;
The night is dark, and I am far from home,
    Lead Thou me on.
Keep Thou my feet ; I do not ask to see
The distant scene ; one step enough for me.

I was not ever thus, nor pray'd that Thou
      Shouldst lead me on ;
I loved to choose and see my path ; but now
      Lead Thou me on.
I loved the garish day, and, spite of fears,
Pride ruled my will : remember not past years.

So long Thy power hath blest me, sure it still
      Will lead me on,
O'er moor and fen, o'er crag and torrent, till
      The night is gone ;
And with the morn those angel faces smile,
Which I have loved long since, and lost awhile.
                     Amen.

483   *Lord, save us.*

JESU, meek and gentle,
    Son of God most High,
Pitying, loving Saviour,
    Hear Thy children's cry.

Pardon our offences,
    Loose our captive chains,
Break down every idol
    Which our soul detains.

Give us holy freedom,
    Fill our hearts with love,
Draw us, Holy Jesus,
    To the realms above.

Lead us on our journey,
    Be Thyself the Way
Through this world of darkness
    To the heav'nly day.

Jesu, meek and gentle,
    Son of God most High,
Pitying, loving Saviour,
    Hear Thy children's cry.   Amen.

484   *Thou art a place to hide me in.*

Dignare me, O Jesu, rogo te.

JESU, grant me this, I pray,
  Ever in Thy heart to stay ;
Let me evermore abide
Hidden in Thy wounded side.

If the evil one prepare,
Or the world, a tempting snare,
I am safe when I abide
In Thy heart and wounded side.

If the flesh, more dangerous still,
Tempt my soul to deeds of ill,
Naught I fear when I abide
In Thy heart and wounded side.

Death will come one day to me ;
JESU, cast me not from Thee :
Dying let me still abide
In Thy heart and wounded side.   Amer

485 *O hold thou up my goings in thy paths; that my
footsteps slip not.*

BE Thou my Guardian and my Guide,
  And hear me when I call ;
Let not my slippery footsteps slide,
  And hold me lest I fall.

The world, the flesh, and Satan dwell
  Around the path I tread ;
O save me from the snares of hell,
  Thou Quickener of the dead.

And if I tempted am to sin,
  And outward things are strong,
Do Thou, O LORD, keep watch within,
  And save my soul from wrong.

Still let me ever watch and pray,
And feel that I am frail ;
That if the tempter cross my way,
Yet he may not prevail.   Amen.

486 *Thou hast been my succour; leave me not, neither*
forsake me, O God of my salvation.

WE know Thee Who Thou art,
Lord Jesus, Mary's Son :
We know the yearnings of Thy heart
To end Thy work begun.

That sacred fount of grace,
'Mid all the bliss of heaven,
Has joy whene'er we seek Thy face,
And kneel to be forgiven.

Brought home from ways perverse,
At peace Thine arms within,
We pray Thee, shield us from the curse
Of falling back to sin.

We dare not ask to live
Henceforth from trials free ;
But Oh, when next they tempt us, give
More strength to cling to Thee.

We know Thee Who Thou art,
Our own redeeming Lord ;
Be Thou by will, and mind, and heart,
Accepted, loved, adored.   Amen.

487 *If any man serve me, let him follow me; and where I*
am, there shall also my servant be.

O JESUS, I have promised
To serve Thee to the end ;
Be Thou for ever near me,
My Master and my Friend ;
I shall not fear the battle
If Thou art by my side,
Nor wander from the pathway
If Thou wilt be my Guide.

GENERAL HYMNS.

O let me feel Thee near me :
  The world is ever near ;
I see the sights that dazzle,
  The tempting sounds I hear ;
My foes are ever near me,
  Around me and within ;
But, Jesus, draw Thou nearer,
  And shield my soul from sin.

O let me hear Thee speaking
  In accents clear and still,
Above the storms of passion,
  The murmurs of self-will ;
O speak to re-assure me,
  To hasten or control ;
O speak, and make me listen,
  Thou Guardian of my soul.

O let me see Thy features,
  The look that once could make
So many a true disciple
  Leave all things for Thy sake ;
The look that beam'd on Peter
  When he Thy Name denied ;
The look that draws Thy loved ones
  Close to Thy piercèd side.

O Jesus, Thou hast promised
  To all who follow Thee,
That where Thou art in glory
  There shall Thy servant be ;
And, Jesus, I have promised
  To serve Thee to the end ;
O give me grace to follow,
  My Master and my Friend.

O let me see Thy foot-marks,
  And in them plant mine own ;
My hope to follow duly
  Is in Thy strength alone ;

O guide me, call me, draw me,
    Uphold me to the end ;
And then in heav'n receive me,
    My Saviour and my Friend.   Amen.

38 *A man shall be as an hiding place from the wind,*
and a covert from the tempest.

JESU, Lover of my soul,
    Let me to Thy bosom fly,
While the gath'ring waters roll,
    While the tempest still is high :
Hide me, O my Saviour, hide,
    Till the storm of life be past ;
Safe into the haven guide,
    O receive my soul at last.

Other refuge have I none ;
    Hangs my helpless soul on Thee ;
Leave, ah ! leave me not alone,
    Still support and comfort me.
All my trust on Thee is stay'd,
    All my help from Thee I bring ;
Cover my defenceless head
    With the shadow of Thy wing.

Thou, O CHRIST, art all I want,
    More than all in Thee I find :
Raise the fallen, cheer the faint,
    Heal the sick, and lead the blind.
Just and holy is Thy Name,
    I am all unrighteousness ;
False and full of sin I am,
    Thou art full of truth and grace.

Plenteous grace with Thee is found,
    Grace to cleanse from every sin ;
Let the healing streams abound ;
    Make and keep me pure within ;

Thou of life the fountain art ;
  Freely let me take of Thee ;
Spring Thou up within my heart,
  Rise to all eternity.   Amen

489 *Let my supplication come before thee; deliver me,*
according to thy word.

JESUS, LORD of life and glory,
    Bend from heav'n Thy gracious ear;
While our waiting souls adore Thee,
    Friend of helpless sinners, hear :
      By Thy mercy,
    O deliver us, good LORD.

From the depths of nature's blindness,
    From the hardening power of sin,
From all malice and unkindness,
    From the pride that lurks within,
      By Thy mercy,
    O deliver us, good LORD.

When temptation sorely presses,
    In the day of Satan's power,
In our times of deep distresses,
    In each dark and trying hour,
      By Thy mercy,
    O deliver us, good LORD.

When the world around is smiling,
    In the time of wealth and ease,
Earthly joys our hearts beguiling,
    In the day of health and peace,
      By Thy mercy,
    O deliver us, good LORD.

In the weary hours of sickness, .
    In the times of grief and pain,
When we feel our mortal weakness,
    When the creature's help is vain,
      By Thy mercy,
    O deliver us, good LORD.

In the solemn hour of dying,
In the awful judgment day,
May our souls, on Thee relying,
Find Thee still our Rock and Stay :
By Thy mercy,
O deliver us, good LORD.   Amen.

490 *Surely he hath borne our griefs and carried our*
sorrows.

WHEN our heads are bow'd with woe,
When our bitter tears o'erflow,
When we mourn the lost, the dear,
JESU, Son of Mary, hear.

Thou our throbbing flesh hast worn,
Thou our mortal griefs hast borne,
Thou hast shed the human tear ;
JESU, Son of Mary, hear.

When the solemn death-bell tolls
For our own departed souls,
When our final doom is near,
JESU, Son of Mary, hear.

Thou hast bow'd the dying head,
Thou the blood of life hast shed,
Thou hast fill'd a mortal bier ;
JESU, Son of Mary, hear.

When the heart is sad within
With the thought of all its sin,
When the spirit shrinks with fear,
JESU, Son of Mary, hear.

Thou the shame, the grief, hast known,
Though the sins were not Thine own ;
Thou hast deign'd their load to bear ;
JESU, Son of Mary, hear.   Amen.

(421)

491 *Unto you therefore which believe he is precious.*

HOW sweet the Name of JESUS sounds
   In a believer's ear !
It soothes his sorrows, heals his wounds,
   And drives away his fear.

It makes the wounded spirit whole,
   And calms the troubled breast ;
'Tis manna to the hungry soul,
   And to the weary rest.

Dear Name ! the rock on which I build,
   My shield and hiding-place,
My never-failing treasury fill'd
   With boundless stores of grace.

JESUS ! my Shepherd, Husband, Friend,
   My Prophet, Priest, and King,
My Lord, my Life, my Way, my End,
   Accept the praise I bring.

Weak is the effort of my heart,
   And cold my warmest thought ;
But when I see Thee as Thou art,
   I'll praise Thee as I ought.

Till then I would Thy love proclaim
   With every fleeting breath ;
And may the music of Thy Name
   Refresh my soul in death.   Amen.

492   *He is altogether lovely.*
      Jesu dulcedo cordium.

JESU, Thou Joy of loving hearts !
   Thou Fount of life, Thou Light of men !
From the best bliss that earth imparts
   We turn unfill'd to Thee again.

Thy truth unchanged hath ever stood ;
　Thou savest those that on Thee call ;
To them that seek Thee Thou art good ;
　To them that find Thee All in all.

We taste Thee, O Thou living Bread,
　And long to feast upon Thee still ;
We drink of Thee, the Fountain-head,
　And thirst our souls from Thee to fill.

Our restless spirits yearn for Thee,
　Where'er our changeful lot is cast,
Glad when Thy gracious smile we see,
　Blest, when our faith can hold Thee fast.

O JESU, ever with us stay ;
　Make all our moments calm and bright ;
Chase the dark night of sin away ;
　Shed o'er the world Thy holy light.　Amen.

93　*Thy name is as ointment poured forth.*

Jesu, dulcis memoria.

JESU, the very thought of Thee
　With sweetness fills the breast ;
But sweeter far Thy face to see,
　And in Thy presence rest.

No voice can sing, no heart can frame,
　Nor can the memory find
A sweeter sound than JESU's Name,
　The Saviour of mankind.

O Hope of every contrite heart,
　O Joy of all the meek,
To those who ask how kind Thou art,
　How good to those who seek !

But what to those who find? Ah! this
  Nor tongue nor pen can show;
The love of JESUS, what it is
  None but His loved ones know.

JESU, our only joy be Thou,
  As Thou our prize wilt be;
In Thee be all our glory now,
  And through eternity.

PART 2.

O JESU, King most wonderful,
  Thou Conqueror renown'd,
Thou Sweetness most ineffable,
  In Whom all joys are found!

When once Thou visitest the heart,
  Then truth begins to shine,
Then earthly vanities depart,
  Then kindles love divine.

O JESU, Light of all below,
  Thou Fount of living fire,
Surpassing all the joys we know,
  And all we can desire;

JESU, may all confess Thy Name,
  Thy wondrous love adore,
And, seeking Thee, themselves inflame
  To seek Thee more and more.

Thee, JESU, may our voices bless,
  Thee may we love alone,
And ever in our lives express
  The image of Thine own.

PART 3.

O JESU, Thou the Beauty art
  Of Angel-worlds above;
Thy Name is music to the heart,
  Inflaming it with love.

Celestial Sweetness unalloy'd,
  Who eat Thee hunger still;
Who drink of Thee still feel a void
  Which only Thou canst fill.

O most sweet JESU, hear the sighs
  Which unto Thee we send;
To Thee our inmost spirit cries,
  To Thee our prayers ascend.

Abide with us, and let Thy light
  Shine, LORD, on every heart;
Dispel the darkness of our night,
  And joy to all impart.

JESU, our Love and Joy, to Thee,
  The Virgin's Holy Son,
All might, and praise, and glory be,
  While endless ages run.   Amen.

494 *Thine, O Lord, is the greatness, and the power, and
the glory, and the victory, and the majesty.*

O GOD, of good th' unfathom'd sea,
  Who would not give his heart to Thee?
Who would not love Thee with his might?
O JESU, Lover of mankind,
Who would not his whole soul and mind,
  With all his strength, to Thee unite?

High throned on heav'n's eternal hill,
In number, weight, and measure still
  Thou sweetly ord'rest all that is:
And yet Thou deign'st to come to me,
And guide my steps, that I with Thee
  Enthroned may reign in endless bliss.

Primeval Beauty, in Thy sight
The first-born fairest sons of light
  See all their brightest glories fade.
What then to me Thine eyes could turn,
In sin conceived, of woman born,
  A worm, a leaf, a blast, a shade ?

Fountain of good ! all blessing flows
From Thee ; no want Thy fulness knows :
  What but Thyself canst Thou desire ?
Yet, self-sufficient as Thou art,
Thou dost desire my worthless heart ;
  This, only this dost Thou require.

O GOD, of good th' unfathom'd sea,
Who would not give his heart to Thee ?
  Who would not love Thee with his might ?
O JESU, Lover of mankind,
Who would not his whole soul and mind,
  With all his strength, to Thee unite ?   Amen.

495   *God is love.*
Liebe, die Du mich zum Bilde.

O LOVE, Who formedst me to wear
  The image of Thy GODHEAD here ;
Who soughtest me with tender care
  Through all my wanderings wild and drear ;
O LOVE, I give myself to Thee,
Thine ever, only Thine to be.

O LOVE, Who ere life's earliest morn
  On me Thy choice hast gently laid ;
O LOVE, Who here as Man wast born,
  And wholly like to us wast made ;
O LOVE, I give myself to Thee,
Thine ever, only Thine to be.

O LOVE, Who once in time wast slain,
  Pierced through and through with bitter woe ;
O LOVE, Who wrestling thus didst gain
  That we eternal joy might know ;
O LOVE, I give myself to Thee,
Thine ever, only Thine to be.

O LOVE, Who lovedst me for aye,
  Who for my soul dost ever plead ;
O LOVE, Who didst that ransom pay
  Whose power sufficeth in my stead ;
O LOVE, I give myself to Thee,
Thine ever, only Thine to be.

O LOVE, Who once shalt bid me rise
  From out this dying life of ours ;
O LOVE, Who once o'er yonder skies
  Shalt set me in the fadeless bowers ;
O LOVE, I give myself to Thee,
Thine ever, only Thine to be.   Amen.

496   *Lovest thou me?*

HARK, my soul ! it is the LORD ;
    'Tis thy Saviour, hear His word ;
JESUS speaks, and speaks to thee,
"Say, poor sinner, lov'st thou Me ?

"I deliver'd thee when bound,
And, when bleeding, heal'd thy wound ;
Sought thee wandering, set thee right,
Turn'd thy darkness into light.

"Can a woman's tender care
Cease towards the child she bare ?
Yes, she may forgetful be,
Yet will I remember thee.

" Mine is an unchanging love,
Higher than the heights above
Deeper than the depths beneath,
Free and faithful, strong as death.

" Thou shalt see My glory soon,
When the work of grace is done ;
Partner of My throne shalt be ;
Say, poor sinner, lov'st thou Me ? "

LORD, it is my chief complaint
That my love is weak and faint ;
Yet I love Thee, and adore ;
O for grace to love Thee more.   Amen.

497 *Mary hath chosen that good part, which shall not be taken away from her.*

O LOVE Divine, how sweet Thou art !
   When shall I find my willing heart
  All taken up by Thee ?
I thirst, I faint, I die to prove
The greatness of redeeming love,
  The love of CHRIST to me.

Stronger His love than death or hell ;
Its riches are unsearchable ;
  The first-born sons of light
Desire in vain its depths to see ;
They cannot reach the mystery,
  The length, and breadth, and height.

GOD only knows the love of GOD ;
O that it now were shed abroad
  In this poor stony heart !
For love I sigh, for love I pine ;
This only portion, LORD, be mine,
  Be mine this better part.

For ever would I take my seat
With Mary at the Master's feet ;
  Be this my happy choice ;
My only care, delight, and bliss,
My joy, my heav'n on earth, be this,
  To hear the Bridegroom's voice. Amen.

98   *Visit me with thy salvation.*

LOVE Divine, all loves excelling,
  Joy of heav'n, to earth come down,
Fix in us Thy humble dwelling,
  All Thy faithful mercies crown.

Jesu, Thou art all compassion,
  Pure unbounded love Thou art ;
Visit us with Thy salvation,
  Enter every trembling heart.

Come, Almighty to deliver,
  Let us all Thy grace receive ;
Suddenly return, and never,
  Never more Thy temples leave.

Thee we would be always blessing,
  Serve Thee as Thy hosts above,
Pray, and praise Thee, without ceasing,
  Glory in Thy perfect love.

Finish then Thy new creation,
  Pure and spotless let us be ;
Let us see Thy great salvation,
  Perfectly restored in Thee,

Changed from glory into glory,
  Till in heav'n we take our place,
Till we cast our crowns before Thee,
  Lost in wonder, love, and praise. Amen.

499 *Whom have I in heaven but thee? and there is none upon earth that I desire in comparison of thee.*

JESU, my LORD, my GOD, my All,
   Hear me, Blest Saviour, when I call ;
Hear me, and from Thy dwelling-place
Pour down the riches of Thy grace ;
   JESU, my LORD, I Thee adore,
   O make me love Thee more and more.

JESU, too late I Thee have sought,
How can I love Thee as I ought?
And how extol Thy matchless fame,
The glorious beauty of Thy Name?
   JESU, my LORD, I Thee adore,
   O make me love Thee more and more.

JESU, what didst Thou find in me,
That Thou hast dealt so lovingly?
How great the joy that Thou hast brought,
So far exceeding hope or thought !
   JESU, my LORD, I Thee adore,
   O make me love Thee more and more.

JESU, of Thee shall be my song,
To Thee my heart and soul belong ;
All that I have or am is Thine,
And Thou, Blest Saviour, Thou art mine.
   JESU, my LORD, I Thee adore,
   O make me love Thee more and more.
                 Amen.

500 *What reward shall I give unto the Lord for all the benefits that he hath done unto me?*

THY life was given for me,
   Thy Blood, O LORD, was shed,
That I might ransom'd be,
   And quicken'd from the dead ;
Thy life was given for me ;
What have I given for Thee?

Long years were spent for me
  In weariness and woe,
That through eternity
  Thy glory I might know ;
Long years were spent for me ;
Have I spent one for Thee ?

Thy FATHER's home of light,
  Thy rainbow-circled throne,
Were left for earthly night,
  For wanderings sad and lone ;
Yea, all was left for me ;
Have I left aught for Thee ?

Thou, LORD, hast borne for me
  More than my tongue can tell
Of bitterest agony,
  To rescue me from hell ;
Thou suff'redst all for me ;
What have I borne for Thee ?

And Thou hast brought to me
  Down from Thy home above
Salvation full and free,
  Thy pardon and Thy love ;
Great gifts Thou broughtest me ;
What have I brought to Thee ?

O let my life be given,
  My years for Thee be spent ;
World-fetters all be riven,
  And joy with suffering blent ;
Thou gav'st Thyself for me,
I give myself to Thee. Amen.

GENERAL HYMNS.

501 *When ye glorify the Lord, exalt him as much as ye can: for even yet will he far exceed: and when ye exalt him, put forth all your strength, and be not weary: for ye can never go far enough.*

OH for a thousand tongues to sing
   My blest Redeemer's praise,
The glories of my GOD and King,
   The triumphs of His grace !

JESUS—the Name that charms our fears,
   That bids our sorrows cease ;
'Tis music in the sinner's ears,
   'Tis life, and health, and peace.

He breaks the power of cancell'd sin,
   He sets the prisoner free :
His Blood can make the foulest clean ;
   His Blood avail'd for me.

He speaks ;—and, listening to His voice,
   New life the dead receive,
The mournful broken hearts rejoice,
   The humble poor believe.

Hear Him, ye deaf ; His praise, ye dumb,
   Your loosen'd tongues employ ;
Ye blind, behold your Saviour come ;
   And leap, ye lame, for joy !

My gracious Master and my GOD,
   Assist me to proclaim
And spread through all the earth abroad
   The honours of Thy Name.   Amen.

502 *God forbid that I should glory, save in the cross of our Lord Jesus Christ.*

WE sing the praise of Him Who died,
   Of Him Who died upon the Cross ;
The sinner's hope let men deride,
   For this we count the world but loss.

Inscribed upon the Cross we see
   In shining letters, "GOD is Love;"
He bears our sins upon the Tree;
   He brings us mercy from above.

The Cross! it takes our guilt away;
   It holds the fainting spirit up;
It cheers with hope the gloomy day,
   And sweetens every bitter cup.

It makes the coward spirit brave,
   And nerves the feeble arm for fight;
It takes the terror from the grave,
   And gilds the bed of death with light;

The balm of life, the cure of woe,
   The measure and the pledge of love,
The sinner's refuge here below,
   The Angels' theme in heav'n above.

To CHRIST, Who won for sinners grace
   By bitter grief and anguish sore,
Be praise from all the ransom'd race
   For ever and for evermore.   Amen.

3   *In everything give thanks.*

Beim frühen Morgenlicht.

WHEN morning gilds the skies,
   My heart awaking cries,
   May JESUS CHRIST be praisèd:
Alike at work and prayer
To JESUS I repair;
   May JESUS CHRIST be praisèd.

Whene'er the sweet church bell
Peals over hill and dell,
    May JESUS CHRIST be praisèd :
O hark to what it sings,
As joyously it rings,
    May JESUS CHRIST be praisèd.

*My tongue shall never tire
Of chanting with the choir,
    May JESUS CHRIST be praisèd :
This song of sacred joy,
It never seems to cloy,
    May JESUS CHRIST be praisèd.

When sleep her balm denies,
My silent spirit sighs,
    May JESUS CHRIST be praisèd :
When evil thoughts molest,
With this I shield my breast,
    May JESUS CHRIST be praisèd.

*Does sadness fill my mind ?
A solace here I find,
    May JESUS CHRIST be praisèd :
Or fades my earthly bliss ?
My comfort still is this,
    May JESUS CHRIST be praisèd.

The night becomes as day,
When from the heart we say,
    May JESUS CHRIST be praisèd :
The powers of darkness fear,
When this sweet chant they hear,
    May JESUS CHRIST be praisèd.

In heav'n's eternal bliss
The loveliest strain is this,
    May JESUS CHRIST be praisèd :
Let earth, and sea, and sky
From depth to height reply,
    May JESUS CHRIST be praisèd.

*Be this, while life is mine,
My canticle divine,
   May JESUS CHRIST be praisèd :
Be this th' eternal song
Through ages all along,
   May JESUS CHRIST be praisèd.   Amen.

     * *These verses can be omitted.*

1 *Every day will I give thanks unto thee, and praise*
       thy name for ever and ever.

SAVIOUR, Blessèd Saviour,
    Listen whilst we sing,
Hearts and voices raising
   Praises to our King ;
All we have we offer ;
   All we hope to be,
Body, soul, and spirit,
   All we yield to Thee.

Nearer, ever nearer,
   CHRIST, we draw to Thee,
Deep in adoration
   Bending low the knee ;
Thou for our redemption
   Cam'st on earth to die ;
Thou, that we might follow,
   Hast gone up on high.

Great and ever greater
   Are Thy mercies here ;
True and everlasting
   Are the glories there ;
Where no pain, nor sorrow,
   Toil, nor care, is known,
Where the Angel-legions
   Circle round Thy throne.

Dark and ever darker
  Was the wintry past,
Now a ray of gladness
  O'er our path is cast ;
Every day that passeth,
  Every hour that flies,
Tells of love unfeignèd,
  Love that never dies.

Clearer still and clearer
  Dawns the light from heaven,
In our sadness bringing
  News of sin forgiven ;
Life has lost its shadows,
  Pure the light within ;
Thou hast shed Thy radiance
  O'er a world of sin.

Brighter still and brighter
  Glows the western sun,
Shedding all its gladness
  O'er our work that's done ;
Time will soon be over,
  Toil and sorrow past ;
May we, Blessèd Saviour,
  Find a rest at last.

Onward, ever onward,
  Journeying o'er the road
Worn by Saints before us,
  Journeying on to GOD ;
Leaving all behind us,
  May we hasten on,
Backward never looking
  Till the prize is won.

Higher then and higher
  Bear the ransom'd soul,
Earthly toils forgotten,
  Saviour, to its goal ;

Where in joys unthought of
Saints with Angels sing,
Never weary raising
Praises to their King. Amen.

;05 *O praise the Lord, laud ye the name of the Lord;*
praise it, O ye servants of the Lord.

THANKSGIVING.

REJOICE to-day with one accord,
Sing out with exultation ;
Rejoice and praise our mighty LORD,
Whose arm hath brought salvation ;
His works of love proclaim
The greatness of His Name ;
For He is GOD alone
Who hath His mercy shown ;
Let all His saints adore Him !

When in distress to Him we cried,
He heard our sad complaining ;
O trust in Him, whate'er betide,
His love is all-sustaining ;
Triumphant songs of praise
To Him our hearts shall raise ;
Now every voice shall say,
"O praise our GOD alway ;"
Let all His saints adore Him !

Rejoice to-day with one accord,
Sing out with exultation ;
Rejoice and praise our mighty LORD,
Whose arm hath brought salvation ;
His works of love proclaim
The greatness of His Name ;
For He is GOD alone
Who hath His mercy shown ;
Let all His saints adore Him ! Amen.

P 2

GENERAL HYMNS.

503 *O clap your hands together, all ye people ; O sing unto God with the voice of melody.*

Nun danket alle Gott.

THANKSGIVING.

NOW thank we all our GOD,
  With heart, and hands, and voices,
Who wondrous things hath done,
In Whom His world rejoices ;
  Who from our mother's arms
    Hath bless'd us on our way
With countless gifts of love,
    And still is ours to-day.

O may this bounteous GOD
Through all our life be near us,
  With ever joyful hearts
And blessèd peace to cheer us ;
  And keep us in His grace,
    And guide us when perplex'd,
And free us from all ills
    In this world and the next.

All praise and thanks to GOD
The FATHER now be given,
  The SON, and Him Who reigns
With Them in highest heaven,
  The One Eternal GOD,
    Whom earth and heav'n adore,
For thus it was, is now,
    And shall be evermore.   Amen.

NATIONAL ANTHEM.

507 *All the people shouted and said, God save the king.* |

GOD save our gracious King,
  Long live our noble King,
GOD save the King.

(438)

NATIONAL ANTHEM.

Send him victorious,
Happy and glorious,
Long to reign over us ;
    God save the King.

Thy choicest gifts in store
On him be pleased to pour,
    Long may he reign.
May he defend our laws,
And ever give us cause
To sing with heart and voice
God save the King.

THANKSGIVING FOR NATIONAL BLESSINGS.

508 *Thou shalt bless the Lord thy God for the good land*
which he hath given thee.

PRAISE to our God, Whose bounteous hand
    Prepared of old our glorious land ;
A garden fenced with silver sea ;
A people prosperous, strong, and free.

Praise to our God ; through all our past
His mighty arm hath held us fast ;
Till wars and perils, toils and tears,
Have brought the rich and peaceful years.

Praise to our God : the vine He set
Within our coasts is fruitful yet ;
On many a shore her offshoots grow ;
'Neath many a sun her clusters glow.

Praise to our God ; His power alone
Can keep unmoved our ancient throne ;
Sustain'd by counsels wise and just,
And guarded by a people's trust.

THANKSGIVING FOR NATIONAL BLESSINGS.

Praise to our GOD; Who still forbears,
Who still this sinful nation spares;
Who calls us still to seek His face,
And lengthens out our day of grace.

Praise to our GOD; though chastenings stern
Our evil dross should throughly burn;
His rod and staff, from age to age,
Shall rule and guide His heritage!   Amen.

THANKSGIVING FOR PEACE.

509 *The Lord shall give his people the blessing of peace.*
Herr Gott, dich loben wir, Regier.

LORD GOD, we worship Thee!
    In loud and happy chorus
We praise Thy love and power,
Whose goodness reigneth o'er us!
    To heav'n our song shall soar,
For ever shall it be
    Resounding o'er and o'er;
LORD GOD, we worship Thee!

LORD GOD, we worship Thee!
For Thou our land defendest;
    Thou pourest down Thy grace,
And strife and war Thou endest;
    Since golden peace, O LORD,
Thou grantest us to see,
    Our land with one accord,
LORD GOD, gives thanks to Thee!

LORD GOD, we worship Thee!
Thou didst indeed chastise us;
    Yet still Thy anger spares,
And still Thy mercy tries us;

THANKSGIVING FOR PEACE.

Once more our FATHER's hand
Doth bid our sorrows flee
And peace rejoice our land :—
LORD GOD, we worship Thee !

LORD GOD, we worship Thee !
And pray Thee, Who hast blest us,
That we may live in peace,
And none henceforth molest us.
O crown us with Thy love ;
Fulfil our cry to Thee ;
O FATHER, grant our prayer ;
LORD GOD, we worship Thee ! Amen.

HARVEST.

10   *Behold, a sower went forth to sow.*

THE sower went forth sowing,
    The seed in secret slept
Through days of faith and patience,
    Till out the green blade crept ;
And warm'd by golden sunshine,
    And fed by silver rain,
At last the fields were whiten'd
    To harvest once again.
O praise the heav'nly Sower,
    Who gave the fruitful seed,
And watch'd and water'd duly,
    .. And ripen'd for our need.

Behold ! the heav'nly Sower
    Goes forth with better seed,
The word of sure salvation,
    With feet and hands that bleed ;
Here in His Church 'tis scatter'd,
    Our spirits are the soil ;
Then let an ample fruitage
    Repay His pain and toil.

HARVEST.

O fair to Him the harvest
  Wherein all goodness thrives,
And this the true thanksgiving,
  The first-fruits of our lives.

Within a hallow'd acre
  He sows yet other grain,
When peaceful earth receiveth
  The dead He died to gain ;
For though the growth be hidden,
  We know that they shall rise ;
Yea even now they ripen
  In sunny Paradise.
O summer land of harvest,
  O fields for ever white
With souls that wear CHRIST's raiment,
  With crowns of golden light !

One day the heav'nly Sower
  Shall reap where He hath sown,
And come again rejoicing,
  And with Him bring His own ;
And then the fan of judgment
  Shall winnow from His floor
The chaff into the furnace
  That flameth evermore.
O holy, awful Reaper,
  Have mercy in the day
Thou puttest in Thy sickle,
  And cast us not away. Amen.

511 *The eyes of all wait upon thee, O Lord, and t/*
    givest them their meat in due season.

Wir pflügen und wir streuen.

WE plough the fields, and scatter
  The good seed on the land,
But it is fed and water'd
  By GOD's Almighty hand ;

HARVEST.

He sends the snow in winter,
 The warmth to swell the grain,
The breezes and the sunshine,
 And soft refreshing rain.
  All good gifts around us
   Are sent from heav'n above,
  Then thank the LORD, O thank the LORD,
   For all His love.

He only is the Maker
 Of all things near and far ;
He paints the wayside flower,
 He lights the evening star ;
The winds and waves obey Him,
 By Him the birds are fed ;
Much more to us, His children,
 He gives our daily bread.
   All good gifts, &c.

We thank Thee then, O FATHER,
 For all things bright and good,
The seed-time and the harvest,
 Our life, our health, our food ;
Accept the gifts we offer
 For all Thy love imparts,
And, what Thou most desirest,
 Our humble, thankful hearts.
   All good gifts, &c.   Amen.

12 *Thou visitest the earth, and blessest it ; thou makest
it very plenteous.*

FATHER of mercies, GOD of love,
 Whose gifts all creatures share,
The rolling seasons as they move
 Proclaim Thy constant care.
When in the bosom of the earth
 The sower hid the grain,
Thy goodness mark'd its secret birth
 And sent the early rain.

HARVEST.

The spring's sweet influence, LORD, was Thine,
  The seasons knew Thy call ;
Thou mad'st the summer sun to shine,
  The summer dews to fall.

Thy gifts of mercy from above
  Matured the swelling grain ;
And now the harvest crowns Thy love,
  And plenty fills the plain.

O ne'er may our forgetful hearts
  O'erlook Thy bounteous care,
But what our FATHER's hand imparts
  Still own in praise and prayer.

To FATHER, SON, and HOLY GHOST,
  The GOD Whom we adore,
Be glory, as it was, is now,
  And shall be evermore. Amen.

513 *Who giveth food to all flesh, for his mercy endureth
  for ever.*

PRAISE, O praise our GOD and King ;
  Hymns of adoration sing ;
    For His mercies still endure
    Ever faithful, ever sure.

Praise Him that He made the sun
Day by day his course to run :
  For His mercies still endure
  Ever faithful, ever sure.

And the silver moon by night,
Shining with her gentle light ;
  For His mercies still endure
  Ever faithful, ever sure.

HARVEST.

Praise Him that He gave the rain
To mature the swelling grain ;
   For His mercies still endure
   Ever faithful, ever sure.

And hath bid the fruitful field
Crops of precious increase yield ;
   For His mercies still endure
   Ever faithful, ever sure.

Praise Him for our harvest-store,
He hath fill'd the garner-floor ;
   For His mercies still endure
   Ever faithful, ever sure.

And for richer Food than this,
Pledge of everlasting bliss ;
   For His mercies still endure
   Ever faithful, ever sure.

Glory to our bounteous King ;
Glory let creation sing ;
   Glory to the FATHER, SON,
   And Blest SPIRIT, THREE in ONE.
                 Amen.

4   *They joy before thee according to the joy in harvest.*

COME, ye thankful people, come,
   Raise the song of Harvest-home :
All is safely gather'd in,
Ere the winter storms begin ;
GOD, our Maker, doth provide
For our wants to be supplied ;
Come to GOD's own temple, come ;
Raise the song of Harvest-home.

All this world is GOD's own field,
Fruit unto His praise to yield ;
Wheat and tares therein are sown,
Unto joy or sorrow grown ;

HARVEST.

Ripening with a wondrous power
Till the final Harvest-hour :
Grant, O LORD of life, that we
Holy grain and pure may be.

For we know that Thou wilt come,
And wilt take Thy people home ;
From Thy field wilt purge away
All that doth offend, that day ;
And Thine Angels charge at last
In the fire the tares to cast,
But the fruitful ears to store
In Thy garner evermore.

Come then, LORD of mercy, come,
Bid us sing Thy Harvest-home :
Let Thy Saints be gather'd in,
Free from sorrow, free from sin ;
All upon the golden floor
Praising Thee for evermore :
Come, with all Thine Angels come ;
Bid us sing Thy Harvest-home.   Amen.

515   *Thou crownest the year with thy goodness.*

TO Thee, O LORD, our hearts we raise
    In hymns of adoration,
To Thee bring sacrifice of praise
    With shouts of exultation ;
Bright robes of gold the fields adorn,
    The hills with joy are ringing,
The valleys stand so thick with corn
    That even they are singing.

And now, on this our festal day,
    Thy bounteous hand confessing,
Upon Thine altar, LORD, we lay
    The first-fruits of Thy blessing ;

HARVEST.

By Thee the souls of men are fed
  With gifts of grace supernal ;
Thou Who dost give us earthly bread,
  Give us the Bread eternal.

We bear the burden of the day,
  And often toil seems dreary ;
But labour ends with sunset ray,
  And rest comes for the weary ;
May we, the Angel-reaping o'er,
  Stand at the last accepted,
CHRIST's golden sheaves for evermore
  To garners bright elected.

Oh, blessèd is that land of GOD,
  Where Saints abide for ever ;
Where golden fields spread far and broad,
  Where flows the crystal river :
The strains of all its holy throng
  With ours to-day are blending ;
Thrice blessèd is that harvest-song
  Which never hath an ending.   Amen.

516 *The harvest is the end of the world, and the reapers
are the angels.*

LORD of the harvest, once again
  We thank Thee for the ripen'd grain ;
For crops safe carried, sent to cheer
Thy servants through another year ;
For all sweet holy thoughts supplied
By seed-time, and by harvest-tide.

The bare dead grain, in autumn sown,
Its robe of vernal green puts on ;
Glad from its wintry grave it springs,
Fresh garnish'd by the King of kings :
So, LORD, to those who sleep in Thee
Shall new and glorious bodies be.

Nor vainly of Thy word we ask
A lesson from the reaper's task :
So shall Thine Angels issue forth ;
The tares be burnt ; the just of earth,
To wind and storm exposed no more,
Be gather'd to their FATHER'S store.

Daily, O LORD, our prayers be said,
As Thou hast taught, for daily bread ;
But not alone our bodies feed,
Supply our fainting spirits' need :
O Bread of life, from day to day,
Be Thou their comfort, food, and stay.

Amen.

The following Hymns are also suitable:

324 Let all the world rejoice.
326 O worship the King.
333 For the beauty of the earth.
400 O praise our great and gracious LORD.
407 Praise to the LORD, the Almighty.
506 Now thank we all our GOD.

TIMES OF TROUBLE.

517 *Thou that hearest the prayer; unto thee shall all
flesh come.*

GREAT King of nations, hear our prayer,
　While at Thy feet we fall,
And humbly with united cry
　To Thee for mercy call ;
The guilt is ours, but grace is Thine,
　O turn us not away ;
But hear us from Thy lofty throne
　And help us when we pray.

Our fathers' sins were manifold,
　And ours no less we own,
Yet wondrously from age to age
　Thy goodness hath been shown ;

(448)

TIMES OF TROUBLE.

When dangers, like a stormy sea,
  Beset our country round,
To Thee we look'd, to Thee we cried,
  And help in Thee was found.

With one consent we meekly bow
  Beneath Thy chastening hand,
And, pouring forth confession meet,
  Mourn with our mourning land ;
With pitying eye behold our need,
  As thus we lift our prayer ;
Correct us with Thy judgments, LORD,
  Then let Thy mercy spare. Amen.

18   *Arise, O God, maintain thine own cause.*

WAR.

LET GOD arise to lead forth those
    Who march to war !
Let GOD arise, and all His foes
  Be scatter'd far !

So Israel pray'd, and Thou, O LORD,
  Wast with him then :
Be with us now, who draw the sword
  For war again.

Grant Thou our soldiers courage high
  When foes are near,
To strive, to suffer, or to die,
  Untouch'd by fear.

Grant strength to those, who mourn to-day
  Their loved ones lost,—
Yea, those who give their best, nor stay
  To count the cost.

Fight Thou for us, that we may fill
  Thy courts with praise ;
Then teach us mercy, teach us still
  The fall'n to raise.

Yet more and more, as ages run,
    Bid warfare cease,
And give to all beneath the sun
    Love, Freedom, Peace.   Amen.

519 *Thou hast been my defence and refuge in the day of my trouble.*
WAR.

L ORD, while afar our brothers fight,
    Thy Church united lifts her prayer ;
Be Thou their shield by day and night ;
    Guide, guard, and help them everywhere :
O GOD of battles, hear our cry,
And in their danger be Thou nigh.

For those who, wounded in the fray,
    Are ling'ring still on beds of pain,
Who to their loved ones far away
    May nevermore return again,
O GOD of pity, hear our cry,
And in their anguish be Thou nigh.

For wives and mothers sore distress'd,
    For all who wait in silent fear,
For homes bereaved which gave their best,
    For hearts now desolate and drear,
O GOD of comfort, hear our cry,
And in the darkest hour draw nigh.

Spare us, good LORD ! If just the strife,
    Yet still from guilt we are not free ;
Forgive our blind and careless life,
    Our oft forgetfulness of Thee.
O GOD of mercy, hear our cry,
And to our contrite souls draw nigh.

We bow beneath the chastening rod,
    To us the sin and shame belong :
But Thou art righteous, Thou art GOD,
    And right shall triumph over wrong.
In Thee we trust, to Thee we cry ;
LORD, now and ever be Thou nigh. Amen.

TIMES OF TROUBLE.

0 *The Lord shall give his people the blessing of peace.*

R.

GOD of love, O King of peace,
  Make wars throughout the world to cease ;
wrath of sinful man restrain,
e peace, O GOD, give peace again.

nember, LORD, Thy works of old,
wonders that our fathers told,
nember not our sin's dark stain,
e peace, O GOD, give peace again.

om shall we trust but Thee, O LORD ?
ere rest but on Thy faithful word ?
ne ever call'd on Thee in vain,
e peace, O GOD, give peace again.

ere Saints and Angels dwell above,
hearts are knit in holy love ;
ind us in that heav'nly chain,
e peace, O GOD, give peace again.   Amen.

1 *Thou shalt not be afraid . . . for the pestilence that
walketh in darkness; nor for the sickness that
destroyeth in the noon-day.*

PESTILENCE.

IN grief and fear to Thee, O GOD,
  We now for succour fly ;
Thine awful judgments are abroad,
  O shield us lest we die.

The fell disease on every side
  Walks forth with tainted breath ;
And pestilence, with rapid stride,
  Bestrews the land with death.

O look with pity on the scene
  Of sadness and of dread ;
And let Thine Angel stand between
  The living and the dead.

With contrite hearts to Thee, our King,
    We turn who oft have stray'd ;
Accept the sacrifice we bring,
    And let the plague be stay'd.   Amen.

HYMNS FOR THE WORK OF THE CHURCH.

522 *All the ends of the earth shall see the salvation of*
                     our God.

FOREIGN MISSIONS.

FROM Greenland's icy mountains,
    From India's coral strand,
Where Afric's sunny fountains
    Roll down their golden sand,
From many an ancient river,
    From many a palmy plain,
They call us to deliver
    Their land from error's chain.

What though the spicy breezes
    Blow soft o'er Ceylon's isle,
Though every prospect pleases
    And only man is vile,
In vain with lavish kindness
    The gifts of GOD are strown,
The heathen in his blindness
    Bows down to wood and stone.

Can we, whose souls are lighted
    With wisdom from on high,
Can we to men benighted
    The lamp of life deny ?
Salvation ! oh, salvation !
    The joyful sound proclaim,
Till each remotest nation
    Has learn'd Messiah's name.

Waft, waft, ye winds, His story,
  And you, ye waters, roll,
Till, like a sea of glory,
  It spreads from pole to pole ;
Till o'er our ransom'd nature
  The LAMB for sinners slain,
Redeemer, King, Creator,
  In bliss returns to reign. Amen.

23   *So shall he sprinkle many nations.*

SAVIOUR, sprinkle many nations,
  Fruitful let Thy sorrows be ;
By Thy pains and consolations
  Draw the Gentiles unto Thee :
Of Thy Cross the wondrous story,
  Be it to the nations told ;
Let them see Thee in Thy glory,
  And Thy mercy manifold.

Far and wide, though all unknowing,
  Pants for Thee each mortal breast ;
Human tears for Thee are flowing,
  Human hearts in Thee would rest ;
Thirsting, as for dews of even,
  As the new-mown grass for rain,
Thee they seek, as GOD of heaven,
  Thee, as Man, for sinners slain.

Saviour, lo ! the isles are waiting,
  Stretch'd the hand, and strain'd the sight,
For Thy SPIRIT new creating,
  Love's pure flame and wisdom's light ;
Give the word, and of the preacher
  Speed the foot and touch the tongue,
Till on earth by every creature
  Glory to the LAMB be sung. Amen.

524 *Come over into Macedonia, and help us.*

THROUGH midnight gloom from Macedon
 The cry of myriads as of one,
The voiceless silence of despair,
Is eloquent in awful prayer,—
The soul's exceeding bitter cry,
" Come o'er and help us, or we die."

How mournfully it echoes on !
For half the earth is Macedon ;
These brethren to their brethren call,
And by the love which loved them all,
And by the whole world's life they cry,
" O ye that live, behold we die ! "

By other sounds the world is won
Than that which wails from Macedon ;
The roar of gain is round it roll'd,
Or men unto themselves are sold,
And cannot list the alien cry,
" O hear and help us, lest we die ! "

Yet with that cry from Macedon
The very car of CHRIST rolls on ;
" I come ; who would abide My day
In yonder wilds prepare My way ;
My voice is crying in their cry ;
Help ye the dying, lest ye die."

JESU, for men of Man the Son,
Yea, Thine the cry from Macedon ;
O by the kingdom, and the power,
And glory of Thine Advent hour,
Wake heart and will to hear their cry ;
Help us to help them, lest we die ! Amen.

25 *He shall testify of me, and ye also shall bear witness.*

O SPIRIT of the living God,
  In all the fulness of Thy grace,
Where'er the foot of man hath trod,
  Descend on our apostate race.
Give tongues of fire and hearts of love
  To preach the reconciling word ;
Give power and unction from above,
  Whene'er the joyful sound is heard.
Be darkness at Thy coming light,
  Confusion order in Thy path ;
Souls without strength inspire with might :
  Bid mercy triumph over wrath.
O Spirit of the Lord, prepare
  All the round earth her God to meet ;
Breathe Thou abroad like morning air,
  'Till hearts of stone begin to beat.
Baptize the nations ; far and nigh
  The triumphs of the Cross record ;
The Name of Jesus glorify
  Till every kindred call Him Lord.   Amen.

26 *And God said, Let there be light; and there was light.*

THOU Whose Almighty Word
  Chaos and darkness heard,
    And took their flight ;
Hear us, we humbly pray,
And where the Gospel-day
Sheds not its glorious ray,
  Let there be light.
Thou Who didst come to bring
On Thy redeeming wing
  Healing and sight,
Health to the sick in mind,
Sight to the inly blind,
Oh now to all mankind
  Let there be light.

SPIRIT of truth and love,
Life-giving, Holy DOVE,
  Speed forth Thy flight ;
Move on the waters' face,
Bearing the lamp of grace,
And in earth's darkest place
  Let there be light.

Holy and Blessèd THREE,
Glorious TRINITY,
  Wisdom, Love, Might ;
Boundless as ocean's tide
Rolling in fullest pride,
Through the earth far and wide
  Let there be light.   Amen.

527 *Waiting for the coming of our Lord Jesus Christ.*

LORD, her watch Thy Church is keeping ;
  When shall earth Thy rule obey ?
When shall end the night of weeping ?
  When shall break the promised day ?
See the whitening harvest languish,
  Waiting still the labourers' toil ;
Was it vain, Thy SON's deep anguish ?
  Shall the strong retain the spoil ?

Tidings, sent to every creature,
  Millions yet have never heard ;
Can they hear without a preacher ?
  LORD Almighty, give the word :—
Give the word ; in every nation
  Let the Gospel-trumpet sound,
Witnessing a world's salvation
  To the earth's remotest bound.

Then the end : Thy Church completed,
  All Thy chosen gather'd in,
With their King in glory seated,
  Satan bound, and banish'd sin ;
Gone for ever parting, weeping,
  Hunger, sorrow, death, and pain ;
Lo ! her watch Thy Church is keeping ;
  Come, LORD JESUS, come to reign. Amen.

28 *He shall set up an ensign for the nations.*

LIFT up your heads, ye gates of brass ;
  Ye bars of iron, yield,
And let the King of glory pass ;
  The Cross is in the field.

That banner, brighter than the star
  That leads the train of night,
Shines on the march, and guides from far
  His servants to the fight.

A holy war those servants wage ;
  In that mysterious strife,
The powers of heav'n and hell engage
  For more than death or life.

Ye armies of the living GOD,
  Sworn warriors of CHRIST's host,
Where hallow'd footsteps never trod,
  Take your appointed post.

Though few and small and weak your bands,
  Strong in your Captain's strength,
Go to the conquest of all lands :
  All must be His at length.

The spoils at His victorious feet
  You shall rejoice to lay,
And lay yourselves as trophies meet,
  In *His* great judgment day.

(457)

Then fear not, faint not, halt not now ;
   In JESUS' Name be strong !
To Him shall all the nations bow,
   And sing the triumph song :—
Uplifted are the gates of brass,
   The bars of iron yield ;
Behold the King of glory pass ;
   The Cross hath won the field.   Amen.

529 *The earth shall be filled with the knowledge of the glory of the Lord, as the waters cover the sea.*

GOD is working His purpose out as year
   succeeds to year,
GOD is working His purpose out and the time is
   drawing near ;
Nearer and nearer draws the time, the time that
   shall surely be,
When the earth shall be fill'd with the glory of
   GOD as the waters cover the sea.

From utmost east to utmost west where'er man's
   foot hath trod,
By the mouth of many messengers goes forth the
   voice of GOD,
"Give ear to Me, ye continents, ye isles, give ear
   to Me,
That the earth may be fill'd with the glory of GOD
   as the waters cover the sea."

What can we do to work GOD's work, to prosper
   and increase
The brotherhood of all mankind, the reign of the
   Prince of peace ?
What can we do to hasten the time, the time that
   shall surely be,
*When the earth shall be fill'd with the glory of
   GOD as the waters cover the sea?*

[arch we forth in the strength of GOD with the
    banner of CHRIST unfurl'd,
hat the light of the glorious Gospel of truth may
    shine throughout the world.
ight we the fight with sorrow and sin, to set
    their captives free,
hat the earth may be fill'd with the glory of GOD
    as the waters cover the sea.

ll we can do is nothing worth unless GOD
    blesses the deed ;
ainly we hope for the harvest-tide till GOD gives
    life to the seed ;
et nearer and nearer draws the time, the time
    that shall surely be,
Then the earth shall be fill'd with the glory of
    GOD as the waters cover the sea.   Amen.

30 *The ransomed of the Lord shall return, and come
with singing unto Zion.*

TRUMPET of GOD sound high ;
    Till the hearts of the heathen shake,
And the souls that in slumber lie
    At the voice of the LORD awake.
    Till the fencèd cities fall
      At the blast of the Gospel call,
Trumpet of GOD sound high !

Hosts of the LORD go forth :
    Go, strong in the power of His rest.
Till the south be at one with the north,
    And peace upon east and west ;
    Till the far-off lands shall thrill
      With the gladness of GOD's " Goodwill,"
Hosts of the LORD go forth.

Come, as of old, like fire ;
    O Force of the LORD, descend,
Till with love of the world's Desire
    Earth burn to its utmost end ;
      Till the ransom'd people sing
      To the glory of CHRIST the King,
Come, as of old, like fire.   Amen.

531 *He hath not dealt so with any nation: neither hal*
      the heathen knowledge of his laws.

O LIVING GOD, Whose voice of old
    Was heard in Sinai's thunder,
Who to the nations didst unfold
    Thine Israel's tale of wonder ;
While in Thy temple we rejoice
    To see Thee in Thy beauty,
O make us hear Thy still small voice—
    A nation's call to duty.

In childhood's days with glowing hearts
    We listen'd to the story,
How men of alien speech and arts
    To England show'd Thy glory ;
They to an island dark with sin
    Thy light and truth imparted,
May we to larger realms akin
    Be ever larger hearted.

To many a realm by Thy decree
    Our kith and kin are wending,
'Neath many a toil by land and sea
    An English life is bending ;
LORD, grant that they who onward press
    To tasks of Thy creation,
May onward bear through toil and stress
    The faith that made their nation.

FOREIGN MISSIONS.

For not by preachers' word alone
 Thou speak'st to men benighted,
'Tis Thine each faithful task to own
 By truth and mercy lighted ;
O light in us such love to Thee,
 That we Thy truth confessing
May to the nations ever be
 An earnest of Thy blessing. Amen.

The following Hymns are suitable :

28 The day Thou gavest, LORD, is ended.
370 Thy kingdom come, O GOD.
372 GOD of mercy, GOD of grace.
373 JESUS shall reign where'er the sun.
374 Hail to the LORD's Anointed.
501 Oh for a thousand tongues to sing.

2 *Blessed be his glorious name for ever: and let the whole earth be filled with his glory; Amen and Amen.*

NKSGIVING FOR MISSIONS.

ORD of the harvest ! it is right and meet
 That we should lay our first-fruits at Thy feet
  With joyful Alleluia !

et is the soul's thanksgiving after prayer ;
et is the worship that with heav'n we share,
  Who sing the Alleluia !

Thee, O LORD of harvest, Who hast heard,
l to Thy white-robed reapers given the word,
  We sing our Alleluia.

HRIST, Who in the wide world's ghostly sea
t bid the net be cast anew, to Thee
  We sing our Alleluia.

Thee, Eternal SPIRIT, Who again
t moved with life upon the slumbrous main,
  We sing our Alleluia.

(461)

Yea, west and east the companies go forth :
"We come !" is sounding to the south and north:
To God sing Alleluia.

The fishermen of Jesus far away
Seek in new waters an immortal prey ;
To Christ sing Alleluia.

The Holy Dove is brooding o'er the deep,
And careless hearts are waking out of sleep ;
To Him sing Alleluia.

Yea, for sweet hope new-born, blest work begun,
Sing Alleluia to the Three in One,
Adoring Alleluia.

Glory to God ! the Church in patience cries ;
Glory to God ! the Church at rest replies,
With endless Alleluia.   Amen.

533 *The gifts and calling of God are without repentance.*

MISSIONS TO THE JEWS.

UNCHANGING God, hear from eternal
    heaven :
We plead Thy gifts of grace, for ever given,
Thy call, without repentance, calling still,
The sure election of Thy sovereign will.

Out of our faith in Thee Who canst not lie,
Out of our heart's desire, goes up our cry,
From hope's sweet vision of the thing to be,
From love to those who still are loved by Thee.

Bring Thy belovèd back, Thine Israel,
Thine own elect who from Thy favour fell,
But not from Thine election !—O forgive,
Speak but the word, and lo ! the dead shall live.

ather of mercies ! these the long-astray,
hese in soul-blindness now the far away,
hese are not aliens, but Thy sons of yore,
' by Thy Fatherhood, restore, restore !

reathe on Thy Church, that it may greet the day,
tir up her will to toil, and teach, and pray,
ill Zionward again salvation come,
.nd all her outcast children are at home.

riune JEHOVAH, Thine the grace and power,
hine all the work, its past, its future hour,
' Thou Who failest not, Thy gifts fulfil,
.nd crown the calling of Thy changeless will.

       Amen.

34   *God is able to graft them in again.*

THOU, the CHRIST for ever one,
  Mary's Child and Israel's GOD,
Daniel's Prince and David's Son,
  Jacob's Star and Jesse's Rod,
Thou of Whom the Prophets spake,
  Thou in Whom their words came true,
Hear the pleading prayer we make,
  Hear the Gentile for the Jew !

Knowing what the SPIRIT saith,
  Sure of Thee, our CHRIST Divine,
Lo, we stand, by right of faith,
  Heirs of Abraham's charter'd line ;
Can we then his sons forget,
  Branches sever'd from their tree,
Exiles from their homes, and yet
  Kinsmen, LORD, in flesh to Thee ?

Though the Blood, betray'd and spilt,
  On the race entail'd a doom,
Let its virtue cleanse the guilt,
  Melt the hardness, chase the gloom ;

(463)

Lift the veil from off their heart,
　Make them Israelites indeed,
Meet once more for lot and part
　With Thy household's genuine seed.

Thou that didst Thy dews outpour,
　Crowning alien grafts with fruit,
Soon the native growths restore,
　Making glad the parent root :
Ah ! but let not pride ensnare
　Souls that need to mourn their sin ;
Still the boughs adopted spare,
　And the outcasts—graft them in !

Speed the day of union sweet
　When, with us in faith allied,
Israel's heart shall turn to greet
　Thee, Whom Israel crucified :
Thee, in all Thy truth and grace,
　Own'd at last as Salem's King,
While her children find their place
　Gather'd safe beneath Thy wing.　Amen.

535 *Take . . . the sword of the Spirit, which is the word*
of God.

HOME MISSIONS.

SOLDIERS of the Cross, arise !
　Gird you with your armour bright ;
Mighty are your enemies,
　Hard the battle ye must fight.

O'er a faithless fallen world
　Raise your banner in the sky ;
Let it float there wide unfurl'd ;
　Bear it onward ; lift it high.

HOME MISSIONS.

'Mid the homes of want and woe,
  Strangers to the living word,
Let the SAVIOUR's herald go,
  Let the voice of hope be heard.

Where the shadows deepest lie,
  Carry truth's unsullied ray ;
Where are crimes of blackest dye,
  There the saving sign display.

To the weary and the worn
  Tell of realms where sorrows cease ;
To the outcast and forlorn
  Speak of mercy and of peace.

Guard the helpless ; seek the stray'd ;
  Comfort troubles, banish grief ;
In the might of GOD array'd,
  Scatter sin and unbelief.

Be the banner still unfurl'd,
  Still unsheath'd the SPIRIT's sword,
Till the kingdoms of the world
  Are the kingdom of the LORD.   Amen.

6   *The ways of the Lord are right.*

CHURCH WORKERS.

OH, it is hard to work for GOD,
    To rise and take His part
Upon this battlefield of earth,
  And not sometimes lose heart !

He hides Himself so wondrously,
  As though there were no GOD ;
He is least seen when all the pow'rs
  Of *ill* are most abroad.

(465)

Ah ! GOD is other than we think,
His ways are far above,
Far beyond reason's height, and reach'd
Only by childlike love.

Workman of GOD ! O lose not heart,
But learn what GOD is like,
And in the darkest battlefield
Thou shalt know where to strike.

Then learn to scorn the praise of men,
And learn to lose with GOD ;
For JESUS won the world through shame,
And beckons thee His road.

For right is right, as GOD is GOD,
And right the day must win ;
To doubt would be disloyalty,
To falter were to sin.   Amen.

537 *Stand fast in one spirit, striving together for
the faith of the Gospel.*

THE call to arms is sounding,
The foemen muster strong,
While Saints beneath the altar
Are crying " LORD, how long ? "
The living and the loving
CHRIST's royal standard raise,
And marching on to conflict
Shout forth their Captain's praise.

No time for self-indulgence,
For resting by the way ;
Repose will come at even,
But toil is for the day :
Work, like the blessèd JESUS,
Who from His earliest youth
Would do His FATHER's business
And witness for the truth.

For the one Faith, the true Faith,
  The Faith which cannot fail,
For the one Church, the true Church,
  'Gainst which no foes prevail ;
Made one with GOD Incarnate,
  We in His might must win
The glory of self-conquest,
  Of victory over sin.

Behold ! upon Mount Sion
  A glorious people stand,
A crown on every forehead,
  A palm in every hand ;
Lo ! these are they who boldly
  The Name of CHRIST confess'd,
And now triumphant praise Him
  In heav'n's unresting rest.

O JESU, Who art waiting
  Thy faithful ones to crown,
Vouchsafe to bless our conflict,
  Our loving service own ;
Come in each heart for ever
  As King adored to reign,
Till we with Saints triumphant
  Uplift the victor strain. Amen.

8   *Go work to-day.*

COME, labour on !   [plain,
  Who dares stand idle on the harvest
le all around him waves the golden grain ?
l to each servant does the Master say,
  " Go, work to-day ! "

Come, labour on !
m the high calling Angels cannot share,
young and old the Gospel-gladness bear :
eem the time : its hours too swiftly fly,
  The night draws nigh.

Come, labour on !
The enemy is watching night and day,
To sow the tares, to snatch the seed away ;
While we in sleep our duty have forgot,
    He slumber'd not.

Come, labour on !
Away with gloomy doubts and faithless fear !
No arm so weak but may do service here ;
By feeblest agents can our GOD fulfil
    His righteous will.

Come, labour on !
No time for rest, till glows the western sky,
Till the long shadows o'er our pathway lie,
And a glad sound comes with the setting sun—
    "Servants, well done !"

Come, labour on !
The toil is pleasant, the reward is sure ;
Blessèd are those who to the end endure ;
How full their joy, how deep their rest shall be,
    O LORD, with Thee !   Amen.

539   *Turn us then, O God our Saviour.*

ALMIGHTY GOD, Whose only SON
  O'er sin and death the triumph won,
And ever lives to intercede
For souls who Thy sweet mercy need ;

In His dear Name to Thee we pray
For all who err and go astray,
For sinners, wheresoe'er they be,
Who do not serve and honour Thee.

There are who never yet have heard
The tidings of Thy blessèd word,
But still in heathen darkness dwell,
Without one thought of heav'n or hell ;

And some within Thy sacred fold
To holy things are dead and cold,
And waste the precious hours of life
In selfish ease, or toil, or strife ;

And many a quicken'd soul within
There lurks the secret love of sin,
A wayward will, or anxious fears,
Or lingering taint of bygone years :

O give repentance true and deep
To all Thy lost and wandering sheep,
And kindle in their hearts the fire
Of holy love and pure desire.

That so from Angel-hosts above
May rise a sweeter song of love,
And we, with all the Blest, adore
Thy Name, O GOD, for evermore.   Amen.

40   *My helpers in Christ Jesus.*

LORD, speak to me, that I may speak
   In living echoes of Thy tone ;
As Thou hast sought, so let me seek
   Thy erring children lost and lone.

O lead me, LORD, that I may lead
   The wandering and the wavering feet ;
O feed me, LORD, that I may feed
   Thy hungering ones with manna sweet.

O strengthen me, that while I stand
   Firm on the Rock, and strong in Thee,
I may stretch out a loving hand
   To wrestlers with the troubled sea.

O teach me, LORD, that I may teach
   The precious things Thou dost impart :
And wing my words, that they may reach
   The hidden depths of many a heart.

O give Thine own sweet rest to me,
  That I may speak with soothing power
A word in season, as from Thee,
  To weary ones in needful hour.

O fill me with Thy fulness, LORD,
  Until my very heart o'erflow
In kindling thought and glowing word,
  Thy love to tell, Thy praise to show.

O use me, LORD, use even me,
  Just as Thou wilt, and when, and where,
Until Thy blessèd face I see,
  Thy rest, Thy joy, Thy glory share.   Amen.

541 *The word that I shall speak unto thee, that thou shalt*
speak.

SHINE Thou upon us, LORD,
  True Light of men, to-day ;
And through the written word
  Thy very self display ;
That so from hearts which burn
  With gazing on Thy face,
Thy little ones may learn
  The wonders of Thy grace.

Breathe Thou upon us, LORD,
  Thy SPIRIT's living flame,
That so with one accord
  Our lips may tell Thy Name ;
Give Thou the hearing ear,
  Fix Thou the wandering thought,
That those we teach may hear
  The great things Thou hast wrought.

Speak Thou for us, O LORD,
  In all we say of Thee ; .
According to Thy word
  Let all our teaching be ;

That so Thy lambs may know
  Their own true Shepherd's voice,
Where'er He leads them go,
  And in His love rejoice.

Live Thou within us, LORD;
  Thy mind and will be ours;
Be Thou beloved, adored,
  And served, with all our powers:
That so our lives may teach
  Thy children what Thou art,
And plead, by more than speech,
  For Thee with every heart. Amen.

The following is also suitable:
639 The Litany of the Church.

2 *As my Father hath sent me, even so send I you.*

EMBER DAYS.

CHRIST is gone up; yet ere He pass'd
  From earth, in heav'n to reign,
He form'd one holy Church to last
  Till He should come again.

His twelve Apostles first He made
  His ministers of grace;
And they their hands on others laid,
  To fill in turn their place.

So age by age, and year by year,
  His grace was handed on;
And still the holy Church is here,
  Although her LORD is gone.

Let those find pardon, LORD, from Thee,
  Whose love to her is cold:
Bring wanderers in, and let there be
  One Shepherd and one fold. Amen.

543 *He gave some, apostles; . . . and some, pastors and teachers; for the perfecting of the saints, for the work of the ministry, for the edifying of the body of Christ.*

O THOU Who makest souls to shine
   With light from lighter worlds above,
And droppest glistening dew divine
On all who seek a Saviour's love ;

Do Thou Thy benediction give
On all who teach, on all who learn,
That so Thy Church may holier live,
And every lamp more brightly burn.

Give those who teach pure hearts and wise,
Faith, hope, and love, all warm'd by prayer ;
Themselves first training for the skies,
They best will raise their people there.

Give those who learn the willing ear,
The spirit meek, the guileless mind ;
Such gifts will make the lowliest here
Far better than a kingdom find.

O bless the shepherd ; bless the sheep ;
That guide and guided both be one,
One in the faithful watch they keep,
Until this hurrying life be done.

If thus, good LORD, Thy grace be given,
In Thee to live, in Thee to die,
Before we upward pass to heaven,
We taste our immortality.   Amen.

544 *The harvest truly is plenteous, but the labourers are few*

THE earth, O LORD, is one wide field
   Of all Thy chosen seed ;
The crop prepared its fruit to yield ;
The labourers few indeed.

EMBER DAYS.

We therefore come before Thee now
    With fasting and with prayer,
Beseeching of Thy love that Thou
    Wouldst send more labourers there.

Not for our land alone we pray,
    Though that above the rest ;
The realms and islands far away,
    O let them all be blest.

Endue the bishops of Thy flock
    With wisdom and with grace,
For truth and justice, like a rock,
    To set the heart and face :

To all Thy priests Thy truth reveal,
    And make Thy judgments clear ;
Make Thou Thy deacons full of zeal
    And humble and sincere :

And give their flocks a lowly mind
    To hear and to obey ;
That each and all may mercy find
    At Thine appearing-day.   Amen.

5   *Let thy priests be clothed with righteousness.*

LORD, pour Thy SPIRIT from on high,
    And Thine ordainèd servants bless ;
Graces and gifts to each supply,
And clothe Thy priests with righteousness.

Within Thy temple when they stand,
To teach the truth as taught by Thee,
Saviour, like stars in Thy right hand,
Let all Thy Church's pastors be.

Wisdom, and zeal, and faith impart,
Firmness with meekness, from above,
To bear Thy people in their heart,
And *love the souls* whom Thou dost love :

(473)

To watch, and pray, and never faint,
By day and night their guard to keep,
To warn the sinner, cheer the saint,
To feed Thy lambs, and tend Thy sheep.

So, when their work is finish'd here,
May they in hope their charge resign ;
So, when their Master shall appear,
May they with crowns of glory shine.   Amen.

546 *Unto every one of us is given grace according to the measure of the gift of Christ.*

O GUARDIAN of the Church Divine,
    The sevenfold gifts of grace are Thine,
And kindled by Thy hidden fires
The soul to highest aims aspires.

Thy priests with wisdom, LORD, endue,
Their hearts with love and zeal renew ;
Turn all their weakness into might,
O Thou the source of life and light.

SPIRIT of truth, on us bestow
The faith in all its power to know ;
That with the saints of ages gone,
And those to come, we may be one.

Protect Thy Church from every foe,
And peace, the fruit of love, bestow ;
Convert the world, make all confess
The glories of Thy righteousness.

All praise to GOD the FATHER be,
All praise, Eternal SON, to Thee,
Whom with the SPIRIT we adore
For ever and for evermore.   Amen.

These Hymns for Ember Days are also suitable for need
of Clergy.

(474)

ALMSGIVING.

ALMSGIVING.

O LORD of heav'n, and earth, and sea,
To Thee all praise and glory be ;
How shall we show our love to Thee,
    Who givest all ?

The golden sunshine, vernal air,
Sweet flowers and fruit, Thy love declare ;
When harvests ripen, Thou art there,
    Who givest all.

For peaceful homes, and healthful days,
For all the blessings earth displays,
We owe Thee thankfulness and praise,
    Who givest all.

Thou didst not spare Thine Only Son,
But gav'st Him for a world undone,
And freely with that Blessèd One
    Thou givest all.

Thou giv'st the Holy Spirit's dower,
Spirit of life, and love, and power,
And dost His sevenfold graces shower
    Upon us all.

For souls redeem'd, for sins forgiven,
For means of grace and hopes of heaven,
Father, what can to Thee be given,
    Who givest all ?

We lose what on ourselves we spend,
We have as treasure without end
Whatever, Lord, to Thee we lend,
    Who givest all ;

To Thee, from Whom we all derive
Our life, our gifts, our power to give :
O may we ever with Thee live,
    Who givest all. Amen.

548 *Ye ought . . . to remember the words of the I*
Jesus, how he said, It is more blessed to give tha
receive.

LORD of glory, Who hast bought us
    With Thy life-blood as the price,
Never grudging for the lost ones
    That tremendous Sacrifice,
And with that hast freely given
    Blessings countless as the sand
To th' unthankful and the evil
    With Thine own unsparing hand ;

Grant us hearts, dear LORD, to yield Thee
    Gladly, freely of Thine own ;
With the sunshine of Thy goodness
    Melt our thankless hearts of stone ;
Till our cold and selfish natures,
    Warm'd by Thee, at length believe
That more happy and more blessèd
    'Tis to give than to receive.

Wondrous honour hast Thou given
    To our humblest charity
In Thine own mysterious sentence,
    "Ye have done it unto Me."
Can it be, O gracious Master,
    Thou dost deign for alms to sue,
Saying by Thy poor and needy,
    "Give as I have given to you ? "

Yes : the sorrow and the suffering,
    Which on every hand we see,
Channels are for tithes and offerings
    Due by solemn right to Thee ;
Right of which we may not rob Thee,
    Debt we may not choose but pay,
Lest that face of love and pity
    Turn from us another day.

(478)

ALMSGIVING.

Lord of glory, Who hast bought us
  With Thy life-blood as the price,
Never grudging for the lost ones
  That tremendous Sacrifice,
Give us faith, to trust Thee boldly,
  Hope, to stay our souls on Thee;
But oh best of all Thy graces,
  Give us Thine own charity. Amen.

49   *The Lord remember all thy offerings.*

A WIDOW'S hand in days of old
  Gave more than all beside;
Her gift more costly far than gold
  Bestow'd with careless pride.
So love that yieldeth all must be
The first free gift we bear to Thee.

Thy treasury is open still,
  And there our gifts we pour;
The contrite heart, the subject will
  Are offerings evermore,
Which even Thine all-searching eyes
May gaze upon and not despise.

Within one broadening stream unite
  The alms of rich and poor,
All equal in Thy holy sight,
  Who press Thy temple floor;
How vain all earthly pride and place
When God and man are face to face!

The silver and the gold are Thine;
  Thine own we give to Thee,
Whene'er before Thy sacred shrine
  We bow th' adoring knee;
O merciful High Priest, receive
The lowly *gifts* Thy children give. Amen.

550 *Whoso hath this world's goods, and seeth his brother have need, and shutteth up his bowels of compassion from him, how dwelleth the love of God in him?*

WE give Thee but Thine own,
　Whate'er the gift may be :
All that we have is Thine alone,
　A trust, O LORD, from Thee.

May we Thy bounties thus
　As stewards true receive,
And gladly, as Thou blessest us,
　To Thee our first-fruits give.

Oh hearts are bruised and dead,
　And homes are bare and cold,
And lambs, for whom the Shepherd bled,
　Are straying from the fold.

To comfort and to bless,
　To find a balm for woe,
To tend the lone and fatherless,
　Is Angels' work below.

The captive to release,
　To GOD the lost to bring,
To teach the way of life and peace,
　It is a Christ-like thing.

And we believe Thy word,
　Though dim our faith may be ;
Whate'er for Thine we do, O LORD,
　We do it unto Thee.

All might, all praise be Thine,
　FATHER, Co-equal SON,
And SPIRIT, Bond of love divine,
　While endless ages run.　Amen.

51 *They brought unto him all sick people that were taken with divers diseases . . . and he healed them.*

HOSPITALS.

THOU to Whom the sick and dying
   Ever came, nor came in vain,
Still with healing word replying
   To the wearied cry of pain,
     Hear us, JESU, as we meet
     Suppliants at Thy mercy-seat.

Still the weary, sick, and dying
   Need a brother's, sister's care ;
On Thy higher help relying
   May we now their burden share,
     Bringing all our offerings meet,
     Suppliants at Thy mercy-seat.

May each child of Thine be willing,
   Willing both in hand and heart,
All the law of love fulfilling,
   Ever comfort to impart ;
     Ever bringing offerings meet,
     Suppliant to Thy mercy-seat.

So may sickness, sin, and sadness
   To Thy healing virtue yield,
Till the sick and sad, in gladness,
   Rescued, ransom'd, cleansèd, heal'd,
     One in Thee together meet,
     Pardon'd at Thy judgment-seat.   Amen.

52 *They brought unto him all that were diseased, and besought him that they might only touch the hem of his garment; and as many as touched were made perfectly whole.*

THINE arm, O LORD, in days of old,
   Was strong to heal and save ;
It triumph'd o'er disease and death,
   O'er darkness and the grave ;

To Thee they went, the blind, the dumb,
  The palsied and the lame,
The leper with his tainted life,
  The sick with fever'd frame.

And lo ! Thy touch brought life and health,
  Gave speech, and strength, and sight ;
And youth renew'd and frenzy calm'd
  Own'd Thee, the LORD of light ;
And now, O LORD, be near to bless,
  Almighty as of yore,
In crowded street, by restless couch,
  As by Gennesareth's shore.

Be Thou our great Deliverer still,
  · Thou LORD of life and death :
Restore and quicken, soothe and bless
  With Thine Almighty Breath ;
To hands that work, and eyes that see,
  Give wisdom's heav'nly lore,
That whole and sick, and weak and strong
  May praise Thee evermore.   Amen.

The following Hymn is suitable :
30 At even, when the sun did set.

553 *I heard the voice of the Lord, saying, Whom shall I
send, and who will go for us?   Then said I, Here
am I, send me.*

FOR THEOLOGICAL COLLEGES.

ONE Thy Light, the temple filling,
  Holy, Holy, Holy, THREE :
Meanest men and brightest Angels
  Wait alike the word from Thee ;
Highest musings, lowliest worship,
  Must their preparation be.

(480)

THEOLOGICAL COLLEGES.

Now Thou speakest—hear we trembling—
  From the glory comes a voice,
Who accepts th' Almighty's mission ?
  Who will make CHRIST's work his choice ?
Who for Us proclaim to sinners,
  Turn, believe, endure, rejoice ?

Here are we, Redeemer, send us !
  But because Thy work is fire,
And our lips, unclean and earthly,
  Breathe no breath of high desire,
Send Thy Seraph from the altar,
  Veil'd, but in his bright attire.

Cause him, LORD, to fly full swiftly
  With the mystic coal in hand,
Sin-consuming, soul-transforming
  (Faith and love will understand) ;
Touch our lips, Thou awful Mercy,
  With Thine own keen healing brand.

Thou didst come that fire to kindle ;
  Fain would we Thy torches prove,
Far and wide Thy beacons lighting
  With th' undying spark of love :
Only feed our flame, we pray Thee,
  With Thy breathings from above.

Now to GOD, the soul's Creator,
  To His WORD and WISDOM sure,
To His all-enlightening SPIRIT,
  Patron of the frail and poor,
THREE in ONE, be praise and glory
  Here and while the heav'ns endure. Amen.

554 *Blessed are the pure in heart: for they shall see God.*

TEMPERANCE.

O LORD, our strength in weakness,
　We pray to Thee for grace ;
For power to fight the battle,
　For speed to run the race ;
When Thy baptismal waters
　Were pour'd upon our brow,
We then were made Thy children,
　And pledged our earliest vow.

CHRIST with His own Blood bought us,
　And made the purchase sure ;
His are we ; may He keep us
　Sober, and chaste, and pure.
He, GOD in Man, has carried
　Our nature up to heaven ;
And thence the HOLY SPIRIT
　To dwell in us has given.

Conform'd to His own likeness,
　May we so live and die,
That in the grave our bodies
　In holy peace may lie,
And at the Resurrection
　Forth from those graves may spring
Like to the glorious Body
　Of CHRIST, our LORD and King.

The pure in heart are blessèd,
　For they shall see the LORD,
For ever and for ever
　By Seraphim adored ;
And they shall drink the pleasures,
　Such as no tongue can tell,
From the clear crystal river,
　And Life's eternal well.

TEMPERANCE.

Sing therefore to the FATHER,
  Who sent the SON in love;
And sing to GOD the SAVIOUR,
  Who leads to realms above:
Sing we with Saints and Angels,
  Before the heav'nly throne,
To GOD the HOLY SPIRIT;
  Sing to the THREE in ONE. Amen.

55 *This kind goeth not out but by prayer and fasting.*

O FATHER, in Whose great design
   Our hearts are fill'd with love divine,
Teach us to give our love to those
By sin beset and all its woes;
On Thee for them to cast our care,
By fasting and by lowly prayer.

LORD JESU, grant us eyes to see
In our poor brethren Thine and Thee—
To give ourselves where others need;
Where others sin to intercede;
And thus, by fasting and by prayer,
Our brethren's burden seek to bear.

O SPIRIT, by Whose grace alone
The many members are made one;
O warm our hearts, inspire our will,
That we Thy purpose may fulfil;
And thus by fasting and by prayer,
Through Thee the glorious Church prepare.

O GOD, all-loving THREE in ONE,
Whom we shall see beyond the sun;
Where walk in white the blood-bought throng,
Where soars to Thee the sweet new song,
Grant that we find the brethren there
We sought by fasting and by prayer. Amen.

556 *The Lord hath done great things for us already.*

O THOU before Whose presence
   Naught evil may come in,
Yet Who dost look in mercy
   Down on this world of sin ;
O give us noble purpose
   To set the sin-bound free,
And CHRIST-like tender pity
   To seek the lost for Thee.

Fierce is our subtle foeman :
   The forces at his hand
With woes that none can number
   Despoil the pleasant land ;
All they who war against them,
   In strife so keen and long,
Must in their Saviour's armour
   Be stronger than the strong.

So hast Thou wrought among us
   The great things that we see !
For things that are we thank Thee,
   And for the things to be :
For bright Hope is uplifting
   Faint hands and feeble knees,
To strive beneath Thy blessing
   For greater things than these.

Lead on, O Love and Mercy,
   O Purity and Power !
Lead on till Peace eternal
   Shall close this battle-hour :
Till all who pray'd and struggled
   To set their brethren free,
In triumph meet to praise Thee,
   Most HOLY TRINITY. Amen.

¡57 *Bear ye one another's burdens, and so fulfil the law of Christ.*

BENEFIT SOCIETIES.

O PRAISE our GOD to-day,
His constant mercy bless,
Whose love hath help'd us on our way,
And granted us success.

His arm the strength imparts
Our daily toil to bear ;
His grace alone inspires our hearts
Each other's load to share.

O happiest work below,
Earnest of joy above,
To sweeten many a cup of woe
By deeds of holy love !

LORD, may it be our choice
This blessèd rule to keep,
" Rejoice with them that do rejoice,
And weep with them that weep."

O praise our GOD to-day,
His constant mercy bless,
Whose love hath help'd us on our way,
And granted us success.   Amen.

The following Hymns are suitable for Men's Services:

439 SON of GOD, Eternal Saviour.
440 O GOD of Truth, Whose living word.
442 Through the night of doubt and sorrow.
443 Brothers, joining hand to hand.
444 O LORD, how joyful 'tis to see.

558 *The Lord himself give you peace always by all means.*

FOR A SERVICE OF FAREWELL.

WITH the sweet word of Peace
We bid our brethren go ;
Peace as a river to increase,
And ceaseless flow.

With the calm word of Prayer
We earnestly commend
Our brethren to Thy watchful care,
Eternal Friend !

With the dear word of Love
We give our brief farewell ;
Our love below, and Thine above,
With them shall dwell.

With the strong word of Faith
We stay ourselves on Thee,
That Thou, O LORD, in life and death
Their help shalt be.

Then the bright word of Hope
Shall on our parting gleam,
And tell of joys beyond the scope
Of earth-born dream.

Farewell ! in hope and love,
In faith and peace and prayer,
Till He Whose home is ours above,
Unite us there ! Amen.

FOR ABSENT FRIENDS.

559 *The Lord shall preserve thy going out and thy coming in.*

FOR ABSENT FRIENDS.

FOR the dear ones parted from us
   We would raise our hymns of prayer ;
By the tender love which watcheth
   Round Thy children everywhere,
      Holy FATHER,
   Keep them ever in Thy care.

Through each trial and temptation,
   Dangers faced by night and day,
By the infinite compassion
   Pleading for the souls that stray,
      Loving SAVIOUR,
   Keep them in the narrow way.

In their hours of doubt and sorrow,
   When their faith is sorely tried,
By the grace divine which strengthens
   Souls for whom the Saviour died,
      Gracious SPIRIT,
   Be Thou evermore their guide.

In their joys, by friends surrounded,
   In their strife, by foes oppress'd,
May Thy blessing still be with them,
   May Thy presence give them rest,
      GOD Almighty,
   FATHER, SON, and SPIRIT blest.   Amen.

560 *The Lord watch between me and thee, when we are absent one from another.*

HOLY FATHER, in Thy mercy
   Hear our anxious prayer ;
Keep our loved ones, now far absent,
      'Neath Thy care.

Jesus, Saviour, let Thy p esen e
  Be their light and guide;   c
Keep, O keep them, in their weakness,
          At Thy side.

When in sorrow, when in danger,
  When in loneliness,
In Thy love look down and comfort
          Their distress.

May the joy of Thy salvation
  Be their strength and stay ;
May they love and may they praise Thee
          Day by day.

Holy Spirit, let Thy teaching
  Sanctify their life ;
Send Thy grace, that they may conquer
          In the strife.

Father, Son, and Holy Spirit,
  God the One in Three,
Bless them, guide them, save them, keep them
          Near to Thee. Amen.

ON BEHALF OF THOSE AT SEA.

561   *Thou rulest the raging of the sea.*

ETERNAL Father, strong to save,
  Whose arm hath bound the restless wave,
Who bidd'st the mighty ocean deep
Its own appointed limits keep ;
  O hear us when we cry to Thee
  For those in peril on the sea.

O Christ, Whose voice the waters heard
And hush'd their raging at Thy word,
Who walkedst on the foaming deep,
And calm amid the storm didst sleep ;
  O hear us when we cry to Thee
  For those in peril on the sea.

ON BEHALF OF THOSE AT SEA.

O HOLY SPIRIT, Who didst brood
Upon the waters dark and rude,
And bid their angry tumult cease,
And give, for wild confusion, peace ;
  O hear us when we cry to Thee
  For those in peril on the sea.

O TRINITY of love and power,
Our brethren shield in danger's hour ;
From rock and tempest, fire and foe,
Protect them wheresoe'er they go ;
  Thus evermore shall rise to Thee
  Glad hymns of praise from land and sea.
                          Amen.

FOR USE AT SEA.

562 *Thou shalt shew us wonderful things in thy right-*
eousness, O God of our salvation: thou that art the
hope of all the ends of the earth, and of them that
remain in the broad sea.

ALMIGHTY FATHER, hear our cry,
  As o'er the trackless deep we roam ;
Be Thou our haven always nigh,
  On homeless waters Thou our home.

O JESU, Saviour, at Whose voice
  The tempest sank to perfect rest,
Bid Thou the fearful heart rejoice,
  And cleanse and calm the troubled breast.

O HOLY GHOST, beneath Whose power
  The ocean woke to life and light,
Command Thy blessing in this hour,
  Thy fostering warmth, Thy quickening might.

Great GOD of our salvation, Thee
  We love, we worship, we adore ;
Our Refuge on time's changeful sea,
  Our Joy on heav'n's eternal shore.   Amen.

3 *The sea is his.*

O LORD, be with us when we sail
    Upon the lonely deep,
Our Guard when on the silent deck
    The midnight watch we keep.

We need not fear, though all around
    'Mid rising winds we hear
The multitudes of waters surge,
    For Thou, O GOD, art near.

The calm, the breeze, the gale, the storm,
    That pass from land to land,
All, all are Thine, are held within
    The hollow of Thy hand.

If duty calls from threaten'd strife
    To guard our native shore,
And shot and shell are answering fast
    The booming cannon's roar,

Be Thou the mainguard of our host,
    Till war and danger cease :
Defend the right, put up the sword,
    And through the world make peace.

To Thee the FATHER, Thee the SON,
    Whom earth and sky adore,
And SPIRIT, moving o'er the deep,
    Be praise for evermore.   Amen.

564 *Pray that ye enter not into temptation.*

O SAVIOUR ! when Thy loving hand
    Has brought us o'er the sea,
Through perils many, safe to land—
    The land we long'd to see ;

O help us, for Thy help we need
    Each moment more and more,
In perils that we scarcely heed,
    More deadly, on the shore.

FOR USE AT SEA.

LORD, save us ! and the Christian name,
　　O help us pure to keep,
On sea or land, alike the same,
　　Till we in death shall sleep.

Then through Thy merits, wash'd and clean
　　From sin's polluting stain,
In raiment white may we be seen
　　With all Thy Saints to reign.　Amen.

The following is also suitable:
643 Litany for use at Sea.

FOR THE YOUNG.

565 *To him that is able to keep you from falling.*

SING to the LORD the children's hymn ;
　　His gentle love declare,
Who bends amid the Seraphim
　　To hear the children's prayer.

He at a mother's breast was fed,
　　Though GOD'S own SON was He ;
He learnt the first small words He said
　　At a meek mother's knee.

Close to His loving heart He press'd
　　The children of the earth ;
He lifted up His hands and bless'd
　　The babes of human birth.

Lo ! from the stars His face will turn
　　On us with glances mild ;
The Angels of His presence yearn
　　To bless the little child.

Keep us, O JESUS, LORD, for Thee,
　　That so, by Thy dear grace,
We, children of the font, may see
　　Our heav'nly FATHER'S face.　Amen.

FOR THE YOUNG.

The child Jesus.

ONCE in royal David's city
    Stood a lowly cattle shed,
Where a Mother laid her Baby
    In a manger for His bed ;
Mary was that Mother mild,
JESUS CHRIST her little Child.

He came down to earth from heaven
    Who is GOD and LORD of all,
And His shelter was a stable,
    And His cradle was a stall ;
With the poor, and mean, and lowly,
Lived on earth our Saviour Holy.

And through all His wondrous Childhood
    He would honour and obey,
Love, and watch the lowly Maiden,
    In whose gentle arms He lay ;
Christian children all must be
Mild, obedient, good as He.

For He is our childhood's pattern,
    Day by day like us He grew,
He was little, weak, and helpless,
    Tears and smiles like us He knew ;
And He feeleth for our sadness,
And He shareth in our gladness.

And our eyes at last shall see Him,
    Through His own redeeming love,
For that Child so dear and gentle
    Is our LORD in heav'n above ;
And He leads His children on
To the place where He is gone.

(492)

Not in that poor lowly stable,
  With the oxen standing by,
We shall see Him ; but in heaven,
  Set at GOD's right hand on high ;
When like stars His children crown'd
All in white shall wait around.   Amen.

567   *The love of Christ.*

I LOVE to hear the story
    Which Angel voices tell,
How once the King of glory
    Came down on earth to dwell.
I am both weak and sinful,
    But this I surely know,
The LORD came down to save me,
    Because He loved me so.
        I love to hear the story
            Which Angel voices tell,
        How once the King of glory
            Came down on earth to dwell.

My Blessèd LORD and SAVIOUR
    Was once a Child like me,
To show how pure and holy
    His little ones might be ;
And if I try to follow
    His footsteps here below,
He never will forget me,
    Because He loves me so.
        I love to hear the story
            Which Angel voices tell,
        How once the King of glory
            Came down on earth to dwell.

To tell His love and mercy
    My sweetest songs I raise ;
And though I cannot see Him,
    I know He hears my praise ;

For He Himself has promised
That even I may go
To sing among His Angels,
Because He loves me so.
I love to hear the story
Which Angel voices tell,
How once the King of glory
Came down on earth to dwell.
Amen.

568 *Let this mind be in you which was also in Christ Jesus.*

BEHOLD a little Child,
Laid in a manger bed ;
The wintry blasts blow wild
Around His infant head.
But Who is this so lowly laid ?
'Tis He by Whom the worlds were made.

Alas ! in what poor state
The SON of GOD is seen ;
Why doth the LORD so great
Choose out a home so mean ?
That we may learn from pride to flee,
And follow His humility.

Where Joseph plies his trade,
Lo ! JESUS labours too ;
The hands that all things made
An earthly craft pursue,
That weary men in Him may rest,
And faithful toil through Him be blest.

Among the doctors see
The Boy so full of grace ;
Say, wherefore taketh He
The scholar's lowly place ?
That Christian boys, with rev'rence meet
May sit and learn at JESUS' feet.

FOR THE YOUNG.

CHRIST ! once Thyself a Boy,
　Our boyhood guard and guide ;
Be Thou its light and joy,
　And still with us abide,
That Thy dear love, so great and free,
May draw us evermore to Thee.　Amen.

69 *Children crying in the temple, and saying, Hosanna*
to the Son of David.

WHEN, His salvation bringing,
　To Zion JESUS came,
The children all stood singing
　Hosanna to His Name ;
Nor did their zeal offend Him,
　But, as He rode along,
He let them still attend Him,
　And listen'd to their song.
　　Hosanna to JESUS they sang.

And since the LORD retaineth
　His love for children still,
Though now as King He reigneth
　On Zion's heav'nly hill :
We'll flock around His banner,
　Who sits upon the throne,
And cry aloud " Hosanna,"
　To David's royal Son.
　　Hosanna to JESUS we'll sing.

For should we fail proclaiming
　Our great Redeemer's praise,
The stones, our silence shaming,
　Would their Hosannas raise.
But shall we only render
　The tribute of our words ?
No ! while our hearts are tender,
　They, too, shall be the LORD's.
　　Hosanna to JESUS, our King.　Amen.

570 *While we were yet sinners, Christ died for us.*

THERE is a green hill far away,
　　Outside a city wall,
Where the dear LORD was crucified,
　　Who died to save us all.

We may not know, we cannot tell,
　　What pains He had to bear,
But we believe it was for us
　　He hung and suffer'd there.

He died that we might be forgiven,
　　He died to make us good,
That we might go at last to heaven,
　　Saved by His precious Blood.

There was no other good enough
　　To pay the price of sin ;
He only could unlock the gate
　　Of heav'n, and let us in.

Oh, dearly, dearly has He loved,
　　And we must love Him too,
And trust in His redeeming Blood,
　　And try His works to do.　Amen.

571 *Let us hold fast the profession of our faith without wavering.*

I WAS made a Christian
　　When my name was given,
One of GOD's dear children,
　　And an heir of heaven.

In the name of Christian
　　I will glory now,
Evermore remember
　　My baptismal vow.

FOR THE YOUNG.

I must, like a Christian,
  Shun all evil ways,
Keep the faith of JESUS,
  Serve Him all my days.

Call'd to be a Christian,
  I will praise the LORD,
Seek for His assistance
  So to keep my word.

All a Christian's blessings
  I will claim for mine :
Holy work and worship,
  Fellowship divine.

FATHER, SON, and SPIRIT,
  Give me grace, that I
Still may live a Christian,
  And a Christian die.   Amen.

'2   *He took them up in his arms.*

CHRIST, Who once amongst us
    As a Child did dwell,
Is the children's Saviour
  And He loves us well ;
If we keep our promise
  Made Him at the font,
He will be our Shepherd,
  And we shall not want.

There it was they laid us
  In those tender arms,
Where the lambs are carried
  Safe from all alarms ;
If we trust His promise,
  He will let us rest
In His arms for ever,
  Leaning on His breast.

(497)

FOR THE YOUNG.

Though we may not see Him
　For a little while,
We shall know He holds us,
　Often feel His smile ;
Death will be to slumber
　In that sweet embrace,
And we shall awaken
　To behold His face.

He will be our Shepherd
　After as before,
By still heav'nly waters
　Lead us evermore,
Make us lie in pastures
　Beautiful and green,
Where none thirst or hunger,
　And no tears are seen.

Jesus, our good Shepherd,
　Laying down Thy life,
Lest Thy sheep should perish
　In the cruel strife,
Help us to remember
　All Thy love and care,
Trust in Thee, and love Thee
　Always, everywhere.　Amen.

573 *My sheep hear my voice, and I know them, and they*
follow me.

LOVING Shepherd of Thy sheep,
　Keep Thy lamb, in safety keep ;
Nothing can Thy power withstand,
None can pluck me from Thy hand.

Loving Saviour, Thou didst give
Thine own life that we might live,
And the hands outstretch'd to bless
Bear the cruel nails' impress.

(498)

FOR THE YOUNG.

I would praise Thee every day,
Gladly all Thy will obey,
Like Thy blessèd ones above,
Happy in Thy precious love.

Loving Shepherd, ever near,
Teach Thy lamb Thy voice to hear;
Suffer not my steps to stray
From the straight and narrow way.

Where Thou leadest I would go,
Walking in Thy steps below,
Till before the FATHER's throne
I shall know as I am known.   Amen.

574 *He shall give his angels charge over thee, to keep thee in all thy ways.*

AROUND the throne of GOD a band
Of glorious Angels ever stand;
Bright things they see, sweet harps they hold,
And on their heads are crowns of gold.

Some wait around Him, ready still
To sing His praise and do His will;
And some, when He commands them, go
To guard His servants here below.

LORD, give Thy Angels every day
Command to guide us on our way,
And bid them every evening keep
Their watch around us while we sleep.

So shall no wicked thing draw near,
To do us harm or cause us fear;
And we shall dwell, when life is past,
With Angels round Thy throne at last.
                              Amen.
                                 R.

FOR THE YOUNG.

575 *Praise our God, all ye his servants, and ye that*
him, both small and great.

ABOVE the clear blue sky,
  In heaven's bright abode,
The Angel host on high
  Sing praises to their GOD ;
    Alleluia !
    They love to sing
    To GOD their King
    Alleluia !

But GOD from infant tongues
  On earth receiveth praise ;
We then our cheerful songs
  In sweet accord will raise :
    Alleluia !
    We too will sing
    To GOD our King
    Alleluia !

O Blessèd LORD, Thy truth
  To us betimes impart,
And teach us in our youth
  To know Thee as Thou art.
    Alleluia !
    Then shall we sing
    To GOD our King
    Alleluia !

O may Thy holy word
  Spread all the world around ;
And all with one accord
  Uplift the joyful sound,
    Alleluia !
    All then shall sing
    To GOD their King
      Alleluia ! Amen.

6 *Jesus . . . took a child, and set him by him.*

THERE'S a Friend for little children
    Above the bright blue sky,
A Friend Who never changes,
    Whose love will never die ;
Our earthly friends may fail us,
    And change with changing years ;
This Friend is always worthy
    Of that dear Name He bears.

There's a rest for little children
    Above the bright blue sky,
Who love the Blessèd Saviour,
    And to the FATHER cry ;
A rest from every turmoil,
    From sin and sorrow free,
Where every little pilgrim
    Shall rest eternally.

There's a home for little children
    Above the bright blue sky,
Where JESUS reigns in glory,
    A home of peace and joy ;
No home on earth is like it,
    Nor can with it compare ;
And every one is happy,
    For all are holy there.

There's a crown for little children
    Above the bright blue sky,
And all who look for JESUS
    Shall wear it by and by ;
A crown of brightest glory,
    Which He will then bestow
On those who found His favour
    And *loved* His Name below.

R 2

FOR THE YOUNG.

There's a song for little children
    Above the bright blue sky,
A song that will not weary,
    Though sung continually ;
A song which even Angels
    Can never, never sing ;
They know not CHRIST as Saviour,
    But worship Him as King.

There's a robe for little children
    Above the bright blue sky :
And a harp of sweetest music,
    And palms of victory.
All, all above is treasured,
    And found in CHRIST alone ;
LORD, grant Thy little children
    To know Thee as their own.   Amen.

577 *The Son of man shall come in his glory, and all t.*
        holy angels with him.

UP in heaven, up in heaven,
    In the bright place far away,
He Whom bad men crucified
Sitteth at His FATHER'S side,
    Till the Judgment Day.

And He loves His little children,
    And He pleadeth for them there,
As their great High Priest in heaven,
That their sins may be forgiven,
    And He hears their prayer.

Never more a helpless Baby,
    Born in poverty and pain,
But with awful glory crown'd,
With His Angels standing round,
    He shall come again.

Then the wicked souls shall tremble,
    And the good souls shall rejoice ;
Parents, children, every one,
Then shall stand before His throne
    And shall hear His voice.

And all faithful, holy Christians,
    Who their Master's work have done,
Shall appear at His right hand
And inherit the fair land
    That His love has won.   Amen.

578   *Even a child is known by his doings.*

WE are but little children weak,
    And He is King above the sky ;
What can we do for JESUS' sake,
Who is so good, and great, and high ?

We know the Holy Innocents
Laid down for Him their infant life,
And Martyrs brave, and patient Saints
Have stood for Him in fire and strife.

We wear the Cross they wore of old,
Our lips have learn'd like vows to make ;
We are not call'd like them to die,
What may we do for JESUS' sake ?

Oh, day by day each Christian child
Has much to do, without, within ;
A death to die for JESUS' sake,
A weary war to wage with sin.

When deep within our swelling hearts
The thoughts of pride and anger rise,
When bitter words are on our tongues,
And tears of passion in our eyes ;

(503)

Then we may stay the angry blow,
Then we may check the hasty word,
Give gentle answers back again,
And fight a battle for our LORD.

With smiles of peace, and looks of love,
Light in our dwellings we may make,
Bid kind good humour brighten there,
And still do all for JESUS' sake.

There's not a child so small and weak
But has his little cross to take,
His little work of love and praise
That he may do for JESUS' sake. Amen.

579 . *Looking unto Jesus.*

LAMB of GOD, I look to Thee,
  Thou shalt my example be :
Thou art gentle, meek, and mild,
Thou wast once a little Child.

Fain I would be as Thou art ;
Give me Thy obedient heart ;
Thou art pitiful and kind,
Let me have Thy loving mind.

Meek and lowly may I be ;
Thou art all humility :
Let me to my betters bow,
Subject to Thy parents Thou.

Let me above all fulfil
GOD my heav'nly FATHER's will ;
Never His good SPIRIT grieve,
Only to His glory live.

FOR THE YOUNG.

Loving JESU, gentle LAMB,
In Thy gracious hands I am ;
Make me, Saviour, what Thou art ;
Live Thyself within my heart.

I shall then show forth Thy praise,
Serve Thee all my happy days ;
Then the world shall always see
CHRIST, the Holy Child, in me.   Amen.

*My song shall be alway of the loving-kindness of the
Lord.*

COME, sing with holy gladness,
  High Alleluias sing,
Uplift your loud Hosannas
  To JESUS, LORD and King ;
Sing, boys, in joyful chorus
  Your hymn of praise to-day,
And sing, ye gentle maidens,
  Your sweet responsive lay.

O boys, be strong in JESUS ;
  To toil for Him is gain,
And JESUS wrought with Joseph
  With chisel, saw, and plane.
O maidens, live for JESUS,
  Who was a maiden's Son ;
Be patient, pure, and gentle,
  And perfect grace begun.

'Tis good for boys and maidens
  Sweet hymns to CHRIST to sing ;
'Tis meet that children's voices
  Should praise the children's King ;
For JESUS is salvation,
  And glory, grace, and rest ;
To babe, and boy, and maiden
  The one Redeemer Blest.   Amen.

FOR THE YOUNG.

581 *Thine eyes shall see the King in his beauty; they sh[*
behold the land that is very far off.

EVERY morning the red sun
    Rises warm and bright;
But the evening cometh on,
    And the dark, cold night.
There's a bright land far away,
Where 'tis never-ending day.

Every spring the sweet young flowers
    Open bright and gay,
Till the chilly autumn hours
    Wither them away.
There's a land we have not seen,
Where the trees are always green.

Little birds sing songs of praise
    All the summer long,
But in colder, shorter days
    They forget their song.
There's a place where Angels sing
Ceaseless praises to their King.

CHRIST our LORD is ever near
    Those who follow Him;
But we cannot see Him here,
    For our eyes are dim;
There is a most happy place,
Where men always see His face.

Who shall go to that bright land?
    All who do the right:
Holy children there shall stand
    In their robes of white;
For that heav'n, so bright and blest,
Is our everlasting rest. Amen.

32 *There is mercy with thee, therefore shalt thou be feared.*

AS now Thy children lowly kneel,
    And all for mercy pray,
O Father, make us truly feel
    The solemn words we say.

Teach us to hate the power of sin,
    Which parts our souls from Thee ;
Help us to make our life within
    What Thou wilt love to see.

Teach us to trust the Lamb of God,
    Who takes our sins away ;
Help us to choose the path He trod,
    And so Thy will obey.

Teach us to keep Thy holy laws
    Because we trust Thy love ;
Help us to rise, when Jesus draws
    To better joys above.

O teach us more our sin to fear,
    And more Thy word to love :
Help us on earth the cross to bear,
    And win the crown above.   Amen.

33   *Cease to do evil, learn to do well.*

DO no sinful action,
    Speak no angry word ;
Ye belong to Jesus,
    Children of the Lord.

Christ is kind and gentle,
    Christ is pure and true ;
And His little children
    Must be holy too.

FOR THE YOUNG.

There's a wicked spirit
　Watching round you still,
And he tries to tempt you
　To all harm and ill.

But ye must not hear him,
　Though 'tis hard for you
To resist the evil,
　And the good to do.

For ye promised truly
　In your infant days
To renounce him wholly,
　And forsake his ways.

Ye are new-born Christians,
　Ye must learn to fight
With the bad within you,
　And to do the right.

CHRIST is your own Master,
　He is good and true,
And His little children
　Must be holy too.　Amen.

584　　*Speak, Lord, for thy servant heareth.*

HUSH'D was the evening hymn,
　　The temple courts were dark ;
The lamp was burning dim
　Before the sacred ark ;
When suddenly a voice divine
Rang through the silence of the shrine.

The old man meek and mild,
　The priest of Israel, slept ;
His watch the temple child,
　The little Levite, kept ;
And what from Eli's sense was seal'd,
The LORD to Hannah's son reveal'd.

(508)

FOR THE YOUNG.

O give me Samuel's ear,
  The open ear, O Lord,
Alive and quick to hear
  Each whisper of Thy word ;
Like him to answer at Thy call,
And to obey Thee first of all.

O give me Samuel's heart,
  A lowly heart, that waits
Where in Thy house Thou art,
  Or watches at Thy gates,—
By day and night, a heart that still
Moves at the breathing of Thy will.

O give me Samuel's mind,
  A sweet unmurmuring faith,
Obedient and resign'd
  To Thee in life and death ;
That I may read with child-like eyes
Truths that are hidden from the wise.
                              Amen.

585   *The Lord made all things.*

ALL things bright and beautiful,
    All creatures great and small,
All things wise and wonderful,
  The Lord God made them all.

Each little flower that opens,
  Each little bird that sings,
He made their glowing colours,
  He made their tiny wings.
          All things bright, &c.

The rich man in his castle,
  The poor man at his gate,
God made them high or lowly,
  And order'd their estate.
          All things bright, &c.

FOR THE YOUNG.

The purple-headed mountain,
  The river running by,
The sunset, and the morning
  That brightens up the sky ;—
      All things bright, &c.

The cold wind in the winter,
  The pleasant summer sun,
The ripe fruits in the garden,—
  He made them every one ;
      All things bright, &c.

He gave us eyes to see them,
  And lips that we might tell,
How great is GOD Almighty,
  Who has made all things well.
      All things bright, &c.   Amen.

586 *The cup which my Father hath given me shall I not
drink it ?*

SOME time o'er our pathway
    Passing clouds must fall ;
Some time pain and sorrow
  Come to each and all.

GOD, our FATHER, gives us
  Ever what is best ;
We in faith and patience
  Find our only rest.

If the cup be bitter
  It is meant to heal ;
And our good Physician
  Pities all we feel.

What are all our troubles,
  What our greatest loss,
When we think of JESUS
  Dying on the Cross ?

(510)

So our great Example
  We must follow still ;
When our FATHER calls us
  Yielding up our will.

Then, through joy or sorrow,
  By His SPIRIT led,
We shall rise to glory
  With our royal Head.   Amen.

$7   *Give ear, O Shepherd of Israel.*

FAITHFUL Shepherd, feed me
  In the pastures green ;
Faithful Shepherd, lead me
  Where Thy steps are seen.

Hold me fast, and guide me
  In the narrow way ;
So, with Thee beside me,
  I shall never stray.

Daily bring me nearer
  To the heav'nly shore ;
May my faith grow clearer,
  May I love Thee more.

Hallow every pleasure,
  Every gift and pain ;
Be Thyself my treasure,
  Though none else I gain.

Day by day prepare me
  As Thou seest best,
Then let Angels bear me
  To Thy promised rest.   Amen.

FOR THE YOUNG.

588 *Be ye therefore followers of God, as dear childre*

HEAV'NLY FATHER, send Thy blessi
   On Thy children gather'd here ;
May they all, Thy Name confessing,
   Be to Thee for ever dear :
May they be, like Joseph, loving,
   Dutiful, and chaste, and pure ;
And their faith, like David, proving,
   Steadfast unto death endure.

Holy SAVIOUR, Who in meekness
   Didst vouchsafe a Child to be,
Guide their steps, and help their weaknes
   Bless and make them like to Thee ;
Bear Thy lambs when they are weary,
   In Thine arms and at Thy breast :
Through life's desert, dry and dreary,
   Bring them to Thy heav'nly rest.

Spread Thy golden pinions o'er them,
   HOLY SPIRIT, from above,
Guide them, lead them, go before them,
   Give them peace, and joy, and love :
Thy true temples, HOLY SPIRIT,
   May they with Thy glory shine,
And immortal bliss inherit,
   And for evermore be Thine.   Amen.

589 *Thou shalt not delay to offer the first of thy ripe f*

FAIR waved the golden corn
   In Canaan's pleasant land,
When full of joy, some shining morn,
   Went forth the reaper-band.

To GOD so good and great
   Their cheerful thanks they pour ;
Then carry to His temple-gate
   The choicest of their store.

FOR THE YOUNG.

Like Israel, LORD, we give
  Our earliest fruits to Thee,
And pray that, long as we shall live,
  We may Thy children be.

Thine is our youthful prime,
  And life and all its powers ;
Be with us in our morning time,
  And bless our evening hours.

In wisdom let us grow,
  As years and strength are given,
That we may serve Thy Church below,
  And join Thy Saints in heaven.   Amen.

*O Master, we would that thou shouldest do for us
    whatsoever we shall desire.*

FOR A SCHOOL FEAST.

LORD JESUS, GOD and Man,
    For love of man a Child,
The Very GOD, yet born on earth
  Of Mary undefiled ;

LORD JESUS, GOD and Man,
  In this our festal day
To Thee for precious gifts of grace
  Thy ransom'd people pray.

We pray for childlike hearts,
  For gentleness and love,
For strength to do Thy will below
  As Angels do above.

We pray for simple faith,
  For hope that never faints,
For true communion evermore
  With all Thy blessèd Saints.

(513)

On friends around us here
O let Thy blessing fall;
We pray for grace to love them well,
But Thee beyond them all.

O joy to live for Thee !
O joy in Thee to die !
O very joy of joys to see
Thy face eternally !

LORD JESUS, GOD and Man,
We praise Thee and adore,
Who art with GOD the FATHER One
And SPIRIT evermore.   Amen.

591   *Suffer the little children to come unto me.*
FOR LITTLE CHILDREN.

OUR GOD of love Who reigns above
    Comes down to us below ;
'Tis sweet to tell He loves so well,
    And 'tis enough to know.

So deep, so high—like air and sky,
    Beyond us, yet around ;
He Whom our mind can never find,
    Can in our heart be found.

LORD GOD, so far, past sun and star,
    Yet close to all our ways !
In love so near, be pleased to hear
    Thy little children's praise !

O may that sign that we are Thine—
    Our FATHER, SAVIOUR, FRIEND—
Which seal'd our brow, be on us now,
    And with us to the end.

Through all our way, and every day
    Believed, beloved, adored ;
Be this our grace to see Thy face
    In JESUS CHRIST our LORD.   Amen.

FOR THE YOUNG.

Vhen thou liest down thou shalt not be afraid; yea,
thou shalt lie down and thy sleep shall be sweet.

EVENING.

NOW the day is over,
   Night is drawing nigh,
Shadows of the evening
   Steal across the sky.

Now the darkness gathers,
   Stars begin to peep,
Birds and beasts and flowers
   Soon will be asleep.

JESU, give the weary
   Calm and sweet repose;
With Thy tenderest blessing
   May mine eyelids close.

Grant to little children
   Visions bright of Thee;
Guard the sailors tossing
   On the deep blue sea.

Comfort every sufferer
   Watching late in pain;
Those who plan some evil
   From their sin restrain.

Through the long night watches
   May Thine Angels spread
Their white wings above me,
   Watching round my bed.

When the morning wakens,
   Then may I arise
Pure, and fresh, and sinless
   In Thy holy eyes.

Glory to the FATHER,
   Glory to the SON,
And to Thee, Blest SPIRIT,
   Whilst all ages run. Amen.

593 *There shall be showers of blessing.*

LORD, I hear of showers of blessing
 Thou art scattering full and free,
Showers the thirsty land refreshing ;
 Let some drops descend on me—Even me.

Pass me not, O gracious FATHER,
 Sinful though my heart may be ;
Thou might'st leave me, but the rather
 Let Thy mercy light on me—Even me.

Pass me not, O gracious SAVIOUR !
 Let me love and cling to Thee ;
I am longing for Thy favour ;
 Whilst Thou'rt calling, O call me--Even me.

Pass me not, O mighty SPIRIT !
 Thou canst make the blind to see ;
Witnesser of JESU'S merit,
 Speak the word of power to me—Even me.

Have I long in sin been sleeping,
 Long been slighting, grieving Thee ?
Has the world my heart been keeping ?
 O forgive and rescue me—Even me.

Love of GOD, so pure and changeless ;
 Blood of CHRIST, so rich and free :
Grace of GOD, so strong and boundless,
 Magnify it all in me—Even me.

Pass me not ; but, pardon bringing,
 Bind my heart, O LORD, to Thee ;
Whilst the streams of life are springing,
 Blessing others, O bless me—Even me. Amei

FOR MISSION SERVICES.

94 *Return unto the Lord thy God: for thou hast fallen by thine iniquity.*

RETURN, O wanderer, to thy home,
 Thy FATHER calls for thee :
No longer now an exile roam
 In guilt and misery :
  Return, return.

Return, O wanderer, to thy home,
 'Tis JESUS calls for thee :
The SPIRIT and the Bride say, Come ;
 O now for refuge flee :
  Return, return.

Return, O wanderer, to thy home,
 'Tis madness to delay :
There are no pardons in the tomb,
 And brief is mercy's day :
  Return, return. Amen.

95   *I have set before thee an open door.*

TO-DAY Thy mercy calls us
 To wash away our sin,
However great our trespass,
 Whatever we have been ;
However long from mercy
 Our hearts have turn'd away,
The precious Blood can cleanse us,
 And make us white to-day.

To-day Thy gate is open,
 And all who enter in
Shall find a FATHER'S welcome,
 And pardon for their sin.
The past shall be forgotten,
 A present joy be given,
A future grace be promised,
 A glorious crown in heaven.

FOR MISSION SERVICES.

To-day our FATHER calls us,
  His HOLY SPIRIT waits;
His blessèd Angels gather
  Around the heav'nly gates;
No question will be ask'd us
  How often we have come;
Although we oft have wander'd,
  It is our FATHER'S home!

O all-embracing mercy!
  O ever-open door!
What should we do without Thee
  When heart and eye run o'er?
When all things seem against us,
  To drive us to despair,
We know one gate is open,
  One ear will hear our prayer!   Amen.

596 *If we confess our sins, he is faithful and just to forgive*
us our sins, and to cleanse us from all unrighteousness.

O GOD, to know that Thou art just
    Gives hope and peace within;
We could not in a mercy trust
  Which takes no count of sin.

I fain would open to Thy sight
  My utmost wickedness;
Set, LORD, in Thy most searching light
  What I have done amiss.

No stern and needless law was Thine—
  Hard to be understood—
But plainly read in every line,
  Holy, and just, and good.

Though basely weak my fallen race,
  And masterful my foes,
I had th' omnipotence of grace
  To conquer, if I chose.

Well did I know the tender heart
  I outraged by my sin,
Yet with the world I would not part,
  Nor rein my passions in.

My fault it was, O LORD most High,
  And not my fate alone :
Thou canst not suffer sin, nor I
  In any way atone.

Yet there's a plea that I may trust—
  CHRIST died that I might live !
Cleanse me, my GOD, for Thou art just ;
  Be faithful, and forgive. Amen.

97 *So shall I make answer unto my blasphemers : for my
trust is in thy word.*

APPROACH, my soul, the mercy-seat,
  Where JESUS answers prayer ;
There humbly fall before His feet,
  For none can perish there.

Thy promise is my only plea,
  With this I venture nigh :
Thou callest burden'd souls to Thee,
  And such, O LORD, am I.

Bow'd down beneath a load of sin,
  By Satan sorely press'd,
By war without, and fears within,
  I come to Thee for rest.

Be Thou my Shield and Hiding-place,
  That, shelter'd near Thy side,
I may my fierce accuser face,
  And tell him Thou hast died.

O wondrous love, to bleed and die,
  To bear the Cross and shame,
That guilty sinners, such as I,
  Might plead Thy gracious Name ! Amen.

598 *The Son of man is come to seek and to save that u*
was lost.

RESCUE the perishing,
　　Care for the dying,
Snatch them in pity from sin and the grave ;
　　Weep o'er the erring one,
　　Lift up the fallen,
Tell them of JESUS the mighty to save.
　　　　Rescue the perishing,
　　　　Care for the dying ;
　　　　JESUS is merciful,
　　　　JESUS will save.

　　Though they are slighting Him,
　　Still He is waiting,
Waiting the penitent child to receive ;
　　Plead with them earnestly,
　　Plead with them gently ;
He will forgive if they only believe.
　　　　Rescue the perishing, &c.

　　Down in the human heart,
　　Crush'd by the tempter,
Feelings lie buried that grace can restore ;
　　Touch'd by a loving heart,
　　Waken'd by kindness,
Chords that were broken will vibrate once m
　　　　Rescue the perishing, &c.

　　Rescue the perishing,
　　Duty demands it ;
Strength for thy labour the LORD will provid
　　Back to the narrow way
　　Patiently win them ;
Tell the poor wanderer a Saviour has died.
　　　　Rescue the perishing, &c.　Ame

599 *Be of good comfort; rise, he calleth thee.*

O COME to the merciful Saviour Who calls
  you,
O come to the LORD Who forgives and forgets ;
Though dark be the fortune on earth that befalls
  you,
  There's a bright home above, where the sun
  never sets.

O come then to JESUS, Whose arms are extended
  To fold His dear children in closest embrace ;
O come, for your exile will shortly be ended,
  And JESUS will show you His beautiful face.

Yes, come to the Saviour, Whose mercy grows
  brighter
  The longer you look at the depth of His love ;
And fear not ! 'tis JESUS ! and life's cares grow
  lighter
  As you think of the home and the glory above.

Have you sinn'd as none else in the world have
  before you ?
  Are you blacker than all other creatures in guilt ?
O fear not, and doubt not ! the mother who
  bore you
  Loves you less than the Saviour Whose Blood
  you have spilt !

Then come to His feet, and lay open your story
  Of suffering and sorrow, of guilt and of shame ;
For the pardon of sin is the crown of His glory,
  And the joy of our LORD to be true to His
  Name. Amen.

FOR MISSION SERVICES.

600 *O Lord, though our iniquities testify against us.*
thou it for thy name's sake; for our backslid
are many.

WEARY of wandering from my GOD,
　　And now made willing to return,
I hear, and bow me to the rod ;
　　For Thee, not without hope, I mourn ;
I have an Advocate above,
A Friend before the throne of love.

O JESUS, full of pardoning grace,
　　More full of grace than I of sin,
Yet once again I seek Thy face ;
　　Open Thine arms, and take me in,
And freely my backslidings heal,
And love the faithless sinner still.

Thou know'st the way to bring me back,
　　My fallen spirit to restore ;
O for Thy truth and mercy's sake
　　Forgive, and bid me sin no more ;
The ruins of my soul repair,
And make my heart a house of prayer.

The stone to flesh again convert,
　　The veil of sin once more remove ;
Sprinkle Thy Blood upon my heart,
　　And melt it with Thy dying love ;
This rebel heart by love subdue,
And make it soft, and make it new.

Ah, give me, LORD, the tender heart
　　That trembles at the approach of sin ;
A godly fear of sin impart,
　　Implant, and root it deep within,
That I may dread Thy gracious power,
And never dare offend Thee more. Amen.

FOR MISSION SERVICES.

301 *In that day there shall be a fountain opened . . .*
for sin and for uncleanness.

THERE is a fountain fill'd with Blood,
    Drawn from Emmanuel's veins,
And sinners plunged beneath that flood
    Lose all their guilty stains.

The dying thief rejoiced to see
    That fountain in his day ;
And there may I, as vile as he,
    Wash all my sins away.

Dear dying LAMB, Thy precious Blood
    Shall never lose its power,
Till all the ransom'd Church of GOD
    Be saved' to sin no more.

E'er since by faith I saw the stream
    Thy flowing wounds supply,
Redeeming love has been my theme.
    And shall be till I die.

Then in a nobler, sweeter song,
    I'll sing Thy power to save,
When this poor lisping, stammering tongue
    Lies silent in the grave.

LORD, I believe Thou hast prepared,
    Unworthy though I be,
For me a blood-bought free reward,
    A golden harp for me.

'Tis strung and tuned for endless years,
    And form'd by power divine,
To sound in GOD the FATHER's ears
    No other name but Thine. Amen.

602 *If any man sin, we have an advocate with the Father
Jesus Christ the righteous.*

WHEN at Thy footstool, LORD, I bend,
 And plead with Thee for mercy there,
Think of the sinner's dying Friend,
And for His sake receive my prayer.

O think not of my shame and guilt,
My thousand stains of deepest dye ;
Think of the Blood which JESUS spilt,
And let that Blood my pardon buy.

Think, LORD, how I am still Thine own,
The trembling creature of Thy hand ;
Think how my heart to sin is prone,
And what temptations round me stand.

O think upon Thy holy word,
And every plighted promise there ;
How prayer should evermore be heard,
And how Thy glory is to spare.

O think not of my doubts and fears,
My strivings with Thy grace divine ;
Think upon JESUS' woes and tears,
And let His merits stand for mine.

Thine eye, Thine ear, they are not dull ;
Thine arm can never shorten'd be ;
Behold me here ; my heart is full ;
Behold, and spare, and succour me. Amen.

603 *Him that cometh to me I will in no wise cast out.*

JUST as I am, without one plea
 But that Thy Blood was shed for me,
And that Thou bidd'st me come to Thee,
  O LAMB of GOD, I come.

Just as I am, though toss'd about
With many a conflict, many a doubt,
Fightings and fears within, without,
  O LAMB of GOD, I come.

(524)

Just as I am, poor, wretched, blind;
Sight, riches, healing of the mind,
Yea all I need, in Thee to find,
    O Lamb of God, I come.

Just as I am, Thou wilt receive,
Wilt welcome, pardon, cleanse, relieve:
Because Thy promise I believe,
    O Lamb of God, I come.

Just as I am (Thy love unknown
Has broken every barrier down),
Now to be Thine, yea, Thine alone,
    O Lamb of God, I come.

Just as I am, of that free love
The breadth, length, depth, and height to prove,
Here for a season, then above,
    O Lamb of God, I come.   Amen.

04   *Against thee, thee only have I sinned.*

MY God! my God! and can it be
    That I should sin so lightly now,
And think no more of evil thoughts
    Than of the wind that waves the bough?

I sin, and heav'n and earth go round,
    As if no dreadful deed were done;
As if Thy Blood had never flow'd
    To hinder sin, or to atone.

I walk the earth with lightsome step,
    Smile at the sunshine, breathe the air,
Do my own will, nor ever heed
    Gethsemane and Thy long prayer.

Shall it be always thus, O Lord?
    Wilt Thou not work this hour in me
The grace Thy Passion merited,
    Hatred of self, and love of Thee?

O by the pains of Thy pure love,
  Grant me the gift of holy fear ;
And by Thy woes and bloody sweat,
  Wash Thou my guilty conscience clear !

Ever when tempted make me see,
  Beneath the olives' moon-pierced shade,
My GOD, alone, outstretch'd, and bruised,
  And bleeding, on the earth He made ;

And make me feel it was my sin,
  As though no other sins were there,
That was to Him Who bears the world
  A load that He could scarcely bear. Amen.
  This Hymn is suitable for Passion-tide.

605 *He died for all, that they which live should not hence-*
  forth live unto themselves.

O H, the bitter shame and sorrow,
    That a time could ever be
When I let the Saviour's pity
Plead in vain, and proudly answer'd,
    "All of self, and none of Thee."

Yet He found me : I beheld Him
    Bleeding on the accursèd tree,
Heard Him pray, "Forgive them, FATHER ; "
And my wistful heart said faintly,
    "Some of self, and some of Thee."

Day by day His tender mercy,
    Healing, helping, full and free,
Sweet and strong, and ah ! so patient,
Brought me lower, while I whisper'd,
    "Less of self, and more of Thee."

Higher than the highest heaven,
    Deeper than the deepest sea,
LORD, Thy love at last hath conquer'd ;
Grant me now my supplication,
    "None of self, and all of Thee." Amen.

(528)

6 *The name of the Lord is a strong tower: the righteous runneth into it, and is safe.*

Ἰησοῦ γλυκύτατε.

JESU ! Name all names above,
    Jesu, best and dearest,
Jesu, fount of perfect love,
    Holiest, tenderest, nearest ;
Jesu, source of grace completest,
Jesu purest, Jesu sweetest,
    Jesu, well of power divine,
    Make me, keep me, seal me Thine.

Jesu, open me the gate,
    That the robber enter'd,
Who in that most lost estate
    Wholly on Thee ventured.
Thou Whose wounds are ever pleading,
And Thy Passion interceding,
    From my misery let me rise
    To a home in Paradise.

Jesu, crown'd with thorns for me,
    Scourged for my transgression,
Witnessing through agony
    That Thy good confession ;
Jesu, clad in purple raiment,
For my evil making payment,
    Let not all Thy woe and pain,
    Let not Calvary be in vain.

When I reach death's bitter sea,
    And its waves mount higher,
Earthly help forsaking me
    As the storm draws nigher ;
Jesu, leave me not to languish
Helpless, hopeless, full of anguish ;
    Jesu, let me hear Thee say,
    "Thou shalt be with Me to-day." Amen.

607 *There wrestled a man with him until the breaking*
of the day.

COME, O Thou Traveller unknown,
    Whom still I hold, but cannot see,
My company before is gone,
    And I am left alone with Thee;
With Thee all night I mean to stay,
And wrestle till the break of day.

I need not tell Thee who I am,
    My misery and sin declare;
Thyself hast call'd me by my name;
    Look on Thy hands, and read it there!
But Who, I ask Thee, Who art Thou?
Tell me Thy Name, and tell me now.

In vain Thou strugglest to get free,
    I never will unloose my hold;
Art Thou the Man that died for me?
    The secret of Thy love unfold;
Wrestling, I will not let Thee go,
Till I Thy Name, Thy Nature know.

Yield to me now, for I am weak,
    But confident in self-despair;
Speak to my heart, in blessings speak,
    Be conquer'd by my instant prayer!
Speak, or Thou never hence shalt move,
And tell me if Thy Name is Love?

'Tis Love! 'tis Love! Thou diedst for me!
    I hear Thy whisper in my heart!
The morning breaks, the shadows flee;
    Pure universal Love Thou art;
To me, to all, Thy mercies move;
Thy Nature and Thy Name is Love.   Amen.

08 *Without me ye can do nothing.*

I COULD not do without Thee,
 O Saviour of the lost,
Whose precious Blood redeem'd me
 At such tremendous cost;
Thy righteousness, Thy pardon,
 Thy precious Blood must be
My only hope and comfort,
 My glory and my plea.

I could not do without Thee,
 I cannot stand alone,
I have no strength or goodness,
 No wisdom of my own;
But Thou, belovèd Saviour,
 Art all in all to me,
And weakness will be power
 If leaning hard on Thee.

I could not do without Thee,
 For oh the way is long,
And I am often weary,
 And sigh replaces song:
How could I do without Thee?
 I do not know the way;
Thou knowest, and Thou leadest,
 And wilt not let me stray.

I could not do without Thee,
 O Jesus, Saviour dear;
E'en when my eyes are holden,
 I know that Thou art near;
How dreary and how lonely
 This changeful life would be
Without the sweet communion,
 The secret rest with Thee.

(529)

I could not do without Thee ;
   No other friend can read
The spirit's strange deep longings,
   Interpreting its need ;
No human heart could enter
   Each dim recess of mine,
And soothe, and hush, and calm it,
   O Blessèd LORD, but Thine.

I could not do without Thee,
   For years are fleeting fast,
And soon in solemn loneness
   The river must be pass'd ;
But Thou wilt never leave me,
   And though the waves roll high,
I know Thou wilt be near me,
   And whisper, " It is I."   Amen.

609   *Behold, I stand at the door and knock.*

O JESU, Thou art standing
   Outside the fast-closed door,
In lowly patience waiting
   To pass the threshold o'er :
Shame on us, Christian brethren,
   His Name and sign who bear,
Oh shame, thrice shame upon us
   To keep Him standing there !

O JESU, Thou art knocking :
   And lo ! that hand is scarr'd,
And thorns Thy brow encircle,
   And tears Thy face have marr'd :
O love that passeth knowledge
   So patiently to wait !
O sin that hath no equal
   So fast to bar the gate !

FOR MISSION SERVICES.

O JESU, Thou art pleading
  In accents meek and low,
"I died for you, My children,
  And will ye treat Me so?"
O LORD, with shame and sorrow
  We open now the door:
Dear Saviour, enter, enter,
  And leave us never more. Amen.

*O I, if I be lifted up from the earth, will draw all men
unto me.*

O MY Saviour, lifted
  From the earth for me,
Draw me, in Thy mercy,
  Nearer unto Thee.

Lift my earth-bound longings,
  Fix them, LORD, above;
Draw me with the magnet
  Of Thy mighty love.

LORD, Thine arms are stretching
  Ever far and wide,
To enfold Thy children
  To Thy loving side.

And I come, O JESUS:—
  Dare I turn away?
No! Thy love hath conquer'd,
  And I come to-day;

Bringing all my burdens,
  Sorrow, sin, and care,
At Thy feet I lay them,
  And I leave them there. Amen.

(531)

611 *I came not to judge the world, but to save the world.*

SOULS of men ! why will ye scatter
    Like a crowd of frighten'd sheep ?
Foolish hearts ! why will ye wander
    From a love so true and deep ?

Was there ever kindest shepherd
    Half so gentle, half so sweet,
As the Saviour Who would have us
    Come and gather round His feet ?

There's a wideness in GOD's mercy,
    Like the wideness of the sea ;
There's a kindness in His justice,
    Which is more than liberty.

There is no place where earth's sorrows
    Are more felt than up in heaven ;
There is no place where earth's failings
    Have such kindly judgment given.

There is plentiful redemption
    In the Blood that has been shed ;
There is joy for all the members
    In the sorrows of the Head.

For the love of GOD is broader
    Than the measures of man's mind ;
And the heart of the Eternal
    Is most wonderfully kind.

Pining souls ! come nearer JESUS,
    And oh ! come not doubting thus,
But with faith that trusts more bravely
    His great tenderness for us.

If our love were but more simple,
    We should take Him at His word ;
And our lives would be all sunshine
    In the sweetness of our LORD. Amen.

612 *Oh that my ways were made so direct, that I might keep thy statutes.*

OH for a closer walk with GOD,
  A calm and heav'nly frame ;
A light to shine upon the road
  That leads me to the LAMB !

What peaceful hours I once enjoy'd !
  How sweet their memory still !
But they have left an aching void
  The world can never fill.

Return, O holy DOVE, return,
  Sweet messenger of rest :
I hate the sins that made Thee mourn,
  And drove Thee from my breast.

The dearest idol I have known,
  Whate'er that idol be,
Help me to tear it from Thy throne,
  And worship only Thee.

So shall my walk be close with GOD,
  Calm and serene my frame ;
So purer light shall mark the road
  That leads me to the LAMB. Amen.

613 *Thou hast destroyed thyself: but in me is thy help found.*

GOD made me for Himself, to serve Him here
  With love's pure service and in filial fear ;
To show His praise, for Him to labour now ;
Then see His glory where the Angels bow.

All needful grace was mine, through His dear SON,
Whose life and death my full salvation won ;
The grace that would have strengthen'd me, and
  taught ;
Grace that would crown me when my work was
  wrought.

(533)

s 2

And I, poor sinner, cast it all away ;
Lived for the toil or pleasure of each day ;
As if no CHRIST had shed His precious Blood,
As if I owed no homage to my GOD.

O HOLY SPIRIT, with Thy fire divine,
Melt into tears this thankless heart of mine ;
Teach me to love what once I seem'd to hate,
And live to GOD, before it be too late.   Amen.

614 *I am crucified with Christ, nevertheless I live; yet
not I, but Christ liveth in me.*

THOU hidden love of GOD, whose height,
   Whose depth unfathom'd, no man knows;
I see from far Thy beauteous light,
   Inly I sigh for Thy repose ;
My heart is pain'd, nor can it be
At rest, till it finds rest in Thee.

'Tis mercy all, that Thou hast brought
   My mind to seek her peace in Thee ;
Yet, while I seek but find Thee not,
   No peace my wandering soul shall see ;
O when shall all my wanderings end,
And all my steps to Thee-ward tend ?

Is there a thing beneath the sun
   That strives with Thee my heart to share ?
Ah, tear it thence, and reign alone,
   The LORD of every motion there !
Then shall my heart from earth be free,
When it hath found repose in Thee.

O hide this self from me, that I
   No more, but CHRIST in me, may live ;
My vile affections crucify,
   Nor let one hidden lust survive !
In all things nothing may I see,
Nothing desire, apart from Thee.

Each moment draw from earth away
   My heart, that lowly waits Thy call;
Speak to my inmost soul, and say,
   "I am thy Love, thy GOD, thy All."
To feel Thy power, to hear Thy voice,
To taste Thy love, be all my choice. Amen.

15 *Yield yourselves unto God . . . and your members*
       as instruments of righteousness.

FATHER, SON, and HOLY GHOST,
   ONE in THREE, and THREE in ONE,
As by the celestial host,
   Let Thy will on earth be done;
Praise by all to Thee be given,
Glorious LORD of earth and heaven.

If a sinner such as I
   May to Thy great glory live,
All my actions sanctify,
   All my words and thoughts receive;
Claim me for Thy service, claim
All I have, and all I am.

Take my soul and body's powers;
   Take my memory, mind, and will,
All my goods, and all my hours,
   All I know, and all I feel,
All I think, or speak, or do;
Take my heart;—but make it new!

O my GOD, Thine own I am,
   Let me give Thee back Thine own;
Freedom, friends, and health, and fame,
   Consecrate to Thee alone;
Thine to live, thrice happy I;
Happier still if Thine I die.

FOR MISSION SERVICES.

618 *With one mind striving together . . . and in nothing terrified by your adversaries.*

WE are soldiers of CHRIST, Who is mighty to save,
And His Banner the Cross is unfurl'd ; [brave
We are pledged to be faithful and steadfast and
Against Satan, the flesh, and the world.

We are brothers and comrades, we stand side by side,
And our faith and our hope are the same ;
And we think of the Cross on which JESUS has died,
When we bear the reproach of His Name.

At the font we were marked with the Cross on our
Of our grace and our calling the sign : [brow,
And the weakest is strong to be true to his vow,
For the armour we wear is divine.

We will watch ready arm'd if the tempter draw
If he come with a frown or a smile, [near ;
We will heed not his threats, nor his flatteries hear,
Nor be taken by storm or by wile.

We will master the flesh, and its longings restrain,
We will not be the bond-slaves of sin,
The pure SPIRIT of GOD in our nature shall reign,
And our spirits their freedom shall win.

For the world's love we live not, its hate we defy,
And we will not be led by the throng ;
We'll be true to ourselves, to our FATHER on high,
And the bright world to which we belong.

Now let each cheer his comrade, let hearts beat as one,
While we follow where CHRIST leads the way ;
'Twere dishonour to yield, or the battle to shun,
We will fight, and will watch, and will pray.

ough the warfare be weary, the trial be sore,
In the might of our GOD we will stand ; .
ι, what joy to be crown'd and be pure evermore,
In the peace of our own Fatherland.   Amen.

19   *Fight the good fight.*

ɲIGHT the good fight with all thy might,
   CHRIST is thy strength, and CHRIST thy right ;
y hold on life, and it shall be
y joy and crown eternally.

ιn the straight race through GOD's good grace,
ft up thine eyes, and seek His face ;
ſe with its way before us lies,
IRIST is the path, and CHRIST the prize.

st care aside, lean on thy Guide ;
s boundless mercy will provide ;
ust, and thy trusting soul shall prove
IRIST is its life, and CHRIST its love.

ιnt not nor fear, His arms are near,
ɪ changeth not, and thou art dear ;
ιly believe, and thou shalt see
ιat CHRIST is all in all to thee.   Amen.

20 *Thou wilt keep him in perfect peace, whose mind is*
                     stayed on thee.

ɔEACE, perfect peace, in this dark world of sin ?
   The Blood of JESUS whispers peace within.

ace, perfect peace, by thronging duties press'd ?
 do the will of JESUS, this is rest.

ace, perfect peace, with sorrows surging round ?
ι JESUS' bosom naught but calm is found.

ace, perfect peace, with loved ones far away ?
 JESUS' keeping we are safe and they.

Peace, perfect peace, our future all unknown ?
JESUS we know, and He is on the throne.

Peace, perfect peace, death shadowing us and ours
JESUS has vanquish'd death and all its powers.

It is enough : earth's struggles soon shall cease,
And JESUS call us to heav'n's perfect peace.

Amen.

621 *And so shall we ever be with the Lord.*

" FOR ever with the LORD ! "
    Amen ; so let it be ;
Life from the dead is in that word,
    'Tis immortality.
Here in the body pent,
    Absent from Him I roam,
Yet nightly pitch my moving tent
    A day's march nearer home.

My FATHER'S house on high,
    Home of my soul, how near
At times to faith's foreseeing eye
    Thy golden gates appear !
Ah ! then my spirit faints
    To reach the land I love,
The bright inheritance of Saints,
    Jerusalem above.

" For ever with the LORD ! "
    FATHER, if 'tis Thy will,
The promise of that faithful word
    Even here to me fulfil.
Be Thou at my right hand,
    Then can I never fail ;
Uphold Thou me, and I shall stand ;
    Fight, and I must prevail.

FOR MISSION SERVICES.

So when my latest breath
　　Shall rend the veil in twain,
By death I shall escape from death,
　　And life eternal gain.
Knowing as I am known,
　　How shall I love that word,
And oft repeat before the throne,
　　" For ever with the Lord ! "　Amen.

*Eye hath not seen, nor ear heard, neither have entered
into the heart of man, the things which God hath
prepared for them that love him.*

Τὰς ἑδρὰς τὰς αἰωνίας.

THOSE eternal bowers
　　Man hath never trod,
Those unfading flowers
　　Round the throne of God :
Who may hope to gain them
　　After weary fight ?
Who at length attain them
　　Clad in robes of white ?

He who gladly barters
　　All on earthly ground ;
He who, like the Martyrs,
　　Says, " I will be crown'd : "
He whose one oblation
　　Is a life of love ;
Clinging to the nation
　　Of the blest above.

Shame upon you, legions
　　Of the heav'nly King,
Denizens of regions
　　Past imagining !
What ! with pipe and tabor
　　Fool away the light,
When He bids you labour,
　　When He tells you, " Fight !."

While I do my duty,
   Struggling through the tide,
Whisper Thou of beauty
   On the other side !
Tell me not the story
   Of the now distress :
O the future glory !
   O the loveliness ! Amen.

623   *The night is far spent, the day is at hand.*

HARK ! hark, my soul ! Angelic songs are
    swelling
  O'er earth's green fields, and ocean's wave-beat
    shore :   [telling
How sweet the truth those blessèd strains are
  Of that new life when sin shall be no more !
Angels of JESUS, Angels of light,
Singing to welcome the pilgrims of the night !
Onward we go, for still we hear them singing,
  "Come, weary souls, for JESUS bids you come :"
And through the dark, its echoes sweetly ringing,
  The music of the Gospel leads us home.
Angels of JESUS, Angels of light,
Singing to welcome the pilgrims of the night !
Far, far away, like bells at evening pealing,
  The voice of JESUS sounds o'er land and sea,
And laden souls, by thousands meekly stealing,
  Kind Shepherd, turn their weary steps to Thee.
Angels of JESUS, Angels of light,
Singing to welcome the pilgrims of the night !
Rest comes at length ; though life be long and
    dreary,
  The day must dawn, and darksome night be past
Faith's journey ends in welcome to the weary,
  And heav'n, the heart's true home, will come ₁
Angels of JESUS, Angels of light,   [la
Singing to welcome the pilgrims of the night !

;els ! sing on, your faithful watches keeping,
ing us sweet fragments of the songs above ;
morning's joy shall end the night of weeping,
nd life's long shadows break in cloudless love.
;els of JESUS, Angels of light,
;ing to welcome the pilgrims of the night !

Amen.

4　　　*He was lost, and is found.*

REDEEM'D, restored, forgiven,
　　Through JESUS' precious Blood,
Heirs of His home in heaven,
　　O praise our pardoning GOD !
Praise Him in tuneful measures,
　　Who gave His SON to die ;
Praise Him Whose sevenfold treasures
　　Enrich and sanctify !

Once on the dreary mountain
　　We wander'd far and wide,
Far from the cleansing fountain,
　　Far from the piercèd side ;
But JESUS sought and found us,
　　And wash'd our guilt away ;
With cords of love He bound us
　　To be His own for aye.

Dear Master, Thine the glory
　　Of each recover'd soul ;
Ah ! who can tell the story
　　Of love that made us whole ?
Not ours, not ours the merit ;
　　Be Thine alone the praise,
And ours a thankful spirit
　　To serve Thee all our days.

Now keep us, Holy Saviour,
　　In Thy true love and fear ;
And grant us of Thy favour
　　The grace to persevere ;

Till, in Thy new creation,
    Earth's time-long travail o'er,
We find our full salvation,
    And praise Thee evermore. Amen.

625 *There is joy in the presence of the angels of God o*
        one sinner that repenteth.

THERE was joy in heav'n,
    There was joy in heav'n,
When this goodly world to frame
The LORD of might and mercy came ;
Shouts of joy were heard on high,
And the stars sang from the sky,
    Glory to GOD in heav'n.

There was joy in heav'n,
    There was joy in heav'n,
When the billows heaving dark,
Sank around the stranded ark,
And the rainbow's watery span
Spake of mercy, hope to man,
    And peace with GOD in heav'n.

There was joy in heav'n,
    There was joy in heav'n,
When of love the midnight beam
Dawn'd on the towers of Bethlehem,
And along the echoing hill
Angels sang " On earth good will,
    And glory in the heav'ns ! "

There is joy in heav'n, ·
    There is joy in heav'n
When the soul that went astray
Turns to CHRIST, the living Way,
And, by grace of heav'n subdued,
*B*reathes a prayer of gratitude,
    Oh, there is joy in heav'n. Amen.

PROCESSIONAL.

6 *Be strong and of a good courage. . . . And the Lord,*
he it is that doth go before thee.

ONWARD, Christian soldiers,
　　Marching as to war,
With the Cross of JESUS
　　Going on before.
CHRIST the royal Master
　　Leads against the foe ;
Forward into battle,
　　See, His banners go !
　　　　Onward, Christian soldiers,
　　　　Marching as to war,
　　　　With the Cross of JESUS
　　　　Going on before.

At the sign of triumph
　　Satan's host doth flee ;
On then, Christian soldiers,
　　On to victory.
Hell's foundations quiver !
　　At the shout of praise ;
Brothers, lift your voices,
　　Loud your anthems raise.
　　　　　　　Onward, &c.

Like a mighty army
　　Moves the Church of GOD ;
Brothers, we are treading
　　Where the Saints have trod ;
Though divisions harass,
　　All one body we,
One in hope and doctrine,
　　One in charity.
　　　　　　　Onward, &c.

Crowns and thrones may perish,
　　Kingdoms rise and wane,
But the Church of JESUS
　　Constant will remain ;

(545)

PROCESSIONAL.

Gates of hell can never
  'Gainst that Church prevail ;
We have CHRIST'S own promise,
  And that cannot fail.
Onward, &c.

Onward, then, ye people,
  Join our happy throng,
Blend with ours your voices
  In the triumph song ;
Glory, laud, and honour
  Unto CHRIST the King ;
This through countless ages
  Men and Angels sing.
Onward, &c.   Amen.

627 *Speak unto the children of Israel that they go forward.*

FORWARD ! be our watchword,
  Steps and voices join'd ;
Seek the things before us,
  Not a look behind ;
Burns the fiery pillar
  At our army's head ;
Who shall dream of shrinking,
  By our Captain led ?
    Forward through the desert,
      Through the toil and fight ;
    Jordan flows before us,
      Sion beams with light.

Forward, when in childhood
  Buds the infant mind ;
All through youth and manhood,
  Not a thought behind ;
Speed through realms of nature,
  Climb the steps of grace ;
Faint not, till in glory
  Gleams our FATHER'S face.

(546)

PROCESSIONAL.

Forward, all the life-time,
  Climb from height to height;
Till the head be hoary,
  Till the eve be light.

Forward, flock of JESUS,
  Salt of all the earth,
Till each yearning purpose
  Spring to glorious birth;
Sick, they ask for healing;
  Blind, they grope for day;
Pour upon the nations
  Wisdom's loving ray.
    Forward, out of error,
      Leave behind the night;
    Forward through the darkness,
      Forward into light.

Far o'er yon horizon
  Rise the city towers,
Where our GOD abideth;
  That fair home is ours:
Flash the streets with jasper,
  Shine the gates with gold;
Flows the gladdening river
  Shedding joys untold.
    Thither, onward thither,
      In the SPIRIT's might;
    Pilgrims to your country,
      Forward into light.

Into GOD's high temple
  Onward as we press,
Beauty spreads around us,
  Born of holiness;
Arch, and vault, and carving,
  Lights of varied tone,
Soften'd words and holy,
  Prayer and praise alone:

PROCESSIONAL.

Every thought upraising
To our city bright,
Where the tribes assemble
Round the throne of light.

Naught that city needeth
Of these aisles of stone ;
Where the GODHEAD dwelleth,
Temple there is none ;
All the Saints, that ever
In these courts have stood,
Are but babes, and feeding
On the children's food.
On through sign and token,
Stars amidst the night,
Forward through the darkness,
Forward into light.

To th' Eternal FATHER
Loudest anthems raise ;
To the SON and SPIRIT
Echo songs of praise ;
To the LORD of glory,
Blessèd THREE in ONE,
Be by men and Angels
Endless honours done :
Weak are earthly praises :
Dull the songs of night ;
Forward into triumph,
Forward into light ! Amen.

628 *Now they desire a better country, that is, an heare*
wherefore God is not ashamed to be called their (

*THE GOD of Abraham praise
Who reigns enthroned above,
Ancient of everlasting days,
And GOD of love :

(548)

PROCESSIONAL.

Jehovah, great I Am,
By earth and heav'n confest;
We bow and bless the sacred Name
For ever blest.
The God of Abraham praise,
At Whose supreme command
From earth we rise, and seek the joys
At His right hand:
We all on earth forsake,
Its wisdom, fame, and power;
And Him our only portion make,
Our shield and tower.

Though nature's strength decay,
And earth and hell withstand,
To Canaan's bounds we urge our way
At His command.
The watery deep we pass,
With Jesus in our view;
And through the howling wilderness
Our way pursue.

The goodly land we see,
With peace and plenty blest;
A land of sacred liberty
And endless rest;
There milk and honey flow,
And oil and wine abound,
And trees of life for ever grow,
With mercy crown'd.

There dwells the Lord, our King,
The Lord our Righteousness,
Triumphant o'er the world of sin,
The Prince of peace:
On Sion's sacred height
His Kingdom He maintains,
And glorious with His saints in light
For ever reigns.

PROCESSIONAL.

*He keeps His own secure,
　He guards them by His side,
Arrays in garment white and pure
　　His spotless Bride :
With streams of sacred bliss,
　Beneath serener skies,
With all the fruits of Paradise,
　　He still supplies.

*Before the great THREE-ONE
　They all exulting stand,
And tell the wonders He hath done
　　Through all their land :
The listening spheres attend,
　And swell the growing fame,
And sing, in songs which never end,
　　The wondrous Name.

*The GOD Who reigns on high
　The great Archangels sing,
And " Holy, Holy, Holy," cry,
　　" Almighty King !
Who was, and is the same,
　And evermore shall be :
JEHOVAH, FATHER, Great I AM,
　　We worship Thee."

Before the Saviour's face
　The ransom'd nations bow,
O'erwhelm'd at His almighty grace
　　For ever new ;
He shows His prints of love,—
　They kindle to a flame,
And sound through all the worlds above
　　The slaughter'd LAMB.

PROCESSIONAL.

The whole triumphant host
Give thanks to GOD on high ;
"Hail ! FATHER, SON, and HOLY GHOST,"
They ever cry :
Hail ! Abraham's GOD, and mine !
(I join the heav'nly lays),
All might and majesty are Thine,
And endless praise.   Amen.

* *These verses may be omitted.*

29 *He that hath an ear, let him hear what the Spirit saith unto the churches.*

GLORY to the First-begotten,
Risen CHRIST, Incarnate WORD !
Glory to the Faithful Witness,
Over all dominion LORD,
Who hath loved us, Who hath wash'd us
In His precious Blood outpour'd !

*Glory unto Him Who gave us
Heritage of priest and king !
That for ever in His presence
We our Eucharist may sing,
All our crowns cast down before Him,
To His shrine our incense bring.

*Glory to the LORD ALMIGHTY !
Every foe beneath Him cast,
High He reigns in splendour seated,
He the First and He the Last,
He both Alpha and Omega,
LORD of future, present, past.

Glory unto Him Who holdeth
Mystic stars in His right hand !
Glory unto Him Who walketh
'Midst the lamps that gleaming stand !
Every Church and every pastor
Subject to His dread command.

PROCESSIONAL.

Thou Who knowest how we labour'd,
　Fainting not when foemen strove,
Raise once more our fallen courage,
　Stir again our early love :
Quench not all the light within us,
　Nor our candlestick remove.

*From all subtle evil guard us,
　False Apostles, deeds of ill ;
Grant us every lie to conquer,
　Every hateful lust to kill :
By the Tree of Life sustain us,
　And our hungry spirits fill.

If, wherever Satan dwelleth,
　We confess Thee as our LORD,
Bid us fear not Satan's malice,
　Tribulation, fire, or sword.
Crown Thy faithful patient servants
　With the Martyr's bright reward.

By Thy HOLY SPIRIT cleanse us,
　Pure in heart Thy law to own ;
Grant to us the hidden manna,
　Grant to us the fair white stone,
And the new name newly written,
　Only to Thy servants known.

Thou hast once for our salvation
　On the raging Dragon trod,
Keep us stedfast, faithful, loving,
　Smite our foes with iron rod,
Scatter all the depths of Satan,
　Bright and Morning Star of GOD.

Save us from the name of living
　While the soul within is dead ;
Wash our garments from defilement,
　In the Blood that Thou hast shed ;

PROCESSIONAL.

Then confess us in Thy glory,
　　Members worthy of their Head.

Thou Who hast the key of David,
　　Set for us an open door,
Refuge in the Great Temptation
　　When the testing tempests roar ;
Plant us in Thy FATHER's temple,
　　Pillars firm for evermore.

We are wretched, cold, and naked,
　　Needing all things, poor and blind ;
Thou hast raiment, riches, healing,
　　Meet for body, soul, and mind.
Humbled, shamefast we approach Thee,
　　All our store in Thee to find.

Come, in love rebuke and chasten,
　　At our hearts' door come and stand ;
Knock once more, and bid us open,
　　Knock with Thine own piercèd hand.
We will hear Thee, we will open,
　　Sup with Thee at Thy command.

Grant to us that overcoming
　　By a virtue not our own,
We may with Thee in Thy glory
　　Be Thy crownèd brothers shown,
Even as Thou, overcoming,
　　Sittest on Thy FATHER's throne.

Glory unto Him that reigneth
　　On th' eternal throne on high !
Glory to the LAMB that suffer'd,
　　Living now no more to die !
Glory to the Blessed SPIRIT,
　　One with Both eternally !　Amen.

* *These verses may be omitted.*

PROCESSIONAL.

630 *The voice of them that shall say, Praise the Lo.*
hosts; for the Lord is good.

WITH gladsome feet we press
  To Sion's holy mount,
Where gushes from its deep recess
  The cooling fount.
O happy, happy hill,
  The joy of every saint !
With sweet Siloam's crystal rill
  That cheers the faint !

We love fair Sion well :
  The LORD in her is seen ;
With her is ever fain to dwell
  In radiant sheen !
He there reveals His face,
  There stretches out His arm,
.A lamp to light a darken'd race,
  A shield from harm.

Thou, LORD, dost crown the steep ;
  Thou broodest o'er the stream ;
Then leave us never more to weep
  Thine absent beam.
Refresh the thirsty soul,
  Thou springing Well of life !
Conduct us towards the heav'nly goal
  Amid the strife !

Great city, blest of GOD !
  Jerusalem the free !
With ceaseless step the path be trod
  That leads to thee !
The Martyr's bleeding feet,
. The Saints by blood unstain'd,
Alike have sought thy golden seat,
  And rest have gain'd.

PROCESSIONAL.

The towers that point on high
Our earth-bound spirits teach
To scorn the world, and upward fly,
True bliss to reach ;
To veil Thy shrine of love,
LORD, let no mist arise ;
No cloud to hide the scene above
From longing eyes !

We come, with fervent zeal,
Beneath Thy hallow'd dome,
The pledge of our eternal weal,
Our happy home !
Thine house on Sion stands,
Though rear'd of earthly stone,
The type of that not made with hands,
Yet still Thine own.

There, calming all alarms,
The Cross of love is traced,
Outstretching salutary arms
To bless the waste !
The sinner there can plead
In ever listening ears ;
In hope on Thee can sweetly feed,
And dry his tears.

LORD, while Thy courts we tread,
Array'd in robes of white,
May evil never lift its head
To shame the light,
But all be pure below ;
Each heart from taint be free,
Unsullied, bright as spotless snow,
Meet shrines for Thee !
So this our festal day
Celestial joy shall raise,
While lips and hearts conjoin'd essay
To hymn Thy praise.

PROCESSIONAL.

The very stones shall ring,
Resound each holy wall,
With Thee, Thyself the Rock, the Spring
Our Heav'n, our All !

The FATHER loud adore !
And loud adore the SON !
Exalt the SPIRIT evermore,
The THREE in ONE :
The TRINITY extol
In Unity sublime,
Till circling ages cease to roll,
The death of time ! Amen.

631   *The sign of the Son of man.*

GLIDING through the shadows
    Goes the Cross of CHRIST,
Through the dreary darkness,
    Through the driving mist.
Lo ! the storms are rising ;
    Hark ! the winds are shrill ;
But the Cross is moving
    Onwards, onwards still.

Onwards, upwards, homewards
    Through the striving air,
Press the streaming pennons
    Of that standard fair ;
Tens and tens of thousands,
    'Midst their seething foes
March CHRIST'S warrior legions
    Where that standard goes.

Round that waving banner
    While the war goes on,
Deeds of saintly daring
    Have been wrought and won.

PROCESSIONAL.

Oh, for feet to follow !
  Oh, for hands to fight !
Oh, for strength to wrestle
  Onwards into light !

Onwards where the battle
  Fierce and fiercer grows,
Where the air is parted
  With a thousand blows :
See the swords are flashing,
  See the spears are wet,
But that lofty banner
  Surges onwards yet.

Down the darksome valley
  Streams that sacred sign ;
'Midst the gloom and blackness
  How its splendours shine,
Lighting yonder waters,
  Swift and deep and chill,
As its rays are passing
  Onwards, onwards still !

By Thy pangs and passion,
  By Thy pain and loss,
Crucified, we pray Thee,
  Draw us by that Cross ;
By the wounds of pity,
  By the nail-piercedyhand,
Lead Thy pilgrim soldiers
  Into Holy Land. Amen.

The following are also suitable for Processions:

144, 169, 182, 255 Hail, festal day.
324 Let all the world rejoice.
442 Through the night of doubt and sorrow.
504 Saviour, Blessèd Saviour.

632

G OD the FATHER, GOD the SON,
G   GOD the SPIRIT, THREE in ONE,
Hear us from Thy heav'nly throne ;
    Spare us, Holy TRINITY.

JESU, Life of those who die,
Advocate with GOD on high,
Hope of immortality,
    Save us, Holy JESU.

DEATH.

Thou Whose death to mortals gave
Power to triumph o'er the grave,
Living now from death to save,
    Help us, Holy JESU.

Ere we hear the Angel's call,
Ere the shadows round us fall,
Thou, our Saviour and our All,
    Help us, Holy JESU.

In the gloom Thy light provide ;
Safely through the valley guide ;
Thee we trust, for Thou hast died ;
    Help us, Holy JESU.

JUDGMENT.

Thou Who didst for sin atone,
And before Whose great white throne
All our doings must be shown,
    Save us, Holy JESU.

When Thy summons we obey
On the dreadful Judgment Day,
From confusion and dismay
    Save us, Holy JESU.

(568)

While the lost in terror fly
At the awful majesty
Of Thy doom, O Judge most High,
    Save us, Holy JESU.

HELL.

Thou Whose death was borne that we,
From the power of Satan free,
Might not die eternally,
    Save us, Holy JESU.

From th' accursed pit of hell,
Where in outer darkness dwell
Those who to the end rebel,
    Save us, Holy JESU.

From the Adversary's claim,
From the worm and from the flame,
From the everlasting shame,
    Save us, Holy JESU.

HEAVEN.

Thou Who dost a place prepare,
That we may Thy glory share ;
To those heav'nly mansions fair
    Bring us, Holy JESU.

Where the captives find release,
Where all foes from troubling cease,
Where the weary rest in peace,
    Bring us, Holy JESU.

Where in wondrous light are shown
All Thy dealings with Thine own,
Who shall know as they are known,
    Bring us, Holy JESU.

Where, with loved ones gone before,
We may love Thee and adore
Face to face for evermore,
    Bring us, Holy JESU. Amen.

LITANY OF PENITENCE.

Thou, despised, denied, refused,
And for man's transgressions bruised,
Sinless, yet of sin accused,
  Hear us, Holy JESU.

Thou Who on the Cross didst reign,
Dying there in bitter pain,
Cleansing with Thy Blood our stain,
  Hear us, Holy JESU.

Shepherd of the straying sheep,
Comforter of them that weep,
Hear us crying from the deep,
  Hear us, Holy JESU.

That in Thy pure innocence
We may wash our souls' offence,
And find truest penitence,
  We beseech Thee, JESU.

That we give to sin no place,
That we never quench Thy grace,
That we ever seek Thy face,
  We beseech Thee, JESU.

That, denying evil lust,
Living godly, meek, and just,
In Thee only we may trust,
  We beseech Thee, JESU.

That, to sin for ever dead,
We may live to Thee our Head,
And the narrow pathway tread,
  We beseech Thee, JESU.

When shall end the battle sore,
When our pilgrimage is o'er,
Grant Thy peace for evermore,
  We beseech Thee, JESU. Amen.

GOD the FATHER, GOD the SON,
 GOD the SPIRIT, THREE in ONE,
Hear us from Thy heav'nly throne;
  Spare us, Holy TRINITY.

JESU, Who for us didst bear
Scorn and sorrow, toil and care,
Hearken to our lowly prayer,
  We beseech Thee, JESU.

By the hour of agony,
Spent while Thine Apostles three
Slumber'd in Gethsemane,
  Hear us, Holy JESU.

JESU, by Thy friend betray'd,
JESU, sport for sinners made,
JESU, in mock-robes array'd,
  Hear us, Holy JESU.

By the scourging meekly borne,
By the reed and crown of thorn,
By the malice and the scorn,
  Hear us, Holy JESU.

By the outcry of the Jews,
When a murd'rer they would choose,
And the Prince of life refuse,
  Hear us, Holy JESU.

By the horror of that cry
"Crucify Him, crucify,"
By Thy going forth to die,
  Hear us, Holy JESU.

By Thy nailing to the Tree,
By the title over Thee,
By the gloom of Calvary,
  Hear us, Holy JESU.

By the seven words then said,
By the bowing of Thy head,
By Thy numb'ring with the dead,
 Hear us, Holy JESU.

JESU, Who for us hast died,
And, for ever glorified,
Reignest at the FATHER's side,
 Hear us, Holy JESU. Amen.

636 LITANY FOR THE ROGATION DAYS.

 O Thee our GOD we fly
 For mercy and for grace ;
O hear our lowly cry,
 And hide not Thou Thy face.
O LORD, stretch forth Thy mighty hand,
And guard and bless our fatherland.

 Arise, O LORD of hosts,
 Be jealous for Thy Name,
And drive from out our coasts
 The sins that put to shame.
O LORD, stretch forth Thy mighty hand,
And guard and bless our fatherland.

 Thy best gifts from on high
 In rich abundance pour,
That we may magnify
 And praise Thee more and more.
O LORD, stretch forth Thy mighty hand,
And guard and bless our fatherland.

 The powers ordain'd by Thee
 With heav'nly wisdom bless ;
May they Thy servants be,
 And rule in righteousness.
O LORD, stretch forth Thy mighty hand,
And guard and bless our fatherland.

The Church of Thy dear Son
   Inflame with love's pure fire,
Bind her once more in one,
   And life and truth inspire.
O LORD, stretch forth Thy mighty hand,
And guard and bless our fatherland.

The pastors of Thy fold
   With grace and power endue,
That, faithful, pure, and bold,
   They may be pastors true.
O LORD, stretch forth Thy mighty hand,
And guard and bless our fatherland.

O let us love Thy house,
   And sanctify Thy day,
Bring unto Thee our vows,
   And loyal homage pay.
O LORD, stretch forth Thy mighty hand,
And guard and bless our fatherland.

Give peace, LORD, in our time ;
   O let no foe draw nigh,
Nor lawless deed of crime
   Insult Thy majesty.
O LORD, stretch forth Thy mighty hand,
And guard and bless our fatherland.

Though vile and worthless, still
   Thy people, LORD, are we ;
And for our GOD we will
   None other have but Thee.
O LORD, stretch forth Thy mighty hand,
And guard and bless our fatherland. Amen.

his Hymn may be sung at other seasons as a Supplication
for the Nation.

GOD the FATHER, GOD the SON,
  GOD the SPIRIT, THREE in ONE,
Hear us from Thy heav'nly throne ;
      Spare us, Holy TRINITY.

HOLY SPIRIT, heav'nly Dove,
Dew descending from above,
Breath of life, and Fire of love,
      Hear us, Holy SPIRIT.

Thou by Whom the Virgin bore
Him Whom heav'n and earth adore,
Eve's lost children to restore,
      Hear us, Holy SPIRIT.

Thou Whom JESUS from His throne
Sent to dwell within His own,
That they might not strive alone,
      Hear us, Holy SPIRIT.

Thou Whose sound th' Apostles heard,
Thou Whose power their spirit stirr'd,
Giving them the living word,
      Hear us, Holy SPIRIT.

Coming now with hallowing might
In the new baptismal rite,
Souls with GOD to reunite,
      Hear us, Holy SPIRIT.

Thou from Whom the sevenfold aid
To Thy children is convey'd,
By the hands upon them laid,
      Hear us, Holy SPIRIT.

Thou by Whose o'ershadowing
Of the gifts Thy servants bring,
We receive our LORD and King,
      Hear us, Holy SPIRIT.

Come with grace our hearts to fill,
Bend aright our stubborn will,
All our evil passions kill ;
        Hear us, Holy SPIRIT.

Come to fortify the weak,
Give Thy grace to all who seek,
Teach our faltering tongues to speak ;
        Hear us, Holy SPIRIT.

Come to aid the souls who yearn
More of truth divine to learn,
And with larger love to burn ;
        Hear us, Holy SPIRIT.

Come and be our welcome guest,
Sanctify each longing breast,
Lead us to our heav'nly rest ;
        Hear us, Holy SPIRIT.   Amen.

58 LITANY OF THE BLESSED SACRAMENT OF THE BODY AND BLOOD OF CHRIST.

GOD the FATHER, GOD the SON,
    GOD the SPIRIT, THREE in ONE,
      Spare us, Holy TRINITY.

GOD of GOD, and Light of Light,
King of glory, LORD of might,
      Hear us, Holy JESU.

Very Man, Who for our sake
Didst true Flesh of Mary take,
      Hear us, Holy JESU.

Shepherd, Whom the FATHER gave
His lost sheep to find and save,
      Hear us, Holy JESU.

Priest and Victim, Whom of old
Type and prophecy foretold,
      Hear us, Holy JESU.

LITANY OF THE BLESSED SACRAMENT 01
THE BODY AND BLOOD OF CHRIST.

King of Salem, Priest Divine,
Bringing forth Thy Bread and Wine,
  Hear us, Holy JESU.

Paschal LAMB, Whose sprinkled Blood
Saves the Israel of GOD,
  Hear us, Holy JESU.

Manna, found at dawn of day,
Pilgrim's Food in desert-way,
  Hear us, Holy JESU.

Offering pure, in every place
Pledge and means of heav'nly grace,
  Hear us, Holy JESU.

PART 2.

By the mercy, that of yore
Shadow'd forth Thy gifts in store,
  Save us, Holy JESU.

By the love, on that last night
That ordain'd the better rite,
  Save us, Holy JESU.

By the death, that could alone
For the whole world's sin atone,
  Save us, Holy JESU.

By the wounds, that ever plead
For our help in time of need,
  Save us, Holy JESU.

PART 3.

That we may remember still
Kedron's brook and Calvary's hill,
  Grant us, Holy JESU.

That our thankful hearts may glow
As Thy precious death we show,
  Grant us, Holy JESU.

That, with humble contrite fear,
We may joy to feel Thee near,
> Grant us, Holy JESU.

That in faith we may adore,
Praise, and love Thee more and more,
> Grant us, Holy JESU.

That Thy sacred Flesh and Blood
Be our true life-giving food,
> Grant us, Holy JESU.

That in all our words and ways
We may daily show Thy praise,
> Grant us, Holy JESU.

That, as death's dark vale we tread,
Thou mayst be our strengthening Bread,
> Grant us, Holy JESU.

That, unworthy though we be,
We may ever dwell with Thee,
> Grant us, Holy JESU.   Amen.

39   LITANY OF THE CHURCH.

GOD the FATHER, GOD the SON,
  GOD the SPIRIT, THREE in ONE,
Hear us from Thy heav'nly throne ;
> Spare us, Holy TRINITY.

JESU, with Thy Church abide,
Be her Saviour, LORD, and Guide,
While on earth her faith is tried :
> Grant it, Holy JESU.

Arms of love around her throw,
Guard her safe from every foe,
Comfort her in time of woe :
> Grant it, Holy JESU.

LITANY OF THE CHURCH.

Keep her life and teaching pure,
Grant her patience to endure,
Trusting in Thy promise sure :
    Grant it, Holy Jesu.

May her voice be ever clear,
Telling of a Saviour dear,
Warning of a judgment near :
    Grant it, Holy Jesu.

May she one in doctrine be,
One in truth and charity,
Winning all to faith in Thee :
    Grant it, Holy Jesu.

May she guide the poor and blind,
Seek the lost until she find,
And the broken-hearted bind :
    Grant it, Holy Jesu.

Save her love from growing cold,
Make her watchmen strong and bold,
Fence about her threaten'd fold :
    Grant it, Holy Jesu.

May her priests Thy people feed,
Shepherds of the flock indeed,
Ready where Thou call'st to lead :
    Grant it, Holy Jesu.

Judge her not for work undone,
Judge her not for fields unwon,
Bless her works in Thee begun :
    Grant it, Holy Jesu.

Raise her to her calling high,
Let the nations far and nigh
Listen to her warning cry :
    Grant it, Holy Jesu.

May her lamp of truth be bright,
Bid her bear aloft its light
Through the realms of heathen night :
    Grant it, Holy JESU.

May her scatter'd children be
From reproach of evil free,
Blameless witnesses for Thee :
    Grant it, Holy JESU.

May she holy triumphs win,
Overthrow the hosts of sin,
Gather all the nations in :
    Grant it, Holy JESU.

May she soon all glorious be,
Spotless and from wrinkle free,
As a Bride adorn'd for Thee :
    Grant it, Holy JESU. Amen.

40   LITANIES OF INTERCESSION.
No. 1.

GOD the FATHER, GOD the SON,
    GOD the SPIRIT, THREE in ONE,
Hear us from Thy heav'nly throne,
    Spare us, Holy TRINITY.

JESU, evermore adored,
As we claim Thy promised word,
Gather'd in Thy Name, O LORD,
    Hear us, we beseech Thee.

For Thy Church so dear to Thee,
That she may for ever be
Kept in peace and unity,
    We beseech Thee, JESU.

For the rulers of our land,
That they may at Thy command
Right promote and wrong withstand,
    We beseech Thee, JESU.

LITANY OF INTERCESSION.

For Thy priests in every place,
That relying on Thy grace
They with patience run their race,
  We beseech Thee, JESU.

All our loved ones we commend,
LORD, to Thee, man's truest Friend,
Guard and guide them to the end,
  We beseech Thee, JESU.

Some on beds of sickness lie,
Some in want and hunger cry ;
LORD, their every need supply,
  We beseech Thee, JESU.

Some are lonely, some are sad,
Some have lost the joy they had ;
With true comfort make them glad,
  We beseech Thee, JESU.

Some have fallen from Thy grace,
Wearied in their heav'nward race ;
May they rise and seek Thy face,
  We beseech Thee, JESU.

Some are sunk in deadly sin
With no spark of love within ;
In their souls Thy work begin,
  We beseech Thee, JESU.

That whoever now doth lie
In his mortal agony,
To the last may feel Thee nigh,
  We beseech Thee, JESU.

That the souls for whom we pray
Of the faithful pass'd away
May find mercy in that Day,
  We beseech Thee, JESU.   Amen.

LITANY OF INTERCESSION.

GOD the FATHER, from Thy throne
 Hear us, we beseech Thee ;
GOD the Co-eternal SON,
 Hear us, we beseech Thee ;
GOD the SPIRIT, mighty LORD,
 Hear us, we beseech Thee ;
THREE in ONE, by all adored,
 Hear us, we beseech Thee.

 JESU ! JESU !
By Thy wondrous Incarnation,
By Thy Birth for our salvation,
 We beseech Thee, we beseech Thee,
From every ill defend us,
Thy grace and mercy send us.

 JESU ! JESU !
By Thy Fasting and Temptation,
By Thy nights of supplication,
 We beseech Thee, we beseech Thee,
From every ill defend us,
Thy grace and mercy send us.

 JESU ! JESU !
By Thy works of sweet compassion,
By Thy Cross and bitter Passion,
 We beseech Thee, we beseech Thee,
From every ill defend us,
Thy grace and mercy send us.

 JESU ! JESU !
By Thy Blood for sinners flowing,
By Thy Death true life bestowing,
 We beseech Thee, we beseech Thee,
From every ill defend us,
Thy grace and mercy send us.

LITANY OF INTERCESSION.

Jesu ! Jesu !
By Thy glorious Resurrection,
Earnest of our own perfection,
    We beseech Thee, we beseech Thee,
From every ill defend us,
Thy grace and mercy send us.

Jesu ! Jesu !
To the Father's throne ascended,
All Thy pain and sorrows ended,
    We beseech Thee, we beseech Thee,
From every ill defend us,
Thy grace and mercy send us.

Jesu ! Jesu !
Advocate for sinners pleading,
With the Father interceding,
    We beseech Thee, we beseech Thee,
From every ill defend us,
Thy grace and mercy send us.   Amen.

642   LITANY FOR CHILDREN.

God the Father, God the Son,
    God the Spirit, Three in One,
Hear us from Thy heav'nly throne ;
    Spare us, Holy Trinity.

Jesu, Saviour meek and mild,
Once for us a little Child
Born of Mary undefiled,
    Hear us, Holy Jesu.

Jesu, by that Blessèd Maid
In Thy swaddling-clothes array'd,
And within a manger laid,
    Hear us, Holy Jesu.

Jesu, at Whose infant feet,
Bending low in worship meet,
Shepherds knelt their Lord to greet,
    Hear us, Holy Jesu.

LITANY FOR CHILDREN.

JESU, to Thy temple brought,
Whom the ancient Simeon sought
By Thy Holy SPIRIT taught,
    Hear us, Holy JESU.

JESU, unto Whom of yore
Wise men, hasting to adore,
Gold and myrrh and incense bore,
    Hear us, Holy JESU.

JESU, Who didst deign to flee
From king Herod's cruelty,
When he sought to murder Thee,
    Hear us, Holy JESU.

JESU, Whom Thy Mother found,
'Mid the doctors sitting round,
Marv'lling at Thy words profound,
    Hear us, Holy JESU.

PART 2.

From all pride and vain conceit,
From all spite and angry heat,
From all lying and deceit,
    Save us, Holy JESU.

From all sloth and idleness,
From hard hearts and selfishness,
From all lust and greediness,
    Save us, Holy JESU.

From refusing to obey,
From the love of our own way,
From forgetfulness to pray,
    Save us, Holy JESU.

PART 3.

By Thy birth and early years,
By Thine infant wants and fears,
By Thy sorrows and Thy tears,
    Save us, Holy JESU.

(575)

LITANY FOR CHILDREN.

By Thy pattern bright and pure,
By the pains Thou didst endure
Our salvation to procure,
    Save us, Holy JESU.

By Thy wounds and thorn-crown'd head,
By Thy Blood for sinners shed,
By Thy rising from the dead,
    Save. us, Holy JESU.

By Thy mercies infinite,
By Thine all-surpassing might,
By Thy glory in the height,
    Save us, Holy JESU. Amen.

643   LITANY FOR USE AT SEA.

FATHER, Whose creating hand
    Made the sea and made the land ;
All Thy creatures are Thy care,
Thou art present everywhere ;
    Hear us, we beseech Thee.

CHRIST, Who didst of old appear
On the waters drawing near ;
Thou art able still to save,
Ruler of the wind and wave ;
    Hear us, we beseech Thee.

SPIRIT, Who didst move of old
Where the barren waters roll'd ;
By Thy breath we move and live,
Thou dost light and order give ;
    Hear us, we beseech Thee.

GOD, to Whom our life we owe,
GOD, Whose Blood for man did flow,
GOD, Who dost within us dwell,
Keep us Thine, and all is well ;
    Hear us, we beseech Thee.

LITANY FOR USE AT SEA.

When the deep in slumber lies
Under bright and peaceful skies,
When the winds in fury rave,
Lifting high the rushing wave,
    Hear us, Holy JESUS.

All our honest labour bless,
Give each lawful aim success ;
In our time of need draw nigh,
Saying, " Fear not, it is I ; "
    Hear us, Holy JESUS.

Guard the loved ones left behind,
Give them peace in heart and mind ;
Keep us all in union sweet
At our FATHER'S mercy-seat ;
    Hear us, Holy JESUS.

When temptations round us roll,
Threat'ning shipwreck to the soul,
Grant us faith and holy fear
By Thy word our course to steer ;
    Hear us, Holy JESUS.

Through the gloom of sorrow's night,
Show Thy cheering, guiding light ;
Waft us homeward, LORD, we pray,
Nearer heaven, day by day ;
    Hear us, Holy JESUS.

Mark our course, and keep us true,
Till the haven fair we view ;
Grant us on that peaceful shore
Home and friends for evermore ;
    Hear us, Holy JESUS. Amen.

The Hymns marked * *are the copyright of the Compilers.*
The Translations marked † *have been altered by the Compilers,*
and in this form are copyright.

INDEX OF FIRST LINES.

INDEX.

INDEX.

(580)

INDEX.

INDEX.

INDEX.

INDEX.

INDEX.

INDEX.

INDEX.

INDEX.

INDEX.

INDEX.

(590)

INDEX.

INDEX.

INDEX.

LITANIES.

Applications for grants of books to poor parishes (giving particulars of population, congregation, etc.), and for permission to print copyright HYMNS *and* TUNES *for Choral Festivals, should be addressed to the* CHAIRMAN OF THE COMMITTEE OF HYMNS A. & M., *care of* WM. CLOWES & SONS, Limited, 23, *Cockspur Street, London, S.W.*

LONDON:

WM. CLOWES AND SONS, LTD., TYPE MUSIC AND GENERAL PRINTERS,
DUKE STREET, STAMFORD STREET, S.E.

Lightning Source UK Ltd.
Milton Keynes UK
UKHW021439090119
334994UK00007B/422/P